# THE NORTH AMERICAN ANIMAL ALMANAC

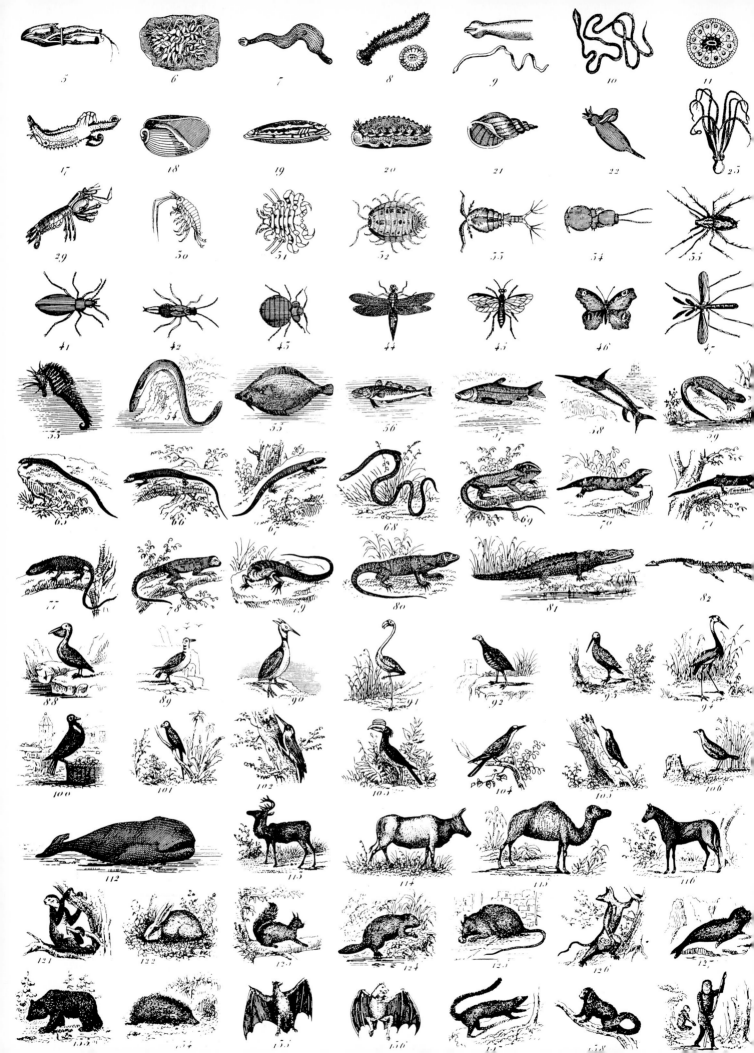

# THE NORTH AMERICAN
# ANIMAL ALMANAC

## BY DARRYL STEWART

### DESIGNED BY J. C. SUARES

# STEWART, TABORI & CHANG

## NEW YORK

Text copyright © 1984 Darryl Stewart
Illustrations copyright © 1984 Stewart,
Tabori & Chang, Inc., for the benefit of the
individual copyright owners who retain
copyright to their material.

*Copyeditor:* Linda Reiman
*Photo researcher:* Sabra Moore

**Library of Congress Cataloging in
Publication Data**

Stewart, Darryl.
　The North American animal almanac.

　Includes index.
　1. Zoology — North America — Miscel-
lanea. 2. Seasons — North America —
Miscellanea. I. Title.
QL151.S74　1984　596.097　83-18178
ISBN 0-941434-43-5 (pbk.)　ISBN 0-941434-58-3

Distributed by Workman Publishing
Company, Inc.
1 West 39th Street, New York, New York
10018.

*Printed and bound in the United States.*

PAGES 2-3: FUR SEAL BULL AND HAREM.
PAGES 4-5: CROCODILE.
PAGES 6-7: WILD TURKEY BY AUDUBON.

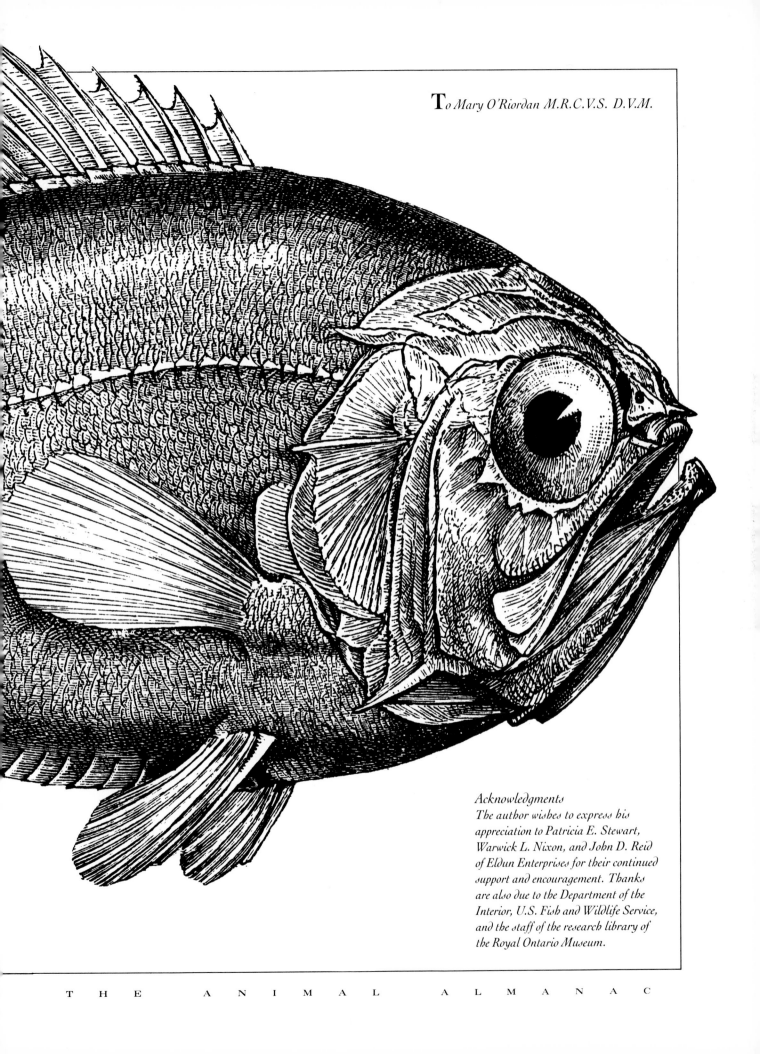

*To Mary O'Riordan M.R.C.V.S. D.V.M.*

*Acknowledgments*
*The author wishes to express his*
*appreciation to Patricia E. Stewart,*
*Warwick L. Nixon, and John D. Reid*
*of Eldun Enterprises for their continued*
*support and encouragement. Thanks*
*are also due to the Department of the*
*Interior, U.S. Fish and Wildlife Service,*
*and the staff of the research library of*
*the Royal Ontario Museum.*

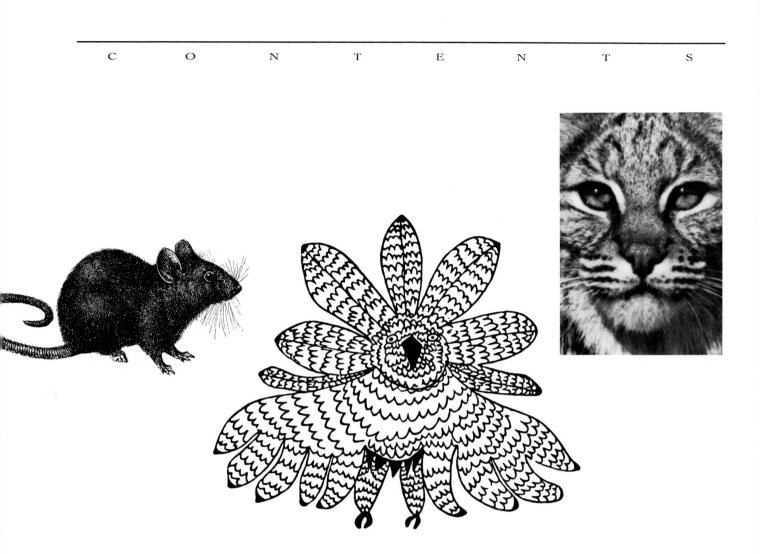

# CONTENTS

# INTRODUCTION

**F**ROM THE ARCTIC CIRCLE AND the northern extremities of Canada and Alaska to the Tropic of Cancer and central Mexico, North America offers a more varied climate and topography than perhaps any other land mass, making it a veritable paradise for the nature lover.

North America is a land of enormous magnitude: together with Greenland and the Hawaiian Islands, the continent covers approximately 8,650,000 square miles. This vast land mass is inhabited by some 461 species of mammals, 927 species of birds, 268 species of reptiles, 192 species of amphibians, 712 species of fresh water fish. This fascinating variety of creatures can be observed all year round, in every corner of the North American continent.

Like the farmer who relies on the calendar in planning for his bounty, the animal watcher also must be attentive to the natural rhythm of wildlife behavior that occurs with changing seasons, from month to month, from year to year. Observing nature is not merely a matter of following a fixed schedule, however. Thus, this handbook for the naturalist is not simply a calendar. Like the farmer, the naturalist turns to an almanac for advice and for information, from the most prosaic to the most obscure.

Through the movement of the seasons, the environment of North America changes; the activities of animals and our observations of them change as well. This almanac contemplates the patterns of the seasons in month by month calendars of events and anniversaries, in specific looks at the animal activity within each month, and in readings suggested by the time of year. The subject is virtually with- out limit, and enjoy- ment of the outdoors can only be enhanced by the stories, facts, and figures found in this book.

# January

January may not be so dark as December or so cold as February, but this tends, nevertheless, to be the cruelest month in most of North America. Most animals try to avoid it altogether. The vast majority of birds capable of long-distance flight abandon North America, and most land-based creatures find sanctuary below the frost line or in protected nests. A few furry creatures, such as the otter, are tough enough to get around during the month, as are some hardy birds — the jays, chickadees, hairy woodpeckers, cardinals, tree sparrows, and starlings. Other furred and feathered species, such as pigeons, brown rats, and house mice, manage to stay alive along the edges of our artificial environment. January is the ideal time to consider creatures of ages past that were unable to survive the climate to which we have grown accustomed. Some of those animals that were successful, such as the winged reptiles, have changed a good deal over time, while some of the ancient sea life, the shark, paddlefish, and horseshoe crab, for example, are still alive and well, even on this continent.

OPPOSITE: COMMON LOON.

# JANUARY

## 2

U.S. Department of the Interior designated the grizzly bear a threatened species in 1975.

Record American alligator shot (19 feet 2 inches long) by E. A. McIlhenny at Avery Island, Louisiana, in 1890.

First redshank, Old World shore bird, reported for North America in Halifax County, Nova Scotia, Canada, in 1960.

BALD EAGLE.

## 4

Adult whooping crane, North America's most famous endangered species, shot in error by a duck hunter just north of the Aransas National Wildlife Refuge in Texas in 1968. It was rushed to the hospital but died on the operating table.

One of last 19th-century sightings of an eastern cougar reported in the *Toronto Evening Telegram* in Ontario in 1884. A specimen had been killed near Creemone, Ontario, on the preceding Tuesday.

. . . . . . . . . . . .

## 8

Cahow, or Bermuda petrel, rediscovered in Bermuda by conservation officer David Wingate in 1951. It was believed to have been extinct since 1615.

Lewis and Clark expedition found a 105-foot skeleton of a blue whale near the mouth of the Columbia River, Oregon, in 1806. The whale had been washed ashore a few days earlier, and the meat had been removed by the local Indians.

Alfred Russel Wallace, co-founder of the theory of evolution, born in England in 1823.

29 pilot whales died after beaching themselves at Pyramid Cove, San Clemente Island, California, in 1971.

WHOOPING CRANE.

## 9

First recorded sightings of manatees made by Christopher Columbus off the coast of the Dominican Republic and Haiti in 1493. Columbus believed they were mermaids.

Winter range of rare and very local Kirtland's warbler discovered on Andros Island in the Bahamas in 1879. This bird breeds solely in a small area in north-central Michigan.

Wind Cave National Park, South Dakota, established in 1903.

**10**

A black-footed ferret, perhaps America's rarest mammal, collected at Box Elder, Pennington County, South Dakota, in 1913 — the tenth official sighting for that state.

. . . . . . . . . . . .

**13**

Bald eagle survey begun by the National Wildlife Federation, Washington, D.C., in 1979 to record the total number of specimens in the continental United States over a two-week period. 9,836 bald eagles were recorded.

. . . . . . . . . . . .

**19**

Lafayette National Park, Maine, changed its name to Acadia National Park in 1929.

. . . . . . . . . . . .

**26**

Rocky Mountain National Park, Colorado, established in 1915.

BLUE WHALE.

**27**

John James Audubon, America's most famous 19th-century bird artist, died in New York City in 1851.

A female blue whale — 268,400 pounds, 89 feet — weighed piecemeal aboard a factory ship in the Ross Sea in 1948. It took 80 men 3¾ hours to flense, dismember, and weigh this huge specimen.

**29**

Largest bowfin (21 pounds 8 ounces) caught with rod and line taken at Florence, South Carolina, in 1980.

. . . . . . . . . . . .

**30**

Largest bluefish (31 pounds 12 ounces) caught with rod and line taken in Hatteras Inlet, North Carolina, in 1972.

**31**

First legal auction of sea otter pelts conducted at Seattle, Washington, in 1968. Neiman-Marcus, the famous Dallas department store, paid $9,200 for four pelts from Alaska.

21

BEAR.

## AN ANIMAL FOR ALL SEASONS
*Otter*

Perhaps the animal that is least bothered by winter's deep freeze is the otter (*Lutra canadensis*). This animal, the largest of the weasels, moves about a good deal on land but has webbed feet and is more at home in the water.

Almost all other animals have to change their way of life in winter; they must eat different food, work harder, and often travel farther in order to stay alive. But not the otter! The otter follows its year-round hunting trails as usual. It can always find a soft spot in the ice, where it goes down into the water, often swimming a long way and popping up through another hole. Below the ice it finds the same kind of food as in summer, and it doesn't mind coming out of the water to lie in the snow and eat a fish or a frog when the temperature is below zero.

The winter holds no fear for this rather lovable animal. In fact, it really seems to enjoy the snow, rolling around in it just for fun and sliding along.

........................

## THE CAMP ROBBER
*Gray Jay*

A most characteristic bird of the northern woods is the gray jay (*Perisoreus canadensis*), one of the few northern residents that remains with us throughout the year.

The gray jay has a good many popular names, including whisky john, whisky-jack, carrion bird, meat hawk, and camp robber. The last name was bestowed on the bird because of its habit of visiting the camps of trappers and lumberjacks to steal anything remotely edible. It regards humans as benevolent providers of food and can become quite tame in their presence.

About 12 inches long, the gray jay bears a strong superficial resemblance to an overgrown chickadee. Its feathers are a soft gray, its neck is sooty black, and the forepart of its head is white. The wings and tail are of a darker shade of gray than the body. The gray jay possesses a wide variety of strange notes and calls but most frequently utters a soft *whee-ah*. It is something of a mimic, and any strange, unidentifiable sound can generally be attributed to this bird.

It is one of our earliest nesting birds. Mating occurs in late winter, usually around February, when the snow is still thick on the ground. The nest is bulky and substantial. One parent bird always remains with the greenish-gray, heavily spotted eggs until they hatch. It is remarkable that these birds prevent the eggs from freezing in temperatures that may reach minus 30 degrees Fahrenheit.

These curious birds tend to follow birders throughout their wanderings, repeatedly perching just above their heads and coming readily to the hand for food. They will often fly away with morsels of food in their bills, only to return seconds later for additional handouts. When hunger strikes, the gray jay will not disdain carrion. Its diet also includes a large number of injurious insects.

........................

## THE MOST COLORFUL BIRD
*Painted Bunting*

A very small bird that breeds in the southern United States and often winters in southern Florida is the most brilliantly plumaged bird on the continent. Its very name is suggestive — the painted bunting (*Passerina ciris*). In some parts of its range, it is known as the "nonpareil," which means "without equal."

Unlike other birds whose colors blend into one another, the painted bunting has a bright blue head, flaming red underparts, brownish wings, and a shining yellow-green back patch, all sharply defined, as though painted with a brush. It belongs to the great finch family, and has the stout, seed-crushing beak of the sparrows, grosbeaks, and other members of the family.

The female painted bunting is so different from

her gaudy mate that one would never think the two belong to the same species; she is a plain greenish-backed, sparrowlike bird with yellowish underparts. This is all part of nature's plan to make her inconspicuous on the nest.

..........................

## COLUMBUS AND THE MERMAIDS
### *Manatees*

When Christopher Columbus traveled past the coast of Hispaniola (now the Dominican Republic and Haiti) on January 9, 1493, he saw what he thought were three mermaids lift their heads above the water.

The admiral recorded the event in his journal, adding somewhat wistfully, "They are not so beautiful as they are painted; though to some extent they have the form of a human face." Nine years passed before Columbus encountered the mermaids again, this time at Azua on the south coast of Hispaniola, but by this time the legendary mermaids had been identified as large aquatic mammals known today as manatees or sea cows. Columbus's brief statement appears to be the first record of a manatee sighting.

Manatees (*Trichechus manatus*) and their cousin the dugong (*Dugong dugong*) are the only remaining members of the order Sirenia. They are the only large herbivorous mammals living in shallow areas of both fresh and salt waters. They have been exploited by humans in all parts of their range to the verge of extinction. The one other member of the Sirenia was the Steller's sea cow, which became extinct in 1768, only 27 years after its discovery.

At the time that Ponce de Leon rounded Florida, the Florida manatee (*T. m. latirostris*) was commonly distributed throughout the coastal waters and lagoons from the Florida Keys to North Carolina and was even found in Virginia, although these were probably stragglers. Today the Florida manatee is an officially recognized endangered species that congregates in sparse numbers only at the southern tip of Florida.

Recently, scientists at Florida Atlantic University believed they had found a way to make use of the manatee, and at the same time save it from extinction. Since an adult manatee can eat a ton of aquatic vegetation in a day, the scientists' idea was to use manatees to eliminate the introduced water hyacinths that are choking up the many estuaries and canals in Florida. Whereas chemical and mechanical controls can eliminate the water hyacinths for one to three months, a hungry manatee uproots entire plants and prevents new growth for six to eight months.

In 1964 the manatees were used to help clear Florida's choked waterways of water hyacinths, but seven of the eight animals involved in the project died, most from pneumonia caught during the cooler months of that year. Two of the manatees were maliciously killed.

Wildlife biologist Daniel S. Hartman states that although Florida manatees are protected within the United States, the 1,000 or so native specimens are still in danger: Not only are they shot at, a great many are killed or maimed each year by the propellers of motorboats. Also contributing to their demise are the increasing appropriation of territory by developers and the pollution of Florida's waterways.

*23*

# January Reading

## LOST FOR LOVE
*Steller's Sea Cow*

**Up to the present, only one species of sea cow has been totally exterminated — the Steller's sea cow (*Hydrodamalis stelleri*), a coarse-skinned sirenian, 25 feet long, which dwelt in the Bering Sea and along the coast of Kamchatka.** Unlike other members of its order, which dwell in tropical or subtropical climes, the Steller's sea cow was strictly a far northern species.

This largest-known sirenian was discovered by Georg Wilhelm Steller in 1741, during one of the Russian exploration voyages that led to the discovery of Alaska. Steller noted that these sea mammals lived in herds and fed together on kelp. When a sailor hooked one, the others tried to save it, circling the victim or jostling the boat; once, for two days, a male of the species continued to swim in close to a beach where its mate lay dead.

Shortly after Steller's voyage, the fate of the big, defenseless, and edible sea cow was sealed. By 1755 it had been hunted almost to extinction, and finally, in 1768, just 27 years after its discovery, Steller's sea cow was seen for the very last time.

## WHY DID THE DINOSAURS DIE OUT?

**Dinosaurs were reptiles that lived and died in the Mesozoic era, between 65 million and 215 million years ago.** Remains of these prehistoric animals have been found on every continent from the Arctic to Patagonia, and from Great Britain to China.

Although all dinosaurs were reptiles, not all reptiles were dinosaurs. (Reptiles that lived in the sea, such as the ichthyosaurs and pleisiosaurs, and reptiles that glided on naked wings, such as the pterosaurs, were not dinosaurs.) Dinosaurs varied greatly in size and structure: Some were no bigger than a large dog, while others, like the diplodocus, reached an enormous length of 87 feet, and a weight of 30 or more tons. Yet, the largest of the dinosaurs — such as the diplodocus and the brachiosaurus — are small in comparison with the present-day blue whale (*Balaenoptera musculus*), which may exceed a length of 100 feet and a weight of 160 tons and is the largest creature to have ever lived on earth.

24

It is generally believed that most dinosaurs must have been fairly harmless, slow-moving creatures that fed entirely on plants, and that they were in turn preyed upon by ferocious, sharp-toothed carnivores that moved around on strong, muscular hind legs, with their bodies bent forward and their tails off the ground as a counterbalance.

The extinction of the dinosaurs is one of the great mysteries of the world. And yet, if we were to follow the dinosaurs' history, we would find that some kinds were disappearing and diversifying throughout all the stages of their development, so that the last dinosaurs differed greatly from their ancestors.

Throughout their long evolution, dinosaurs became increasingly larger, so that more food and more space were required to accommodate their great bulk. It is well known that there were also changes in the relationship of land and water throughout the Mesozoic era, coupled with changes in vegetation and the inevitable changes in climate. Each and all of these factors must have had an effect on the dinosaurs.

Under these conditions, it would undoubtedly have become more difficult for the large vegetarians to acquire food. And since large animals tend to have fewer young, there would have been increased competition for food among the carnivores as well. The cooling of the climate toward the latter part of the Mesozoic era (the Cretaceous period, 70 million to 136 million years ago), while not affecting the dinosaurs directly if they were warmblooded (as some experts believe), would certainly have affected the vegetation, and thus added to the difficulties of the many different kinds of dinosaurs.

Compounding this was the gradually increasing competition from other animals. In the Cretaceous period, the reptiles themselves produced very large crocodiles, capable of dealing with large dinosaurs, and mammals were also making themselves known. The mammals were mainly small, but their predations on dinosaur eggs and young at such a critical time may have hastened the dinosaurs' demise.

Thus it can be seen that there were many possible reasons for the disappearance of the dinosaurs at a time when the continents were slowly being reshaped. All of the dinosaurs had disappeared by the end of the Cretaceous period.

......................

## THE LARGEST DINOSAUR EVER
### *"Supersaurus"*

**Paleontologists have identified at least fifty new kinds of dinosaurs since 1970.** One of the most astounding of these discoveries occurred in 1972, when a huge, hitherto unknown dinosaur was found in the Dry Mesa quarry of western Colorado by James Jenson of Brigham Young University in Utah.

The animal in question, a 75-foot-long, 75-ton sauropod, was the largest dinosaur ever found, and was unofficially named supersaurus. It appeared to be an enlarged variation of a brachiosaurus, previously the largest known dinosaur. Brachiosaurus stood about 40 feet high and may have weighed up to 70 tons.

In 1979, however, at the same western Colorado site, James Jenson uncovered an 8-foot-long shoulder blade of a dinosaur that must have been even larger. And if built on the same brachiosaurid lines, this dinosaur must have attained a length of 80 feet and a weight of 80 tons. A study of the incomplete series of cervical vertebrae indicated that this dinosaur must have sported a neck approximately 39 feet long (compared to diplodocus, with a neck length of about 22 feet). When it stretched its long neck to the full height, the creature that James Jenson called ultrasaurus probably stood 50 to 60 feet tall. Another shoulder blade from the same site measured 8 feet 10 inches.

......................

## THE LARGEST FLYING REPTILE
### *"Texas Pterosaur"*

**The largest-known creature ever to have taken to the air was discovered in Big Bend National Park, west Texas, between 1972 and 1974.** It was an extinct winged reptile with an estimated wingspan of 51 feet. The size of the creature is derived from calculations based on measurements of many fragmentary and some complete bones found in excavations during the two years at Big Bend.

Graduate student Douglas L. Lawson first spotted a fossilized pterosaur bone during a survey in the area. He left it in place and returned the following spring with his supervisor, Dr. Wann Langston, Jr., of the University of Texas at Austin. "The thing that's so ex-

PTERODACTYL.

traordinary about this thing is its tremendous size," said Dr. Langston. "There's never been anything like this before."

The animal, placed in a new order, Quetzalcoatlus, and tentatively dubbed the "Texas pterosaur," lived more than 60 million years ago. Its wingspan is twice that of the previously biggest known pterosaur, *Pteranodon ingens*, which had a wingspan of about 27 feet.

Most pterosaurs are considered to have been fish eaters, scooping up their prey while gliding above the waves. But the Big Bend reptile was found in nonmarine sediment, suggesting that its habitat was away from open bodies of water. The assumption is that this winged reptile was a carrion eater that fed off the remains of animals that roamed the same area. It is not known whether pterosaurs became airborne by flapping their featherless wings or by climbing on high perches and leaping into the air to soar like gliders. The mammoth size of this creature makes it improbable that it was able to rise into the air by wingpower alone.

BLUE SHARK.

## SALTWATER GOURMANDS
*Sharks*

**Of all the creatures roaming the seas, the most detested and feared are the sharks.** A prehistoric predator that has fired man's imagination for thousands of years, the shark was studied as early as Aristotle, who made precise notes on shark anatomy and behavior.

However, of the 250 present-day species of sharks (according to the file maintained by the U.S. Navy, and the Smithsonian Institution), only 39 have been implicated in attacks on humans. Ironically, the two largest sharks in the world, the whale shark (*Rhineodon typus*) and the basking shark (*Cetorhinus maximus*), growing to 60 feet long and 45 feet long, respectively, are both plankton eaters and perfectly harmless. But the few shark species that have attacked humans are enough to give the entire family a bad name.

Of all the sharks that are dangerous to humans, the great white shark (*Carcharodon carcharias*) has rightfully deserved the title of "most deadly." It is the largest of the man-eaters, occasionally reaching 35 feet in length and weighing more then 3 tons. It is also the most powerful and the most voracious, standing convicted of the greatest number of attacks on humans. In 1916, a great white shark fatally attacked four bathers and mutilated a fifth in a few days along a stretch of the New Jersey coast, setting off the greatest shark hunt in the history of the United States.

The best available evidence suggests that sharks have evolved almost unchanged for 200 million to 300 million years. They are also credited with being the first animals to have developed teeth, which consequently makes them the first predators. Unlike most fish, sharks do not possess bony skeletons but are "cartilaginous," a characteristic they share with other ancient fish such as the sturgeons (*Acipenser* sp.).

The teeth of sharks are embedded in the gums to form four to six rows, and as many as twenty in some species (the teeth of vertebrates are anchored to the jaws by roots). Different species of sharks display tremendous diversity in their dentition. A tiger shark (*Galeocerdo cuvieri*) may produce, use, and shed as many as 24,000 razor-sharp teeth in a ten-year period.

A shark is equipped with a distensible stomach that can expand to several times its normal size. What is more remarkable is that a shark can apparently store food or foreign objects at will for weeks at a time without digesting them. One shark killed off an Australian dock had in its stomach half a ham, several legs of mutton, the head and forelegs of a bulldog with a rope around its neck, a quantity of horseflesh, and a ship's scraper.

## AMERICA'S ONLY FRESHWATER SHARK
### Bull Shark

**The bull shark (*Carcharhinus leucas*) inhabits numerous bodies of fresh and salt water around the world, and in almost every geographic area it bears a different name.** For many years a type of shark inhabiting Lake Nicaragua was considered to be a distinct species, until it was recognized as a freshwater population of the ocean-dwelling bull shark. In the Americas, the bull shark inhabits both the Atlantic and Pacific Oceans, where it ranges from Chesapeake Bay, Maryland, and Anacapa Island, California, south to Brazil and the southern extremity of Ecuador.

This is the only shark species that has entered the fresh waters of the United States. Records of bull sharks exist from the following inland localities: the Atchafalaya River (as far inland as 160 miles) and the Red River, Louisiana; the Mississippi River, Illinois; and the Aucilla River, Tall Timbers Reserve Station, and the Apalachicola River, Florida.

The bull shark preys voraciously on other sharks, rays, porpoises, sea turtles, crustaceans, and mollusks. It is also potentially dangerous to man — there are several accounts of attacks on humans.

## Record Measurements for Sharks

| | Length | Weight |
|---|---|---|
| Whale shark (*Rhineodon typus*) | 59' | 90,000* lb |
| Basking shark (*Cetorhinus maximus*) | 45' | 32,000* |
| Great white shark (*Carcharodon carcharias*) | 37' | 24,000* |
| Greenland shark (*Somniosus microcephalus*) | 21' | 2,250 |
| Tiger shark (*Galeocerdo cuvieri*) | 20'10" | 2,070 |
| Hammerhead shark (*Sphyrna mokarran*) | 18'4" | 1,860 |
| Thresher shark (*Alopias vulpinus*) | 18' | 1,100 |
| Six-gill shark (*Hexanchus griseus*) | 15'5" | 1,300 |
| Gray nurse shark (*Ginglymostoma cirratum*) | 14' | 1,225 |
| Great blue shark (*Prionace glauca*) | 12'7" | 550 |
| Mako (*Isurus oxyrinchus*) | 12' | 1,200 |
| Dusky shark (*Carcharhinus obscurus*) | 11'11" | 850 |
| Whaler shark (*Eulamia brachyura*) | 11'8" | 768 |
| Whitetip shark (*Carcharhinus longimanus*) | 11'6" | 750 |
| Porbeagle (*Lamna nasus*) | 10' | 500 |
| Bull shark (*Carcharhinus leucas*) | 10' | 400 |

*Estimated weight.

## KING OF THE HERRINGS OR SEA SERPENT?
### Oarfish

**Whoever first coined the phrase: "There are stranger things in the sea than ever came out of it," may well have been thinking of the oarfish (*Regalecus glesne*).** The oarfish is a most mysterious fish, responsible for many reports of sea serpents, because of its appearance and the slithery way in which it swims.

The real interest in this fish lies in its extraordinary shape, its large size, and how little is known about its way of life.

There is reason to believe that this is a deep-sea fish that only occasionally comes to the surface in the north Atlantic and the Mediterranean, where specimens have been captured, exciting much comment and often being exhibited.

The oarfish has a flattened body up to a foot high, only 2 inches thick, and possibly 50 feet long (although about 21 feet is the greatest recorded length).

Extending the entire length of its long, ribbon-shaped body (it is sometimes called the

### Record Weights for Saltwater Fish From North America*

| Species | Weight | Location | Date |
|---|---|---|---|
| Black sea bass | 8 lb 12 oz | Oregon Inlet, N.C. | Apr. 21, 1979 |
| Giant sea bass | 563 lb 8 oz | Anacapa Island, Calif. | Aug. 20, 1968 |
| Striped bass | 72 lb | Cuttyhunk, Mass. | Oct. 10, 1969 |
| Bluefish | 31 lb 12 oz | Hatteras Inlet, N.C. | Jan. 30, 1972 |
| Cod | 98 lb 12 oz | Isle of Shoals, N.H. | June 8, 1969 |
| Black drum | 113 lb 1 oz | Lewes, Del. | Sept. 15, 1975 |
| Red drum | 90 lb | Rodanthe, N.C. | Nov. 7, 1973 |
| Summer flounder | 22 lb 7 oz | Montauk, N.Y. | Sept. 15, 1975 |
| American halibut | 250 lb | Gloucester, Mass. | July 3, 1981 |
| California halibut | 42 lb | Santa Rosa Island, Calif. | May 24, 1981 |
| Crevalle jack | 51 lb | Lake Worth, Fla. | June 20, 1978 |
| Jewfish | 680 lb | Fernandina Beach, Fla. | May 20, 1961 |
| Kawakawa | 21 lb | Kauai, Hawaii | Aug. 21, 1975 |
| King mackerel | 90 lb | Key West, Fla. | Feb. 16, 1976 |
| Blue Atlantic marlin | 1,282 lb | St. Thomas, Virgin Is. | Aug. 6, 1977 |
| Permit | 51 lb 8 oz | Lake Worth, Fla. | Apr. 28, 1978 |
| Pollock | 46 lb 7 oz | Brielle, N.J. | May 26, 1975 |
| African pompano | 41 lb 8 oz | Ft. Lauderdale, Fla. | Feb. 15, 1978 |
| Oarfish | 114 lb | La Paz, Mexico | June 1, 1960 |
| Rainbow runner | 33 lb 10 oz | Clarion Islands, Mexico | Mar. 14, 1976 |
| White sea bass | 83 lb 12 oz | San Felipe, Mexico | Mar. 31, 1953 |
| Spotted sea trout | 16 lb | Mason's Beach, Va. | May 28, 1977 |
| Hammerhead shark | 717 lb | Jacksonville Beach, Fla. | July 27, 1980 |
| Shortfin mako shark | 1,080 lb | Montauk, N.Y. | Aug. 26, 1979 |
| Tiger shark | 1,780 lb | Cherry Grove, S.C. | June 14, 1964 |
| Black skipjack | 14 lb 8 oz | Baja, Mexico | May 24, 1977 |
| Tautog | 21 lb 6 oz | Cape May, N.J. | June 12, 1954 |
| Atlantic bigeye tuna | 375 lb 8 oz | Ocean City, Md. | Aug. 26, 1977 |
| Bluefin tuna | 1,496 lb | Aulds Cove, Nova Scotia | Oct. 26, 1979 |
| Yellowfin tuna | 388 lb 12 oz | San Benedicto Islands, Mexico | Apr. 1, 1977 |
| Little tunny | 27 lb | Key Largo, Fla. | Apr. 20, 1976 |
| California yellowtail | 71 lb 15 oz | Alijos Rocks, Mexico | June 24, 1979 |

*Caught with rod and line.

"ribbonfish") is a bright red dorsal fin. Its head is topped with a high crest, which may be erected at will. This may well be the sea serpent described as having the head of a horse and a red mane.

The oarfish has been called the "king of the herrings" because it was once believed that it swam in front of the herring shoals, as if leading them.

It appears that an oarfish can lose nearly half its body and still survive. Many captured oarfish had lost part of the tail or had scars on the rear half of the body. The internal organs are all packed into the front of the body; therefore, an oarfish can survive provided only the rear half is bitten, even if it is bitten right off.

. . . . . . . . . . . . . . . . . . . . . .

## LIVING FOSSILS
### *Horseshoe Crab and Paddlefish*

**First applied to certain trees, the term *living fossil*\* is now applied to a number of animals as well.** To qualify as a living fossil, an animal must have certain credentials. It must represent the persistence, in nearly unchanged form, of an ancient and comparatively primi-

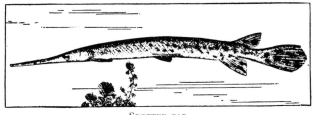
SPOTTED GAR.

tive structural type. It must have fossil relatives that date back to a remote geological period, as close as possible to the beginnings of fossil records of complex animals. The true

\*Charles Darwin first used the term *living fossil* in connection with the gingko, or maidenhair, tree (*Gingko biloba*), which existed worldwide during the Permian period 200 million years ago. Eighteenth-century Europeans found the gingko tree still surviving in China and Japan.

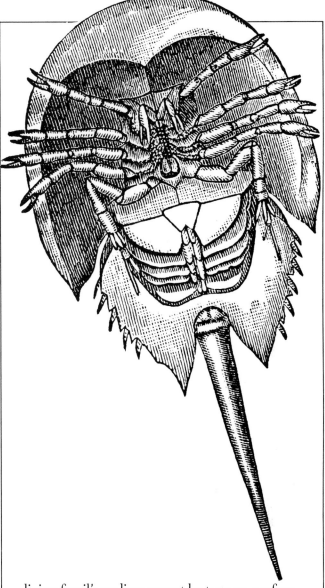

living fossil's pedigree must be tens or, preferably, hundreds of millions of years old, and it must have no, or at least very few, close living relatives. Two such animals are the horseshoe crab, an arachnid, and the paddlefish, which is referred to as an archaic fish.[†]

### *Horseshoe Crab*

The North American horseshoe crab (*Limulus ployhemus*), which occurs commonly along the eastern seaboard of the United States and around the shores of the Gulf of Mexico, has persisted essentially unchanged for hundreds of millions of years. Virtually the only

[†]Other archaic fish in North America are the sturgeons (family Acipenseridae), the gars (*Lepisosteus* sp.), and the bowfin (*Amia calva*).

difference between the modern-day horseshoe crab and its 300-million-year-old relative Palaeolimulus is its size. A fully grown living horseshoe crab is at least five times the size of its ancestor.

Incidentally, this creature is not a true crab; it is the sole modern representative of an arachnid, distantly related to spiders and scorpions, that was abundant in the Paleozoic seas 300 million years ago.

### Paddlefish

Left over from the Cretaceous period of the Mesozoic era, the paddlefish has existed almost unchanged in American waters for over 100 million years and is still found today in the Mississippi Valley basin.

Two species of paddlefish are known to exist: the American paddlefish (*Polyodon spathula*), from the Mississippi Valley, and the Chinese paddlefish (*P. gladius*), which inhabits the Yangtze River. They are included in the order Acipenseriformes, along with the

sturgeons, with which they share the cartilaginous skeleton; and neither the sturgeon nor the paddlefish has ever developed a swim bladder.

The paddlefish are the only surviving members of an order of fish whose ancestors are the sharks and the bony fish. There are, however, small details of anatomy that link the paddlefish with the sharks, although in other respects they are more like the bony fish; they are, in fact, "missing links" connecting these two main groups.

The name of this fish is derived from the shape of its snout, which is like the blade of a canoe paddle and is a third to a half the total length of the fish. With its paddle-topped mouth the paddlefish engulfs freshwater shrimp and other small aquatic animals. The skin of the paddlefish is scaleless, except for a few vestigial scales and patches of scales on the tail fin.

Although it seldom weighs more than 50 pounds now, the paddlefish once weighed three times that amount; a 6-foot-long specimen weighing 184 pounds has been recorded. The paddlefish was once common in large bodies of water throughout much of the Mississippi Valley and the adjacent San Jacinto River in Texas, east to Mobile Bay in Alabama. It was known with certainty in Lake Erie prior to 1903, and is of uncertain occurrence in other Great Lakes, where it was reported around the turn of the century.

Today the paddlefish is confined to the larger streams and connected waters of the Mississippi Valley basin, where it appears to have been declining in recent years because of habitat loss, river pollution, and overfishing. The fact that there are only two widely separated species of paddlefish suggests that these fish are a dying breed.

## OUR MOST PRIMITIVE BIRDS
### Loons

**Of all our native birds, the loons are rated first on the scale of evolution by ornithologists, since their bones show striking similarities to the fossilized remains of prehistoric birds.** The loons are, therefore, our most primitive birds.

COMMON LOON.

The common loon (*Gavia immer*) is a characteristic bird of the north woods. Its far-echoing call is best heard before you turn in for the night. Hours later you awaken to its loud derisive laugh. And its voice also belongs to the early morning and the afternoon. It seems as if the loon never sleeps — and when it does, it does so on the water.

The loon's legs are set far back close to the tail, making it awkward and clumsy on land but superbly adapted for life in the water. Its ability to dive is, in fact, equaled by few other water birds, as many hunters can attest.

A loon can actually dive at the flash of a gun before the bullet can reach it. As soon as it sees the flash, it propels itself into the water, where it remains fully submerged for several seconds, only to reappear 50 or 100 feet from where it went down. It appears to be impossible to shoot a loon when it is looking at you.

......................

## THE MOST MODERN BIRDS
### *Sparrows*

**The sparrow family is the largest bird family in the world.** Of its more than 600 species, 93 have been recorded in North America.

Among the songbirds, sparrows stand high on the evolutionary scale, and they are considered by ornithologists to be the farthest removed of any birds from their primitive ancestors.

Although many of these birds are colored in drab browns and grays, this is greatly compensated for by such exceptions as the rose-breasted grosbeak (*Pheucticus ludovicianus*), purple finch (*Carpodacus purpureus*), indigo bunting (*Passerina cyanea*), lazuli bunting (*P. amoena*), blue grosbeak (*Guiraca caerulea*), evening grosbeak (*Coccotbraustes vespertina*), and American goldfinch (*Carduelis tristis*), dressed in combinations of black, white, red, yellow, and blue.

In addition to their decorative and musical contributions, these birds are among the most

OVERLEAF: BUNTINGS.

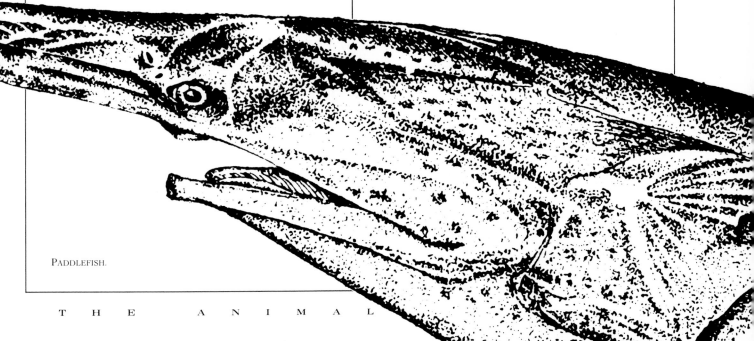

PADDLEFISH.

G. Mützel gez.

X. J. & K. JAHRMARGT
M. Ringe sc

useful to humans in their never-ending war against weeds and insects. Many birds destroy insects but eat nothing else. Sparrows eat both insects and weed seeds. This enables them to survive in colder climates than can be tolerated by entirely insectivorous birds, and gives us our attractive assortment of "winter finches."

Whether we call them sparrows, finches, buntings, grosbeaks, or longspurs, they are one of the most fascinating groups of birds and are of great value to humankind.

. . . . . . . . . . . . . . . . . . . . . .

## UNDESIRABLE ALIENS?
### *House Sparrow and Starling*

**Neither the house sparrow (*Passer domesticus*) nor the starling (*Sturnus vulgaris*), two of our most abundant resident bird species, is native to North America.** Both were introduced on this continent during the last century.

### *House Sparrow*

The house sparrow was introduced first. Its current occupation on the continent has been completed within 40 years of its introduction. According to earliest records, eight pairs of house sparrows were brought to the Brooklyn Institute in New York from England in 1850. However, this and a number of other experiments failed. But in 1854, house sparrows were introduced into Portland, Maine, and they began to thrive and multiply. By 1872 the house sparrow had reached California.

The largely grain-eating birds traveled extensively from place to place along the highways, where they could pick up grain dropped by horse-drawn vehicles. They also fed on semi-digested grain found in horse droppings. The advent of the motor vehicle brought a decrease in their numbers in the towns and cities, as they were forced away from the highways into the surrounding rural and suburban regions.

The house sparrow is never found far from human habitation and cultivated lands, on which it depends largely for food; it is almost completely absent in the far north. It is, however, reported in Churchill, Manitoba, because of the presence of grain fields in the area. At present, the northern breeding limit of the house sparrow corresponds roughly with the east–west course of the Canadian National Railway, which broadly coincides with the limit of cultivation. The starling is more tolerant of northern conditions than the house sparrow, and has been reported about 200 miles south of the Barren Ground country.

### *Starling*

The individual chiefly responsible for the starling's presence in North America was Eugene Scheifflin of New York City, who imported and liberated about a hundred starlings in Central Park in 1890 and 1891. For the next six years the starling was wholly confined to the limits of the Greater New York area, but little over half a century later it had reached the Pacific coast.

The progress of the starling across the continent was much slower and more deliberate than that of the house sparrow, but it was equally effective. The starling first reached Canada at Brockville, Ontario, in 1919. By 1925 it was breeding in Ottawa and had arrived in Nova Scotia. In January 1947 a flock of eight birds wandered up the Okanagan Val-

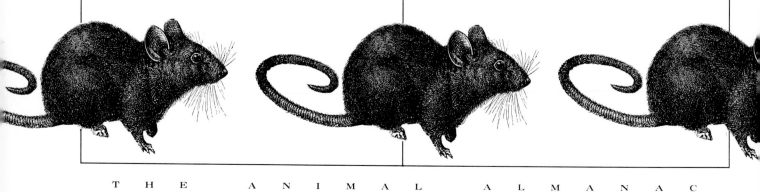

ley to Oliver in British Columbia. By 1963 the starling had reached the Arctic Ocean.

Both starlings and house sparrows are noisy, aggressive birds and have deposed and decreased the numbers of more desirable native birds that use tree cavities as nesting sites; the bluebird (*Sialia* sp.) in particular, has suffered from this intervention. The decrease in the population of the red-headed woodpecker (*Melanerpes erythrocephalus*) since the 1920s is very likely due to the deposing habits of the starling. The flicker (*Colaptes auratus*) has also been victimized, for the starling shows a distinct predilection for woodpecker cavities.

However, the excessive wrath and unpopularity that these immigrant birds incur is often unwarranted; these birds do have better sides to their nature. The starling can even be considered beneficial, for it consumes large quantities of noxious insects, and less than half its food consumption is vegetable — and only a small proportion of this is cultivated fruit. It is often blamed for eating cultivated crops when the culprits are usually red-winged blackbirds (*Agelaius phoeniceus*) and common grackles (*Quiscalus quiscula*).

In defense of house sparrows, it can be said that they often share nesting quarters with other birds and live together in peaceful coexistence. Most frequently, they will occupy the lower level of martin (*Progne subis*) houses and, surprisingly, will even build their nests inside the much larger nests of hawks (*Buteo* sp.). Particular cases on record concern the osprey (*Pandion haliaetus*) and the Swainson's hawk (*Buteo swainsoni*). They do not appear to interfere with the martins; neither do they show any fear of the large hawks.

NORWAY RAT.

## STOWAWAYS
### *Brown Rat and House Mouse*

**The brown, or Norway, rat (*Rattus norvegicus*) and the house mouse (*Mus musculus*) are immigrants to this continent.** Both species have adapted especially well to man-made habitats and may be found close to human habitation.

It is believed that the Norway rat is native to the more temperate climate of Asia. It appeared in continental Europe and the British Isles during the eighteenth century; in 1727, it swept westward across the Volga River. Boarding ships bound for America from numerous European and British ports, the Norway rat reached the Upper St. Lawrence region about 1775 and Ottawa about 1890. Once established, local populations of this opportunistic animal exploded with remarkable rapidity.

The house mouse originally hailed from southwestern Iran (then Persia), and probably stowed away on the first caravans and ships that carried goods on land and water routes to most parts of the world. Weighing only half an ounce, it is no wonder that this tiny rodent traveled undetected in shipments of clothing, food, and household effects until the items were unpacked and its ravages discovered.

39

# February

As the hemisphere begins to tilt once again toward the direction of the sun, the days lengthen slightly during February. Yet this last full month of winter can often be the coldest and bleakest of the year. Nevertheless, a vigilant eye can detect indications of spring, even during the coldest days of the month. The stirring of a timid, sometimes bothersome creature known as the groundhog (or woodchuck), for example, signals the onset of spring. Not only has this stolid beast survived last year's neighborhood dogs, shotguns, and hawks, eagles, and owls, he's even managed to survive the winter, as he now emerges from his safe burrow in the earth. This is surely a welcome sign for the winter-weary.

The groundhog's cousin — another rodent, the prairie dog — also depends on the holes and burrows of the earth for its safekeeping, while other animals, such as the porcupine and skunk, have developed sufficient weaponry to creep along the surface of the ground in slow but sure self-confidence.

Wherever the snow has begun to recede, you may observe the first summer visitor, the horned lark, a small brown bird with a yellow face, as it forages for food on the ground.

Opposite: A white weasel.

# FEBRUARY

## 1

Henry Redding reported seeing a flock of Carolina parakeets on Fort Drum Creek, Florida, in 1920 (according to Bent's *Life History of North American Birds*). However, the bird was officially declared extinct when the last specimen in the Cincinnati Zoo, Ohio, died in 1918.

. . . . . . . . . . . .

## 2

Groundhog Day

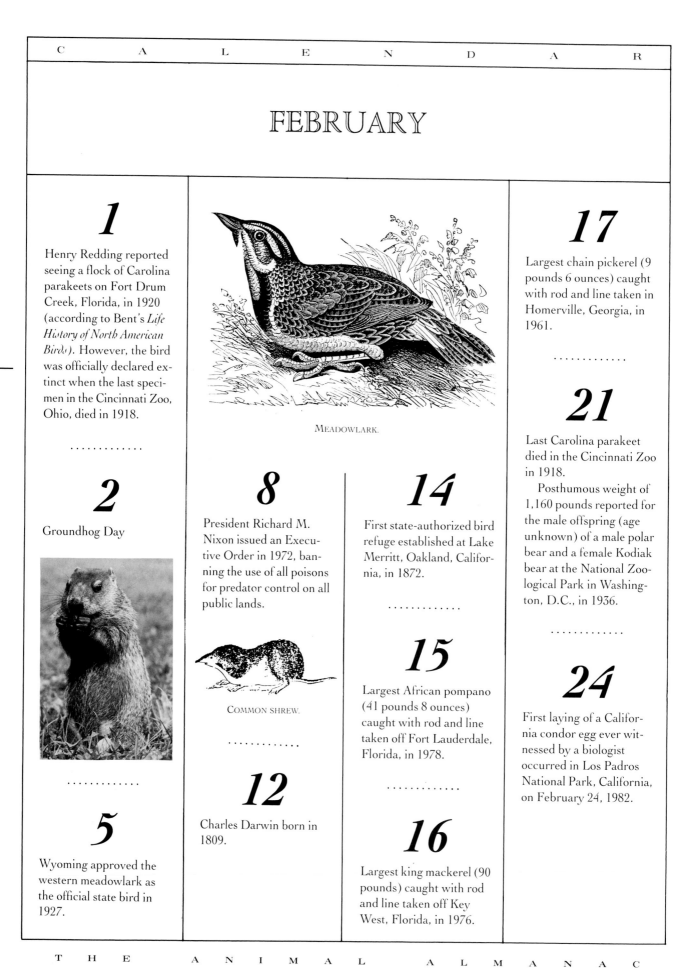

## 5

Wyoming approved the western meadowlark as the official state bird in 1927.

MEADOWLARK.

## 8

President Richard M. Nixon issued an Executive Order in 1972, banning the use of all poisons for predator control on all public lands.

COMMON SHREW.

. . . . . . . . . . . .

## 12

Charles Darwin born in 1809.

## 14

First state-authorized bird refuge established at Lake Merritt, Oakland, California, in 1872.

. . . . . . . . . . . .

## 15

Largest African pompano (41 pounds 8 ounces) caught with rod and line taken off Fort Lauderdale, Florida, in 1978.

. . . . . . . . . . . .

## 16

Largest king mackerel (90 pounds) caught with rod and line taken off Key West, Florida, in 1976.

## 17

Largest chain pickerel (9 pounds 6 ounces) caught with rod and line taken in Homerville, Georgia, in 1961.

. . . . . . . . . . . .

## 21

Last Carolina parakeet died in the Cincinnati Zoo in 1918.

Posthumous weight of 1,160 pounds reported for the male offspring (age unknown) of a male polar bear and a female Kodiak bear at the National Zoological Park in Washington, D.C., in 1936.

. . . . . . . . . . . .

## 24

First laying of a California condor egg ever witnessed by a biologist occurred in Los Padros National Park, California, on February 24, 1982.

MT. MCKINLEY.

## 26

Kentucky approved the cardinal as the official state bird in 1926.

Mount McKinley, Grand Canyon, and Grand Teton national parks all established on this day in 1917, 1919, and 1929, respectively.

## 28

Idaho approved the mountain bluebird as the official state bird in 1931.

43

ALASKAN BROWN BEAR AND HER CUBS.

# GROUNDHOG DAY

Popular superstition has it that the groundhog, or woodchuck *(Marmota monax)*, arises from its winter torpor on February 2. It comes to the surface and if it sees its shadow on the snow, it goes back into its hole for another six weeks of slumber — and another six weeks of winter. If it doesn't see its shadow, it continues more or less actively above ground until spring, which will come early now.

It is true that the groundhog awakens earlier than most ground animals, sometimes as early as the first week in February. It is also true that after looking about, it may return to its den, but probably not for long, certainly not to sleep for six weeks. The groundhog is unaccountably erratic in its hibernation; it often seems to retire for the season while the sun still casts considerable warmth and to push its way to the surface while the ground is still buried under several feet of snow.

Although of short duration, the torpor of the animal is quite profound. Renowned nineteenth-century naturalists John James Audubon and John Bachman tell of a groundhog in captivity aroused only with the greatest difficulty after six weeks' slumber by being placed near an open fire, and then, as quickly, when the source of the heat was removed, curling up into a round ball.

Because they are North America's largest true hibernators, groundhogs are the subject of much medical research, particularly with regard to their ability to lower their body temperature and heart rate and to reduce their oxygen consumption. If it were possible to induce the same sort of reactions in humans, even for brief periods, certain forms of heart surgery and other treatments could be conducted more easily.

In America, the legend of Groundhog Day is a variation on the traditional belief, which sometimes includes the bear or the badger, and is associated with Candlemas (also February 2) in England. According to an old English song:
If Candlemas be fair and bright,
Come, Winter, have another flight;
If Candlemas bring clouds and rain,
Go, Winter, and come not again.

GROUNDHOG.

HOARY MARMOT.

## THE GROUNDHOG'S RARE COUSIN
### *Vancouver Island Marmot*

A close relative of the groundhog, the Vancouver Island marmot (*Marmota vancouverensis*), is the only large mammal species whose entire population is confined within the boundaries of Canada.° In fact, its habitat is restricted to the alpine and subalpine regions of Vancouver Island, where only fifty to a hundred individuals are known to exist. It is regarded as one of the world's rarest mammals and consequently is protected under the British Columbia Wildlife Act and Regulations.

Adult Vancouver Island marmots are black or very dark brown, with patches of white on the muzzle, forehead, and breast. The animal was first discovered in 1910 on the peak of Mount Douglas, south of Alberni, by Harry Schlewald Swarth, a trapper who was working as a field collector for the University of California. He published his findings in 1911, but it was another 20 years before this animal was reported again. Currently, active colonies are known to exist in only four general locations.

This species, which has probably always been rare, appears to be declining in population. The decline may have been caused by the encroachment of trees but is more likely due to wanton killing. The greatest threat to this marmot's survival appears to be advancing logging operations in the immediate vicinity of colonies. Although the companies responsible have agreed to leave the timber immediately adjacent to the colonies intact, the influence of the nearby disturbances is quite unknown.

More study must be done to determine whether some animals could be successfully moved from existing colonies to a vacant habitat to establish new colonies. In this way, the continued existence of the Vancouver Island marmot would be more assured.

........................

## THE AIR-RAID SIREN
### *Hoary Marmot*

The hoary marmot (*Marmota caligata*), a western counterpart of the groundhog, inhabits the upper slopes of the western Rocky Mountains, where it is commonly preyed upon by the golden eagle (*Aquila chrysaetos*) and the grizzly bear (*Ursus arctos horribilis*). Large raptors and other carnivores are a constant threat to the marmots whenever these gregarious rodents go into the open to feed.

° Two small mammal species are also endemic to Canada, the Gaspé shrew (*Sorex gaspensis*) and the Labrador collared lemming (*Dicrostonyx hudsonius*).

In order to guard themselves against these ma-
raudings, the marmots have devised an air-raid
protection system. Whenever a marmot observes
a predator, it emits a piercing whistle, which acts
as an air-raid warning to other marmots. The rodents then take shelter in their shallow burrows,
where they are well protected. The hoary marmot's
whistle is the shrillest sound issued by a mammal;
the sound can easily be heard a mile away, and
under the most favorable conditions it can be heard
at twice that distance.

Once the sentry marmot has given the alarm, it
also goes underground. When the danger has
passed, it utters another, somewhat lower-pitched
whistle — the "all clear." Then gray heads pop up
all over the mountainside, and normal marmot activities resume.

. . . . . . . . . . . . . . . . . . . . . .

## ITS OWN WORST ENEMY
*California Condor*

The California condor (*Gymnogyps californianus*) is one of the rarest and most endangered of all birds; a total population of
fewer than 50 individuals is almost entirely confined
to Los Padres National Forest, northeast of Ventura
in California.

In many ways the condor is its own worst enemy!
Efforts to conserve it were dealt a serious setback
on February 26, 1982, when the first condor egg
of the season was accidentally destroyed by the
breeding pair.

A biologist with the Condor Research Center
witnessed the laying of the condor egg on February 14. This was the first time anyone had ever
observed this rarest of rare birds laying an egg.

Both parent birds took turns incubating the egg
until February 24, when the male condor refused
to relinquish it to the female. After disputing the
incubation rights to the egg for two days, the female managed to work the egg out from under
her mate. Unfortunately, the egg rolled out of the
cave nest, and despite efforts by both condors to
work the egg back inside, it rolled over the cliff;
most of the remains were subsequently consumed
by ravens (*Corvus corax*) and the female condor.

A second egg was laid by the same pair of condors in early April of 1982, but, unfortunately,
invading ravens made this attempt a failure also.

The egg was first observed on April 8, when
the female rolled it out of a dark corner of the
cave nest into view. The egg was probably laid on
the previous day. On April 29, when the female
condor approached the nest to take her turn at
incubating the egg, she was rebuffed and chased
away by the male. A raven, taking full advantage
of the situation, entered the cave nest and began to
peck at the unattended egg, apparently punctur-
ing it. When the female condor returned to the
nest, she first tried to incubate the damaged egg,
but it was soon apparent that the egg was crushed.
The following day, a pair of ravens approached
the nest site and managed to drag away portions
of the eggshell.

Despite the double setback, all does not appear
to be lost. The Condor Research Center has
confirmed the presence of a chick produced by a
second pair of California condors and is optimis-
tic about the nesting behavior exhibited by a third
pair, which indicates the possible existence of an
egg. The nest of the third pair is in a cave and
mainly hidden from view, but biologists are opti-
mistic about the possibility of a successful hatching in the future.

MOUNTED CONDOR.

## THE MOST POPULAR AMERICAN BIRD
### *Cardinal*

The cardinal (*Cardinalis cardinalis*), with its brilliant red plumage (in the male), black face, and jaunty crest, can perhaps be called the most popular bird in America; it represents seven states of the U.S.

This bird, which has its roots in the tropics, has been steadily extending its range northward, until it now occurs in the sphagnum bog country of central Ontario in Canada.

It was a rare bird in Canada prior to the turn of the century. The first active cardinal's nest in that country was discovered at Point Pelee, Ontario, in 1901. The cardinal was breeding in Toronto by 1922.

Cardinals received a big boost in the fall of 1938, when there was a mass influx into the Niagara Falls area. This great invasion of cardinals resulted in the first breeding records for many areas in southern Ontario. Just how much further into Canada cardinals will expand nobody knows, but this expansion is expected to continue. The cardinal has also nested as far north as Winnipeg, Manitoba, and has summered in Montreal, Quebec.

. . . . . . . . . . . . . . . . . . . . . .

### State Birds of the United States

| | |
|---|---|
| Alabama | Common flicker |
| Alaska | Willow ptarmigan |
| Arizona | Cactus wren |
| Arkansas | Mockingbird |
| California | California quail |
| Colorado | Lark bunting |
| Connecticut | American robin |
| Delaware | Blue hen |
| Florida | Mockingbird |
| Georgia | Brown thrasher |
| Hawaii | Hawaiian goose |
| Idaho | Mountain bluebird |
| Illinois | Cardinal |
| Indiana | Cardinal |
| Iowa | Eastern goldfinch |
| Kansas | Western meadowlark |
| Kentucky | Cardinal |
| Louisiana | Eastern brown pelican |
| Maine | Chickadee |
| Maryland | Northern oriole |
| Massachusetts | Chickadee |
| Michigan | American robin |
| Minnesota | Common loon |
| Mississippi | Mockingbird |
| Missouri | Eastern bluebird |

CHICKADEES.

| | |
|---|---|
| Montana | Western meadowlark |
| Nebraska | Western meadowlark |
| Nevada | Mountain bluebird |
| New Hampshire | Purple finch |
| New Jersey | Eastern goldfinch |
| New Mexico | Roadrunner |
| New York | Eastern bluebird |
| North Carolina | Cardinal |
| North Dakota | Western meadowlark |
| Ohio | Cardinal |
| Oklahoma | Scissor-tailed flycatcher |
| Oregon | Western meadowlark |
| Pennsylvania | Ruffed grouse |
| Rhode Island | Rhode Island red |
| South Carolina | Carolina wren |
| South Dakota | Ring-necked pheasant |
| Tennessee | Mockingbird |
| Texas | Mockingbird |
| Utah | Gull |
| Vermont | Hermit thrush |
| Virginia | Cardinal |
| Washington | Willow goldfinch |
| West Virginia | Cardinal |
| Wisconsin | American robin |
| Wyoming | Western meadowlark |

.........................

# THE RODENT THAT BARKS
*Prairie Dog*

**A prairie dog is not a dog at all, but a rodent that got its name because of its shrill, yappy bark.**

Five prairie dog species are known to exist, all of them native to this continent: the black-tailed prairie dog (*Cynomys ludovicianus*), white-tailed prairie dog (*C. leucurus*), Gunnison's prairie dog (*C. gunnisoni*), Mexican prairie dog (*C. mexicanus*), and Utah prairie dog (*C. parvidens*), the last-mentioned an officially recognized endangered species.

Prairie dogs used to be enormously abundant; their burrows were found on the high plains from southern Alberta and Saskatchewan south to the Mexican border and beyond. The renowned Canadian naturalist Ernest Thompson Seton went so far as to say that a century ago an estimate of 5 billion black-tailed prairie dogs alone wouldn't have been an exaggeration.

With the coming of the Europeans, the prairie dog at first multiplied alarmingly because of the wholesale slaughter of its predators: badgers, bobcats, weasels, hawks, eagles, and snakes. But continuing to act in ignorance of prairie ecology, the farmer blamed the prairie dog for the destruction of ranges, and a wholesale campaign of prairie dog extermination began. Prairie dogs were mistakenly persecuted as pests for over a century. Bounties were paid for them, and strychnine and cyanide of potassium were used to kill them.

In turn, as prairie dog colonies began to disappear, other animals went too. The black-footed ferret (*Mustela nigripes*) used to be the prairie dog's most deadly predator, entering the burrows with ease and dining on the hapless rodents. Ferrets have now been extirpated from Canada, and are exceedingly rare in the United States because of the destruction of the prairie dogs, the ferret's major food source.

Prairie dogs, burrowing owls (*Athene cunicularia*), and rattlesnakes (*Crotalus* sp.) all live together in a prairie dog town, but not agreeably. The burrowing owl lives in the burrow so it does not have to dig one itself. The rattlesnake lives there so it can feed on the prairie dogs. And occasionally the prairie dogs will kill an owl. It is just a case of each species taking advantage of the situation.

BLACK-TAILED PRAIRIE DOG.

## THE RODENT THAT LIKES SALT
### *Porcupine*

**The American porcupine (*Erethizon dorsatum*) invaded this continent from South America late in the Pleistocene period, when a flood of animals moved to and from North America.** It is firmly established today as an integral part of our native fauna, and is an especially characteristic feature of the north woods.

The porcupine is a strong and heavy animal that may weigh up to 30 pounds. Except for the damage it does by chewing any article that may contain a trace of salt, it is quite harmless as long as you keep your distance. (The effects of the porcupine's sharp quills can cause great discomfort.)

It may seem like a strange comparison, but the porcupine and the elephant have this much in common: They both have a very low reproductive rate and yet continue to thrive in the face of much opposition and increase rapidly under undisturbed conditions. The porcupine does not breed until it is 3 years old, and it produces only one offspring at a time (rarely two). Porcupine young are very well developed at birth and are able to use their quills for protection within a few hours. They become independent of their mothers within a few months.

Only one species of porcupine is found in North America, but similar animals are found throughout the world, and a variety of these creatures are found in Central and South America. Contrary to popular opinion, porcupines are not able to shoot their quills.

...........................

## IT PREYS ON PORCUPINES
### *Fisher*

**The fisher (*Martes pennanti*), a large species of weasel, has a distinction that no other meat-eating animal has: It is the only creature that habitually dines on porcupine.**

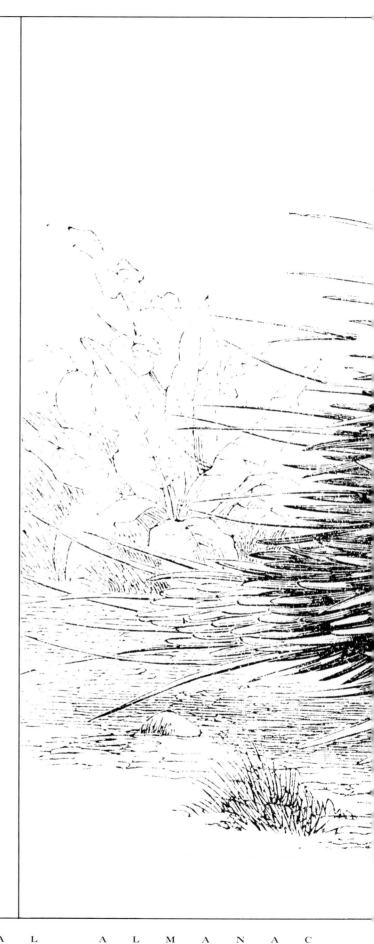

FISHER.

Its method is to flip the spiny rodent over on its back and attack the soft, unprotected belly. The rodent is quickly dispatched, and the fisher settles down to its meal. The entire procedure may take more than thirty minutes.

Very often, fishers have been observed with porcupine quills embedded in their fur, but the quills appear to create little inconvenience, and they generally work their way free in time. Neither do they seem to cause the terrible festering wounds that are suffered by most animals that have run-ins with porcupines. Nevertheless, mistakes do happen, and dead fishers with porcupine quills imbedded in them are reported from time to time.

. . . . . . . . . . . . . . . . . . . . . . .

## DRACULA OF THE ANIMAL KINGDOM
### *Weasel*

**Although weasels are the smallest carnivores, they have acquired a well-deserved reputation as the most bloodthirsty of killers.** They more than make up for their lack of size by their agility, strength, and courage. Adult weasels (*Mustela* sp.) may weigh less than half a pound, but the tenacity of these tiny mam-

WHITE WEASEL.

mals is utterly amazing; they do not hesitate to attack animals several times their size, and not infrequently they emerge victorious.

Many biologists believe that these animals exhibit true blood lust and actually kill for the sheer joy of it. Weasels have been known to enter and completely destroy a colony of rats. Frequently they are forced to move from one place to another because they have killed all the natural prey in that area.

One weasel nest contained eight mice plus the remains of six other rodents. A weasel, whose tracks a biologist was following in the snow, left eleven dead rabbits along its trail. Weasels usually drink a little blood from each victim before continuing the slaughter. Sometimes weasels will raid a chicken house; one little demon has been known to destroy more than forty fowls in a single night. This occasional outlaw has brought the wrath of farmers down on the heads of all weasels, and many people kill them on sight.

This is most unfortunate because weasels are generally extremely beneficial to farmers as destroyers of noxious rodents. One biologist has asserted that were it not for weasels, rats and mice would multiply so rapidly that they would overrun the earth. It has been estimated that the 300,000 weasels in New York State account for 60 million rats and mice every year.

. . . . . . . . . . . . . . . . . . . . . . .

## A GOOD SHOT
### *Skunks*

**Skunks are best known for their undesirable trait of discharging evil-smelling secretions into the atmosphere from their anal glands.** This defense is most effective in deterring would-be predators, and skunks are able to direct the substance with astonishing accuracy.

The method that a skunk employs in releasing the foul secretion varies with the species. The striped skunk (*Mephitis mephitis*), found throughout the United States and southern

Canada, simply turns its back and presents its anal glands in the most direct manner. The spotted skunk (*Spilogale putorius*) of the southwestern United States rises on its front feet, lowers its hind feet to the ground, and aims its noxious fluid at its enemies, often at the eyes. Both species can hit accurately within a range of 12 feet.

What is less well known about skunks is that they have probably made the greatest contribution in our fight against insect pests: It has been said that skunks destroy more in-

STRIPED SKUNK.

sects than do all other mammals combined.

Harmful insects that skunks consume include grasshoppers, crickets, potato beetles, cutworms, and white grubs. From an intensive survey in Canada made on an 8-acre tract, it was estimated that skunks were responsible for the destruction of more than 115,000 white grubs within a relatively short time. In New York, skunks were so effective in controlling the hop grub, a serious pest of hop plants, that the people showed their appreciation by demanding that the mammals receive full protection by law.

. . . . . . . . . . . . . . . . . . . . . .

## OWL MOBBING
*Owls*

**Eighteen species of owls are native to North America.** The largest is the great gray owl (*Strix nebulosa*) of the northwestern pine and spruce forests, with a length approaching 30

inches; the smallest is the elf owl (*Micrathene whitneyi*) of the southwestern desert area, which may grow to only 5¼ inches.

Owls can be separated from all other birds by their "facial disks," which conceal large external ear flaps. The large eyes of the owl are fixed in their sockets, so that the bird has to move its entire head in order to shift its gaze. A major characteristic of owls is their flight feathers, which are constructed in such a way as to make flight almost noiseless. These feathers have downy edges that eliminate most of the whir caused by the stiff primaries of other birds as they cut the air. This appears to apply mainly to nocturnal owls, however. Burrowing owls (*Speotyto cunicularia*), elf owls, pygmy owls (*Glaucidium gnoma*), and hawk owls (*Surnia ulula*), which are active during the day, all make an audible swishing noise when they fly.

Owls that roost in the open during the day are often persistently mobbed by smaller birds. The participants make frantic wing and tail cocking movements while uttering loud and repetitive alarm calls. The effect of this harassment on the owls is unpredictable. Sometimes they attempt to flee the mobbers, but usually they just stand their ground and do nothing. The smaller birds eventually lose interest.

ABOVE: BURROWING OWL AT PRAIRIE DOG TOWN.

OVERLEAF: GREAT HORNED OWL.

Mobbing is a common response of birds to certain predators that pose some degree of threat. It probably carries with it some survival value in that the mobbers draw attention to the whereabouts of the predator. Hawks may also be subject to mobbing, but less often because hawks are generally active during the day.

Not all owls are equally subject to mobbing. The great horned owl usually escapes harassment because it seldom attacks small birds, and the hecklers seem to be aware of that fact. The burrowing owl seems almost immune to attack, probably because small birds know this owl is of no danger to them.

One of the prime targets for mobbing is the pygmy owl, a diurnal species that specializes in preying on small birds. For that reason, anyone who can imitate the call of this small owl can often attract any number of small birds into his line of vision. Conversely, by listening to the excited scolding of songbirds, you can usually trace the commotion to the mobbing of an owl.

For many centuries, hunters have made good use of other birds' dislike of owls by tethering an owl, so that otherwise-wary birds can be lured within the range of guns or nets. This method is still employed today in Italy to lure migrating songbirds to the ground.

Owls have also been used to catch various kinds of hawks in Europe and were once an indispensable part of a team for hunting kites. While the kites were mobbing the owl, peregrine and lanner falcons were set loose to ground them. In North America, the great horned owl was used to entrap marsh hawks and ospreys.

. . . . . . . . . . . . . . . . . . . . . .

## THE TIGER OF THE AIR
### Great Horned Owl

**The great horned owl (Bubo virginianus) is a large and powerful bird ranging in length from 18 to 25 inches, the female being much the larger.** It is probably the fiercest and most savage of our predatory birds and has earned for itself the name of "tiger of the air."

This species is usually fairly common in woodland tracts throughout North America, from the timberline in the far north down into South America. Mainly nonmigratory, it will shift its range to find better hunting when there is a scarcity of food.

The bulk of its prey consists of rabbits, rats, and mice, though it is classified as a general feeder. It will include in its diet a wide range of animals, such as squirrels, groundhogs, cats, shrews, bats, grasshoppers, beetles, and birds ranging in size from sparrows to geese. The great horned owl also preys on snakes, fish, and scorpions.

Attacks on such adversaries as skunks and porcupines are not uncommon, encounters with the latter often having a fatal outcome for one or both participants. This owl does, however, appear to have some immunity against the ill effects of the skunk's defensive weapon dreaded by many other creatures. When food is especially scarce, the great horned owl will attack poultry and game birds, a practice frowned on by poultrymen, farmers, and gamekeepers.

The great horned owl has the distinction of being our earliest nesting bird; in parts of the northern United States and southern Canada it will often nest as early as late February, and in Virginia, as early as late January. The nest is usually the deserted domicile of a hawk or a crow, and both male and female birds share in the incubation of the eggs.

The reason for the extremely early mating habits may be the long dependence that the young birds have on their parents. From the time the eggs hatch, it generally takes ten weeks or so before the youngsters are able to fly away and fend for themselves. Consequently, the maturity of the great horned owl coincides with that of birds that breed later and reach adulthood sooner.

HORNED OWL.

# FEAR OF OWLS

**Owls, more than any other order of birds, are the subjects of superstitious beliefs.** They have been connected with witch-related characters bringing bad news and death by alighting on and calling from the housetops at night.

The mournful hooting of these birds, together with their predilection for roosting and hunting in churchyards and derelict buildings, has doubtless played a great part in creating this sinister reputation.

Pliny the Elder wrote of the owl: "When it appears, [it] foretells nothing but evil . . . and is more to be dreaded than any other bird." In the folklore of many ancient civilizations, there is a relationship between owls and death, and there still is today. In Sicily, the scops owl (*Otus scops*) is especially feared; should one call near the house of a sick man, it is believed that he will die three days later.

## SHIFT WORKERS
### *Owls and Hawks*

**A great many bird watchers maintain that birds of prey, or raptors, are the most exciting birds to observe.** Many of them are very large, and most are too rarely seen ever to become commonplace. In North America these are eagles, ospreys, buteo hawks, falcons, accipiters, kites, harriers, carcaras, vultures, and owls.

Although owls are generally grouped with hawks as birds of prey, they are, in fact, not directly related. Owls have much closer affinities with the goatsuckers, a family of birds that includes the whip-poor-will and the common nighthawk.

Owls and hawks have pursued independent lines of development but complement each other in that hawks have become specialized as daytime (diurnal) hunters, depending upon sight and speed to surprise their prey, and owls, using hearing to supplement vision, have become nighttime (nocturnal) hunters.

Where both the red-shouldered hawk (*Buteo lineatus*) and the barred owl (*Strix varia*) abide, the hawk is active during the day and the owl at night, hunting the same habitat in pursuit of similar prey. Both species have a predilection for large woods and require stands of trees that are sufficiently mature to provide numerous nesting and roosting hollows.

RED-TAILED HAWK AND PREY.

Similarly, short-eared owls (*Asio flammeus*) are the nocturnal equivalent of marsh hawks (*Circus cyaneus*), both in their hunting methods and prey. Both marsh hawks and short-eared owls roost on the ground. Also, the rough-legged hawk (*Buteo lagopus*) and the American kestrel (*Falco sparverius*) are replaced at night by the barn owl (*Tyto alba*) and the screech owl (*Otus asio*), respectively.

At night, the great horned owl (*Bubo virginianus*) replaces two diurnal species, the red-tailed hawk (*Buteo jamaicensis*) and the Cooper's hawk (*Accipiter cooperii*).Great horned owls compete with red-tailed hawks for nesting sites, since the owl builds no nest of its own and must appropriate large nests built by other birds, often by red-tails.

With the possible exception of eagles, the great horned owl is the most dominant North American raptor. The owl will tolerate a red-tailed hawk only at a distance of at least 350 to 700 yards of its nesting site, and will tolerate no raptor at all near its nest during the breeding season. One observer noted that out of eleven confrontations over nests and sites, the owls won nine times and the hawks only twice.

. . . . . . . . . . . . . . . . . . . . . . .

## THE BALANCE OF NATURE
*From Scarcity to Abundance and Back*

**The numbers of nearly all animals vary over a period of time, responding to favorable weather and many other things, but some animals are outstanding for their violent fluctuations between scarcity and abundance.**

There is no simple explanation for why excessive population buildups occur. They are most noticeable among herbivores such as rabbits, deer, and mice, whose main purpose is to produce food for flesh-eaters such as hawks, owls, weasels, and foxes. We can imagine that evolutionary processes might have long ago established a system whereby plant-eaters multiplied at a vast rate in order to keep pace

DEER.

with the heavy demand on their numbers, but here nature seems to have gone to extremes. A surplus of prey species is often far greater than can be taken care of by predators.

Eventually, however, starvation and disease will bring the population numbers back to normal. In the case of deer, starvation caused by overforaging of the winter food supply is likely to be the deciding factor. With rabbits, studies have shown that various diseases spreading quickly under crowded conditions drastically reduce the population almost overnight.

The value of predators, especially birds of prey, to our entire economy is easily traceable to the rodent depredations to which we would be subjected were it not for these birds.

The meadow mouse (*Microtus pennsylvanicus*), also known as the field mouse, field vole, or meadow vole, is an excellent example of an animal that has great fluctuations in numbers and merits a word by itself in any discussion of the habits of our native birds of prey, since mice form such a large proportion of their diet, especially the diet of owls. The meadow mouse is the most numerous mammal on the North American continent. It is also among the most destructive of the forces of nature that food-stuffs producers must contend with. Not only do meadow mice destroy grass; they also feed voraciously on roots, bulbs, tubers, twigs, flowers, seeds, and foliage, and they cause great injury by girdling trees, shrubs, and vines. The effects of removing or diminishing the natural enemies of this creature would be devastating.

OPPOSITE: HARVEST MICE.

# March

As the sun approaches and passes the vernal equinox on March 21, the days continue to lengthen and the weather gradually becomes more benign — seasonal changes that wildlife quickly responds to. Shortly before this important day each year, the turkey vultures wing their way back to Hinckley, Ohio, and — as legend has it — the famous cliff swallows return to San Juan Capistrano, California.

In March the red-breasted robin becomes a common sight in the backyard. Larger backyards — on the order of Yellowstone National Park in the mountains of the northwestern United States and the Okefenokee swamp in the flats of the southeastern United States — have more than their share of winged dwellers. Elsewhere the earliest summer visitors return to their summer breeding grounds: red-winged blackbirds, grackles, bobolinks, and Cooper's hawks. Milder March days will bring squirrels, groundhogs, chipmunks, and other hibernating mammals into the open.

OPPOSITE: GRAY SQUIRREL.

# MARCH

## 1

World's first national park, Yellowstone National Park, Wyoming, founded in 1872.

. . . . . . . . . . . .

## 2

Indiana and Ohio approved the cardinal as the official state bird in 1933.

. . . . . . . . . . . .

## 3

21 Bachman's warblers, possibly the rarest songbird in North America, perished when they struck a lighthouse in the Florida Keys in 1889. This number of the elusive spe-

CALIFORNIA CONDOR.

cies was greater than any seen since that time.

A boreal owl discovered near the Agapuk River, Alaska, in an abandoned igloo in 1905.

. . . . . . . . . . . .

## 4

Hot Springs National Park, Arkansas, and Kings Canyon National Park, California, established on this day in 1921 and 1940, respectively.

Heavy migration of yellow-rumped warblers witnessed along the coastal islands of South Carolina in 1920 by Charles L.

Whittle: "24,000 myrtle (yellow-rumped) warblers passed northward between nine in the morning and one in the afternoon."

. . . . . . . . . . . .

## 5

In 1971 the director of Iceland's Natural History Museum purchased a mounted specimen of a great auk in Sotheby's London auction rooms for £9,000 — the highest price ever paid for a stuffed bird. (The great auk became extinct in 1844, and disappeared from North America in 1785.)

## 6

Spotted owl discovered by Xantus, a pioneer naturalist to the Pacific coast area near Fort Tejon, in the southern Sierra Nevada, California, in 1858. It wasn't seen again for another 14 years.

. . . . . . . . . . . .

## 7

First whaling expedition departed from Southampton, Long Island, New York, in 1644.

. . . . . . . . . . . .

## 11

Last heath hen died on Martha's Vineyard, Massachusetts, in 1932.

FINBACK WHALE.

SEA OTTER.

## 14

President Theodore Roosevelt established Pelican Island as the first National Wildlife Refuge in 1903.

Lewis and Clark expedition left St. Louis, Missouri, in 1804, the start of a monumental 2½-year journey.

. . . . . . . . . . . .

## 15

On this day every year the turkey vultures return to Hinckley, Ohio.

. . . . . . . . . . . .

## 16

Arizona designated the cactus wren as the state bird in 1931.

## 18

Largest spotted bass (8 pounds 15 ounces) caught with rod and line taken in Lewis Smith Lake, Alberta, Canada, in 1978.

. . . . . . . . . . . .

## 19

According to legend, this is the day the cliff swallows arrive at San Juan Capistrano in California every year.

94 Sea otters observed near the mouth of Bixby Creek on California's Monterey Peninsula in 1938, after the animal had been generally regarded as extinct.

. . . . . . . . . . . .

## 21

Almost extinct Eskimo curlew observed on Galveston Island, Texas, by

Dudley Deaver and Ben Feltner in 1959 — the first sighting since 1915.

Nebraska approved the western meadowlark and Iowa the eastern goldfinch as official state birds on March 2, 1929 and 1933, respectively.

. . . . . . . . . . . .

## 23

A law prohibiting the teaching of the theory of evolution proposed by John Washington Butler was passed and signed by the Tennessee legislature in 1925.

. . . . . . . . . . . .

## 24

One of last passenger pigeons killed by a boy near Sargents, Pike County, Ohio, in 1900. This specimen is preserved in the Ohio State Museum.

. . . . . . . . . . . .

## 28

Immigrant European house sparrow first appeared in St. Louis, Missouri, in 1878, when it dislodged a pair of immigrant European tree sparrows from their nesting site.

## 29

First California condor chick born in captivity hatched at the San Diego Zoo, California, in 1983.

Bonaventure Island, Gaspé, Quebec, declared a federal migratory bird sanctuary in 1919. Bonaventure Island has the largest gannetry in the world.

. . . . . . . . . . . .

## 30

Okefenokee Swamp declared a National Wildlife Refuge by order of President Franklin D. Roosevelt in 1937.

Maryland approved the northern oriole and Missouri the eastern bluebird as official state birds on this day in 1882 and 1927, respectively.

. . . . . . . . . . . .

## 31

Largest white sea bass (83 pounds 12 ounces) caught with rod and line taken at San Felipe, Mexico, in 1953.

Largest white bass (5 pounds 9 ounces) caught with rod and line taken from the Colorado River in Texas.

BABY ROBIN.

# THIS ROBIN IS A THRUSH
## *American Robin*

O f all North American birds, there is none that comes into more intimate contact with humans than the American robin (*Turdus migratorius*).

But this robin is not a robin at all. It is a thrush. The early English colonists gave the bird its name doubtless because of its resemblance in coloration to the robin or redbreast (*Erithacus rubecula*) of England; but they failed to notice the close relationship between the American robin and the European blackbird (*Turdus merula*). These two birds, both thrushes, are very similar in habit, general deportment, and voice, although different in plumage. They are, in fact, equivalent species ecologically; the spotted breasts of these birds are indicative of their affiliation with the thrushes, a characteristic that all members of the genus *Turdus* show in the younger stages.

Forty-two percent of the robin's food is animal, mostly insects; the remainder is largely berries and other soft, small fruits, of which a little more than 1 percent is cultivated fruit. Although the American robin is an efficient aid to the agriculturalist because of its taste for insects, its fondness for fruit, especially cherries, occasionally gets it into trouble with growers of small fruit.

# RABBIT OR HARE?
## *Varying Hare*

T he varying hare or snowshoe rabbit (*Lepus americanus*) is classed as a hare, although if you follow local usage, you will call it a rabbit. The European hare (*L. europaeus*), introduced into this continent from Germany in 1912, is known to everyone as a jackrabbit, and the most typical North American hares, inhabiting the western part of the continent, are also known as jackrabbits.

It may seem odd to refer to the same animal as a hare and as a rabbit, but there is really no clearcut difference between the two. At one extreme is a hare that has long legs and ears and does not use a den or burrow but depends on speed to escape from its enemies. Its young are born in an uncovered nest with their eyes open, and they are able to look after themselves within a few days. At the other extreme is a rabbit that has shorter ears and legs and uses brushpiles, hollow logs, and burrows for concealment. Its young are born blind and helpless in a hidden nest. In between these two extremes there are many animals not quite typical of either.

# AMERICA'S FIRST NATIONAL PARK

Yellowstone National Park was established on March 1, 1872—first and largest of America's national parks, with an area of 2,221,773 acres. It borders three states, Wyoming, Montana, and Idaho, and is renowned for its hot springs, its geysers, its geographical attractions, and—by no means least—its wildlife.

The name *Yellowstone* is derived from a Minnetaree Indian word *Mi tsi a-da-zi*, which translates as "Rock Yellow River." The first full rendering of the river's name into English was made by explorer-geographer David Thompson, who located the stream during the winter of 1797–1798, and from information obtained from the Indians, called it "Yellow Stone."

Old Faithful, the most famous geyser in the park, erupts regularly twenty-one or twenty-two times a day, every day, year after year. Although many other great geysers have been dormant for months and even years, Old Faithful continues to be active. Some geysers erupt to a greater height than Old Faithful, but none erupts nearly as regularly and consistently.

The most remarkable thing about Yellowstone is that no matter when you visit it, no matter how many times you come, you will find something new to experience. The richness of the wildlife is perhaps the park's greatest attraction, together with some of the most breathtaking scenery in America.

The characteristic large mammals of Yellowstone are grizzly bear (*Ursus arctos horribilis*), black bear

ELK WITH NEW ANTLERS.

GRIZZLY BEAR.

(*Ursus americanus*), coyote (*Canis latrans*), bison (*Bison bison*), moose (*Alces alces*), wapiti (*Cervus canadensis*), mule deer (*Odocoileus hemionus*), bighorn sheep (*Ovis canadensis*), and pronghorn (*Antilocapra americana*). Other year-round residents include the marten (*Martes americana*), long-tailed weasel (*Mustela frenata*), ermine (*M. erminea*), mink (*M. vison*), wolverine (*Gulo gulo*), badger (*Taxidea taxus*), river otter (*Lutra canadensis*), Canada lynx (*Lynx canadensis*) and bobcat (*L. rufus*). The timber wolf (*Canis lupus*) and the cougar (*Felis concolor*)

are seen only occasionally in the northern part of the park.

Bears are undoubtedly the greatest danger to the tourist at Yellowstone. Like most animals in protected areas, bears tend to lose their natural fear of humans and can become extremely dangerous. However tame a bear may appear to be, it is best to remember that it is still wild and as such is totally unpredictable. Never approach or feed bears, and photograph them only at very safe distances.

Yellowstone is excellent birding country; no less than 227 avian species have been recorded within the confines of the park. Some of the rarer and

OVERLEAF: COYOTE.

LYNX.

most sought-after of the park's breeding species include: the bald eagle (*Haliaeetus leucocephalus*), peregrine falcon (*Falco peregrinus*), prairie falcon (*F. mexicanus*), osprey (*Pandion haliaetus*), ferruginous hawk (*Buteo regalis*), trumpeter swan (*Olor buccinator*), harlequin duck (*Histrionicus histrionicus*), Barrow's goldeneye (*Bucephala islandica*), white pelican (*Pelecanus erythrorhynchos*), great gray owl (*Strix nebulosa*), Wilson's phalarope (*Steganopus tricolor*), Clark's nutcracker (*Nucifraga columbiana*), Townsend's solitaire (*Myadestes townsendi*), American dipper (*Cinclus mexicanus*), mountain chickadee (*Parus gambeli*), mountain bluebird (*Sialia currucoides*), Lewis's woodpecker (*Asyndesmus lewis*), Williamson's sapsucker (*Sphyrapicus thyroideus*), and Mac-Gillivray's warbler (*Oporornis tolmiei*).

The park's finest birding localities are Hayden Valley, Lamar Valley, the upper reaches of the Absaroka Mountains, the Mammoth Hot Springs area, Squaw Lake, and the Mount Washburn Trails.

The best time to visit Yellowstone National Park is between May and October, when the major roads are usually open. However, adverse conditions can delay the spring opening dates or step up the fall closing dates. In winter, the only road open to automobiles is from the North Entrance at Gardiner, Montana, to Mammoth Hot Springs and to Cooke City, Montana, near the Northeast Entrance. Early and late snowstorms can close the road at any time. Reservations are not necessary to enter the park.

For further information on Yellowstone National Park, write: Superintendent, Yellowstone National Park, P.O. Box 168, Wyoming 82190.

## THE BUZZARDS OF HINCKLEY
*Turkey Vultures*

For most of the year the tiny hamlet of Hinckley, Ohio, is hardly more than a wide spot on the road. Two state highways cross in its midst, Ohio 303 and State Route 3, and if there were no traffic light at this intersection, an out-of-towner might pass by Hinckley without being aware of its existence.

But every March 15, Hinckley becomes the setting for one of the most important ornithological events of the year. The Ides of March is "Buzzard Day," traditionally and officially the day when the turkey vultures (*Cathartes aura*) return to Hinckley each year. Local lore has it that the vultures started flocking here around 1818, attracted by the tons of game refuse left by an early band of careless hunters. Most ornithologists point instead to Hinckley's favorable setting, remote yet close to farmlands and water, part forested and part cleared. It probably helps, too, that the nearby caves at Hinckley Ridge and Whip's Ledges provide easy roosting.

Excitement starts to run high in Hinckley toward the end of February, and by mid-March it reaches a high frenzy. There are prizes offered for the person who most accurately clocks the arrival of the first buzzards. Newspapers and radio announcers from Cleveland, 28 miles to the north, are concerned with little else, and the Hinckley Chamber of Commerce prepares for its one big annual celebration, the Buzzard Festival. A poet from Cleveland was even inspired to write a poem entitled "The Buzzards of Hinckley."

The turkey vulture is blackish brown, with wing coverts and linings of ashen gray, is approximately 30 inches long, with a wingspan that often reaches 5 to 6 feet, and is easily identified by its red and wrinkled head and neck. A fully grown turkey vulture can weigh up to 20 pounds.

Though ugly in repose, turkey vultures are as beautiful and graceful in flight as any bird you will ever see. On still days the birds can be seen riding the air currents for hours on end, without ever moving their wings. The local inhabitants of Hinckley have come to look upon the vulture with enlightened self-interest: The bird may not be a beauty, but it is a great tourist attraction.

Turkey vulture.

Vultures were once accused of spreading hog cholera, but actually no more efficient sanitary squad exists than these birds. Their digestive system destroys bacteria, and even their excretions probably are an effective antiseptic. Instead of squirting clear as an eagle does, they whitewash their own legs. The head, which comes into contact with putrid flesh, is naked, exposing infectious bacteria to the purifying rays of the sun.

## THE BIRDS OF OKEFENOKEE

**In southeastern Georgia, near the Florida border, lies Okefenokee, perhaps the world's most spectacular swamp.** It extends about 38 miles from north to south and is about 25 miles across at its widest part; 377,528 acres of this vast area are contained in Okefenokee National Wildlife Refuge, established by order of President Franklin D. Roosevelt on March 30, 1937.

Incredibly rich in wildlife, this primitive wilderness area is home to 225 species of birds, over 42 species of mammals, 58 species of reptiles, 32 species of amphibians, and 34 species of fish. There is also a flourishing population of over 10,000 alligators. Above all, this area is phenomenally rich in plant life, causing Okefenokee to be called, appropriately, "America's greatest natural botanical garden."

It is really surprising that Okefenokee still exists at all, for many attempts have been made to clear its timber and drain the life-sustaining water. More than 423 million board feet of lumber, most of it cypress, was removed between 1908 and 1926. Happily, the trees have grown back, illustrating that left to her own resources, nature has the power to restore and heal herself.

Okefenokee is a magically beautiful place, with its tangled forest of cypress, bay, and gum trees and hanging streamers of Spanish moss. The entire swamp is covered with a bed of peat, ranging from a thin layer to a depth of 20 feet. Thus the Seminole Indians, who made Okefenokee their home until 1838, called this wondrous place "land of the trembling earth."

Liston Elkins, a local naturalist, relates: "Just a little after World War II, a Greek artist came down here by bus to do some sketching of Okefenokee. He hired a boat, took a chicken lunch with him, and went into the swamp. Within an hour he was back. 'What happened?' he was asked. 'I don't like it,' he replied. 'Why not?' 'The damned place is beautiful!' 'Well, isn't that what you hoped to see?' 'Certainly not! I thought the place was a swamp!'"

Of the 225 species of birds recorded at Okefenokee, 78 have bred in the refuge. Of these, 41 are regarded as rare, and an additional 23 species are listed as very rare or accidental. Most spectacular of the swamp's avian life are its great wading birds: Flocks of white ibis (*Eudocimus albus*) and the wood stork (*Mycteria americana*) wing from one cypress stand to another. Great egrets (*Casmerodius albus*), cattle egrets (*Bubulcus ibis*), great blue herons (*Ardea herodius*), black-crowned night herons (*Nycticorax nycticorax*), and anhingas (*Anhinga anhinga*) are also seen in large numbers.

MALLARD.

The swamp is also very valuable as a migratory waterfowl sanctuary: Mallards (*Anas platyrhynchos*), black ducks (*A. rubripes*), pintails (*A. acuta*), green-winged teals (*A. crecca*),

YOUNG RED-SHOULDERED HAWK.

ring-necked ducks (*Aythya collaris*) and hooded mergansers (*Lophodytes cucullatus*) all overwinter here. And the wood duck (*Aix sponsa*), North America's most beautiful species, lives here the year round.

Both vulture species, the turkey vulture (*Cathartes aura*) and the black vulture (*Coragyps atratus*), are commonly observed riding the air currents. Okefenokee's most familiar birds of prey, however, are the red-shouldered hawk (*Buteo lineatus*) and the barred owl (*Strix varia*), which can usually be relied on to make an appearance.

That most beautiful warbler, the prothonotary warbler (*Protonotaria citra*), commonly nests in the hollow cypress trees of Okefenokee and never fails to thrill even the most blasé bird watcher. This is just one of the thirty-two warbler species recorded here, although only half a dozen can be regarded as common. Other sought-after birds that can be expected at Okefenokee include: the mockingbird (*Mimus polyglottos*), Carolina wren (*Thryothorus ludovicianus*), sandhill crane (*Brus canadensis*), yellow-throated warbler (*Dendroica dominica*), white-eyed vireo (*Vireo griseus*), chuck-will's-widow (*Caprimulgus carolinensis*), brown-headed nuthatch (*Sitta pusilla*), red-cockaded woodpecker (*Dendrocopus borealis*), swallow-tailed kite (*Elanoides forficatus*), southern bald eagle (*Haliaeetus l. leucocephalus*), osprey (*Pandion haliaetus*), glossy ibis (*Plegadis falcinellus*), limpkin (*Aramus guarauna*), Swainson's warbler (*Limnothlypis swainsonii*), and Bachman's sparrow (*Aimophila aestivalis*).

Early records indicate that the near-extinct ivory-billed woodpecker (*Campephilus principalis*) was once a familiar sight around the swamp. During his early days at Okefenokee, the swamp's first refuge manager, John Hopkins, saw ivory-bills several times, once "within a few yards." But he never saw any after 1903.

Perhaps the most sought-after bird at Okefenokee is the endangered red-cockaded woodpecker, of which only an estimated 3,000

OVERLEAF: GREAT BLUE HERON AND IBISES.

to 10,000 are believed to exist. This small woodpecker is between 7 and 8 inches long, with white bars on a black back, white spots on the wings, and white underparts. The cheeks are white. In the male, red feathers on both sides of the crown give the bird a rather jaunty appearance and form a sort of cockade, which gives the bird its name.

This woodpecker should be looked for where there are stands of longleaf pine; however, since it tends to stay deep within the pines, it is seldom seen.

The bird is most easily located during the breeding season (usually from March to early May), when an active pair of these woodpeckers converse in noisy chattering notes, so that the air resounds with their shrill, clear calls.

The red-cockaded woodpecker is endangered because its highly specialized habitat is being destroyed. Once found commonly throughout most of the south central and southeastern United States, it is now confined to old pine woods from southeastern Oklahoma, Arkansas, western Kentucky, southeastern Virginia, south to the Gulf Coast and southern Florida. This species chooses pine trees that are generally more than 70 years old and dying of "red heart," a disease that softens the heartwood.

With their strong chisel beaks, a pair of woodpeckers bore into the trunk and hollow out a nest cavity 8 to 12 inches deep, some 20 to 70 feet above the ground. Pine pitch oozes from the bark surrounding this hole; this sticky pitch possibly repels would-be predators and traps insects for food. If the nest tree dies, the birds desert it for living tree nearby. Unfortunately, these trees are cut for pulp before they are old enough to develop red heart: Timber management practices have not allowed any significant retention of old-growth pine, and have thus seriously reduced the available habitat. Okefenokee is one of a number of special areas designated to preserve habitat for this rare woodpecker. Currently, in some national forests, recognized nest trees are being

WHITE-FACED IBIS.

saved, and some unoccupied aging pines are being left close to nests for later use.

Undoubtedly, one of the most striking birds of Okefenokee is the Florida sandhill crane. This bird is one of three recognized subspecies of sandhill cranes and is rare throughout much of its limited range—due to shooting and egg collection, which not only reduced

its numbers but also its range. It may, however, be seen frequently at Okefenokee. In addition to making its home at Okefenokee, the Florida sandhill crane is found locally west of Pascagoula, Mississippi; in Baldwin County, Alabama; and in several parts of Florida.

This bird presents a stirring sight as it stands fully erect and motionless, alert to any ap-proach of danger. From the tip of the tail to the tip of the 6-inch bill, the bird measures from 40 to 48 inches. It is all gray save for the top of its head, which is crowned with red. It also sports a wingspan of 6 to 7 feet.

The best time to view the Florida sandhill crane is during the mating time, which begins in January and may continue into April. At this time the birds congregate on an elevated spot and perform a most intricate dance prior to choosing their partners. The dance consists of a series of prances executed very daintily, with intermittent bowing in every direction.

During the nesting season the sandhill crane appears to be quite tame and may allow an intruder to approach the nest. At this point, the female bird may rest her long neck on the ground in an effort to escape detection. Should this strategy fail, she will take a few strides before rising into the air while uttering the alarm call. Then the male bird will usually arrive on the scene, and their whooping calls become so frenzied that the intruder is only too glad to retreat.

The whip-poor-will, common throughout most of eastern North America, occurs at Okefenokee only as a rare winter visitor: at other times, it is replaced by the larger, buff-colored chuck-will's-widow.

The chuck-will's-widow belongs to a family of birds known commonly as goatsuckers — a name they were given because they were once believed to milk goats. These birds have small bills and large mouths bordered with stiff bristles.

Being nocturnal, the chuck-will's-widow is more often heard than seen. It may, however, be unexpectedly encountered during the day while roosting on the ground. But with its leaflike coloration, it may be taken for dead foliage heaped together by the wind. The sound of the chuck-will's-widow is heard long and often between dusk and dawn, from the first of March until the end of August; its call says "Chuck-will's-widow." It is the habit of these birds to hawk for insects after dark, flying just a few feet above the ground on noiseless wings.

The nesting season of the chuck-will's-widow begins early in March, when two eggs are laid on the bare ground or on dead leaves in hammocks or pine woods. If the eggs or young birds are disturbed, the parent birds may remove them to another locality.

Of the thirty-two species of warblers recorded within the swamp area, only seven are known to have bred here. They are the yellow-throated warbler, Swainson's warbler, prothonotary warbler, northern parula warbler (*Parula americana*), common yellowthroat (*Geothlypis trichas*), hooded warbler (*Wilsonia citrina*), and pine warbler (*Dendroica pinus*).

One of the commonest of these is the pine warbler, although it is perhaps less often observed than the others. This bird is difficult to locate because it prefers to keep to the top of pine trees on which it feeds and is also less distinctly marked than other warblers. The male has an olive-colored back with pale yellowish underparts, lightly streaked with black. The dull brownish black wings have dull white bars. The female is somewhat duller on the back, and her underparts are gray, and she may have a wash of yellow on her breast.

The pine warbler is a slow-moving species as it climbs about the pine needles and pries into the crevices of tree trunks. It will, however, sometimes fly to the ground to gather insects. This warbler is a permanent resident at Okefenokee, where its faint, slow but musical, song can usually be heard throughout the year; the song is uttered as the bird perches high in the topmost branches of a pine.

Bird watching can be very rewarding at Okefenokee at any time, although the activity among the birds is greatest during the spring months (March to May). Access to the refuge may be made at the north entrance, where tourists can, in an hour or two, get a good idea of what Okefenokee is like. The North Entrance to the refuge at Okefenokee Swamp Park, is 8 miles south of Waycross via U.S. 1 or U.S. 23. The visitor center and interpretive facilities are at Suwanee Canal Recreation Area, 11 miles southwest of Folkston (East Entrance via State Route 23).

For further information, write: Okefenokee National Wildlife Refuge, P.O. Box 117, Waycross, Georgia 31501.

CHUCK-WILL'S-WIDOW BY AUDUBON.

# FIN-FOOTED
*Seals*

**Seals, sea lions, and walruses (suborder Pinnipedia — meaning "fin-footed") represent thirty-two species of carnivorous mammals that are adapted for life at sea, but are still dependent on land, especially at breeding time.** They propel themselves through the water with their flippers and also by movements of their flexible bodies. They can dive to depths of 600 feet and can stay under water without breathing for almost three quarters of an hour.

Since pinnipeds are poorly equipped to defend themselves against large land carnivores, they tend to frequent small, isolated breeding grounds usually on an island or on ice, rather than along mainland shorelines. They are distinctly more sociable and gregarious than land animals.

True seals differ from eared seals (sea lions and fur seals) in that they have no earflap and their bodies are usually more streamlined, making them more fully aquatic than sea lions. In addition, the front flippers of true seals are shorter, and instead of moving forward by paddling with their front flippers, as sea lions do, they employ a sideways motion of their hind flippers to propel their bodies forward.

Sea lions have a tiny earflap on either side of the head, a longer neck, and long, strong front flippers that they use as powerful paddles to propel themselves through the water. Sea lions' most characteristic feature is that their hind flippers are capable of rotating forward like feet, enabling them to be far more mobile on land than seals. Because the hind flippers of seals cannot be turned forward, they are virtually helpless on land.

The most familiar pinniped is the California sea lion (*Zalophus californianus*), the "trained seal" of oceanariums, circuses, and zoos, and also the fastest swimmer of the family, having been clocked at a speed of 25 m.p.h.

The giant of the group, and among the largest of mammals, is the southern elephant seal (*Mirounga leonina*). The largest specimen on record is a bull killed in Possession Bay, South Georgia, on February 28, 1913, that measured about 22½ feet long and weighed about 12,200 pounds. North America's largest pinniped, the northern elephant seal (*Mirounga angustirostris*), which is found off southern California and the west coast of Mexico, is only slightly smaller.

Because of the distinct differences between seals and sea lions, current thinking has the former arising from an otterlike ancestor and the sea lions and their kin (fur seals and walruses) evolving independently from a creature distinctly related to a bear. This likeness to bears is well illustrated in the northern fur seal (*Callorhinus ursinus*), a species of eared seal, whose scientific name means "bearlike with a beautiful snout." The description alludes to the pointed noses of the fur seals, compared to the blunt snouts of sea lions and walruses.

BULL FUR SEAL.

# IT WALKS WITH ITS TEETH
*Walrus*

**The walrus (*Odobenus rosmarus*), a large Arctic-dwelling member of the "pinnipeds" (a suborder of marine carnivores consisting of seals, sea lions, and walrus), is quite distinctive by virtue of its ivory tusks and big bristly moustache.** The large ivory tusks, which may reach a length of 3 feet, are used principally for hauling the animal along on the ice; the walrus belongs to the family Odobenidae, meaning "those that walk with their teeth."

One walrus species contains two races, one native to the Atlantic (*O. r. rosmarus*), the other to the Pacific (*O. r. divergens*).

To most people, the walrus is intimately associated with ice floes and arctic waters, and the idea of vast sandy beaches seems to be out of keeping with what is known of its present-day distribution. However, many historical sources show that the walrus occurred as far south as Sable Island, off the coast of Nova Scotia, and probably remained there until perhaps the end of the eighteenth century.

On a cold, blustery day in early February 1963, Arthur Mansfield, of the Fisheries Research Board of Canada, and his assistant, were trudging along the exposed western spit of Sable Island when they stumbled on a small, sharp object projecting from the sand. It was a highly-polished and well-worn walrus tusk, firmly attached to a large buried skull. This was by no means the first walrus skull to turn up on Sable Island, but what Mansfield found particularly interesting was that it was discovered on the very same exposed site, well out on the western spit, that is now frequented by many hundred gray seals (*Halichoerus grypus*) throughout the year.

The walrus was also known to have inhabited the shallow waters of the Gulf of St. Lawrence, and was found in large numbers on Magdalen Island, and on Miscou Island and near the northwestern tip of Prince Edward Island. The large populations of the St. Lawrence and of Sable Island suffered severely at the hands of early mariners and settlers, and few survived beyond the eighteenth century.

The Eskimo prizes the walrus above all other marine creatures, not only for its massive bulk and rich store of food, but also for its magnificent aggressiveness when hunted. The art of hunting walrus from a kayak is lost now, except perhaps to the Polar Eskimos of Greenland and to a few of the Belcher Island Eskimos. Instead, the use of fragile canvas and wood freight canoes is increasing. Whaleboats are also popular craft, and these, together with canoes, form the chief means of hunting walrus in the loosely packed ice.

Such hunting practice is common during the spring and early summer months. After sighting a suitable small group of walruses sprawled out on the ice floe, the Eskimos close in to it as silently as possible and try to shoot the animals before they can plunge into the water.

Natural mortality must be low for, apart from humans, the killer whale (*Orca orcinus*) and the polar bear (*Ursus maritimus*) are the two most important predators. The killer whale is occasionally a menace around Bering Sea walrus herds; the polar bear can be dangerous only to calves and immature walruses.

The chief diet of the walrus consists of clams and sea snails. Occasionally a walrus, for reasons not fully understood, will turn carnivorous and feed on whale carcasses or prey on small ringed seals (*Pusa hispida*) or bearded seals (*Erignathus barbatus*). Such specimens are almost always solitary, adult bulls. The act of predation has never been witnessed by a biologist, but tales of seal-killing walruses abound in Eskimo folklore and in contemporary stories, and sea mammal remains have been found in the stomachs of dead walrus. The liver of a seal-eating walrus is dangerous to humans because, like the liver of the polar bear, it may contain a toxic amount of vitamin A.

# April

April witnesses the emergence of the insect world, the beginning of intense activity that does not subside until autumn. Trillions of flies now appear, to the consternation of the fresh-water fisherman, who prefers to eradicate the little pests with sprays and powders, but very much to the delight of hungry birds recently arrived from their long journey north. Birds will feast on new generations of flies, moths, and butterflies, and underwater, grubs, trout, bass, pike, perch, sunfish, and carp will try to consume any of the tiny creatures that come within their reach — whether or not they're attached to strings and hooks.

If the weather is warm enough, the first snakes of the season can be observed as they move silently through the underbrush in search of a safe place to soak up the sun.

BROAD-TAILED HUMMINGBIRDS.

OPPOSITE: RACCOON.

# APRIL

**1**

Largest yellowfin tuna (388 pounds 12 ounces) caught with rod and line taken off San Benedicto Island, Mexico, in 1977.

. . . . . . . . . . . .

**3**

Isle Royale National Park, Michigan, established in 1940. This is one of the few areas where wolves still thrive in the United States.

. . . . . . . . . . . .

**6**

Maine declared the black-capped chickadee as the official state bird in 1927.

**8**

Michigan designated the American robin as the official state bird in 1931.

. . . . . . . . . . . .

**9**

Two cougars believed to be endangered eastern cougars sighted at Indian Head, 40 miles east of Regina, Saskatchewan, Canada, in 1969.

Largest bluegill (4 pounds 12 ounces) caught with rod and line taken in Ketona Lake, Alberta, Canada, in 1950.

. . . . . . . . . . . .

**10**

A nest of the almost extinct ivory-billed woodpecker (America's rarest bird) containing four eggs discovered by S. W. Wilson at Altamaha Swamp, Georgia, in 1892.

84

TIMBER WOLF.

## 13

Archibald Belaney, better known as Grey Owl, died in 1938. This Englishman, who passed himself off as an Indian, was Canada's best-known conservationist.

. . . . . . . . . . . .

## 17

Specimen of almost extinct Eskimo curlew collected near Norfolk, Nebraska, in 1915. The species was not sighted again until 1959.

. . . . . . . . . . . .

## 18

First whooping crane egg laid in captivity, at the Patuxent Wildlife Research Center, Laurel, Maryland, in 1975.

Great San Francisco earthquake occurred in 1906.

. . . . . . . . . . . .

## 19

Olive-backed warbler, a Mexican species, first discovered north of the border when three specimens were shot at Hidalgo, Texas, in 1877.

Tennessee adopted the mockingbird as the official state bird in 1933.

IVORY-BILLED WOODPECKER.

Largest freshwater drum (54 pounds 8 ounces) caught with rod and line taken in Nicka-jack Lake, Tennessee, in 1972.

First Eurasian golden plover reported for North America on the Avalon Peninsula, Newfoundland, Canada, in 1961.

. . . . . . . . . . . .

## 23

Florida approved the mockingbird as the state bird in 1907.

## 25

20 European tree sparrows brought to and liberated in Lafayette Park, St. Louis, Missouri, by a bird dealer on April 25, 1870. None were seen again until April 24, 1871, when a single bird was spotted 1 mile east of the park.

. . . . . . . . . . . .

## 26

John James Audubon, probably America's most well known bird painter, born at Les Cayes, Haiti, in 1785.

Largest American shad (9 pounds 4 ounces)

caught with rod and line taken in the Delaware River, Pennsylvania, in 1979.

. . . . . . . . . . . .

## 28

Largest permit (51 pounds 8 ounces) caught with rod and line taken in Lake Worth, Florida, in 1978.

. . . . . . . . . . . .

## 29

Captain William Clark's entry in his journal regarding the grizzly bear in 1805, reads: "Of the strength and ferocity of this animal, the Indians had given us dreadful accounts. They never attack him but in parties of six or eight persons, and then are often defeated with a loss of one or more of their party."

Colorado designated the lark bunting as the official state bird in 1931.

. . . . . . . . . . . .

## 30

A little brown bat found in a cave on Mount Aeoles, East Dorset, Vermont, in 1960; it had been banded in Massachusetts in 1937, making the animal at least 24 years old.

85

## THE FIRST BUTTERFLIES OF SPRING
### *Mourning Cloak*

Certain members of the butterfly family Nymphalidae hibernate throughout the entire winter in the adult butterfly stage (imago), concealing themselves in hollows in tree trunks, under large stones or logs, in the corners of barns and outhouses and other suitable refuges.

They are among the first butterflies to appear in the northern states — they come out as soon as the weather is warm and sunny enough for their liking. Very often, an unusually mild day in midwinter will temporarily bring them forth from their hiding places, and you may witness the incongruous sight of butterflies flying against a background of snow.

By far the most common of this group of butterflies are the mourning cloaks *(Nymphalis antiopa)*, which are fairly widespread through North America in wooded areas and open country. Somewhat sluggish after their long winter sleep, they flitter about for a while, then rest with wings extended on the ground, often remaining motionless for some time.

A freshly emerged adult mourning cloak is a strikingly beautiful insect, although most early-spring adult specimens tend to be rather ragged and worn after their hibernation period. The butterfly is a rich maroon-brown with a light yellow border along the outer margins of the wings. A number of irregularly shaped large blue spots inset in black run along the inside of the pale-colored border.

In England, where this butterfly occurs only as a very rare migrant from Scandinavia, it is known by the delightful name of "Camberwell beauty" and is greatly prized by collectors.

. . . . . . . . . . . . . . . . . . . . . . .

## A NOISY SPRING

By 1962, when Rachel Carson's book *Silent Spring* came out, a few people had already noticed a relationship between elm trees sprayed with DDT to kill bark beetles, which cause Dutch elm disease, and the death of robins.

The top predators, especially fish-eating birds of prey, were most vulnerable to this chemical hazard because they prey mainly on the unwary, the sick, the dying, and the dead, those most heavily laden with pesticide poisons. Each meal added measurably to the concentration held in their own bodies. Even if they grew to maturity and reproduced, the shells of their eggs did not contain the usual amount of calcium. The too-thin eggshells were unable to withstand the wear and tear of incubation, and the eggs failed to hatch. Consequently, raptor populations declined drastically.

However, since the almost total ban on the use of DDT in Canada in 1971, and in the United States in 1972, many of these populations have shown significant signs of a resurgence.

......................

## PIONEER BIRD MAN
### *John James Audubon*

**B**orn at Les Cayes, in tropical Haiti, on April 26, 1785, the son of a French naval captain, planter, and slavetrader, John James Audubon was destined to become the best known and most picturesque of all American naturalists.

In complete dedication to producing a book on North American birds of unparalleled magnitude, Audubon vagabonded through eastern North America for nearly half a century, shooting, preparing, and sketching birds and gathering notes on their habits and distribution. Armed with spyglass, shotgun, notebook, and sketch pad, and traveling mostly on foot or horseback, by boat or stagecoach, Audubon carried out his vast and daring plan in the face of almost insurmountable difficulties.

Though considered by many an incompetent madman, he persisted in his colossal undertaking, never giving up despite setbacks that would have discouraged anybody else: In 1812, for example, a hundred of his drawings were destroyed by rats in Henderson, Kentucky; it took him three years to replace them. In 1819 he was sent to debtors prison (his business ventures were a consistent failure); in 1821, while in New Orleans, he and his family were so poor he couldn't afford to buy himself a new journal, and his wallet was stolen. In 1824 he fell victim to a similar act on the Canadian side of the Niagara River.

Unable to find a publisher for his book, he set out and obtained nearly 200 subscribers at $1 each, on both sides of the Atlantic, on the strength of his personality and the excellence of his paintings. He, was, in fact, not only author and illustrator of the book, but production manager, publisher, salesman, and collector as well.

Armed with a portfolio of 240 drawings, Audubon sailed for England in 1826 and met with instant acclaim there. In Paris in 1828, distinguished zoologist Baron Georges Cuvier said that Audubon's paintings "surpass[ed] in magnificence anything of the kind ever likely to be painted."

*The Birds of America* was published by Audubon himself in London (at a cost of $100,000) between 1827 and 1838 in eighty-seven parts (comprising four volumes measuring 39½ inches by 29½ inches), containing 435 life-size, hand-colored plates of birds, based on his own dramatic paintings. Fewer than 200 sets were printed. Today they are collector's items. Were a set to become available on the market now, it could not be had for under $100,000.

Audubon later collaborated with John Bachman on his two-volume *Viviparous Quadrupeds of North America*, which contains 150 hand-colored plates of mammals. Half the plates were based on paintings by Audubon's son, John Woodhouse Audubon. Between 1846 and 1854 three volumes of text appeared, two of which were published by his other son, Victor Gilford Audubon. These later volumes contained five additional plates.

Birds were Audubon's chief interest, however, and his writings contain descriptions of twenty-three North American species that were new to science. The Audubon's shearwater (*Puffinus lherminieri*), the Audubon's warbler (*Dendroica auduboni*), and the Audubon's caracara (*Caracara cheriway*) were named in his honor by contemporaries. These, plus the numerous Audubon societies that bear his name, attest to the high esteem in which he is held in ornithological and popular natural history circles.

Audubon was personally acquainted with 385 species of North American birds, a remarkable record considering the difficulties under which he operated, the paucity of published information, and the primitive modes of transportation available to him in the early years of his fieldwork.

His paintings, which revolutionized the realm

WHITE PELICAN.

of bird art, were unexcelled until American illustrator Louis Agassiz Fuertes began exhibiting his work in 1895.

Most of Audubon's original watercolors (432 of them) were purchased from his widow in 1863 by the New York Historical Society for $2,000, by public subscription.

Audubon died famous and well-to-do in New York City on January 27, 1851, at age 66.

. . . . . . . . . . . . . . . . . . . . . .

# IT LAYS ITS EGGS IN OTHER BIRDS' NESTS
*Brown-Headed Cowbird*

Nobody has ever found a nest of the brown-headed cowbird *(Molothrus ater)* because there hasn't ever been one. The brown-headed cowbird is the only entirely parasitic North American bird, taking the place here of the notorious cuckoo *(Cuculus canorus)* of Europe, which also lays its eggs in the nests of other birds.

COWBIRD.

The cowbird gets its name from its habit of following cattle about the fields in order to take advantage of the insects stirred up by the feeding animals. In the old days they were called buffalo birds because they followed the bison herds, and it has been suggested that they lost their nest-building habit by following the moving herds and not staying long enough in one place to make a nest.

EASTERN YELLOW WARBLER.

Before we knew much about such things, it was thought that cowbirds were complete gypsies, wandering around the country and laying their eggs in other nests at random. It is now known, however, that they pair as other birds do and claim a certain territory within which the female lays about five eggs in various nests. They usually choose the nests of the smaller birds, such as sparrows, warblers, and vireos. They sneak the eggs in when the rightful owners are absent, and most of these never notice the difference. Even when the aggressive young cowbird takes more than its share of food, or pushes its smaller nest mates out of the nest, the deluded foster parents go right on feeding it.

Cowbirds regularly lay their eggs in the nests of yellow warblers *(Dendroica petechia)*. This common species usually builds its nest in a prominent position near the top of a shrub or small tamarack tree; doubtless, the bird is so frequently victimized by the cowbird because its nest is easy to locate.

Sometimes, however, the yellow warbler builds a platform over the alien eggs and resumes her domestic activities all over again. It is not uncommon for cowbird eggs to be found in a nest that has been completely covered over by a new yellow warbler's nest.

. . . . . . . . . . . . . . . . . . . . . .

## The Young of Animals Other Than Mammals & Birds

| | |
|---|---|
| Butterfly | Caterpillar, larva |
| Codfish | Codling, sprag |
| Dragonfly | Nymph |
| Eel | Elver |
| Fish (generally) | Fingerling, fry |
| Frog | Tadpole, polliwog |
| Mackerel | Spike, blinker, tinker |
| Moth | Caterpillar, larva |
| Salmon | Parr, smolt, grise |
| Shark | Cub |

## BUILT FOR SPEED
*Hummingbirds*

**When a hummingbird hovers over a flower, its wings can hardly be seen because they are beating at an incredible 55 beats per second.** A camera must be set at less than 1/5000 of a second to catch a picture of them. This beating rate gives the bird all the maneuverability of a helicopter, enabling it to hang suspended in midair, fly backwards, dart sideways, and rise vertically.

But this is nothing compared with the beating rate it achieves when flying at a speed of 60 miles an hour, which it does often. Its wings then vibrate about 200 times a second. The hummingbird's top speed is said to be 80 miles an hour, attained when chasing another hummingbird. It can keep up a speed of 60 miles an hour nonstop for hundreds of miles. During the migration north from Central America in spring, ruby-throated hummingbirds (*Archilochus colubris*) frequently pass ships out at sea — traveling four or five times faster than the ships.

The hummingbird is especially pugnacious and will attack birds much larger than itself. It has been known to engage hawks and eagles in aerial combat. Its weapon is its long, needlelike bill, which it uses to attack the eyes of its enemies, and this, coupled with its ability to fly straight up, down, sideways, and backwards, makes it a very dangerous adversary.

Not surprisingly, hummingbirds have the highest energy output per unit of weight of any living warmblooded animal. They also have the lowest blood temperature: Readings as low as 56 degrees Fahrenheit have been recorded.

## CHISEL BILLS
*Woodpeckers*

**All woodpeckers have claws adapted to climbing and some have tails ending in stiff feathers with which they prop themselves upright while working on tree trunks.** The bills of these wood-boring birds are as sharp and effective as chisels, enabling them to dig deep into trees to reach wood-destroying insects. These they extract with a long, barbed tongue that serves as a sort of fork; it is longer than the bird's mouth, so is curled up when not in use.

The Northern three-toed woodpecker (*Picoides tridactylus*) is particularly skillful and is a respected ally of the forester. Implacable foes of the bark beetles, these birds pursue their war against the enemies of the forest the year round. The bill of the sapsucker (*Sphyrapicus* sp.) is shorter than that of the woodpecker and thus its penetration is not so deep. The sapsucker's tongue ends in a brushlike form that it uses as a spoon. These birds can kill young trees by injuring the cambium, the source of the growth cells, but for this they compensate by consuming spiders, caterpillars, moths, and insect larvae.

The downy woodpecker (*Picoides pubescens*) has a still shorter bill; it cannot probe much deeper than the thickness of the bark, from which it takes many crawling things. The common flicker (*Colaptes auratus*) spends less time on trees than on the ground, where it digs immense quantities of ants and beetles.

......................

## OUR CLEVEREST NATIVE ANIMAL
### *Raccoon*

**For the most part the progress of humans and the expansion of their environment in the form of large towns and cities have caused the decline in numbers and even the complete extinction of many of our native animals.**

Not so for the raccoon (*Procyon lotor*), however. This marked bandit, with its shrewd ways and humanlike hands, has learned well to adapt to our mode of living and even uses us to its own advantage. Raccoons may, in fact, be as numerous now as they have ever been in modern times. This is not the case with some other city-dwelling animals, such as the striped skunk (*Mephitis mephitis*) and the red fox (*Vulpes vulpes*), both of which have declined somewhat in numbers over the past 25 years.

Since the raccoon is largely a night prowler, it is more likely to be observed during the hours of darkness. In fact, its eyes often give

PILEATED WOODPECKER.

RACCOON.

it away, since they are lit up by the headlights of cars.

Not everyone likes the raccoon. Many farmers think it is a pest, for it may raid their henhouses at night. The little bandit is also likely to help itself to the farmer's corn patch, as it is especially fond of corn. In its favor, the raccoon is charming and friendly, gets rid of a number of insects, and eats lots of garbage. Many people who are paid regular visits by raccoons are not always happy with this last habit, for the garbage-hunting animals often leave the place looking like a disaster area.

Since the raccoon is highly adaptable, it is likely to make a very good pet. Humane Societies shelter them on occasion. Trying to tame an animal captured in the wild is not suggested, however, unless it is very young or orphaned. And people with dogs should forget the idea of having a raccoon for a pet, for raccoons are generally very wary of dogs and avoid them whenever possible.

As well as being one of our most successful wild animals, the raccoon may well be the most intelligent of North American animals. There are numerous accounts of raccoons unscrewing complicated tops off bird-feeders, unhooking garbage-can tops, opening barn and garage doors, and removing the suet from a tight mesh bag suspended from a fragile tree limb without breaking the limb or tearing the mesh.

Dr. K. L. Michels of Purdue University in Indiana testifies that raccoons learn even more quickly than marmosets and cats. A number of demanding intelligence tests using food as the key were conducted on raccoons. They took just 800 trials to achieve 75 percent success on a given problem. Marmosets required 5,000 trials and cats 7,000 to reach the same success ratio as the raccoons.

. . . . . . . . . . . . . . . . . . . . . .

## NATIVE FRESHWATER FISH

**Fish are ideally equipped for their aquatic existence.** Their tails are adapted in the same way as skulling oars for propelling their streamlined bodies through the water. They have fins to help maintain their balance and direction. And they also have swim bladders, which permit them to go up and down as they please. By expelling air out of their swim bladders, they are able to sink; forcing air in again enables them to rise.

A typical fish has two pairs of fins, corresponding to the limbs of four-footed mammals. These are known as the pectoral and ventral fins. Also, there is usually a single prominent fin on the back (the dorsal fin), and the tail fin itself (the caudal fin).

Unlike mammals and birds, fish continue to grow throughout their lifetime; the older the fish, the greater its size. However, fish vary greatly in size according to their environment. Those inhabiting large bodies of water, such as lakes and rivers, tend to be significantly larger than the same species found in small ponds and brooks. The amount of available food in the water also has a decided bearing on their size.

Fish breathe by way of gills situated at the back of the head and protected by gill covers. Incidentally, almost all fish have ears of a kind, but they are hidden. It is generally believed that fish make little use of their hearing, relying more on their sense of smell to seek out their food.

Young fish feed on plankton (minute plant and animal life), while most adults feed on smaller fish species and other vertebrates. Some fish, however, are strictly plant-eaters. Fish are an important source of food for other animals, their only means of protection being their ability to hide and to swim fast. Very young fish are almost entirely defenseless, and their chances of reaching maturity are extremely slim. This is why many species lay millions of eggs at one time.

Fish and fisheries constitute a valuable part of North America's natural resources, for not only are they of considerable commercial value, they are also of importance as a form of outdoor recreation. This continent contains some of the finest salmon, trout, and char populations available anywhere, although industrial development and technological fallout are

threatening the continued existence of these species in even the most remote places.

Here are just a few of the popular fish species found in the inland waters of North America:

### Rainbow Trout

**The very attractive rainbow trout (*Salmo gairdneri*) is originally a native of the Pacific coastal waters of North America and was introduced into the east in the early part of the century.** It has the typically trout-shaped laterally compressed body and a large mouth with many large teeth. There are variations in color and body form, which are generally believed to be environmentally controlled. Taxonomists conclude that if all the forms were placed in the same environment, they would become quite indistinguishable from one another.

The rainbow trout has a vivid red or purplish broad band that extends from behind the eye across the body and tail. This colored band is only evident in adult fish, especially in spawning males. It is from this distinctive feature that the fish gets its name. Its back is

LARGEMOUTH BASS.

green or greenish blue, blending to silvery on the sides, and the underside is white. Numerous black spots also adorn the top of the head, the body, and the fins.

It generally takes two to three years to reach maturity, and spawning usually takes place about April or May, with the adults migrating upstream to clear rapid water. There, a nest is constructed in the clean gravel. With the completion of spawning, the adults move downstream again, where they usually remain permanently.

The rainbow trout is an exceptionally popular game fish because of its fighting ability and its beauty. This species is one of the top five sport fishes in North America and the most important west of the Rocky Mountains.

The size of rainbow trout varies greatly with the type of habitat: Pacific Ocean specimens tend to be the largest, and the record catch for this species may be one taken many years ago in Jewel Lake in British Columbia, which tipped the scales at 52 pounds. The record for the state of New York is a 21-pound 9-ounce specimen taken in the Salmon River in 1979.

### Northern Pike

**The northern pike (*Esox lucius*) is found throughout most of Europe and northern Asia as well as North America.** It ranges the entire northern part of our continent south to Missouri, where it is easily identified by its very elongated and somewhat compressed body. The head is large, as is the mouth, with its many long, needle-sharp teeth. This species is readily distinguished from the closely related muskellunge (*E. masquinongy*) by its different arrangement of markings and coloration and by the less extensive scaling on its cheeks.

The northern pike's ground color consists of various shades of green graduating to lighter hues on the sides. There are also numerous light horizontal spots along the sides and dark green blotching on the yellowish fins; the underneath is white. Very young pikes have light vertical bars.

Spawning takes place in the early spring in shallow bays and marshy areas. These fish return to spawn in the same area every year. The eggs are scattered at random and then abandoned by the parent fish. In summer, pike can be found in weedy shallows of lakes, hanging motionless just below the surface of the water. They move into deeper water with the onset of winter.

The northern pike is one of our most popular fish, and is of high commercial importance, especially in our northern inland waters. It feeds primarily on other fish, such as yellow perch, minnows, and suckers, and occasionally supplements its diet with frogs, snakes, mice, small ducks, and muskrats.

These fish may grow to a large size: Specimens measuring over 3 feet in length and weighing over 20 pounds are not uncommon. Pike grow much larger in Europe than in North America: A list of large British pike drawn up in 1971 included at least eight individuals that equal or exceed all North American records. The angler record for a pike in New York State, however, is one caught in Great Sacandaga Lake in 1940, which weighed an impressive 46 pounds 2 ounces.

## Largemouth Bass

**The largemouth bass (*Micropterus salmoides*) is a large, deep-bodied fish, which is distinguished from the similar smallmouth bass (*M. dolomieui*) by the larger mouth, which extends beyond the eye.** The fins of the largemouth bass are not uniform in length. And the dorsal fin is very deeply notched. The largemouth also has a broader, more powerful tail than the smallmouth. The largemouth is usually dark green on its back, shading to a lighter green on its side, with the underside a light color. There is a broad dark band of irregular patches on the sides, which is more distinct in younger fish.

The largemouth bass is very adaptable and is found in many different types of localities. However, spawning, which occurs in early May, takes place in warm weedy waters. Before spawning, the male chooses a nesting site that consists of a depression in the muddy bottom. The eggs and young are actively protected for a while by the male fish before he abandons them to fend for themselves.

This species is somewhat cannibalistic, with some specimens eating smaller members of their own kind. Their diet usually consists of other fish species, especially minnows, crayfish, and frogs. Feeding usually occurs in the morning and evening.

The largemouth bass is one of the most popular game fish, and generally tends to be larger than the smallmouth bass. A large specimen may weigh 6 to 8 pounds and be 7 to 10 inches long. The present record size for a largemouth bass in New York State is an individual of 10 pounds 12 ounces caught in Chadwick Lake. However, a specimen from Stoney Lake, Peterborough County, in Ontario, is reported to have weighed 14 pounds 2 ounces.

## Lake Sturgeon

**The lake sturgeon (*Acipenser fulvescens*) is one of our largest and most primitive fish, retaining the cartilaginous skeleton of the earliest fish.** Its elongated, almost cylindrical, body tapers toward the tail. It has a number of bony plates along its back, which are more prominent in younger fish. The snout is long and pointed, and there are four barbels in front of the mouth, which assist the fish in locating its prey.

This species occupies most of the inland waters of eastern North America from eastern Alberta to northern Quebec, south to Alabama and eastern Missouri. The general coloration of adult sturgeons is slate gray, varying to dark

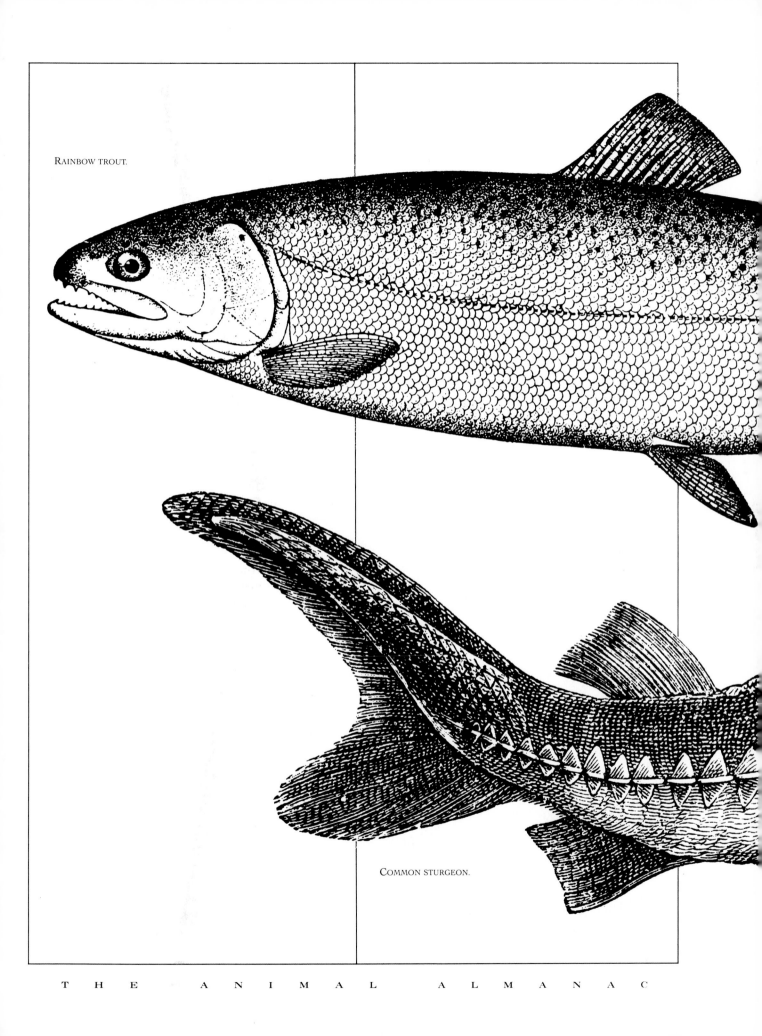

Rainbow trout.

Common sturgeon.

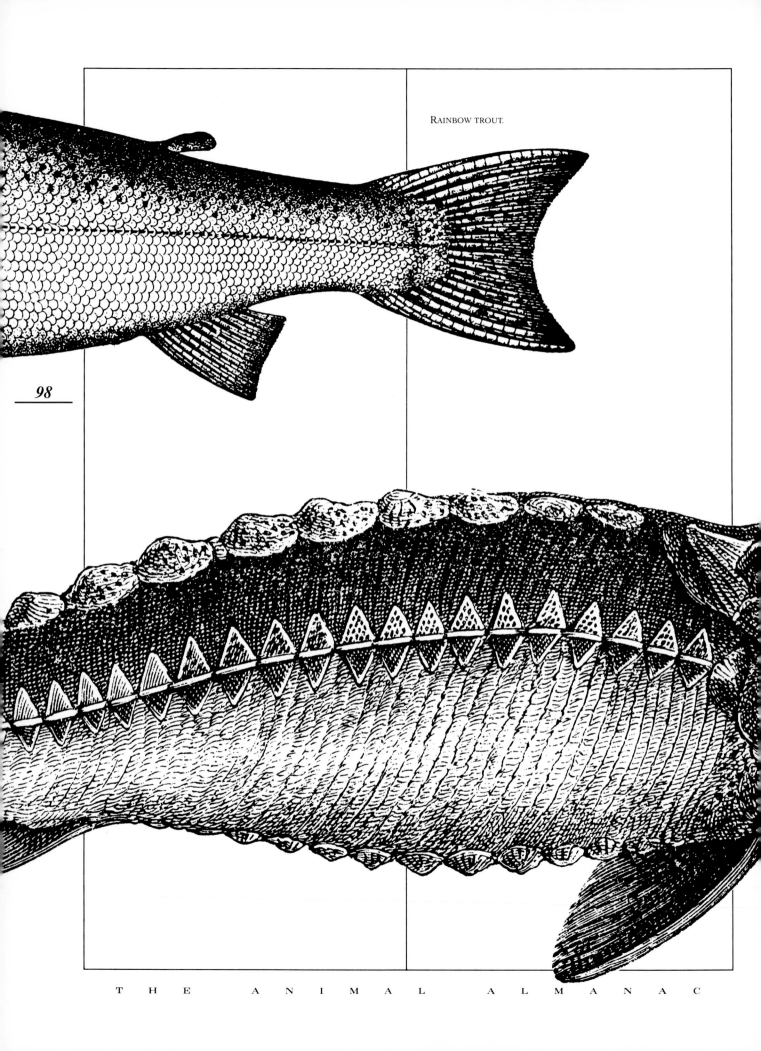

98

gray, black, and even green. It is a long-lived fish and takes many years to reach maturity.

Large females may produce upward of 500,000 eggs at a single spawning. The very young fish feed on minute crustaceans, changing to mayfly nymphs as they get a little older. These fish are especially useful in outdoor ponds as they help considerably in keeping down the amount of algae that collect there.

Before the lake sturgeon was recognized as a desirable food fish, it was indiscriminately destroyed by fishermen because it often became entangled in their nets and ripped great holes in them. It is no longer indiscriminately destroyed, and, in fact, commercial fishing of this species is now strictly regulated, because sturgeon eggs produce the most desirable caviar, commanding very high prices.

In the area of the Great Lakes, lake sturgeon may occasionally grow to an enormous size, sometimes attaining a weight of 300 pounds and a length of 7 feet. Fish of this size, however, are now exceedingly rare. Apparently, the largest lake sturgeon ever re-

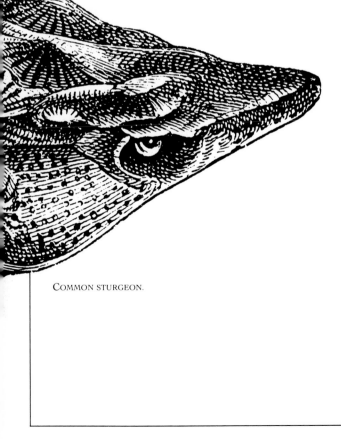

COMMON STURGEON.

corded is a 310-pounder, 7 feet 11 inches long, caught in Batchewana Bay, Lake Superior, in Ontario, on June 29, 1922.

### Pumpkinseed

**The pumpkinseed (*Lepomis gibbosus*) is the most common and most widely distributed of our native sunfish.** It occurs from New Brunswick south along the Atlantic seaboard, west to eastern South Dakota and northern Missouri. It has been introduced into the waters of California, Wyoming, Montana, Washington, and Oregon, and possibly some other western states.

The pumpkinseed is distinctly rounder than other members of the sunfish family and is quite unmistakable. Its body is covered with large scales of many colors: No other species of freshwater fish exhibits such a great variety of colors and markings. Its back is generally greenish, graduating to blue with orange or rust-colored spots on the side, and the cheeks are orange with wavy blue streaks, which are more brilliantly colored in the male. Mature females have distinct vertical bars.

The pumpkinseed is partial to heavily weeded warm water, where there is abundant food and enough shelter in which to hide from its enemies. Spawning takes place quite late, generally in June or July. Like all sunfish, the male pumpkinseed is very aggressive at spawning time. It constructs the nest and possessively stands guard over the newly hatched young, chasing away all intruders.

The pumpkinseed has a prolific reproduction potential; sometimes too many are produced for the available food supply. Under such circumstances the fish then become stunted, rarely attaining lengths of more than 4 to 5 inches. Under optimal conditions lengths of 8 to 9 inches are not unusual. The maximum size for this species is probably about 10 inches long and weighs 17 ounces. Because of their size, pumpkinseeds are usually ignored by anglers, although their flesh is sweet and of excellent flavor.

## Yellow Perch

The yellow perch (*Perca flavescens*) is represented in Europe as well as North America. On this continent it ranges from Great Slave Lake in the Northwest Territories to Nova Scotia, south to Alabama and the Florida panhandle, although it is far more common in the northern and eastern areas.

The young of this species is preyed on by almost all other predatory fish, such as bass, sunfish, crappies, walleyes, sauger, northern pike, muskellunge, lake trout, and even other yellow perch. The adults are prey for many species of water birds. The principal diet of the perch consists of animal plankton, aquatic insects, and other small fish, especially minnows and sticklebacks.

This fish is generally olive green, graduating to yellow on the sides. Six to eight broad, dark vertical crossbars run down the sides. The belly is pale, generally whitish or yellowish, and the very distinctive upper fins are separated and somewhat dusky in color.

It generally takes two years for the yellow perch to attain sexual maturity. Spawning usually occurs at night during April and May in shallow, sheltered areas. The eggs are embedded in a gelatinous covering and hatch in approximately three weeks. No parental care is given to the young fish.

Yellow perch tend to be more numerous where there are expanses of open water with a moderate amount of vegetation, especially in warmer waters. They are very gregarious and usually travel about in large shoals. Although essentially fish of larger lakes, they are often found in small bodies of water as well.

Specimens caught by anglers in Canada tend to be the largest, usually 8 to 12 inches long and weighing 4 to 10 ounces. A 14-inch perch was taken in the Saugeen River (Lake Huron) in Ontario in 1929; and one weighing 4 pounds 1 ounce was caught in Quebec.

## Carp

Closely related to the popular domesticated goldfish (*Carassius auratus*), the carp (*Cyprinus carpio*) was originally a native of Asia. It was first introduced into Europe by way of Cyprus, early in the Middle Ages, and did not reach North America until around 1877. It is now widely distributed throughout the entire eastern part of the continent.

Carp have very robust bodies furnished with many large, overlapping scales. They have moderate-size mouths with slightly protruding upper jaws, and they are toothless. A pair of conspicuous barbels is situated at the corner of the mouth. The ground color of the adult fish ranges from olive green on the back to yellowish on the belly. The lower half of the caudal and anal fins are a distinct reddish hue.

Spawning commences in late spring, sometimes extending into late summer, usually in shallow, heavily weeded waters. There is much violent activity at this time; the thrashings of some of these spawning carp frequently cause them to leap clear out of the water. The record for the species in New York State is a specimen taken in Keuka Lake in 1976 that weighed 35 pounds 4 ounces.

......................

# NORTH AMERICA'S LARGEST FRESHWATER FISH
## White Sturgeon

**North America's largest freshwater fish, and one of the largest fish in the world, is the white sturgeon (*Acipenser transmontanus*). A specimen caught in the Columbia River at Astoria, Oregon, in 1892 was exhibited at the World's Fair in Chicago the following year; its weight was stated as "more than 2,000 pounds," but this weight was never confirmed.**

There are also two claims for 1,500-pound white sturgeons on record — one reportedly

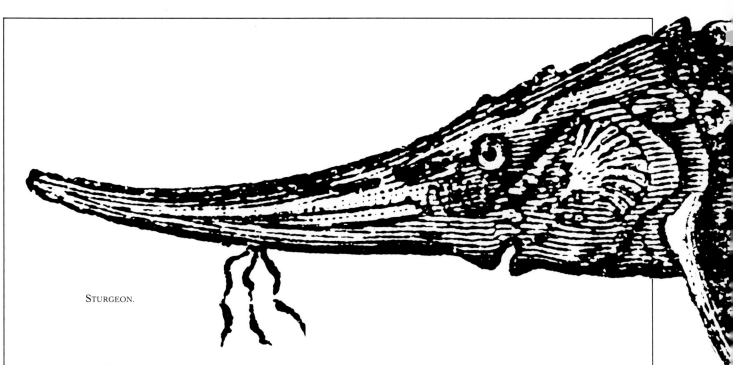

Sturgeon.

taken from the Weiser River, Washington, in 1898, and the other from Snake River, Oregon, in 1911.

A reliable record exists for a 12-foot 6-inch white sturgeon captured in the Columbia River near Vancouver, Washington, in May or June 1912 that weighed 1,285 pounds; however, it is believed that the largest specimen ever reported was taken near Mission, British Columbia, and weighed over 1,800 pounds.

## Record Weights for Freshwater Fish from New York State

| Species | Weight | Body of Water | Year |
|---|---|---|---|
| Brook trout | 8 lb 8 oz | Punchbowl Pond | 1908 |
| Brown trout | 22 lb 4 oz | Keuka Lake | 1979 |
| Lake trout | 31 lb | Follensby Pond | 1922 |
| Rainbow trout | 21 lb 9 oz | Salmon River | 1979 |
| Splake | 11 lb 2 oz | Eagle Lake | 1979 |
| Atlantic landlocked salmon | 18 lb 8 oz | Oswego River | 1978 |
| Chinook salmon | 47 lb | Lake Ontario | 1980 |
| Chain pickerel | 8 lb 1 oz | Toronto Reservoir | 1965 |
| Coho salmon | 21 lb 9 oz | Lake Ontario | 1979 |
| Muskellunge | 69 lb 15 oz | St. Lawrence River | 1957 |
| Northern pike | 46 lb 2 oz | Great Sacandaga Lake | 1940 |
| Largemouth bass | 10 lb 12 oz | Chadwick Lake | 1975 |
| Smallmouth bass | 9 lb | Friends Lake Outlet | 1925 |
| Walleye | 15 lb 3 oz | Chemung River | 1952 |
| Channel catfish | 24 lb | Oneida Lake | 1980 |
| American shad | 5 lb 9 oz | Hudson River | 1980 |
| Lake whitefish | 7 lb 1 oz | Eagle Lake | 1979 |
| Bluegill | 1 lb 13 oz | Wilds Pond | 1977 |
| Carp | 35 lb 4 oz | Keuka Lake | 1976 |
| Crappie | 3 lb 1 oz | Indian Lake | 1977 |
| White bass | 2 lb | Oneida Lake | 1976 |
| Freshwater drum | 12 lb | St. Lawrence River | 1980 |

## Record Weights For Freshwater Fish From North America

| Species | Weight | Location | Date |
|---|---|---|---|
| Largemouth bass | 22 lb 4 oz | Montgomery Lake, Ga. | June 2, 1932 |
| Smallmouth bass | 11 lb 15 oz | Dale Hollow Lake, Ky. | July 9, 1955 |
| Redeye bass | 8 lb 3 oz | Flint River, Ga. | Oct. 23, 1977 |
| Rock bass | 3 lb | York River, Ont. | Aug. 1, 1974 |
| Spotted bass | 8 lb 15 oz | Lewis Smith Lake, Ala. | May 18, 1978 |
| White bass | 5 lb 6 oz | Grenada, Miss. | Apr. 21, 1979 |
| Whiterock bass | 20 lb | Savannah River, Ga. | May 5, 1977 |
| Yellow bass | 2 lb 4 oz | Lake Monroe, Ind. | Mar. 27, 1977 |
| Black bullhead | 8 lb | Lake Waccabuc, N.Y. | Aug. 1, 1951 |
| Bluegill | 4 lb 12 oz | Ketona Lake, Ala. | Apr. 9, 1950 |
| Bowfin | 21 lb 8 oz | Florence, S.C. | Jan. 29, 1980 |
| Bigmouth buffalo | 70 lb 5 oz | Bastrop, La. | Apr. 21, 1980 |
| Smallmouth buffalo | 51 lb | Lawrence, Kans. | May 2, 1979 |
| Burbot | 18 lb 4 oz | Pickford, Mich. | Jan. 31, 1980 |
| Carp | 55 lb 5 oz | Clearwater Lake, Minn. | July 10, 1952 |
| Blue catfish | 97 lb | Missouri River, S.D. | Sept. 16, 1959 |
| Channel catfish | 58 lb | Santee-Cooper Reservoir, S.C. | July 7, 1964 |
| Flathead catfish | 79 lb 8 oz | White River, Ind. | Aug. 13, 1955 |
| White catfish | 17 lb 7 oz | Success Lake, Tulare, Calif. | Nov. 15, 1981 |
| Arctic char | 29 lb 11 oz | Arctic River, N.W.T. | Aug. 21, 1968 |
| Black crappie | 5 lb | Santee-Cooper Reservoir, S.C. | Mar. 15, 1957 |
| White crappie | 5 lb 3 oz | Enid Dam, Miss. | July 31, 1957 |
| Dolly Varden | 33 lb 13 oz | Unalaklett River, Alas. | Aug. 29, 1980 |
| Freshwater drum | 54 lb 8 oz | Nickajack Lake, Tenn. | Apr. 20, 1972 |
| Alligator gar | 279 lb | Rio Grande River, Tex. | Dec. 2, 1951 |
| Florida gar | 21 lb 3 oz | Boca Raton, Fla. | June 3, 1981 |
| Longnose gar | 50 lb 5 oz | Trinity River, Tex. | July 30, 1954 |
| American grayling | 5 lb 15 oz | Katseyedie River, N.W.T. | Aug. 16, 1967 |
| Inconnu | 33 lb 9 oz | Kobuk River, Alas. | Aug. 29, 1981 |

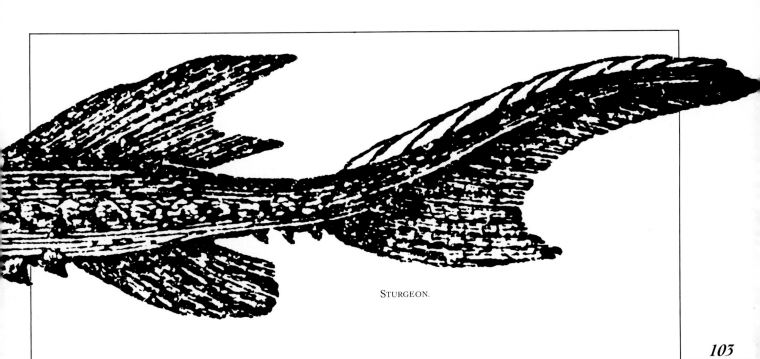

STURGEON.

| Kokanee | 6 lb 9 oz | Priest Lake, Ida. | June 9, 1975 |
| Muskellunge | 69 lb 15 oz | St. Lawrence River, N.Y. | Sept. 22, 1957 |
| Northern pike | 46 lb 2 oz | Sacandaga Reserve, N.Y. | Sept. 15, 1940 |
| White perch | 4 lb 12 oz | Messalonskee Lake, Me. | June 4, 1949 |
| Yellow perch | 4 lb 3 oz | Bordentown, N.J. | May 1865° |
| Chain pickerel | 9 lb 6 oz | Homerville, Ga. | Feb. 17, 1961 |
| Silver redhorse | 5 lb 14 oz | Shelbyville, Ind. | Oct. 20, 1980 |
| " " | " " | Betsie River, Frankfort, Mich. | May 4, 1980 |
| Chinook salmon | 93 lb | Kelp Bay, Alas. | June 24, 1977 |
| Chum salmon | 27 lb 3 oz | Raymond Cove, Alas. | June 11, 1977 |
| Landlocked salmon | 22 lb 8 oz | Sebago Lake, Me. | Aug. 1, 1907 |
| Silver salmon | 31 lb | Cowichan Bay, B.C. | Oct. 11, 1947 |
| Sockeye salmon | 7 lb 14 oz | American River, Alas. | July 19, 1981 |
| Sauger | 8 lb 12 oz | Lake Sakakawea, N.D. | Oct. 6, 1971 |
| American shad | 9 lb 4 oz | Delaware River, Pa. | Apr. 26, 1979 |
| " " | " " | Connecticut River, Conn. | Apr. 20, 1981 |
| White sturgeon | 360 lb | Snake River, Ida. | Apr. 24, 1956 |
| Green sunfish | 2 lb 2 oz | Stockton Lake, Mo. | June 18, 1971 |
| Redbreast sunfish | 1 lb 8 oz | Suwannee River, Fla. | Apr. 30, 1977 |
| Redear sunfish | 4 lb 8 oz | Chase City, Va. | June 19, 1970 |
| Brook trout | 14 lb 8 oz | Nipigon River, Ont. | July 1916° |
| Cutthroat trout | 41 lb | Pyramid Lake, Nev. | Dec. 1925° |
| Golden trout | 11 lb | Cook's Lake, Wyo. | Aug. 5, 1948 |
| Lake trout | 65 lb | Great Bear Lake, N.W.T. | Aug. 8, 1970 |
| Rainbow trout | 42 lb 2 oz | Bell Island, Alas. | June 22, 1970 |
| Sunapee trout | 11 lb 8 oz | Lake Sunapee, N.H. | Aug. 1, 1954 |
| Tiger trout | 17 lb | Lake Michigan, Wis. | Aug. 2, 1977 |
| Walleye | 25 lb | Old Hickory Lake, Tenn. | Aug. 1, 1960 |
| Warmouth | 2 lb | Sylvania, Ga. | May 4, 1974 |
| Lake whitefish | 13 lb | Great Bear Lake, N.W.T. | July 14, 1974 |
| Mountain whitefish | 5 lb | Athabasca River, Alta. | June 3, 1963 |

°Exact date not known.

# May

May is a good month for observing the grizzly bear, as the explorers Lewis and Clark discovered to their dismay in 1805. It is also a splendid month for bird watching, because the spring migration has now reached its peak. Along the flyways, millions of birds — lake birds, shore birds, cuckoos, hummingbirds, hawks, flycatchers, owls, thrushes, and many others — are flying on tight schedules and can be observed at the same points at the same time each year. Each of these winged creatures has its special flight plan and aeronautic record. For example, the Arctic tern travels the longest distance — 11,000 miles each way on its route from the Arctic to the Antarctic — and many other birds, also covering thousands of miles, routinely exceed the legal highway speed limits.

Toward the end of the month, and throughout the next, many young birds may seem lost and abandoned. Do not despair. Their parents are generally very aware of the little ones' whereabouts, and would prefer if you left them untouched.

Opposite: Hawk.

# MAY

The largest bison herd ever recorded was observed moving between Fort Zarah and Fort Larned in Arkansas in May 1871. The herd was reported to be 25 miles wide and 50 miles deep.

In May 1971 two ivory-billed woodpeckers, regarded as extinct by some authorities, were seen in Louisiana. Photographs were produced of one of these birds, well up in the trunk of a large tree.

PRONGHORN.

## 1

Two high school students discovered 7 dead eagles in 1971, in Jackson Canyon, Wyoming; they had been poisoned. 13 more dead specimens were discovered on the following day.

## 3

A female of the rare and endangered black-footed ferret species trapped at Broadus, Montana, in 1920, was said to be carrying unborn young.

Last swift fox positively identified in Canada taken in Alberta in 1938. The animal is now believed extirpated in that country.

. . . . . . . . . . .

## 4

John James Audubon discovered the Bell's vireo during his Missouri River expedition, in 1844, on the same day that the Harris's sparrow had been discovered the year before.

. . . . . . . . . . .

## 5

Captain William Clark had a close encounter with a grizzly bear along the Milk River in Montana in 1805, and narrowly escaped death.

## 6

An egg of the bee hummingbird, the smallest egg laid by any bird, was collected at Boyate, Santiago de Cuba, in 1906, and later presented to the U.S. National Museum in Washington, D.C.

. . . . . . . . . . .

## 8

Tropical kingbird first discovered north of the Mexican border by George B. Sennett at Lomita Ranch, in south Texas, in 1878.

. . . . . . . . . . .

## 10

One of very last nesting records for the ivory-billed woodpecker, an almost extinct species, reported from northern Louisiana by A. A. Allen and P. P. Kellogg in 1935.

Largest freshwater fish ever captured in North America was a white sturgeon (407 pounds) taken in California in 1979.

## 11

Only known specimen of Townsend's bunting collected at New Garden, Pennsylvania, in 1833.

. . . . . . . . . . .

## 13

Kirtland's warbler, America's most local songbird, discovered near Cleveland, Ohio, in 1851.

Wilson's plover first described from a specimen shot on the shore of Cape Island, New Jersey, in 1813.

. . . . . . . . . . .

## 14

Captain Meriwether Lewis first described the prairie dog and the pronghorn in 1806.

## 16

Adult black-footed ferret, America's rarest mammal, killed by a motor vehicle in Jones County, South Dakota, in 1967. The animal appeared to be in heat.

. . . . . . . . . . .

## 17

Captain Meriwether Lewis first described the prairie rattlesnake in 1806: "I was nearly treading on a small fierce rattlesnake different from any I had ever seen."

. . . . . . . . . . .

## 18

Very first black-whiskered vireo discovered in New Providence, Bahamas, by C. J. Maynard in 1884.

## 19

Groove-billed ani, a tropical American bird, first reported from North America near Lomita, Texas, by George B. Sennett in 1878.

. . . . . . . . . . .

## 20

Professor Charles G. Sibley, director of Yale's Peabody Museum and vice president of the American Ornithologists Union, fined $3,000 in 1974, for "illegally importing bird parts taken abroad in violation of foreign wildlife laws."

. . . . . . . . . . .

## 22

Crater Lake National Park, Oregon, established in 1902.

## 26

Black-capped vireo discovered near the source of the Rio San Pedro in western Texas by Captain L. Sitgreaves, who shot two specimens in 1851.

. . . . . . . . . . .

## 28

Largest Alaskan brown bear ever recorded, shot near Cold Bay, Alaska, in 1948. It was 10 feet tall and had an estimated weight of between 1,600 and 1,700 pounds.

. . . . . . . . . . .

## 31

Connecticut proclaimed the European praying mantis as the official state insect in 1977.

BISON HERD.

## CLOSE ENCOUNTERS WITH GRIZZLY BEARS

In 1804 at the time of the monumental Lewis and Clark expedition, the grizzly bear *(Ursus arctos horribilis)* was free to roam throughout the entire North American west. Grizzly bears were then by no means a rare and threatened species, as they are now, and Captains Meriwether Lewis and William Clark had close encounters with them, both narrowly escaping death.

On Sunday evening May 5, 1805, while encamped along the Missouri River below the mouth of the Milk River in Montana, Captain Clark and a hunter named George Drewyer encountered a grizzly bear. After Clark and Drewyer had shot five bullets into its lungs and five more into various parts of its body, the animal was still roaring mad. Mortally wounded, it dove into the water and swam more than halfway across the river to a sandbar, where it lived for 20 minutes more. Cap-

tain Lewis later described the beast as weighing close to 600 pounds and measuring 8 feet 7½ inches from the nose to the hind feet, and 5 feet 10½ inches around the breast. Its claws were 4⅜ inches long. Following this incident, Captain Clark's note in the diary declares: "I must confess that I do not like the gentlemen and had rather fight two Indians than one bear."

Captain Lewis's brush with death came on June 14, 1805, near the Great Falls of the Missouri. He had shot a buffalo and had not reloaded his gun. A grizzly bear had crept to within 20 paces before Lewis discovered the beast. This is the way he described the action:

> In the first moment I drew my gun to shoot, but at the same instant recolected that she was not loaded and that he was too near me to hope to perform this opperation before he reached me, as he was then briskly advancing on me; it was an open level plain, not a bush within miles or a tree within less than three hundred yards of me; the river bank

was sloping and not more than three feet above the level of the water; in short there was no place by means of which I could conceal myself from this monster untill I could charge my rifle; in this situation I thought of retreating in a brisk walk as fast as he was advancing untill I could reach a tree about 300 yards below me, but I had no sooner terned myself about but he pitched at me, open mouthed and full speed. I ran about 80 yards and found that he gained on me fast, I then run into the water — the idea struck me to get into the water to such debth that I could stand and he would be obliged to swim, and that I could in that situation defend myself with my espotoon [a short spear], at this instant he arrived at the edge of the water within 20 feet of me; the moment I put myself in this attitude of defence, he suddenly wheeled about as if frightened, declined to combat on such unequal grounds and retreated with quite as great precipitation as he had just before pursued me.

Although grizzly bears can be extremely dangerous, it is now known that they are generally shy creatures of nocturnal habit and the appearance of a human usually puts them to flight. Unprovoked attacks by grizzlies are very rare; they are most often preceded by one of three acts: approaching a female with young at close range, approaching a bear in possession of a carcass, or surprising a bear at close range.

.........................

## BIRD WATCHING TIPS

**B**ird watching, or birding, as it is more generally known, has become an increasingly popular pastime in recent years. In fact, the number of birders has quadrupled since the end of World War II. According to Roger Tory Peterson, the dean of American ornithologists, an estimated 20 million people on this continent currently participate in birding.

Its charm undoubtedly lies in the fact that everyone can participate, amateur and professional, old and young alike. Also, the necessary equipment is both simple and inexpensive; all you need are a good, serviceable pair of binoculars and a pocket field guide.

The purchase of a pair of binoculars is largely a matter of personal choice. Most birders prefer binoculars with a magnification between 7 x 35 and 8 x 50. Higher-powered binoculars are impractical because they are difficult to control. You may be able to obtain a good secondhand pair, but many of these are of poor quality. There are a number of good foreign-made models at present that can be purchased at a reasonable cost. The rule of thumb with binoculars is to purchase the best that your pocket will allow.

As for field guides, the most popular and widely used are *Birds of North America* by C. S. Robbins, B. Bruun, H. S. Zim, and A. Singer; and *A Field Guide to the Birds of Eastern North America* (Golden Press, New York) and *A Field Guide to the Birds of Western North America* (Houghton Mifflin, Boston) by Roger Tory Peterson. The books by Peterson have recently been revised and are quite excellent. All three publications are well illustrated and specially constructed for easy species identification. They are available in paperback and hard-cover.

OVERLEAF: FUERTES'S DRAWINGS OF CORMORANTS AND ANHINGAS.

Baird's C.

L.A.F.
June 3 — 19

Otto.                    Brandt's cormoran

As for wearing apparel, whenever possible, wear subdued colors (except during the hunting season) that blend with the background. Too much emphasis cannot be placed on correct footwear. Many birds inhabit marshy areas, and in order to observe these birds at close range, it may be necessary to get your feet wet. So waterproof boots are a must. Also, birds have excellent eyesight and hearing and are easily startled, so approach with caution.

## Bird Occurrences

The New York Federation of Bird Clubs has ascribed these various terms and references to denote the relative abundance or scarcity of birds:

| | |
|---|---|
| Very abundant | 501 or more seen daily |
| Abundant | 201 to 500 seen daily |
| Very common | 101 to 200 in a single day |
| Common | 26 to 100 in a single day |
| Occasional | less than once in 5 years |
| Sporadic | less than once in 10 years |
| Casual | less than once in 20 years |
| Accidental | Not expected to occur again |

........................

## LOST BIRDS?

Many persons, finding a young bird without its parents, think that it has been deserted and feel they must take it home and feed it. This is a mistaken kindness, for usually it merely signifies that the brood is somewhat scattered and that the parents are busy feeding the other young. And particularly if the young bird is quiet, indications are that it has recently been fed

BABY RED-SHOULDERED HAWK.

EASTERN KINGBIRD.

and that the adult birds may not be back for a while. If the young bird is put out of the reach of cats, the parents will sooner or later find it and care for it, for its food-call will carry as far as it could possibly have flown since its last feeding.

Young birds (and mammals) should be left where they belong, undisturbed in the forest with their parents.

........................

## FLYWEIGHT CHAMPION OF THE BIRD WORLD
### *Eastern Kingbird*

The eastern kingbird (*Tyrannus tyrannus*) is a member of the tyrant flycatchers, and a common bird throughout eastern North America. This bird may be seen frequently during the late spring and summer months. It feeds mainly on insects and selects for itself an ideal vantage point, such as a telegraph wire or a perch on a tall tree, from which it can survey the surrounding area for possible prey.

Though smaller than a robin, the eastern kingbird has an unusually aggressive disposition. If a hawk or a crow ventures within its chosen territory, the kingbird rises above the intruder and darts at it savagely, swooping and diving with such determination and ferocity that the much larger bird is only too happy to make its escape. It will even swoop at an eagle, alighting on its back while pecking at its neck feathers.

Consequently, the eastern kingbird is looked upon with great favor by farmers and agriculturalists: It consumes large quantities of noxious insects, and it also keeps the hawks and crows away from the chicken yards.

# May Reading

## BIRD MIGRATION AND THE CONTINENTAL DRIFT

**Bird migration is without doubt a perplexing subject, and many theories have been advanced to explain this amazing phenomenon.** Food appears to be the driving force behind the migration of birds — and the need to raise young where there is a plentiful supply. Bird migration might be defined as a form of adaptation to the changing demands of the seasons.

It is clear that migration has been in progress since earlier times, and it has been popular to relate its origins to the Pleistocene ice ages. One theory holds that migratory birds originally evolved in the more northern regions but retreated from there with the coming of the ice, only to move northward again as the ice melted and land became available. If this theory is correct, then the yearly migration as we know it is simply a continuation of what has been going on for tens of thousands of years since the glaciation.

An alternative theory states that birds evolved not in the Temperate Zones but in the Tropics, and that their movement north is but a repetition of their original period of colonization prior to the ice ages, while their movement south is a repetition of their retreat after the ice ages began. Whatever theory one subscribes to, there can be no doubt that bird migration was a part of life long before the birds were dispossessed by the glaciers.

Continental drift as a possible factor in the origin of bird migration is quite reasonable, and was proposed as a theory as early as the 1940s. Certainly, the understanding of continental drift has satisfactorily answered some

ARCTIC TERN.

questions on why birds travel such long distances annually.

The arctic tern (*Sterna paradisaea*) embarks each year on the longest migratory journey of any bird, traveling a round-trip distance about 22,000 miles from the Arctic Ocean to the Antarctic Ocean. This bird follows a most unusual path: It flies east across the North Atlantic, then south along the west coasts of Europe and Africa to Antarctica. The reason for all that unnecessary distance might well be explained by what an early proponent of the continental drift theory described as being "in accord with the pattern of the drift."

Formerly, all the land masses of the earth were composed of two subcontinents, known as Laurasia (in the north) and Gondwanaland (in the south). In keeping with the theory of the drift, the arctic tern's flight across the north Atlantic represents the east–west drift of the parts of Laurasia and is thus a natural route for this bird to take, since it produces the same flight pattern it always has even before the separation and drifting apart of the two subcontinents.

........................

## BUTTERFLIES OF THE BIRD WORLD
### *Wood Warblers*

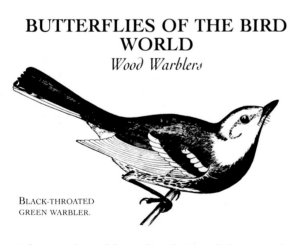

BLACK-THROATED GREEN WARBLER.

**The wood warblers (family Parulidae) are the only truly endemic family of American birds: They are not represented at all outside the Western Hemisphere.** The Old World warblers (family Sylviidae), which are dull olive green or brownish, form a different family.

There are 118 known species of wood

FEMALE PINE WARBLERS.

warblers, 55 of which nest on this continent. Their bold, brightly colored patterns and fluttering movements have earned them the title of "butterflies of the bird world."

These birds are generally the high point of any spring migration, and bird watchers often determine whether or not they have had a successful day's birding by the number of warblers they have listed. All warblers, with a few exceptions, are migratory, traveling far from their winter quarters, which may be the southern United States or Central or South America. Their breeding grounds are for the most part the northern coniferous forests and mixed woodlands of Canada and the northern United States.

Unfortunately, there are many fatalities during the warblers' long migratory flights, especially in stormy weather, for these small birds are not built for rugged conditions. However, many miraculously survive and arrive here in sufficient numbers to delight us with their beauty and song. Some species are hardier than others. The occasional yellow-rumped warbler, for instance, will remain in the more northern climes throughout the winter and survive perfectly well, instead of moving southward with most of its species.

During migration, warblers generally collect in flocks of many different kinds. In fact, a flock composed of a single species is most unusual. It is perhaps this variety that gives warbler spotting its special charm. Male warblers are generally the more brightly colored

OPPOSITE: WARBLERS.

and distinctly marked, and it is therefore not too difficult to identify them as to species. Female warblers, on the other hand, are of a more somber hue and can cause a certain amount of confusion, even among seasoned professionals.

Although most of our resident wood warblers are common and widespread, such as the yellow-rumped warbler (*Dendroica coronata*), black-throated green warbler (*D. virens*), yellow warbler (*D. petechia*), magnolia warbler (*D. magnolia*), pine warbler (*D. pinus*), palm warbler (*D. palmarum*), blackpoll warbler (*D. striata*), black and white warbler (*Mniotilta varia*), ovenbird (*Seiurus aurocapillus*), northern waterthrush (*S. noveboracensis*), and American redstart (*Geothlypis trichas*), a few species comprise some of the rarest and most local of all our native birds.

. . . . . . . . . . . . . . . . . . . . . . .

## OUR RAREST WARBLERS

**The distinction of North America's rarest warbler must go to the Bachman's warbler (*Vermivora bachmanii*).** This small bird is known to have bred in the swamps of the south, but is now so rare that its current breeding habits are almost unknown. At no time in this century have more than a few birds been recorded anywhere.

The reasons for the rarity of this attractive black-throated warbler are difficult to understand. As far as one can tell, its habitat is not unduly specialized; and as for its vulnerability to human predation, it is considered the most difficult of all native birds to locate. Yet it has been a rare bird from the time of its discovery in 1833. It disappeared for over a half-century before Charles Galbraith shot thirty-one specimens in Louisiana for the millinery trade in 1883.

The nest of the Bachman's warbler was first discovered in 1897 in both Arkansas and Missouri, and breeding has since been reported in five other states. A few wanderers have oc-

curred as far north as Indiana, and a few may winter in Florida and Georgia. This species' predilection for remote, inaccessible swamp areas only accentuates the mystery surrounding it. Only one thing is known for certain: The Bachman's warbler is growing rarer.

The Kirtland's warbler (*Dendroica kirtlandii*), an officially recognized endangered species, is another candidate for rarest warbler. It breeds only in three counties of Michigan.

Many wildlife communities and habitats have been destroyed by rampaging forest fires. Ironically, the Kirtland's warbler actually benefits from forest fires, which foster the growth of jack pines, which this warbler appears to require in order to survive. Heat from the fire opens jack pine cones, thus releasing the seed, and also prepares the ground for the germination of that seed.

It has been said that ounce for ounce this handsome, bright yellow-breasted bird, with a striped gray-blue back and sides, has drawn more official interest than any other songbird in history. This species nests only at the base of young jack pines (*Pinus banksiana*) and will not nest in any area where the pines are more than 18 feet tall. Therefore, it must constantly shift its territory.

Theoretically, if it fails to adapt to a less specialized habitat, and if fire is entirely controlled within its range, the Kirtland's warbler will become extinct.

The golden-cheeked warbler (*D. chrysoparia*), a sibling species to the far more familiar black-throated green warbler (*D. virens*), is another rare and local warbler. It is confined to the canyon areas of the Edwards Plateau in west-central Texas and adjacent areas to the north.

When British ornithologist Osbert Salvin first found the golden-cheeked warbler in the highlands of Guatemala in 1859, he did not know that it nested only in the juniper-clad areas of central Texas. Of the 254 Texas counties, the golden-cheeked warbler has been recorded in only 41, of which 31 are now con-

BACHMAN'S WARBLER BY AUDUBON.

Drawn from Nature by J.J.Audubon, F.R.S. F.L.S. *Bachman's Warbler.* SYLVIA BACHMANII. And. *Male 1. Female, 2.* *Gordonia pubescens.* Engraved, Printed, & Coloured by R.Havell, 1833.

Louis Agassiz Fuertes.

sidered to be within the bird's currently known breeding range. It is officially classified by the U.S. Fish and Wildlife Service as a rare bird.

........................

## THE PREACHER BIRD
### Vireo

**Vireos are small passerine birds that superficially are very similar to warblers.** The word *vireo* literally means "I am green," and is an apt name for these olive-backed birds with white underparts tinged with yellow or gray.

Some vireos have wingbars, and some do not. Most have eye rings with a connecting band, giving them a somewhat spectacled look. They are best distinguished from warblers by their thicker, slightly hooked bill, and slower, more deliberate movements; they are far less fluttery and active than warblers.

The most familiar bird of the family is the red-eyed vireo (*Vireo olivaceus*), which is generally regarded as the most abundant nesting bird of the eastern deciduous forests of North America. Its distinctive features are its red iris, prominent eye stripe, and blue-gray cap. The red-eyed vireo has acquired the nickname of "preacher bird" because of the monotonous repetition of its song. One male bird is reported to have repeated its refrain 22,197 times between dawn and dusk, a record not likely to be challenged, except by another red-eyed vireo.

........................

## MYSTERIOUS BIRDS

**Very occasionally a new species of bird is discovered and then, quite mysteriously, is never encountered again.** This is the case with at least three small birds.

One is the Townsend's bunting (*Spiza townsendi*), a description of which was supported by a specimen that was shot in 1833 near West Chester, Pennsylvania, by John K.

FUERTES'S VIREO.

Townsend. The bird hasn't been seen from that time to this and has often been dismissed as either a hybrid form or an aberrant dickcissel (*S. americana*).

Audubon, however, was convinced of the bird's authenticity and called it a "fine specimen of a new species." Recently, ornithologists have suggested that the bird is not a hybrid, but a distinct species that may have become extinct before a second example could be obtained. According to Dr. Elliot Coues, an eminent nineteenth-century ornithologist, "The solitary bird having been killed, it represents a species which died at birth." The U.S. Department of the Interior officially lists the Townsend's bunting as an extinct species.

Two other birds, the Brewster's linnet, collected near Waltham, Massachusetts, in 1870, and the Cincinnati warbler, are also hypothetical forms known from solitary specimens only. They have been accepted as hybrid forms.

In more recent years, the role of most mysterious bird has been taken over by the Sutton's warbler (*Dendroica potomac*), which authorities feel may be a distinct species; they disagree with the popularly held view that it is a hybrid form between the yellow-throated warbler (*D. dominica*) and the northern parula warbler (*Parula americana*). If it is indeed a distinct species, the Sutton's warbler is almost certainly the very last native bird that will ever be discovered in North America.

Two specimens of this bird were collected 18 miles apart in West Virginia in May 1939. Those who believe that the Sutton's warbler is a valid species, and not a hybrid, point out that one of these birds was a female with frayed brood feathers, which indicates the presence of a nest. (Hybirds are almost invariably sterile.) Moreover, a case against its being a hybrid form is that one of the alleged parent species, the yellow-throated warbler, has never been recorded in the state. Since the time of its discovery, at least half a dozen sight records of the Sutton's warbler have been made from West Virginia, about half of which can be considered valid.

## A Plurality of Birds

Over the years people have coined a host of special terms to describe birds in groups. Here are some that still survive in the English language:

A gaggle of geese
A skein of geese (flying)
A plump of waterfowl
A siege of herons or bitterns
A herd of swans, cranes, or curlews
A badelyng of ducks
A sord (or sute) of mallards
A spring of teal
A company of widgeon
A covert of coots
A bazaar of murres
A rafter of turkeys
A bevy of quail
A covey of partridges

A muster of peacocks
A nye of pheasants
A brood of chickens
A congregation of plovers
A desert of lapwings
A cast of hawks
A chattering of choughs
A host of sparrows
A charm of goldfinches
An exaltation of larks
A watch of nightingales
A building of rooks
A wisp (or walk) of snipe
A fall of woodcock
A flight of doves or swallows
A murmuration of starlings
A murder of crows
A descent of woodpeckers
A parliament of owls
A flight of birds
A sedge (or siege) or cranes
A volery of birds

WHISTLING SWANS.

# A NATURALIST'S PARADISE
## *Point Pelee*

**Canada is generally considered to be a northern country, and for the most part this is correct.** Vast spruce-fir forests extend from coast to coast in a never-ending chain. In the extreme north are the tundra and high arctic, a wilderness of ice and snow, almost inaccessible and visited only on a rare occasion by a few stouthearted individuals.

There is, however, a small area of Canada with an environment similar to that of parts of the United States, with the same latitude as northern California and the same favorable, balmy weather.

When the first settlers arrived in Canada, they found a thickly wooded area of hardwood trees in a continuous belt along the northern shore of Lake Erie in southwestern Ontario, extending north to Sarnia and Toronto, the only true region of deciduous forest in Canada. Unfortunately, this unique area was chosen as the center of urban and industrial development, and most of the virgin forest soon came under the axe. Today there are only a few scattered areas where any sizable hardwood forests still remain in Canada; Point Pelee is such an area.

Geographically, Point Pelee is a spit of sand, about 9 miles long, jutting into Lake Erie; the terrain is mostly marsh and woodland. The major part of the area is a 2,000-acre marsh with numerous large ponds. Many forms of wildlife are found at Point Pelee. Undoubtedly, its greatest claim to fame is that it is one of the finest bird-watching spots on the continent; certainly, it is the finest in Canada.

According to world-renowned ornithologist Roger Tory Peterson: "No other spot in the interior of the continent can offer the bird lister more action on a good day in May or in September. Funnelled into the longer finger of land that probes Lake Erie, thousands of small migrants enliven the woods and thickets. No other vantage point in the Great Lakes region has produced as many rarities."*

From March to June, warm air currents carry many rare birds northward across Lake Erie to Point Pelee, where they arrive exhausted and hungry. Birds of all species can be found in profusion, and rarities turn up so often they are almost taken for granted. The height of the spring migration occurs around mid-May, when the warbler wave is under way. At this time the place is literally alive with birds, and the early morning choruses have to be heard to be believed. On a good day it is not unusual to record over a hundred different species of birds.

* *Roger Tory Peterson's Ten Birding Hot Spots* by George H. Harrison.

Sometimes waves of birds will appear in astronomical numbers. As many as 20,000 white-throated sparrows (*Zonotrichia albicollis*) have been recorded in a single day, as well as 6,000 red-breasted mergansers (*Mergus serrator*), 1,000 barn swallows (*Hirundo rustica*), and 650 whistling swans (*Cygnus columbianus*).

Though most of the birds are migrants and end their journey farther north, many remain at Point Pelee to breed. Essentially southern birds such as the orchard oriole (*Icterus spurius*), yellow-breasted chat (*Icteria virens*), Carolina wren (*Thryothorus ludovicianus*), and blue-gray gnatcatcher ((*Polioptila caerulea*) are summer residents and almost never breed outside the area of Point Pelee National Park.

The autumnal migration is, in its way, as interesting as that of the spring migration. During the latter part of September, large gatherings of hawks, in particular, the sharp-shinned hawk (*Accipiter striatus*), put on a spectacular show before their long flight south.

OPPOSITE: MOLE CRICKET.

Reptiles and amphibians are also well represented at Point Pelee; in fact, more turtles are found here than anywhere else in Canada. Characteristic reptiles include the five-lined skink (*Eumeces fasciatus*), eastern spiny softshell turtle (*Trionyx spiniferus*), and Fowler's toad (*Bufo woodhousei fowleri*), a smaller and much rarer cousin of the familiar American toad (*Bufo americanus*). The five-lined skink is eastern Canada's only lizard, and when young is endowed with a vivid blue tail, hence its other common name: blue-tailed skink. Other rare and indigenous animals include the Blanchard's cricket frog (*Acris crepitans blanchardi*), eastern mole (*Scalopus aquaticus*), eastern fox squirrel (*Sciurus niger*), evening bat (*Nycticeius humeralis*) (probably accidental), and northern katydid (*Pterophylla camellefolia*).

Point Pelee is, of course, a bonanza for botanists; the growth of shrubs in the park is luxuriant. At least 600 plant species are found here, mostly along the woodland nature trail. Wildflowers grow profusely. Among the most notable are flowering spurge, wild potato-vine, swamp mallow, and prickly pear cactus (probably the only area in eastern Canada where it is found). Characteristically southern trees include black walnut, red mulberry, cottonwood, sycamore, white sassafras, chestnut oak, and red cedar.

Butterflies and other insects abound at Point Pelee, and in some years the giant swallowtail (*Heraclides cresphontes*), North America's largest butterfly, is not uncommon in the park. It is boldly colored, with yellow blotches and spots on a brown background; similar species almost identical in appearance are found commonly throughout tropical America. While on the subject of butterflies, let us not ignore the familiar monarch (*Danaus plexippus*). Sometimes huge congregations of migrating monarchs festoon the shrubs and trees, resting before their long flight to central Mexico.

One particularly interesting insect found here is the mole cricket (*Gryllotalpa hexadactyla*), a dark brown insect about an inch long that burrows and tunnels in the damp soil along the margins of streams and ponds, sometimes to a depth of 8 inches. It is called the mole cricket because its method of burrowing is similar to that of the mole, with its short, broad front legs. It chirps in the same way as other crickets. Again, this is a southern species, found in Canada only around Point Pelee and the surrounding district.

Collecting plants or other specimens or molesting the animals in any way is strictly forbidden; the park wardens are especially alert to any infringement and strongly enforce this ruling. Many an avid butterfly collector has been evicted from the park.

During the late spring and summer, an interpretive service is maintained, and park naturalists are on hand to help with questions and illustrated talks and field trips. The purpose of Point Pelee National Park is to preserve this unique part of Canada's wild environment and to afford visitors a better understanding and appreciation of the local natural treasures.

Point Pelee National Park is located 6 miles south of Leamington, which can be reached from Highway 401, west from Detroit and Windsor and east from Toronto. For further information, write: Superintendent, Point Pelee National Park, Rural Route 1, Leamington, Ontario, Canada N8H 3V4.

......................

## Bird Migration Dates at Point Pelee National Park

Migration patterns for birds have remained the same over the years, with arrival and departure times varying by only a few days. The following are the migration dates for the species that pass through Point Pelee National Park, which is a focal point in migration. This spot lies along both the Mississippi and Atlantic flyways and is frequented by species nesting from the prairies to Quebec and the Arctic.

| Spring | Start of Buildup | Peak |
|---|---|---|
| Loons, grebes | Apr. 1 | Apr. 15 |
| Swans, geese, ducks | Apr. 10 | Apr. 20 |
| Shore birds | May 5 | May 20 |

| | | |
|---|---|---|
| Gulls | Mar. 20 | May 20 |
| Terns | | |
| Cuckoos | | |
| Hummingbirds | Apr. 15 | May 1 |
| Flycatchers | | |
| Jays | | |
| Thrushes | | |
| Wrens | | |
| Waxwings | | |
| Vireos | May 5 | May 15 |
| Warblers | | |
| Finches | | |

*Fall*

| | | |
|---|---|---|
| Ducks | Sept. 10 | Sept. 30 |
| Geese | Oct. 10 | Oct. 20 |
| Hawks | Oct. 25 | Nov. 10 |
| Shore birds | Sept. 10 | Sept. 20 |
| Yellowlegs | | |
| Pectoral sandpiper | July 30 | Aug. 5 |
| Sanderlings | | |
| Plovers | Oct. 1 | Oct. 10 |
| Terns | | |
| Cuckoos | Aug. 25 | Sept. 10 |
| Hummingbirds | | |
| Flycatchers | | |
| Wrens | Aug. 15 | Sept. 5 |
| Vireos | | |
| Warblers | | |
| Owls | Oct. 15 | Oct. 25 |
| Blackbirds | Oct. 15 | Oct. 30 |
| Sparrows | Oct. 15 | Oct. 30 |
| Thrushes | Sept. 15 | Sept. 25 |

CANADA GOOSE.

# PROTECTED BY LAW
*Migratory Birds*

**North American birds have the good fortune to be protected by an international law, which developed from a convention between the United States and Canada in 1916. The re-sulting Migratory Bird Convention Act (1917) protects migrating birds on both sides of the border.**

This new international recognition of nature's disregard for political boundaries was enlarged in 1936, when the United States and Mexico signed a similar treaty protecting migratory birds in the southern half of North America.

For obvious reasons, nonmigratory birds could not be included in an international agreement, but these few birds come under state or local government legislation, as in the case of the ruffed grouse (*Bonasa umbellus*). Insectivorous birds that are only partly migratory, such as chickadees and woodpeckers, are protected by the Migratory Bird Convention Act, in which they are given specific mention, and just to make sure that no bird is forgotten, the act says "and all other perching birds which feed entirely or chiefly on insects."

It should also be emphasized that the act not only prohibits killing birds, but also "chasing, pursuing, worrying, following after, stalking, trapping, buying, selling, or having in possession." Even a well-intentioned bird watcher might technically be infringing the law by stalking and pursuing birds.

........................

## Record Speeds for Birds in Level Flight

| | |
|---|---|
| Spine-tailed swift (*Chaetura caudacuta*) | 106 mph |
| Frigate-bird (*Fregata* sp.) | 95 |
| Spur-wing goose (*Plectropterus gambiensis*) | 88 |
| Red-breasted merganser (*Mergus serrator*) | 80+ |
| White-rumped swift (*Caffrapus caffer*) | 77 |
| Canvasback (*Aythya valisineria*) | 72 |
| Eider duck (*Somateria mollissimer*) | 70 |
| Teal (*Anas crecca*) | 68 |
| Pintail (*Anas acuta*) | 65 |
| Mallard (*Anas platyrhyncha*) | 65 |
| Golden plover (*Charadrius apricarius*) | 60 |
| Peregrine falcon (*Falco peregrinas*) | 60 |
| Canada goose (*Branta canadensis*) | 60 |
| Racing pigeon (*Columbia livia*) | 60 |
| Quail (*Lophortyx* sp.) | 57 |
| Sandgrouse (*Pterocles* sp.) | 55 |
| Merlin (*Falco columbarius*) | 55 |
| Swan (*Cygnus* sp.) | 55 |
| Lapwing (*Vanellus vanellus*) | 50 |
| Snow goose (*Anser hyperboreus*) | 50 |
| Gannet (*Sula bassana*) | 48 |

## BIRD BANDING

**Approximately 2,000 bird-banding stations are maintained by the U.S. Fish and Wildlife Service throughout the country, and the service organizes and stores on computer discs the vast statistics generated by bird banding.** Forty million birds have been banded since the program was started in the 1930s, and each year a million more are banded. Sixty-five thousand reports recording the observation or retrieval of banded birds are received each year.

Bird banding was originally developed by the Audubon Society and the National Wildlife Federation as a means of monitoring the activities of breeding and migrating birds. The practice has now been expanded in the effort to protect birds against human-made dangers, such as pesticides, toxic chemicals, and radiation.

........................

## SONGBIRDS' SONG

**Songbirds are not born with innate knowledge of the melodies they sing. They learn these by imitating their parents or other members of the same species.**

A number of species, including the mockingbird, starlings, catbirds, and wrens, imitate the calls of other species of birds that they overhear. Crows kept in captivity will imitate the human voice as well as the sounds of cows, horses, chickens, and other farm animals.

Although they learn by imitating, songbirds tend to filter out the sounds made by birds or other creatures not of the same species. Their brains are predisposed to memorize and repeat the songs of their families. However, at times there may be good reasons for imitating the songs of other birds—particularly aggressive ones—in order to discourage competitors from approaching a nest or entering a protected territory.

# POPULATION FLUCTUATIONS
*Muskrat*

**The muskrat (*Ondatra zibethica*) is a fairly large rodent found in the wetlands and waterways of North America.** It is more widely distributed than any other mammal on the continent, ranging from the Arctic Ocean to the Gulf of Mexico, and from the Pacific Ocean to the Atlantic Ocean. In this respect, the muskrat is a very successful species.

The name of this animal derives from the fact that it has two special musk glands (also called anal glands) situated beneath the skin in the region of the anus. These glands enlarge during the breeding season and produce a yellowish, musky-smelling substance that is deposited at stations along travel routes used by muskrats.

Before the colonization of North America, the muskrat was hunted occasionally for food. With the coming of the early settlers and the introduction of guns and traps, the muskrat was hunted intensively for its fur. This activ-

MUSKRAT.

ity has persisted to the present day, and muskrat fur (known as "musquash") is still in great demand as a luxury item.

Like many other wildlife species, muskrats show large fluctuations in numbers that follow what appears to be a regular pattern. Muskrat numbers decrease dramatically about every seven to ten years. At such times, few or no muskrats can be found where two or three years earlier there were thousands.

These catastrophes are often blamed on predators or on overtrapping. But scientists believe these are not the real causes. Instead, they believe that for some as yet unknown reason, the quality and health of individuals decreases, causing widespread death and reproductive failure. After one or two years reproductive and death rates return to normal, leading to an increase in muskrat numbers once again.

..........................

## FRIEND AND FOE
*Pocket Gophers*

**Pocket gophers (family Geomyidae) are small ground squirrels characterized by two external fur-lined cheek pouches extending from the face to the shoulder.** This loose skin and thick hair afford them some protection from the many predators that habitually dine on them. The best protection a gopher has against its enemies, however, is its underground mode of living.

Predators such as coyotes, badgers, and skunks sometimes succeed in digging gophers out, and on the occasions that they roam above ground, hawks and owls make short shrift of them. Snakes and weasels also prey on pocket gophers, pursuing them into their underground burrows.

Gophers can be very destructive, eating crops, burrowing through dikes, and contributing to soil erosion. On the credit side, however, they do sterling work in improving the soil by loosening and aerating it and mixing it with organic matter. They also contribute to water conservation: After a heavy snowfall, the melted water sinks deep into the earth through the maze of gopher tunnels instead of flowing straight into the nearest stream.

Despite its many natural predators, humans are by far the greatest enemy of the pocket gopher. All manner of snares, traps, and slingshots have been used to eliminate the animal. In Mexico, the *tucero*, whose official job is to hunt pocket gophers, is a highly respected member of the village community.

# June

The month with the most hours of daylight offers the naturalist more time each day for observing wildlife. Now that bird migration has virtually come to an end, birds turn their energies toward courtship and nest building. This focus on family may mean that birds are somewhat less visible, but they are by no means less plentiful. For example, during the month of June the total number of birds in the United States and Canada is thought to be in the range of 20 billion, about 80 for each man and woman. From this multitude, we chose the bald eagle as the king of birds in the United States. The golden eagle may be more fierce, and the wild turkey more courageous, but the fact that the bald eagle is near extinction makes this bird a more poignant symbol. June is a good month for observing all large mammals, particularly the black bear, the grizzly bear, and the muskox.

Opposite: Black bear.

# JUNE

The largest fish ever recorded in North America was a 37-foot-long whale shark that was found trapped in a herring net off White Head Island, New Brunswick, Canada, in June 1930.

. . . . . . . . . . . .

## 3

Four captive-bred peregrine falcons released on Carroll Island, 20 miles northeast of Baltimore, Maryland, in 1975.

A young man died in a Worcester, Massachusetts, hospital from what was claimed to be the self-induced bite of a black widow spider in 1935.

. . . . . . . . . . . .

## 4

Last great auk exterminated on Eldey Island off Iceland in 1844. (The great auk disappeared from North America — Funk Island, Newfoundland — in 1785.)

First record of a rattlesnake bite at Independence Creek, Missouri, during the Lewis and Clark expedition in 1804, when "Jos Fields got bit by a Snake which was quickly doctored with

bark by Captain [Meriwether] Lewis." Bark is a poultice of tree bark and gun powder.

Largest white perch (4 pounds 12 ounces) caught with rod and line taken in Messalouskee Lake, Maine, in 1949.

Illinois approved the cardinal as the official state bird in 1929.

. . . . . . . . . . . .

## 5

Most northerly record for a Cassin's kingbird at Algonquin Provincial Park, Ontario, Canada, in 1953.

. . . . . . . . . . . .

## 6

Charlotta checkerspot butterfly was extirpated in Ontario, Canada, in 1891.

. . . . . . . . . . . .

## 8

Sodium fluoroacetate "1080" first tested as a means of pest control in 1944.

First black-throated sparrow reported in Canada — in Wells Gray Park, British Columbia, in 1959.

## 9

A whale shark, largest fish species in the world, killed near Marathon in the Florida Keys in 1923, after a 54-hour fight.

First nest of Hudsonian godwit discovered by Roderick MacFarlane (the discoverer of the first Eskimo curlew's nest) at Fort Anderson, Mackenzie District, Northwest Territories, in 1862.

## 12

Largest tautog (21 pounds 6 ounces) caught with rod and line taken off Cape May, New Jersey, in 1954.

California approved the valley quail as the official state bird in 1931.

Big Bend National Park, Texas, established in 1944.

HERRING GULL.

## 13

*Life* magazine carried an article in 1960 about a snake handler in California who was bitten by a tiger snake; he was the only person ever bitten by this deadliest of all snakes outside Australia.

. . . . . . . . . . . .

## 14

Captain Meriwether Lewis had an encounter with a grizzly bear near the Great Falls of the Missouri in 1805, from which he was lucky to have escaped untouched.

Largest tiger shark (1,780 pounds) caught with rod and line taken off Cherry Grove, South Carolina, in 1964.

First nest of an orchard oriole found in Canada — at Point Pelee National Park, Ontario — by L. L. Snyder in 1920.

. . . . . . . . . . . .

## 16

First nest of an Aplomado falcon discovered near Brownsville, Texas, by J.C. Merrill in 1877.

First nest of a black

WHITE-TAILED DOE.

swift discovered a few miles west of Santa Cruz, California, by A. G. Vrooman in 1901.

. . . . . . . . . . . .

## 17

Muskox first described by Henry Kelsey of the Hudson's Bay Company in 1689.

. . . . . . . . . . . .

## 20

Bald eagle became the emblem of the United States in 1782.

Largest turtle ever recorded was a Pacific leatherback turtle captured near San Diego, California, in 1907. It measured 9 feet overall and weighed 1,902 pounds 8 ounces.

## 21

First nest of black-eared bushtit discovered in Presidio County, Texas, by William Lloyd in 1887.

First orange sulphur butterfly for Canada observed and photographed in Quetico Park, Ontario, in 1978.

. . . . . . . . . . . .

## 23

First incident concerning bats carrying rabies in the United States occurred when a 7-year-old boy was bitten in the chest by a Mexican species of bat while in Florida in 1953. The boy was put on a course of immunization therapy and recovered.

Banff National Park, Canada's first national

park, established in 1887.

Namu, the killer whale, the largest marine mammal ever held in captivity, captured in Fitzhugh Sound, British Columbia, in 1965 and sold to the Seattle Public Aquarium, Washington. Namu was 21 feet 4 inches long.

. . . . . . . . . . . .

## 28

A red deer died at the Milwaukee Zoo in 1954; it was 26 years 8 months 23 days — the greatest known age for a deer.

. . . . . . . . . . . .

## 29

Greatest authenticated longevity record for a wild sea bird is for a herring gull that was banded at Duck Rock, Monhegan Island, Maine, in 1930. The bird was found dead 36 years later.

Olympic National Park, Washington, was established on this day in 1938.

. . . . . . . . . . . .

## 30

Nesting area of whooping crane inadvertently discovered in Wood Buffalo National Park, Northwest Territories, Canada, in 1954, as a result of a fire.

U.S. Fish and Wildlife Service established in 1940.

## A TOUCH OF LARCENY
*Bald Eagle*

The value of birds of prey in our ecosystem cannot be overemphasized; their benefit is easily traced to the depredations of rodents to which we would be subject were it not for these vital animals.

The bald eagle (*Haliaeetus leucocephalus*) is a scavenger as well as a predator, so it is doubly useful. Scavengers are nature's garbage collectors, without which the earth would become a breeding ground for pestilence and disease. The bald eagle will eat small rodents and a crippled duck when it can, but 90 percent of its food is fish, usually dead fish, which it finds washed up on the shore.

Occasionally, the bald eagle will have a taste for fresh fish. But it is a poor fisherman: Any live fish that it can manage to capture are usually spawned-out salmon, which require no real fishing at all. It will harass an airborne osprey (*Pandion haliaetus*) that is carrying a fish, forcing the far more skillful fish-catching bird to drop its catch. As the fish falls from the osprey's clutches, the eagle swoops down and retrieves it before it hits the water.

Benjamin Franklin opposed the choice of the bald eagle for the nation's national emblem because of this trait of piracy. "I wish the bald eagle had not been chosen for the representative of our country," lamented Benjamin Franklin. "For in truth, the turkey is in comparison a much more respectable bird...a bird of courage."

Nevertheless, the bald eagle became the emblem of the United States on June 20, 1782.

## BIRDS BY THE BILLIONS

James Fisher, renowned British ornithologist, once estimated that the world population of birds was on the order of 100 billion individuals.

Roger Tory Peterson's estimate for the United States, made some years ago, was that there were at least 5 billion breeding birds, and probably around 6 billion during the early part of the summer. These estimates were based on the breeding-bird censuses of the National Audubon Society, which uses single territorial male birds as an index to the number of pairs per acre in the different varieties of habitat. Leonard Wing, using a more complicated method, came up with a comparable summer population figure of about 5.6 billion.

None of these estimates included Canada and Alaska, where in a combined area more than 40 percent larger than the United States, an equally large population must be present. Add an average

STORM PETREL.

of two young birds successfully fledged for each pair, and the late summer figure for North America, north of Mexico, may be as high as 20 billion.

Both James Fisher and Roger Tory Peterson have considered the world's most numerous bird species to be the Wilson's storm petrel (*Oceanites oceanicus*), which makes the journey to the north Atlantic every summer from its breeding grounds at the edge of the Antarctic.

Another candidate for most numerous bird is the little shearwater (*Puffinus assimilis*), whose flights Robert Cushman Murphy of the American Museum of Natural History describes in his classic and encyclopedic *Oceanic Birds of South America* as "filling the air like the flakes of a snowstorm and stretching in all directions toward the circle of the horizon from daybreak until dark."

Undoubtedly, many shearwater species are enor-

OPPOSITE: YOUNG BALD EAGLE.

mously abundant. Charles Darwin believed the northern fulmar (*Fulmarus glacialis*) to be the commonest bird in the world. And a single flock of slender-billed shearwaters (*Puffinus tenvirostris*) off Bass Strait, Australia, was once computed to number more than 150 million birds.

. . . . . . . . . . . . . . . . . . . . . .

## THE LARGEST GANNETRY IN THE WORLD

Just 2 miles from the Quebec village of Percé, in the Gulf of St. Lawrence, lies Bonaventure Island, where some of the most spectacular sea-bird colonies anywhere are found.

In particular, Bonaventure Island is world renowned for its colony of gannets (*Morus bassanus*). Upwards of 18,000 pairs of these birds inhabit this island, making this colony the largest of the twenty-two gannetries known throughout the world.

The adult gannet is a magnificent large white bird, up to 40 inches in length, with a wingspan of up to 6 feet. Its distinctly streamlined body is tapered at both ends. Its wingtips are jet black, and its head and neck are saffron yellow. In the first year, the young bird is dark slaty brown, spotted with white. As the young bird matures, the brown feathers are replaced by the splendid white adult plumage. Gannets feed on fish and obtain their food by making spectacular plunges head first into the ocean from a distance of 100 feet or so.

Bonaventure Island, discovered by Jacques Cartier during his first exploration of the New World in 1534, has suffered for 400 years from human settlement and exploitation. By the early 1900s

GANNET.

some of the bird colonies were showing definite signs of decline. At that time, the gannet colony had been depleted to about 3,000 birds, but with the Migratory Bird Convention Act (1917), the island became a sanctuary.

On March 29, 1919, the eastern and northern cliffs of Bonaventure Island, together with Percé Rock, were declared federal migratory bird sanctuaries under the control of the Canadian Wildlife Service. With this protection, the gannet populations have steadily increased and are now 36,000 to 50,000 strong, enough to whiten the cliff tops and spill over onto the slopes.

Other coastal breeding birds found here include: the common murre (*Uria aalge*), razorbill (*Alca torda*), black guillemot (*Cepphus grylle*), black-legged kittiwake (*Rissa tridactyla*), Atlantic puffin (*Fratercula arctica*), herring gull (*Larus argentatus*), double-crested cormorant (*Phalacrocorax auritus*), great black-backed gull (*Larus marinus*), and Leach's storm petrel (*Oceanodroma leucorhoa*).

Roger Tory Peterson is obviously much impressed with Bonaventure Island. He expresses his enthusiasm in these glowing terms: "I believe the gannet lodges of Bonaventure to be one of the greatest ornithological spectacles on the continent, more impressive even than the populous murre and auk colonies further north. The size and whiteness of the gannets give them a visual impact lacking in lesser fowl."*

The recommended time to visit the gannetry is in June and July. Bonaventure Island is reached by boat from the village of Percé. Regular boat tours run by private operators circle the island and enable passengers to observe the sea-bird colonies from the water. Visitors are also able to ramble along the many trails. A guided tour of the island is conducted by the staff of the Percé Wildlife Center to help visitors explore the varied habitats filled with fascinating stories.

For further information on Bonaventure Island, write: Centre d'Histoire Naturelle de Percé, Percé, Comté, Gaspé, Quebec, Canada G0C2L0.

* *Roger Tory Peterson's Ten Birding Hot Spots* by George H. Harrison.

# June Reading

## THE DEFENSIVE CIRCLE
### *Muskox*

**The muskox was first described by Henry Kelsey of the Hudson's Bay Company, while exploring that region on June 17, 1689:**
"Two buffilo . . . ill shapen beast. Their body being bigger than an ox . . . their Horns not growing like other Beast but joyn together upon their forehead and so come down ye side of their head and turn up till ye tip be even with ye Buts. Their Hair is near a foot long."

It confounded early scientists in 1780, for they named it *Ovibos moschatus*, literally meaning "musky sheep-cow." But the muskox is neither; nor is it closely related to either of these animals. In fact, its closest (and still rather distant) living relative is the takin (*Budorcas taxicolor*) of Tibet, Burma, and China.

Muskoxen were numerous for a century after Kelsey's discovery. Samuel Hearne recorded sighting a herd while trekking from Hudson Bay to the Arctic Ocean: "Saw many herds of them in the course of a day's walk,

MUSKOX COW.

and some of those herds did not contain less than eighty or a hundred head."

Apart from humans, the muskox's principal enemy is the wolf (*Canis lupus*). To protect themselves from wolves, muskoxen travel in packs close together, with the cows and calves in the center, and the bulls, with lowered horns, forming an outer defensive ring. In this way they are able to throw off attacking wolves with powerful thrusts of their horns.

Sadly, this excellent tactical measure against predatory mammals proved fatal to the musk ox when man, with his long-range weapons, appeared on the scene, for it was easy to annihilate a herd that remained stationary in this way.

. . . . . . . . . . . . . . . . . . . . .

# BLACK BEARS THAT AREN'T BLACK

**The typical American black bear (*Ursus americanus*) is a glossy black color.** But black bears can, in fact, be black or white, or in-between shades of dark brown, tan, cinnamon, honey brown, and bright blond, with gray-blue and creamy white being the most unusual color phases.

The blue or glacier bear (*U. a. emmonsii*), restricted to a small area of southeastern Alaska and adjacent Yukon Territory, is a rare gray-blue phase of the typical black bear. Population estimates within this limited range place the number of blue bears at 500 individuals. This number now appears to be stabilized, but overhunting for the animal's unusually colored fur as a curio has contributed in no small way to its rarity; its restricted range, of course, has also been a factor in its demise.

The white or Kermode bear (*U. a. kermodei*)

of Gribble Island, British Columbia, was named in honor of Francis Kermode, for many years the director of the Provincial Museum of British Columbia in Victoria. This unusual color phase, however, forms only a small percentage of the black bear population in that area, although bears with similar physical characteristics are also found along coastal British Columbia, from Burke Inlet to the Nass River.

. . . . . . . . . . . . . . . . . . . . .

## Animal Gestation Periods and Litter Sizes

| | *Gestation Period* | *Litter* |
|---|---|---|
| Elephant | 630 days | 1 young |
| Giraffe | 420–450 | 1 |
| Camel | 360–390 | 1 |
| Zebra | 330–360 | 1 |
| Horse | 330 | 1 |
| Otter | 285–375 | 1–4 |
| Cow | 280 | 1–2 |
| Bison | 270–285 | 1 |
| Dolphin | 270 | 1 |
| Yak | 258 | 1 |
| Gorilla | 255 | 1 |
| Chimpanzee | 226 | 1–2 |
| Black bear | 210 | 1–4 |
| White-tailed deer | 210 | 2 |
| Baboon | 180 | 1–2 |
| Macaque | 160–170 | 1–2 |
| Sheep | 150 | 1–3 |
| Pig | 112–115 | 4–6 |
| Lion | 108 | 1–4 |
| Chinchilla | 105–111 | 1–4 |
| Tiger | 100–108 | 2–4 |
| Cat | 63 | 1–6 |
| Raccoon | 63 | 1–6 |
| Dog | 61 | 1–12 |
| Wolf | 60–63 | 1–13 |
| Fox | 49–55 | 1–8 |
| Skunk | 49 | 4–7 |
| Mink | 48–51 | 4–8 |
| Squirrel | 44 | 2–5 |
| Kangaroo | 38–39 | 1–2 |
| Rabbit | 30 | 1–13 |
| Gerbil | 25–29 | 1–7 |
| Mouse | 19–21 | 1–9 |
| Hamster | 16–19 | 2–12 |
| Opossum | 12–13 | 4–13 |

# SEA PARROTS
*Puffins*

**Puffins are among the most endearing of birds.** At their breeding colonies, they stand around in little groups at the very edge of the cliff top, looking rather like waiters in a restaurant before the lunchtime rush. They are often very tame and will allow a human to approach within a few feet. However, because they inhabit rugged, cliff-bound coasts of the north, where they gather to breed, puffins are not easy to see, and they are unknown to the vast majority of people.

Four species of puffins are officially recognized; they are the common or Atlantic puffin (*Fratercula arctica*) of the North Atlantic coast and the horned puffin (*F. corniculata*), the tufted puffin (*Lunda cirrhata*), and the rhinoceros auklet (*Cerorhinca monocerata*) of the North Pacific coast. Puffins belong to the "alcids," a family of birds that included the famous and now-extinct great auk (*Pinguinus impennis*).

Puffins are best known for their large, gaudy bills, which are responsible for their colloquial name of "sea parrots." In winter, the bill is small and relatively plain, but in summer, during the puffin's breeding season, it becomes greatly enlarged, brightly colored, and embellished with several white crescent-shaped grooves. Other facial adornments are a pink to yellow-orange bristlelike rosette at each corner of the mouth; red, orange, or blue eye rings or scales; and a small, fleshy protuberance above each eye.

For centuries, all species of puffins have been hunted by people, as they make excellent eating, although only the breast and thighs are consumed and three or four birds are required to make a decent meal. While hunting of puffins and their eggs has been largely discontinued, these birds still face human-made problems.

Although not yet classified as an endangered species, puffins — the common puffin, in particular — have been a cause of great concern to naturalists because of changes in the birds' marine environment brought about by pollution. Because of the puffin's methods of feeding and the amount of time spent in the water, it is among the most susceptible of all sea birds to oil pollution. Compounding this problem are the toxic chemicals that are poured into the oceans from land-based sources. A survey from Alaska showed that tufted and horned puffins contain the highest residues of DDE (a derivative of DDT) and PCBs of all tested sea birds.

COMMON PUFFIN WITH HERRING.

TUFTED PUFFIN.

## IS IT A BUTTERFLY OR A MOTH?

**The most obvious difference between butterflies and moths is in the formation of their antennae, or feelers.** All butterflies, which form the suborder Rhopalocera, meaning "club-tipped," have clublike knobs at the ends of their antennae, whereas moths, which form the suborder Heterocera, have antennae of various kinds.

They may be feathered or fernlike (pectinated) like those of the silk moths (family Saturniidae), or smooth and tapering with a hook tip like those of the sphinx moths (family Sphingiidae). Never are their antennae clubbed, however.

There are other differences, not quite so specific. The bodies of butterflies are generally much slimmer and are divided into three quite distinct parts: head, chest (thorax), and abdomen. The bodies of moths are usually stout, with the head and thorax less defined and merging into one part. When resting, butterflies usually fold their wings together above their heads, showing their undersides. Moths usually rest with their wings spread out. Butterflies tend to fly during the day, whereas most moths fly during the evening or at night.

However, there are some moths that fly in broad daylight, and very occasionally the red admiral butterfly (*Vanessa atalanta*) has been found flying to artificial light with the nocturnal moths.

Laypeople generally assume that all butterflies are brilliantly colored and that moths are drab and dingy. But there are many moths, of the tropical day-flying species, that can rival any butterfly for sheer brilliance of color — and there are some butterflies that are quite plain.

...............................

## WINGED JEWELS
*Butterflies*

**Although not comparable to the tropics in variety, North America has a number of attractive butterflies.** And, happily, some of the more splendid species, such as the tiger swallowtail (*Pterourus glaucus*), black swallowtail (*Papilio polyxenes asterias*), monarch (*Danaus plexippus*), and mourning cloak (*Nymphalis antiopa*), are fairly common over most of the continent.

In the distribution of butterflies in North America, there is a faunal change on either side of the Rocky Mountains, with some species on one side not found at all on the other.

In some cases, however, there may be different though very similar species on either side of the Rocky Mountains that to all but the keenest observer may appear to be identical.

In the more northern latitudes, all butterflies, except the monarch, hibernate throughout the winter in their various stages; the majority as chrysalids, but many also hibernate in the egg, caterpillar, and adult stages. Those that hibernate as adults are generally the first to appear in the spring.

The life span of a butterfly is generally two to four weeks, although the hibernators and migrating monarchs may live for up to eight months or more.

A female butterfly may lay from 200 to 500 eggs, but only a minute proportion will ever reach maturity. Butterflies, in both the caterpillar and adult forms, have many predators that take an enormous toll on their population; these are mostly birds, lizards, beetles, mice, and spiders. The greatest peril of all, however, are the parasitic wasps and flies that deposit their eggs in the eggs or caterpillars of butterflies. The emerging parasite eats away at the inside of its host, eventually devouring it.

Longevity in butterflies appears to be directly correlated to the amount of energy expended. Experiments have shown that when certain caterpillars were decapitated in such a way as to cause a minimal loss of blood, they could continue the natural course of their development and, after passing through the chrysalis stage, emerge as perfectly healthy, but headless, butterflies — that live longer than their "headed" counterparts. Scientists have concluded that headless butterflies are long-lived because they lead a much less active life. A perfect butterfly quickly spends its strength in activity, whereas its headless companions, leading much more placid lives, wear out their vital forces at a slower rate, and thus live longer.

..............................

## SUPERMOTHS

**Among the moths found in North America, the silk moths (family Saturniidae) are the largest and most attractive, the most familiar and wide-ranging being the cecropia (*Hyalophora cecropia*), polyphemus (*Telea polyphemus*), and luna (*Tropaea luna*).**

The main characteristics of silk moths are their large, expansive wings marked with eyespots, which are transparent in some cases. Their bodies are stout and furry and often as brightly colored as their wings. Their antennae, or feelers, are strongly feathered (pectinated) in the males, far less so in the females. With a few exceptions, silk moths fly at night and are strongly attracted to light.

The caterpillars are large and stout, usually green, and often ornamented with brightly colored spines called tubercles. Winter is spent as a pupa in long or oval cocoons made of silk; from late fall until spring they can readily be seen as they hang from leafless trees or lie among fallen leaves.

The very handsome cecropia is the largest of our native moths; a large female may reach a span of almost 7 inches. The cecropia is common throughout much of North America east of the Rocky Mountains. The wings are gray, tinged with red, with a wavy white line extending across both wings along the margin; there is a transparent eyespot on each wing. The body is bright red, banded with white.

The female lays between 200 and 300 oval white eggs on the underside of the leaves of its food plant in late spring and early summer. When fully mature, the caterpillar that hatches from the egg is 4 to 5 inches long, green, and decorated with blue, yellow, and red tubercles. The cecropia caterpillar feeds on the leaves of a wide variety of trees, including cherry, plum, apple, willow, maple, birch, and elderberry.

The luna has the undisputed distinction of being the most beautiful of all North American insects. It is noted for its delicate green coloring and exquisite wing symmetry. The green coloration fades rapidly, however, to a yellowish color when exposed to direct sunlight for any length of time. The body of the adult luna is white-furred. The eyespots on its wings are small and transparent and surrounded with rings of pale yellow, blue, and black; the forewings have a purplish outer margin. A large luna can measure 4¾ inches across its wings.

The luna, though well known because of its unique appearance, is seen less often than the other silk moth species because it has a predilection for thickly wooded areas; it is found over much of the continent east of the Rocky Mountains. When flying at night, the luna's unusual shape and floating flight give it a ghostly appearance.

The eggs are a shiny bluish green and are laid individually or in clusters on the host plant, which is usually a walnut, hickory, sweet gum, or persimmon tree. The cocoon is thin and compact and is usually spun among the leaves on the ground.

144

Isabella tiger moth.

The polyphemus is generally the most common of our silk moths and ranges across the continent from coast to coast. It is named after the one-eyed cyclops in Homer's *Odyssey* because of the large eyespot on its hindwing. Only a little smaller than the cecropia, a large polyphemus will measure 5½ to 6 inches. It is very variable in color, ranging from a pale cream to a rich terra cotta. Usually it is a delicate shade of tawny yellow with a large blue and yellow eyespot on the hindwing; on the forewing there is a smaller transparent spot. In the northern states there is only one brood each year, but farther south there are two. The moth is active from May to July; the female lays her eggs, which are shaped like hot cross buns, individually or in clusters.

The caterpillar is accordion-shaped, large and green, often with a bluish cast, with red tubercles. It feeds on a wide variety of food trees including oak, hickory, elm, maple, and birch. The cocoon is oval and parchmentlike, and attached to a twig and rolled up in a leaf. When the leaf dies and falls to the ground, the cocoon falls with it and spends the winter there among the leaves. It was once thought that the silk produced by the polyphemus could be used commercially, but the weave proved not to be continuous and was therefore unsatisfactory.

........................

## ASSEMBLING

**Many of our largest and most attractive moths are easy to breed in captivity.** A popular method of rearing giant silk moths, known as *assembling*, involves the use of a captive female specimen to attract males of the species.

In this method, a recently emerged female moth, such as a cecropia (*Hyalophora cecropia*), has a thin thread fastened to her abdomen; the other end of the thread is attached to a piece of screening that is hung up in a tree. The screen with the attached female is hung out in the late afternoon and allowed to remain through the night.

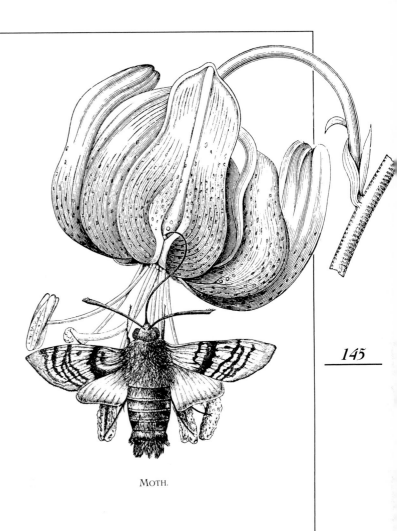

MOTH.

The tethered female broadcasts her existence through her mating odors, thereby attracting large numbers of eligible males in the general vicinity. Under ideal conditions, the scent of the female moth can reach males fully a mile away.

........................

## SOME CHICKS ARE MORE HELPLESS THAN OTHERS

**The young of *altricial* birds are blind, naked, and utterly helpless at birth.** They emerge from the egg in a relatively undeveloped condition and require constant parental care and feeding until they gain strength, grow feathers, and are able to leave the nest. Reflecting the short time that the chicks spend in the egg, and thus their small size when they hatch, their eggs tend to be small. The eastern meadowlark (*Sturnella magna*) is a typical example; the young hatch in about 2 weeks and leave the nest 10 to 12 days later.

Although the killdeer (*Charadrius vociferus*) is about the same size as the meadowlark, its egg is considerably larger, reflecting the longer period, from 24 to 28 days, that the chick will remain in it before hatching, and also the greater amount of yolk needed to feed the larger chick. The young of *precocial* birds such as a killdeer are able to fend for themselves almost immediately after hatching. They can run and feed themselves in an hour, or within two days.

146

......................

### The Young of Birds

| Bird | Nestling |
|------|----------|
| Chicken | Chick, poult |
| Duck | Duckling |
| Eagle | Eaglet |
| Goose | Gosling |
| Grouse | Cheeper, poult |
| Hawk | Eyas |
| Hen | Chick, pullet |
| Owl | Owlet |
| Partridge | Cheeper |
| Peafowl | Peachick |
| Pigeon | Squab |
| Quail | Cheeper |
| Rooster | Cockerel |
| Swan | Cygnet |
| Turkey | Poult |
| Wild fowl | Flapper |

......................

## GUILT BY ASSOCIATION
*Eagles*

**It's a pity that more rural Americans don't hold Benjamin Franklin's opinion of the national bird's trait of piracy.** For Franklin was referring to the fact that far from being a great and glorious hunter, the bald eagle is predominantly a scavenger.

But many people, especially sheep farmers, have traditionally regarded eagles as major predators and shoot them whenever they get the chance. In fact, the chief cause of death among bald eagles in North America is still shooting, even after years of protective legislation and educational programs.

In the worst recorded episode, an investigation of illegal poisonings of eagles in Wyoming in 1970–1971 led U.S. Fish and Wildlife Service investigators further than they could have imagined in the matter of predator persecution. While questioning one of the suspects in the poisonings, they were informed about a group of farmers who would regularly charter a helicopter to go out shooting at eagles from the air. Some 770 bald and golden eagles had been shot from one helicopter in a 12-month period; and there were other incidents as well.

Although this is history now, and people's attitudes have changed greatly for the better, the underlying misunderstanding about eagles is still there and should be cleared up. No self-respecting eagle, least of all a bald eagle, will disdain the chance to scavenge a recently expired lamb. Farmers observing eagles on the corpses of their dead livestock naturally — but mistakenly — assume that the livestock was killed by the eagles. This misunderstanding has led to the wholesale persecution and slaughter of all large birds of prey.

Farmers are now compensated by the Agriculture Department for any livestock depleted by predators, presumably as a measure to prevent them from taking the law into their own hands.

The value of a scavenger like the bald eagle in the nature of things cannot be overemphasized. Scavengers are nature's garbage collectors; without them the earth would become a breeding ground for disease, and plague would run rampant.

BALD EAGLE.

## BIRD OF JOVE
### *Golden Eagle*

**Of all the birds of the air, it is the golden eagle (*Aquila chrysaetos*) that has most inspired the human imagination.** It appears in myths and legends the world over and has been adopted as the emblem of majesty by emperors and kings throughout history. The Roman legends carried the eagle on their standards in the form of silver and golden ensigns. To the Romans, the golden eagle belonged to Jupiter; to Shakespeare, it was the "bird of Jove."

Contrary to general belief, golden eagles do not nest on mountaintops. Many aeries are built on crags only a few hundred feet above

sea level. A new nest is generally small and may be easily overlooked. However, each year the bird will add to the nest, until it becomes a truly monumental structure.

The staple diet of the golden eagle consists largely of rabbits, hares, and large game birds. Very occasionally, a golden eagle develops lamb-killing propensities, but this is the exception rather than the rule and generally occurs in areas where the eagle's natural prey is scarce. All eagles are, however, attracted to carrion; the sight of an eagle feeding on a lamb should not automatically be taken to mean that the bird had a part in killing the animal.

The size of an animal that the golden eagle is capable of killing is often exaggerated. A large golden eagle weighs 10 to 12 pounds, and it is very doubtful that it could lift more than its own weight. It is most unlikely, therefore, that it would kill a creature too large for it to carry away. The golden eagle can kill hares that weigh up to 8 pounds, but it does not usually do so. It normally preys on mountain hares of around 6 pounds.

There is some confusion concerning the longevity of eagles. The golden eagle is without doubt a long-lived bird: It is believed to be at least 4 years old before it reaches sexual maturity. A golden eagle shot in France in 1845 had a collar around its neck with the date 1750 inscribed on it. If the date on the collar of what was presumably an escaped specimen was the year of its capture, then this eagle was 95 years old. It is generally conceded that under optimum conditions in the wild, the golden eagle has a life span of from 40 to 50 years.

# July

Although the earth is some 4 million miles farther from the sun in July than it is in January, this happens to be the hottest month of the year in North America, and some of the most ferocious inhabitants of the continent are most active at this time as a result. Because people are most active at this time too, shark attacks are most frequent, as are stings from the man-o'-war.

All coldblooded creatures seem to do well in the hot weather. Alligators glower from the swamps of the Everglades, and croco- diles from the waters of Florida Bay; and rattle- snakes are at their peak of activity in most of the United States, particularly in their favorite environment, the deserts of the West.

If such creatures seem frightening, consider the smallest mammal on the continent, the shrew, a ferocious animal that can actually weigh as little as an eighth or even a sixteenth of an ounce (a good deal less than a dime weighs). Shrews devote half their lives to eating — they consume the equivalent of at least twice their weight each day!

OPPOSITE: PELICAN.

# JULY

The Bachman's warbler, North America's rarest warbler, was discovered by Dr. John Bachman, friend and co-worker of John James Audubon, a few miles from Charleston, South Carolina, in July 1833.

. . . . . . . . . . . .

## 1

International Trade in Endangered Fauna and Flora came into force in 1975.

Mammoth Cave National Park, Kentucky, and Haleakala National Park, Hawaii, established on this day in 1941 and 1961, respectively.

. . . . . . . . . . . .

## 3

A definite crossing of the Atlantic Ocean has been recorded for a common tern banded at Eastern Egg Rock, Maine, in 1913, and found dead in August 1917 at the mouth of the Niger River in West Africa.

. . . . . . . . . . . .

## 4

Xerces Society's Fourth of July Butterfly Count.

## 5

Great auk last recorded in North America at Funk Island, Newfoundland, in 1785.

. . . . . . . . . . . .

## 6

Largest western diamondback rattlesnake on record was one killed near Brownsville, Texas, on July 6, 1926. It weighed 24 pounds and was 7 feet 5 inches long (excluding the rattle).

. . . . . . . . . . . .

## 7

Largest channel catfish (58 pounds) caught with rod and line taken in the Santee-Cooper Reserve, South Carolina, in 1964.

. . . . . . . . . . . .

## 8

Audubon Society warden Guy Bradley murdered near Oyster Key, Florida, by a plume hunter in 1905.

Hazel R. Ellis of Cornell University was the first person to observe the hatching of a Hudsonian

PEREGRINE FALCON.

godwit at Churchill, Manitoba, Canada, in 1947.

. . . . . . . . . . . .

## 9

Namu, the killer whale, largest marine mammal ever kept in captivity, drowned in the Seattle Public Aquarium in 1966 after getting entangled in the netting surrounding his pen while trying to escape.

Largest smallmouth bass (11 pounds 15 ounces) caught with rod and line taken in Dale Hollow Lake in Kentucky in 1955.

## 10

Largest carp ever recorded was taken in Clearwater Lake, Minnesota, in 1952. It weighed 55 pounds 5 ounces.

. . . . . . . . . . . .

## 12

Georg Wilhelm Steller, famous naturalist and explorer, dissected a carcass of a Steller's sea cow on the beach of Bering Island in 1741, and estimated the animal's weight at 8,000 pounds: "The stomach was so stuffed with food and seaweed that forty strong men with a rope attached could scarcely move it from its place and drag it out."

12-year-old Lester Stilwell attacked by a great white shark in Matawan Creek, New Jersey, in 1916. Both he and his would-be rescuer were killed.

. . . . . . . . . . . .

## 15

Lake sturgeon caught in Lake of the Woods, Kenora, Ontario, Canada, in 1953, believed to be 150 years old, based on a growth ring count of its pectoral fin.

. . . . . . . . . . .

**16**

Georg Wilhelm Steller discovered the Steller's jay on Kayak Island, Alaska, in 1741.

. . . . . . . . . . .

**18**

Only record for a crested caracara in Canada occurred at Port Arthur, Ontario, in 1892.

SHARK.

**19**

Perhaps the earliest-known record of the nest of the great gray owl was made by Roderick Mac-Farlane near Lockhart River, en route to Fort Good Hope, Northwest Territories, in 1862.

. . . . . . . . . . .

**21**

Arctic warbler, a Eurasian bird, first reported for North America at Prince Patrick Island, Northwest Territories, in 1949.

**22**

Largest California halibut (37 pounds 8 ounces) caught with rod and line taken off San Diego, California, in 1979.

. . . . . . . . . . .

**25**

Anaho Island National Wildlife Refuge, Nevada, established in 1940 to preserve North America's largest white pelican colony.

A Hudsonian godwit sighted at Moosonee, Ontario, Canada, in 1942, by Terence Shortt and C. E. Hope, after the species had been presumed extinct.

**27**

8-year-old boy attacked by a tiger shark in shallow water off Longboat Key, Florida, in 1958. His leg had to be amputated.

Largest hammerhead shark (717 pounds) caught with rod and line was taken off Jacksonville Beach, Florida, in 1980.

. . . . . . . . . . .

**28**

Rare and endangered black-footed ferret photographed in Mellette County, South Dakota, in 1966.

*Dallas Weekly Herald*, in 1877, reported a rattlesnake killed in the Cherokee Nation near Eufaula that was 18 feet long, with 37 distinct rattles on its tail. This report is believed to have been greatly exaggerated.

Clem and Jethro, pet wolves of conservationist John Harris, poisoned by a wolf hater who gave them chicken laced with strychnine in New York City in 1973.

. . . . . . . . . . .

**30**

Captive-bred peregrine falcon released on Carroll Island seen perching on an office building in Baltimore, Maryland, on July 30, 1975.

*151*

BROWN
PELICAN.

## RIVER OF GRASS
*The Florida Everglades*

If there were a Mecca for naturalists in North America, it would surely be the Florida Everglades. This semitropical paradise contains an enormous number of wildlife species, and more rare and endangered animals than are found anywhere else on the continent. These include the Florida panther (*Felis concolor coryi*), Everglades kite (*Rostrhamus sociabilis plumbeus*), Florida manatee (*Trichechus manatus latirostris*), Florida sandhill crane (*Grus canadensis pratensis*), brown pelican (*Pelecanus occidentalis*), southern bald eagle (*Haliaeetus leucocephalus leucocephalus*), American peregrine falcon (*Falco peregrinus anatum*), Cape Sable sparrow (*Ammospiza mirabilis*), and American crocodile (*Crocodylus acutus*).

Encompassing nearly all of south Florida, including Lake Okeechobee, the Everglades extend south for 120 miles to Florida Bay and the sea and cover an area of 7 million acres, 1.4 million of which were dedicated to the nation by President Harry S. Truman in 1947.

The Everglades, which appears to be a marshy land covered in places with tall grasses, is, in fact, a river of grass — a saw-grass prairie rooted in a giant river, only 6 inches deep and 50 miles wide. Climate governs the life of the Everglades. The nearly uniform climate makes the area a year-round attraction, but there are two distinct seasons: summer, which is wet, and winter, which is dry.

During the wet season the river flows almost imperceptibly along its course before entering Florida Bay. The heavy rains fall in late May through October, and the warm, humid conditions bring an abundance of insects. So while from the naturalist's point of view, July is an excellent time to visit the Everglades because of the abundance of wildlife, the best time for everyone else to come is between September and April, for it is drier and cooler and the wildlife congregates in the still-wet area.

AMERICAN CROCODILE.

The region is not truly tropical; the southern-most point of the Everglades is 75 miles north of the Tropic of Cancer, which by definition is the northern limit of the Tropical Zone. However, much of the vegetation is more typical of the West Indies than it is of the United States.

Of the several trails leading off the road, the one nearest to the park entrance, called the Anhinga Trail, is the most interesting and popular because of its excellent close-ups of the wildlife. But Pineland Trail, Pa-hay-okee Overlook, Mahogany Hammock, Parotis Pond, Nine Mile Pond, and the West Lake Trail each have something different and interesting to offer.

The Anhinga Trail, named for the bird of that name, includes an elevated boardwalk from which, during the winter months, you can see alligators, snowy egrets, and a wealth of other wildlife, including softshell turtles and diamondback terrapins, which often form part of the alligators' diet.

The best-known denizen of the Florida Everglades is the American alligator (*Alligator mississippiensis*). Unfortunately, the hide of this animal has been greatly prized for high-fashion shoes and handbags. This giant reptile once waged a losing battle against poachers and habitat loss, but it has now staged a dramatic comeback under nationwide protection. In recent years, 75 percent of the nation's alligators have been removed from the endangered species list and reclassified as threatened.

The alligator has earned for itself the title of "keeper of the Everglades," for it serves a vital function in the Everglades ecology. During the dry winter season, the alligator clears out large "alligator holes" from the limestone bed, which function as oases for fish, turtles, snails, and other freshwater animals. In turn, these smaller creatures are preyed upon by the alligators, as well as the neighboring birds and mammals, until the return of the rains.

Crocodiles are far less common in the Everglades than alligators. In Florida, crocodiles are shy and secretive reptiles and are found mostly in the Florida Bay area. The survival of this species hangs on the preservation of its dwindling habitat, which sometimes overlaps that of the alligators.

Large mammals rank high among the most precious inhabitants of the Everglades. The shy and docile Florida manatee weighs close to a ton, is over 12 feet long, and is entirely herbivorous. Propellers of motorboats pose the greatest threat to this peaceful sea cow in the shallow water. Many are maimed and killed every year.

The Florida panther, a subspecies of the cougar, is among North America's rarest mammals.

The major threat to the few remaining panthers that are occasionally seen in the pinelands, along the park road, has been the destruction of their habitat.

Raccoons, bobcats, otters, and smaller mammals are common in the Everglades. You are most likely to see them by taking a walk or driving slowly along the trails, early in the morning or late evening. They are rarely seen during the heat of day.

The abundance and variety of birdlife, especially water birds, have made the Everglades world-famous. At Flamingo, on the southern tip of the peninsula, roseate spoonbills (*Ajaia ajaia*) can be observed. The uninitiated often mistake these large pink birds for flamingos, but wild flamingos are only occasional visitors to Florida. It is quite probable that Flamingo was named for the roseate spoonbill — and was a case of mistaken identity. The only flock of semi-wild flamingos in Florida are the famous birds at Hialeah racetrack.

The anhinga (*Anhinga anhinga*), a familiar bird of the Everglades, is known for its habit of perching in trees and spreading out its wings to dry after every fishing expedition. When hunting for food, the anhinga goes under water, only to reappear moments later with a fish impaled on its spearlike bill. The bird is commonly known as "snakebird" because it holds its long neck outstretched while swimming underwater.

Cape Sable sparrows were once found at Cape Sable and Big Cypress in large numbers, but they are now all but gone, save a few widely scattered individuals. Taylor Slough's grass prairie supports an active population, but exotic plants threaten to close in the open prairie this small bird depends on for its survival. Short-tailed hawks (*Buteo brachyurus*) prey on the sparrow, and ants can kill the nestlings. When the Cape Sable sparrows were abundant, this natural predation posed no serious threat to the species.

Everglades National Park provides the most successful nesting area for the southern bald eagle in the entire United States. Currently, about fifty pairs of these magnificent birds nest along the coast. A good vantage point from which to view them is the breezeway of the Flamingo Visitor Center.

The Everglades is easily accessible from Miami by going west along U.S. 41 to Everglades City on the northern edge of the national park, or south along U.S. 1 or the Florida Turnpike into the very heart of the park. This is the most popular and attractive route because it cuts through a representative cross section of the Everglades. The en-

trance to the national park is about 90 minutes' drive from downtown Miami.

For further information on the Everglades, write: Superintendent, Everglades National Park, P.O. Box 279, Homestead, Florida 33030.

## MURDER IN THE EVERGLADES

Among the four wardens employed by the Audubon Society was Guy Bradley, age 35. A guardian of wildlife in the Florida Everglades, Bradley became the first human martyr in the egrets' cause.

ANHINGA PREENING.

OVERLEAF: GREAT EGRET IN FLIGHT.

On July 8, 1905, Warden Bradley spotted a suspicious-looking schooner near Oyster Key, off the tip of the Florida mainland. He set out in his skiff and reached the schooner just as two plume hunters were loading dead egrets aboard. When Bradley tried to arrest them, the skipper shot him at point-blank range and set sail, leaving the warden dead in his drifting boat. His body was not discovered until 24 hours later, when two curious boys rowed over to investigate the reason for hovering vultures. Bradley's killer went free.

"Heretofore," cried Audubon President William Dutcher, when he heard the news, "the price has been the life of the birds. Now human blood has been added." The murder of Guy Bradley may have been responsible for turning the tide of public opinion in favor of the egrets. Shortly thereafter, the National Association of Audubon Societies was able to push through a law prohibiting the use of wild-bird feathers in New York, the center of the millinery trade.

........................

## HORRORS OF THE MILLINERY TRADE

One of the saddest chapters in the history of North American wildlife was the mass destruction of birds for their feathers to adorn ladies' spring and summer hats. Toward the end of the last century, 5 million birds died annually to satisfy the demands of the millinery trade; these ranged from the arctic tern to the hummingbirds, but it was the great egret *(Casmerodius albus)* and the snowy egret *(Leucophoyx thula)* that suffered the most.

Before the feather fad started around 1875, great and snowy egrets were subjected to little other than sport hunting. Then suddenly they were recognized as the most accessible and the most lucrative of all bird species for the millinery trade. The abundant heronries of the Gulf Coast and Florida (especially those of the Everglades) were invaded by plume hunters, who shot the adult birds and left the young to starve in their nests. Only during the breeding season do the birds carry the graceful nuptial feathers, known in the trade as "aigrettes," which at the peak of demand were worth their weight in gold. In one breeding season in Florida, 130,000 egrets were slaughtered to supply feathered hats to the fashionable women of New York.

"The horrors attending the collection of plumes of Herons are beyond the powers of language to describe, and can best be shown pictorially. The paltry price in money that is paid for the plumes is not to be compared to the price paid in blood and suffering." Thus wrote William Dutcher, president of the National Association of Audubon Societies, around the turn of the century. "Women must remember that the white Herons wear the coveted plumes only during the breeding season, and that the parent birds must be shot in order to obtain the plumes. The young birds in the nest starve, in consequence of the death of the parents."

The dictates of fashion had created an industry that became worldwide. In a few years, this industry grew so much that Florida, swiftly followed by Texas, passed a law to protect plume-bird eggs and young, but these laws were hard to implement and were largely ignored. In spite of state and citizen concern, the shooting continued. Women, intent on following the style, continued to purchase the fine feathered hats. Egrets were altogether too easy to kill and continued to perish in horrendous numbers.

The first to raise his voice against the killings was George Bird Grinnell in 1886. Grinnell was the editor of *Forest and Stream* when he published an editorial suggesting that an organization be formed to protect wild birds and their eggs. Nearly 40,000 people enrolled in that U.S. Audubon Society, but the society died out. In the late 1890s Mrs. Augustus Hemenway of Boston read a witness's account of the horrors of the slaughter of egrets in Florida that prompted her to act on their behalf. From a copy of Boston's *Blue Book*, she drew up a list of acquaintances and then urged them to form a society for the protection of birds, especially the victimized egrets. In this way the Massachusetts Audubon Society was born.

In 1896 the outlook for the egrets improved with the resurrection of the Audubon Societies. These societies sprang up in state after state until by 1905 thirty-five state Audubon Societies had merged into a national association with enough power to influence public opinion. At least ten states appointed wardens to protect nesting colonies and enforce what laws existed. The first steps to save the egrets had been taken.

FASHIONABLE LADY
WITH FEATHER FAN.

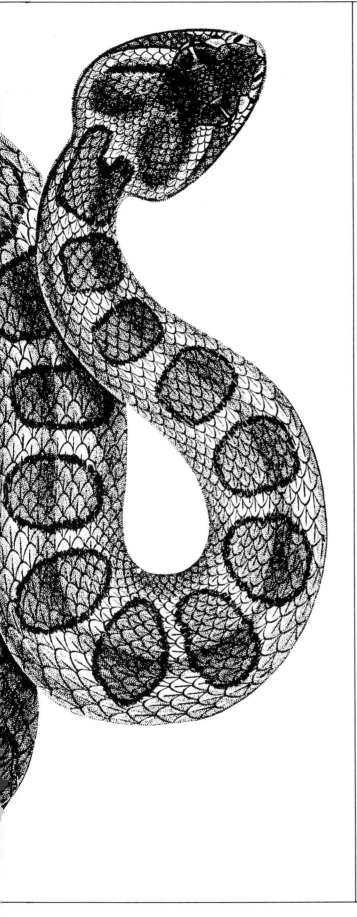

## MONSTER RATTLESNAKES

**A**uthenticated records for the length of rattlesnakes don't exceed 8 feet, although there have been many substantiated reports of monster rattlers.

The *Dallas Weekly Herald* of July 28, 1877, reported a rattler killed in the Cherokee Nation, near Eufaula, 18 feet long, with 37 distinct rattles on its tail. That report must have been exaggerated, but there is an old tradition that a rattler 10 feet long with 50 rattles was killed by early settlers on the Colorado River of Texas.

It is quite possible that in the Rio Grande Valley of Texas and in northern Mexico rattlesnakes attain a larger size than they do anywhere else in the world. W. S. ("Snake") King of Brownsville, Texas, who handled more rattlesnakes than any other man in the world, claims to have captured alive, in Mexico, a rattler 9 feet 6½ inches long.

About 1914 Domingo Roach was running a steer in the lower Rio Grande Valley. When Domingo caught up with the steer, he saw two gigantic rattlesnakes fastened on either side of the steer's jaws. He shot the rattlesnakes with a Winchester he carried in his saddle, but the steer had died.

The skin of one of these snakes, removed and dried, measured 10 feet 3 inches from the tip of its nose to the last button of its rattle; the other skin measured 9 feet 8 inches. For several years the skins were displayed in a drugstore at Harlingen, Texas.

Captain Frank Hamer of the Texas Rangers had a rattlesnake skin, taken from the same region, 9 feet 8 inches long and 16½ inches across its widest spread. Also, in the express car that used to run on the St. Louis and Brownsville railroad into Brownsville, there was a stuffed rattlesnake said to be between 14 and 15 feet long. A snake's skin will stretch, but probably not more than an inch and a half per foot.

. . . . . . . . . . . . . . . . . . . . . .

## THE FOURTH OF JULY BUTTERFLY COUNT

**T**he Xerces Society, founded on December 9, 1971, was established as "an international non-profit organization dedicated to the conservation of 'terrestrial arthropods' and their habitats."

161

The society is largely concerned with rare and endangered lepidoptera (butterflies and moths) of local occurrence. The name is taken from the xerces blue butterfly *(Glaucopsyche xerces)*, which has the dubious distinction of being the first butterfly on this continent to have become extinct at the hand of man.

Every summer, the Xerces Society holds its annual Fourth of July Butterfly Count, although this event can take place any time between the third week in June and the middle of July. The purpose of the count is to acquire accurate records on the variations in butterfly species and populations in specific areas. Endangered butterfly species of particular concern to the Xerces Society include: the El Segundo blue butterfly *(Shijimiaeoides bat-*

*toides allyni)*, Smith's blue butterfly *(S. enoptes smithi)*, Lange's metalmark butterfly *(Apodemia mormo langei)*, Lotis blue butterfly *(Lycaeides argyrognomon lotis)*, Mission blue butterfly *(Icaricia icarioides missionensis)*, and San Bruno elfin butterfly *(Callophrys mossii bayensis)*.

The Fourth of July Butterfly Count for 1981 covered the period from June 20 to July 12. Fourty-four counts were reported, involving 260 participants from 20 states, Colorado and California being best represented with 9 and 5 counts, respectively. The number of species observed ranged from as few as four in Portland, Oregon, to 97 in Lower Circle, Gilpin County, Colorado. The average number of butterfly species for the count was 32.8 species per area.

The number of individual butterflies per count ranged from 18 seen on the University of California at Los Angeles campus to 2,588 seen in Berkeley, California, with an average of 748.3 specimens per count.

For further information on the Fourth of July Butterfly Count, write: Butterfly Count Coordinator, 38 Laconia Street, Lexington, Massachusetts 02173.

For information on the Xerces Society, write: Xerces Society, Secretary, Department of Zoology and Physiology, University of Wyoming, Laramie, Wyoming 82071.

LARVA AND BUTTERFLY.

# July Reading

## TINY TERRORS
### *Shrews*

**The short-tailed shrew (*Blarina brevicauda*), a common mouselike animal found in burrows, fields, and woods, has, despite its innocuous appearance, a bite that is poisonous to its prey**. A large dose of saliva drawn from the glands of its lower jaw can kill a good-sized mouse, but will not harm humans.

Shrews are the smallest of all mammals, and are often mistaken for mice. However, careful examination of a shrew will show no external ears. It has very tiny eyes, and a long, pointed nose, and its tail is usually much shorter than a mouse's. Also, it has five toes on the front feet, compared to a mouse's four.

For its size, no animal is fiercer or more voracious. It will eat anything from fish eggs and insects to birds. On occasion it will even turn cannibalistic. The shrew is cursed with an amazingly fast metabolism, and must eat two to three times its own weight each day or it will die. It eats for three hours and rests for three hours throughout the day and night.

The water shrew (*Neomys* sp.) actually walks on the surface of the water by means of a fringe of bristly hairs on its broad hind feet. This is the same principle employed by the water strider, an insect commonly found in streams.

Shrews have been the subject of many myths and superstitions. Eskimos fear the shrew for they believe it can burrow into a man's flesh to his heart. If they see a shrew, they will stand still until it passes. The shrew was sacred to the ancient Egyptians, who thought the animal to be blind, and so made it into the symbol of night and darkness. The Greek historian Herodotus wrote about the Egyptian city of Buto, which contained a burial ground for shrews; the mummified remains of these animals have been found in the ruins of the city of Thebes.

Small insectivorous animals such as shrews, moles, and hedgehogs are of particular evolutionary significance, as they are the living relics of the animals from which all other mammals descended.

WATER SHREW.

COMMON MOLE.

## ELUSIVE MOLES

**Most people can very quickly count the number of times they have seen a live mole (*Talpa* sp.), although we walk over their underground homes every day.**

The only signs we see of their presence are little mounds of earth or low ridges on the surface. The mounds are made of earth pushed up from their permanent burrows, which may be 2 feet from the surface; the ridges are simply displaced soil heaved up by the animal's body as it goes from one place to another.

Trying to find a mole, even where there are many surface signs, and even if you use a shovel, is generally not successful, because they make their nests and spend most of their time where their young are born, far below the reach of surface excavations. For this reason, many details of mole life history are still not well known to mammalogists.

Although they cause annoyance and some minor damage to lawns, golf courses, and gardens, moles are, in general, far more beneficial than harmful, as their food consists entirely of worms and insects, and they do much to open the hard-packed subsoil so that it can absorb air and water.

......................

## THE POWERFUL EXCAVATOR
*American Badger*

**The American badger (*Taxidea taxus*), one of eight badger species found throughout the world, has extremely powerful digging claws.** In fact, pound for pound, badgers may be the most efficient digging machines in the animal kingdom.

Given the right kind of soil, this animal can literally dig itself out of sight in a matter of minutes. Some time ago biologist J. R. Alcorn from Nevada attempted to dig out a badger but without success. In an experiment to determine how fast a badger can dig, Alcorn di-

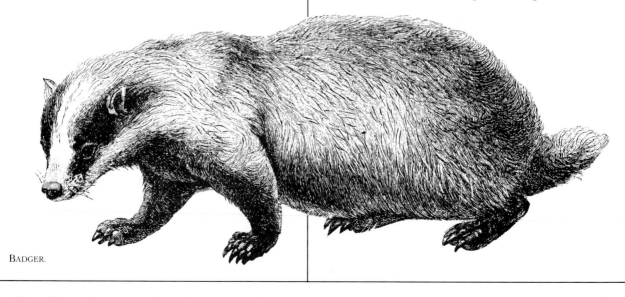

BADGER.

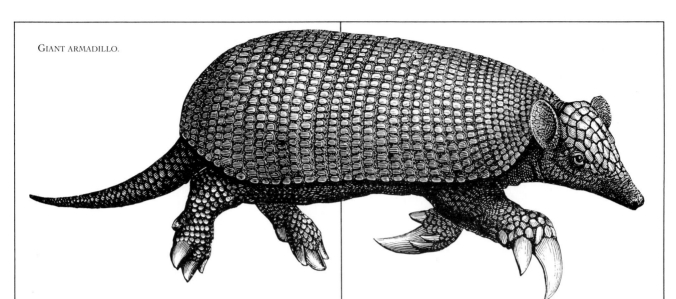

rected ten men with shovels to pursue a specimen as it dug into some very soft soil. The men never found the animal even though they dug continually for several hours.

### The Young of Mammals

| | |
|---|---|
| Antelope | Calf |
| Ass | Foal, hinny |
| Bear | Cub |
| Beaver | Kitten |
| Cat | Kitten |
| Cow | Calf |
| Deer | Fawn |
| Dog | Puppy |
| Elephant | Calf |
| Fox | Cub, kit |
| Goat | Kid |
| Hare | Leveret |
| Hippopotamus | Calf |
| Horse | Colt, foal, filly, filt |
| Kangaroo | Joey |
| Lion | Cub |
| Monkey | Baby |
| Moose | Calf |
| Otter | Whelp |
| Pig | Piglet, shoat, farrow |
| Rabbit | Leveret, bunny |
| Rhinoceros | Calf |
| Seal | Pup |
| Sheep | Lamb |
| Tiger | Cub |
| Whale | Calf |
| Wolf | Cub, whelp |
| Zebra | Colt |

## A PIG INSIDE A TURTLE'S SHELL
### *Armadillo*

**As the climate of the United States became cooler over thousands of years, most tropical species moved southward.** A few, however, continued to extend their range northward.

Perhaps the most interesting of the northward-ranging animals is the nine-banded armadillo (*Dasypus novemcinctus*). This bizarre, armor-plated creature was not discovered in the United States until 1844, when it was first reported by John James Audubon in southern Texas and was painted by him as somewhat resembling a pig inside a turtle's shell.

It was still only an obscure border mammal in the 1930s, but it has since burrowed its way north to Oklahoma, Kansas, and Arkansas and east to Louisiana and Mississippi; and in its indomitable fashion, it gives every indication of pushing on farther. The animal's range extension has also been inadvertently assisted by humans in Florida and Alabama. A few armadillos brought into Florida as pets about the time of World War I have so multiplied that they are now found throughout most of the state.

The armadillo is generally regarded as a slow-witted creature, no doubt due to the fact that its hearing and eyesight are poor. In order to compensate, the animal is strongly protected by bands of bony plates that sheath its back, its head, its tail, its legs, and even its ears.

In the event of danger, a notch in the back plate where the armadillo can insert its head enables it to roll itself into a ball. Although this protective mechanism works perfectly well against natural predators, the armadillo's armor plate is no match for automobiles, and many of these unfortunate animals become road casualties on busy highways.

.......................

## ALLIGATOR OR CROCODILE?

**North America is the natural home of two crocodilians, the American alligator (*Alligator mississipiensis*) and the American crocodile (*Crocodylus acutus*).** But whereas the alligator is found in fresh and brackish waters of the southeastern United States north to South Carolina, the crocodile is confined to the extreme tip of southern Florida.

Alligators and crocodiles are superficially very much alike, and distinguishing one species from the other may present some difficulty to the nonherpetologist.

The main distinguishing feature is the teeth. In both animals the fourth lower tooth on each side is perceptibly longer than the rest. In the crocodile, this tooth fits into a notch on the outside of the upper jaw and is clearly visible when the mouth is closed; in the alligator, the fourth tooth in the lower jaw fits inside a socket in the upper jaw and cannot be seen when the mouth is shut.

In addition, the head of the alligator is substantially broader and shorter, and the snout consequently blunter; the head of the crocodile tapers noticeably toward the snout. Alligators tend to keep more to fresh water than crocodiles and show little tendency to spread along the coastline or to reach offshore islands. Sometimes the ranges of the two animals overlap, however, in brackish water.

Alligators are a grayish brown color. Crocodiles tend to be more of a grayish green.

In recent years, the spectacled caiman (*Caiman crocodilus*) was inadvertently introduced into Florida, where it is living in a wild, free state. Caimans are part of the alligator group and are, in fact, the South American equivalents of our alligators. They differ from alligators in only minor ways. Caimans lack the bony septum between the nostrils that is present in alligators, and the bony plates that make up the armor of a crocodilian are in a far more advanced stage of development on the underside of the caiman.

The order Crocodilia comprises fourteen species of true crocodiles, two gavials (exclusively fish-eaters), two alligators, and seven caimans.

It is purely by accident that two such similar reptiles as the alligator and the crocodile should so early in their history have been given different common names. When the Spanish seafarers, who presumably had no knowledge of crocodiles, first encountered large reptiles in the New World, they spoke of them as lizards—*el largato* in Spanish. The English who followed later adopted the Spanish name but ran the two into one word to make *allagarter*, which was later further corrupted to *alligator*.

.......................

## RARE BUTTERFLIES AND MOTHS OF POINT PELEE

**Point Pelee National Park in Ontario, the southernmost point on the Canadian mainland, supports vegetation and wildlife that are more characteristic of parts of the southern United States than of the rest of Canada.** As in the case with other groups of animals, butterflies and moths at Point Pelee include many southern species rare in Canada.

William Saunders reported in the *Canadian Entomologist* in 1883 his first encounter with the giant swallowtail (*Heraclides cresphontes*) and the very local olive hairstreak (*Callophrys gryneus*). He also referred to finding at Point Pelee the Mexican sulphur (*Eurema mexicana*), an extremely rare visitor to Canada.

CROCODILE.

During collecting trips to Point Pelee from 1908 to 1919, Canadian naturalist Percy Taverner, recorded his sugaring activities (a process of collecting moths by luring them to a sweet and intoxicating substance painted on tree trunks — usually a combination of molasses, brown sugar, and stale beer) and reported them in the *Canadian Entomologist*. "That night we sugared the woods across the road from the campgrounds for moths with considerable luck. The first round of sugared route we found underwings *Catocala* spp. on nearly every tree and took five species. *Catocala cara* was the commonest species but so far I have made out *C. grynea* and *C. cerogama* among the spoils." In all, Taverner collected twelve *Catocala* species: *C. cara, cerogama, parta, grynea, habilis, vidua, piatrix, unijuga, amica, concumbens, relicta,* and *amatrix*.

Rare southern migrant butterflies that may be seen at Point Pelee include the snout butterfly *(Libytheana bachmanii)*, buckeye *(Precis coenia)*, dogface *(Colias* [Zerene] *cesonia)*, cloudless sulphur *(Phoebis sennae eubule)*, and the even rarer regal fritillary *(Speyeria idalia)*, zebra swallowtail *(Eurytides marcellus)*, and Mexican sulphur. These species, along with the black witch moth *(Erebus odora)*, frequently end their northward journey across Lake Erie washed up on the shore along with debris. All these insects are summer immigrants from the south, apparently not able to overwinter in southern Ontario. A few have been observed flying south in the fall, sometimes in the company of migrating monarchs *(Danaus plexippus)*.

Whether or not these insects can be termed truly migrational has yet to be determined. The term *migration* in its strictest sense denotes fairly continuous movement from one area to another with periodic return to the original area. However, in the case of insect migration, it means one-way movement from one area to another with no return flight.

OVERLEAF: ALLIGATOR.

## INSECT MUSICIANS

*Grasshoppers*

**As their name suggests, grasshoppers (family Acrididae) inhabit grass and other ground herbage, where they are protected because their green and brown coloration blends with their surroundings**. The term *locust* is loosely applied to any large tropical or subtropical grasshopper that gathers in large swarms and causes catastrophic damage to vegetation.

Short-horned grasshoppers make a rasping sound by rubbing their hind legs against their front wings. When these grasshoppers are at rest, their true wings are folded like a fan underneath their front wings. There are rows of tiny pegs on the hind legs, and when these are scraped against the rough wings, the sound that results is much like the one made when you scrape your thumbnail across the teeth of a comb. Certain short-horned grasshoppers have gaily-colored hind wings, and these they display in flight by rapid opening and closing of the wings — producing a sound that has given them the name of "castanet grasshoppers."

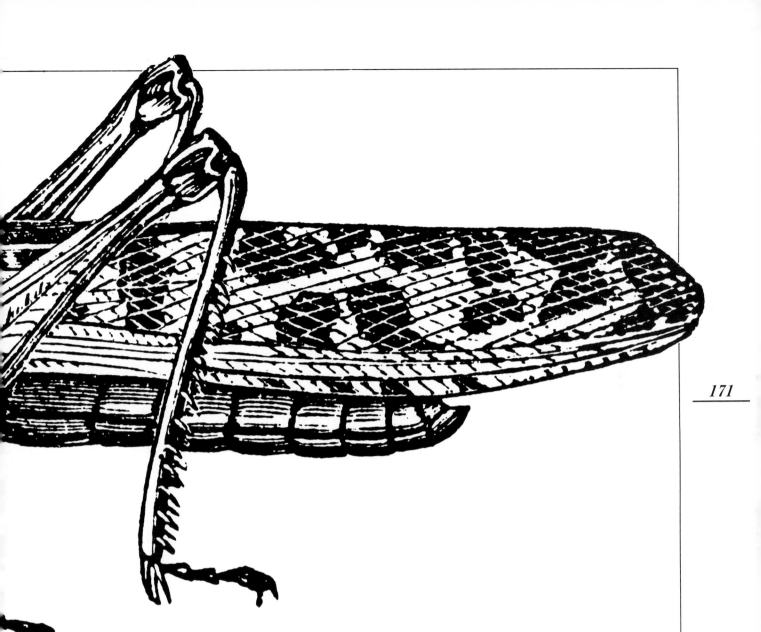

The sound-producing apparatus of long-horned grasshoppers and katydids is quite different from that of their short-horned relatives. Male long-horns "fiddle" by rubbing the underside of one wing on the other. A file-like ridge on one wing rubs against a rough area on the other, the wings themselves acting as sounding boards and producing the familiar high-pitched chirping.

Katydids are bright green, almost transparent, insects that live in trees and so are seldom seen, although their music is loud and clear. By drawing a "bow" on the left wing across a "string" on the right wing, these creatures produce a noise that sounds a little like "Katy did, she didn't, she did," from which they get their name.

Crickets are perhaps the best-known insect musicians, and many species contribute to the ensemble. As with most insects, their activities rise and fall with the temperature, and a reasonably accurate estimate of the Fahrenheit temperature may be obtained by counting the number of chirps for a specified period, and adding a number that varies with the species of cricket. The formula for the field cricket (*Gryllus* sp.) is the number of chirps in 14 seconds plus 40.

*Mollucca Op.* *Male*

*Didelphis or Opossum*

*Kangooroo*

*Spotted Op.*

*Flying Op.*

*Female*

*Kangooroo Rat*

*Surinam Op.*

## LIFE WITHOUT A DRINK
*Kangaroo Rat*

**The kangaroo rat (*Dipodomys* sp.), of the deserts and plains of western North America, lives its entire lifetime without drinking any water.**

It is able to accomplish this miraculous feat by having kidneys that are superbly efficient — at least four times more efficient than those of a human. The animal, therefore, needs far less water to remove body wastes.

Tests have shown that kangaroo rats can live indefinitely on dried-out food, without any access to water; the water in their bodies comes from the chemical breakdown of their food.

. . . . . . . . . . . . . . . .

## KEEPING A COOL HEAD
*Antelope Ground Squirrel*

**The antelope ground squirrel (*Ammospermophilus harrisii*), an inhabitant of the deserts of the southwestern United States, gets its name from the way it carries its tail high,** exposing a white rump in the same way as the pronghorn (antelope).

This remarkable animal runs a high fever every day and yet never falls sick from it. It is active even when the air temperature is 110 degrees Fahrenheit (43° C) and the ground beneath its feet is 150 degrees Fahrenheit (66° C). Even when its own body temperature rises above 110 degrees, the animal shows no sign of discomfort.

The squirrel copes with exceptionally high temperatures by retiring to a shady spot and flattening itself on the ground, and losing heat by conduction. It may also take refuge down inside its burrow. Under these circumstances, the animal's temperature drops from 107 to 100 degrees Fahrenheit (42° to 33° C) within three minutes.

Another method of cooling that the squirrel has devised is to drool and spread the saliva over its head with its forepaws as if washing itself. The antelope ground squirrel is thereby able to endure several hours of blistering desert heat by dashing around with a soaking wet head.

OPPOSITE: CALIFORNIA GROUND SQUIRREL

# August

August is the ideal month for summer holidays, sports, and recreation and seems to be a good time to consider the sporting capabilities of the animals around us. Although the fastest human may be able to overtake a rat or a mole or a skunk or a porcupine (if a human were foolish enough to try to catch up with one), none of us would be capable of overtaking most larger North American animals. Even the lumbering American black bear would quickly outpace us, and the enormous grizzly would run us down altogether.

175

Although many humans may accomplish little in August, reptiles and amphibians are very busy producing families. If interrupted in their activity, some of these creatures tend to employ handy methods of self-defense: the rattlesnake's venom is injected with hypodermic fangs; the gila monster's poison flows over its gums; and the toad's offensive secretions are in its skin and urine. The Texas horned toad, which is not poisonous, has the disconcerting ability to squirt blood from its eyes to a distance of 7 feet. Other lizards will fool you by discarding their tail if you grab them by it.

# AUGUST

## 1

Largest walleye (25 pounds) caught with rod and line taken in Old Hickory Lake, Tennessee, in 1960.

Zebra swallowtail butterfly captured in Toronto, Ontario, Canada, in 1943, was probably at its northernmost limit.

Largest landlocked salmon (22 pounds 8 ounces) caught with rod and line taken in Sebago Lake, Maine, in 1907.

· · · · · · · · · · ·

## 5

Largest golden trout (11 pounds) caught with rod and line taken in Cook's Lake, Wyoming, in 1948.

· · · · · · · · · · ·

## 6

Largest Atlantic blue marlin (1,282 pounds) caught with rod and line taken at St. Thomas, Virgin Islands, in 1977.

## 7

Robert Cavalier de la Salle and 34 men sailed from what is now La Salle, New York, in 1679. Their destination was Lake Michigan, where they planned to trade for furs.

· · · · · · · · · · ·

## 8

Largest North American lake trout (102 pounds and 49½ inches long) caught with rod and line taken in Lake Athabasca, Saskatchewan, Canada, in 1961.

· · · · · · · · · · ·

## 9

Captain F. D. Langsford, skipper of the schooner *Venus*, accidentally speared by the sword of a swordfish in 1886. He survived the injury but died three days later of peritonitis.

· · · · · · · · · · ·

## 10

Smallest-known reptile, a species of gecko, discov-

BISON BULL.

ered on Virgin Gorda in the Virgin Islands in 1964.

· · · · · · · · · · ·

## 12

Largest tiger trout (20 pounds 13 ounces) caught with rod and line was taken in Lake Michigan, Wisconsin, in 1978.

## 14

Pronghorn speed of 61 mph timed by a car speedometer at Spanish Lake, Lake County, Oregon, in 1936.

Ernest Thompson Seton, renowned Canadian naturalist and author, born in 1860.

## 16

Migratory Bird Convention Act, a treaty for the protection of migrating birds in the United States and Canada, signed in Washington, D.C., in 1916.

Largest American grayling (5 pounds 15 ounces) ever recorded taken in Katseyedie River, Northwest Territories, Canada, in 1967.

. . . . . . . . . . . .

## 17

Buff-bellied hummingbird, a Mexican species, first reported north of the border at Fort Brown, Texas, in 1876.

## 18

Captain Meriwether Lewis, of the Lewis and Clark expedition, born near Charlottesville, Virginia, in 1774.

. . . . . . . . . . . .

## 19

A stray monarch, America's famous migrant butterfly, was captured on a mountain ridge at the northwest corner of Tokyo, Japan, in 1950. The monarch is now found in many countries outside its native home.

. . . . . . . . . . . .

## 20

First recorded sighting of

a bison by a white man made by Henry Kelsey of the Hudson's Bay Company in Manitoba, Canada, in 1691.

Largest giant sea bass (563 pounds 8 ounces) caught with rod and line taken at Anacapa Island, California, in 1968.

. . . . . . . . . . . .

## 24

A rare regal fritillary captured in Kitchener, Ontario, Canada, on August 24, 1952 — probably the most northerly record for this species.

. . . . . . . . . . . .

## 26

Last timber rattlesnake reported for Canada taken

in the Niagara Gorge, Ontario, in 1941.

Largest Atlantic bigeye tuna (375 pounds 8 ounces) caught with rod and line taken at Ocean City, Maryland, in 1977.

. . . . . . . . . . . .

## 28

Lesser yellowlegs banded on Cape Cod, Massachusetts, on this day in 1935, and killed six days later on Martinique, West Indies, 1,900 miles away.

Roger Tory Peterson, America's best-known ornithologist, born in Jamestown, New York, in 1908.

. . . . . . . . . . . .

## 29

Huge numbers of the almost extinct Eskimo curlew appeared at Nantucket, Massachusetts, in 1863 — in such numbers as to "almost darken the sun."

Last recorded Eskimo curlew sighting for Canada at Battle Harbor, Labrador, in 1932.

Captain William Clark reported seeing 20,000 bison feeding on the plains near the Big Bend of the Missouri River in 1806.

Hawk Mountain Sanctuary, first sanctuary set apart for birds of prey, established at Drehersville, Pennsylvania, in 1934.

RATTLESNAKES.

# THE FASTEST LAND MAMMAL
*Pronghorn*

Although the cheetah *(Acinonyx jubatus)* is generally regarded as the fastest mammal on earth over a short distance (up to 600 yards), the title of fastest of all land animals over a sustained distance goes to the pronghorn *(Antilocapra americana)*. It is, however, only when challenged that the pronghorn shows evidence of really high speeds.

Here is a firsthand report by A. S. Einarsen:

On August 14, 1939, I was with a group that paced many Pronghorns on the dried bed of Spanish Lake, in Lake County, Oregon. This lake-bed was as hard as adobe. It was a clear, breezy day, ideal to stir the racing instincts of the Pronghorns, and as we rolled along the lake edge we had many challenges. Small groups here and there raced beside the car, until five, led by a magnificent buck, ran parallel to us, pressing toward the shore from the feeding area in the lake center while we drove on a straight course. As they closed in from the right the buck took a lead of about 50 feet and Meyers [Field Observer of the Research Unit at the School of Agriculture, Oregon State College] increased speed to keep even with the animal. Dean Schoenfeld [also of the School of Agriculture] watched the speedometer, Meyers drove the car and I photographed the moving animals.

The buck was now about 20 feet away and kept abreast of the car at 50 miles an hour. He gradually increased his gait, and with a tremendous burst of speed flattened out so that he appeared as lean and low as a greyhound. Then he turned toward us at about a 45 degree angle and disappeared in front of the car, to reappear on our left. He had gained enough to cross our course as the speedometer registered 61 m.p.h. After the buck passed us he quickly slackened his pace, and when he reached a rounded knoll about 600 feet away he stood snorting, in graceful silhouette, against the sky as though enjoying the satisfaction of beating us in a fair race. No sprinter could have posed in victory with a greater show of gratification. His action was typical and indicated no fright, or he would have continued to run until out of sight.*

This pronghorn must have been traveling about 65 miles per hour as it crossed in front of the car. On other occasions pronghorns have been clocked at 55 miles per hour over a distance of half a mile.

*Arthur S. Einarson, *The Pronghorn Antelope and Its Management* (Washington, D.C.: Wildlife Management Institute, 1948).

ELK RUNNING.

## Record Speeds for Mammals

| | |
|---|---|
| Cheetah (*Acinonyx jubatus*) | 63 mph |
| Pronghorn (*Antilocapra americana*) | 61 + |
| Mongolian gazelle (*Procapra guttorosa*) | 55 |
| Springbok (*Antidorcas marsupialis*) | 52 |
| Thomson's gazelle (*Gazella thomsonii*) | 50 |
| Grant's gazelle (*Gazella granti*) | 47 |
| Red deer (*Cervus elephus*) | 42 |
| Black-tailed deer (*Odocoileus columbinaus*) | 40.5 |
| Mountain zebra (*Equus zebra*) | 40 |
| California jack rabbit (*Lepus californicus*) | 40 |
| Cape hartebeest (*Alcelaphus caama*) | 40 |
| Blue wildebeest (*Gorgon taurinus*) | 37 |
| Mongolian wolf (*Canis lupus* subs.) | 36 |
| Coyote (*Canis latrans*) | 35 |
| Indian jackal (*Canis aureus*) | 35 |
| European rabbit (*Oryxtolagus cuniculus*) | 35 |
| Cape buffalo (*Syncerus caffer*) | 35 |
| Roan antelope (*Hippotragus equinus*) | 35 |
| Bison (*Bison bison*) | 32 |
| Giraffe (*Giraffa camelopardalis*) | 32 |
| Reindeer (*Rangifer tarandus*) | 32 |
| Indian wild ass (*Equus hemionus*) | 32 |
| Snowshow hare (*Lepus americanus*) | 31 |
| American black bear (*Ursus americanus*) | 30 |
| Guanaco (*Lama huanacos*) | 30 |
| Wart hog (*Phachochoerus aethiopicus*) | 30 |
| Black rhinoceros (*Diceros bicornis*) | 28 |
| Timber wolf (*Canis lupus*) | 28 |
| Gray fox (*Urocyon cinereoargentus*) | 26 |
| African elephant (*Loxodonta africana*) | 24.5 |
| Arabian camel (*Camelus dromedarius*) | 20 |
| Rocky Mountain goat (*Oreamnos americanus*) | 20 |
| Kouprey (*Bos sauveli*) | 18 |
| Asiatic elephant (*Elephus maximus*) | 16 |
| Banteng (*Bos banteng*) | 11 |
| Malayan tapir (*Tapirus indicus*) | 10 |
| Rat (*Rattus norvegicus*) | 6 |
| Common mole (*Talpa europaea*) | 2.5 |
| Ai or three-toed sloth (*Bradypus tridactylus*) | 0.1 |

. . . . . . . . . . . . . . . . . . . . . .

## THEY'RE EVERYWHERE!
### *Insects*

Nine tenths of the world's animals are insects. Insects outnumber humans by more than 300,000 to 1. This is a fact that will be disputed by no one who has been in the Canadian north woods at the time of the year when blackflies, sandflies, and mosquitoes are enjoying their brief, bloodthirsty heyday. But as numerous as these three pests are, they comprise an infinitesimal fraction of all the insects that exist: in all, some 10 million varieties, of which fewer than 1 million have been classified.

Countless more insects are microscopic than are visible to the naked eye or through a magnifying glass. In the woods they abound, so numerous that it has been calculated that in 1 square foot of forest soil there are more insects than there are humans in the world.

Each of these little creatures has a job to do, a purpose to serve, and a relationship to maintain both with its own kind and with all other living creatures, including humans. The relationship cannot be disturbed without upsetting, in some way, the delicate balance of nature.

OVERLEAF: INSECTS.

## IDENTIFYING VENOMOUS SNAKES

**Since the number of venomous snakes on this continent is relatively few, it is to everyone's advantage to be able to distinguish nonvenomous from venomous ones, and to always allow the former to roam unhindered.** Venomous snakes should also be spared except when they pose a definite danger, such as when they are in close proximity to children or pets.

Rattlesnakes, moccasins, and copperheads can be distinguished from nonvenomous snakes by the following features: They all possess stout bodies with triangular heads, and their pupils are vertically elliptical like a cat's in the light. Coral snakes, however, are the exception to the rule, as they have slender heads and round pupils.

A rattlesnake's most characteristic distinguishing feature is the series of bony plates or rattle at the end of the tail, which is exclusive to this family.

All venomous snakes have two teeth or fangs, one on each side of the upper jaw, but in the so-called rear-fanged snakes, they are situated in the rear of the upper jaw. This feature is not easily seen, however.

In nonvenomous snakes, all the teeth are nearly the same length, none being noticeably larger than the others. Great care should be taken in examining the mouth of a supposedly dead venomous snake, since reflex muscular action may cause it to bite.

. . . . . . . . . . . . . . . . . . . . . . .

## RATTLESNAKES

**Rattlesnakes are distinctively American, and probably originated on the Mexican plateau**

TIMBER RATTLESNAKE.

**and dispersed chiefly northward.** Of the twenty-seven species of *Crotalus* and three of *Sistrurus*, only one has an extensive range south of Mexico, while fifteen occur in the United States. There are both large and small species. Exceptional specimens of the eastern diamondback rattlesnake *(Crotalus adamanteus)* are 7 to 8 feet long, while the small mountain species of Mexico seldom attain a length of 20 inches.

The rattle is an interlocking series of horny segments attached to the tail tip. When vibrated, it makes a hissing or buzzing sound that serves as a warning that the snake is alert, annoyed, and likely to bite if the annoyance continues.

Contrary to popular belief, the age of a snake cannot be determined by counting the number of buttons on its rattle, a snake may produce several buttons in the course of a year, and these may be broken off during travels through rocky areas.

The fangs of rattlesnakes work in a manner similar to a hypodermic needle! The poison is drained out through the tubelike points. When the fangs are not in use, they are folded back against the roof of the snake's mouth.

## THE CHAPARRAL COCK
*Roadrunner*

**The roadrunner (*Geococcyx californianus*) is one of the most famous birds of the southwestern and western United States.** It takes its name from its habit of running along the road in front of wagons and other slow-moving vehicles.

Known by a number of common names, such as ground cuckoo, snake bird, and chaparral cock, it is one of the most nimble of animals on the ground. It has been clocked at 15 miles an hour at full speed, with head outthrust and tail streaming behind; yet in an instant it can swerve into a turn, using its tail as a rudder.

There are many stories of roadrunners' encounters with rattlesnakes; however, much of what one hears in this regard is undocumented. For example, it is believed that the roadrunner will build a corral of cactus around a sleeping rattlesnake in order to trap it. No biologist has ever seen the bird build a corral around a rattlesnake, and until such an incident has been confirmed, we will have to view the notion with due skepticism.

That roadrunners attack rattlesnakes is definitely true, however. When a roadrunner encounters a rattlesnake, it fluffs up its feathers and extends its wings. The snake strikes at the bird repeatedly, but its bites fall harmlessly on the bird's extended wing feathers. The fight usually ends with the death of the rattlesnake, caused by a well-aimed peck by the bird at a vital spot on the snake's head.

A roadrunner was observed killing a rattlesnake about 3½ feet long — after which it ate the snake's brain but disdained to eat the rest. A snake over a foot long is too large to be swallowed entirely. The bird simply swallows as much as it can and waits until this has been digested before swallowing more. While waiting, the roadrunner may be seen walking about unconcernedly with part of a snake dangling from its mouth.

ROADRUNNER.

183

## DEADLY DEAD OR ALIVE!
*Snakes*

**Snakes are very difficult to kill.** A biologist once decapitated eighteen rattlesnakes—three from each of six different races to determine the reactions of the severed heads and bodies, and the results were positively frightening.

He found that the heads of the rattlesnakes were still dangerous even 20 to 25 minutes after severing. Up to 40 minutes after decapitation, the fangs would erect at the approach of a hand and the pupils of the eyes would contract, and after 43 minutes, one head bit a stick that had been thrust into its mouth and discharged its venom.

The headless bodies were even more persistent of life, although their movements were less functional. A specimen that was turned on its back succeeded in righting itself 7 hours and 43 minutes after losing its head, and even when all bodily movements had ceased, the heart continued to beat strongly for several hours. In one case the heart was still active after 59 hours.

......................

## THE HAM ACTOR
*Eastern Hognose Snake*

**The eastern hognose snake (*Heterodon platyrhinos*) is one of three hognose snakes that are endemic to North America.** Because it bears a strong superficial resemblance to a rattlesnake, it has been greatly maligned and persecuted throughout its range.

Some people believe the eastern hognose snake has poisonous breath, toxic enough to cause illness or death to a human or beast. There are still some people in farming communities who will assure you that the death of a cow, or other animal, was caused by this snake's having breathed on it. This sort of myth has been the cause of much unnecessary killing of the hognose snake, undoubtedly contributing to its rarity in certain areas.

In actual fact, this species is one of the most harmless and docile of snakes, feeding almost exclusively on toads and frogs. If disturbed or cornered, however, it goes into a characteristic bluff routine.

When molested, it hisses, spreads out its hood in the manner of a cobra, and strikes as though to appear dangerous. Yet it never bites. If this performance fails to intimidate, it changes it tactics dramatically. It goes into convulsions, writhing in agony, its mouth wide open and its tongue lolling out. Eventually, it rolls on its back and simulates death. When the danger is passed and the snake feels the way to be clear, it turns itself right side up and makes a quick getaway.

......................

## BEAUTIFUL BUT DEADLY
*Eastern Coral Snake*

**The brilliantly colored eastern coral snake (*Micrurus falvius*) is one of the most venomous snakes in the United States.** It differs radically from other native snakes in two important ways: Its fangs are fixed, and they are situated in front of the mouth. In other venomous snakes, the fangs are either movable or in the rear of the mouth.

The highly toxic venom of this relatively small snake does not necessarily cause pain as intense as that of the moccasin, rattlesnake, or copperhead; instead, it produces a paralyzing effect, and in 15 to 20 percent of all coral snake bites, death occurs within 24 hours.

Fortunately, the coral snake is shy and nonaggressive and does not bite unless it is stepped on or handled, and its fangs are too short to penetrate a leather sole. This snake is secretive and feeds largely on other snakes and lizards, which are held fast in its jaws until they succumb to the paralyzing effect of the venom.

Some harmless snakes seem to take advantage of the venomous nature of the coral snake: The scarlet kingsnake (*Lampropeltis doliata doliata*) and the Louisiana milk snake (*L. d.*

HOGNOSE SNAKE AND BLACK VIPER.

*amaura*) in the southeast, and the Mexican milk snake (*L. ∂. annulata*) and western milk snake (*L. ∂. gentilis*) in the southwest, share the color pattern of the coral snake and may receive an added form of protection from predators because of the superficial resemblance.

The coral snake and its imitators can be distinguished, however, by the different arrangement of the colored bands. In the harmless species the red bands are bordered by black; the red bands of the venomous coral snake are bordered by yellow or white. The arrangement of these colored bands can best be learned from this rhyme: "Red and yellow kill a fellow, red and black venom lack" (or "friend to Jack"). Another useful distinguishing feature of the coral snake is its black face. Also, its pupils are round, not vertically elliptical as are those of other venomous snakes.

Not all scientists believe in the mimicry the-

ory, however. Those in opposition point out that most mammalian predators of snakes are color blind and would not be able to see the distinct patterns as a particularly striking decoration. Those who do support the mimicry theory are not deterred by these objections.

Two species of coral snakes inhabit the United States: the eastern coral snake and the Arizona coral snake (*Micruroides euryxanthus*). The eastern coral snake is by far the more deadly; there are no records of deaths caused by the bite of the Arizona species. Also, the Arizona coral snake is smaller, about 15 inches long, compared with the eastern coral snake, which may grow to a length of 28 inches or more.

The range of the eastern coral snake extends from North Carolina to Florida, Texas, and Mexico, and also up the Mississippi Valley to southern Ohio.

# VENOMOUS SNAKES AND SNAKEBITE

**There are not nearly as many venomous snakes as one might imagine.** Of the 2,700 different kinds of snakes known throughout the world, only about 200 are dangerously poisonous to humans. Over most of the globe, venomous snakes comprise only a small percentage of the snake population. A notable exception, however, is Australia, where the majority of snakes are venomous. Poisonous snakes are represented in North America by rattlesnakes (*Crotalus* sp.), copperheads and water moccasins (*Agkistrodon* sp.), and coral snakes (*Micrurus* sp.).

It has been estimated that from 1,500 to 2,000 people are bitten by snakes in the United States alone every year and that there are 100 to 150 fatalities from snakebite. The actual number of confirmed deaths, however, is considerably smaller.

Throughout most of North America and other Temperate Zone countries, snakebite is a summer complaint, with the most bites occurring during the daylight hours of July and August. Frequency of snakebite is correlated with people's, rather than snakes', outdoor activities, as venomous species are naturally active at twilight and during the early hours of darkness.

In the United States, rattlesnakes account for 85 to 90 percent of all snakebite fatalities. The eastern diamondback rattlesnake (*Crotalus adamanteus*) and the western diamondback rattlesnake (*C. atrox*) are the most dangerous species, because they are both large snakes with extensive distribution in well-populated areas. Copperheads (*Agkistrodon contortrix*) cause more bites than any one species of rattlesnake, but fatalities are almost unknown. They are a fairly common cause of bites in Louisiana, Mississippi, Georgia, and Florida. The eastern coral snake (*Micrurus fulvius*) rarely bites, but considered in relation to the percentage of fatalities it causes, it is as dangerous as most rattlesnakes.

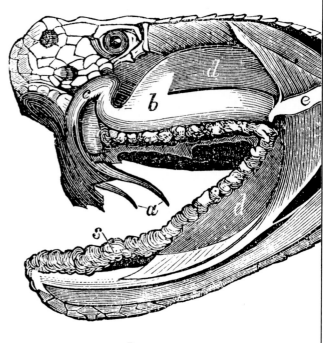

RATTLESNAKE.

There is no such thing as a typical snakebite. When a snake bites a human, the effects are extremely variable and unpredictable. They range from transient and local discomfort, scarcely more than might accompany a brier scratch, to collapse and death within a few minutes.

Despite the fact that snakes kill several thousand people every year, snakebite is insignificant as a medical problem compared with major health situations such as malnutrition, overpopulation, cancer, and heart disease. Even in tropical regions, snakebite is overshadowed by dysentery, malaria, hook worm, and many ailments associated with warm climates.

The total incidence of confirmed snakebite deaths in North America in recent years has been fewer than ten annually, although estimates range up to ten times that amount. Carelessness and inability to identify snakes probably explain the high percentage of bites received by small children, while bravado plays a part in snakebite involving youths.

A venomous snake should never be killed unless small children or pets are present; otherwise it should be *LEFT ALONE!* Don't

186

bother the snake and it won't bother you. It is estimated that at least a third of snakebite incidents in the United States involve deliberate contact with snakes, such as catching, handling, or treading on them.

. . . . . . . . . . . . . . . . . . . . .

## Twenty of the World's Most Venomous Snakes*

| | |
|---|---|
| Australian brown snake | Australia |
| Death adder | Australia |
| Taipan | Australia |
| Tiger snake | Australia |
| Black mamba | Africa |
| Boomslang | Africa |
| Gaboon viper | Africa |

| | |
|---|---|
| Puff adder | Africa |
| Yellow cobra | Africa |
| Saw-tailed viper | Africa and Asia |
| Indian cobra | India and Sri Lanka |
| Indian krait | India and Sri Lanka |
| Many-banded krait | Burma, China, and Taiwan |
| King cobra | Southeast Asia |
| Javan krait | Java |
| Mojave rattlesnake | United States and Mexico |
| Barba amarilla | Central and South America |
| Tropical rattlesnake | Central and South America |
| Jararacussu | South America |
| Island viper | Brazil |

*Not in any particular order of toxicity

# FIRST-AID FOR SNAKEBITE

**In the rare and unfortunate case of a venomous snakebite, keep all physical activity to an absolute minimum, and seek medical attention immediately.** If medical attention is not immediately available, as may be the case when there is distance to be traveled, then apply first-aid. Keep the victim cool and quiet; undue activity will increase the circulation, allowing the venom to spread more rapidly. If the delay in receiving treatment is going to be lengthy, a snakebite kit will be invaluable. The kit consists of a tourniquet, suction devices, an inciser instrument, and an antiseptic.

Apply the suction device directly to the fang punctures and withdraw as much venom as possible. This method is considered far preferable to sucking the venom out by using the mouth, as it eliminates the possibility of the toxic substance entering the system by way of a cut lip or gum. Use medical incision only when a number of hours will pass before medical treatment is received, and follow the instructions in the snakebite kit to the letter.

In any event, the victim must still be taken to a hospital or a doctor, as the lack of proper treatment for venomous snakebite can prove fatal.

. . . . . . . . . . . . . . . . . . . . .

## The World's Largest Snakes

| | |
|---|---|
| Anaconda (*Eunectes murinus*) | 38' + |
| Reticulated python (*Python reticulatus*) | 33' |
| African rock python (*Python sebae*) | 32'2¼" |
| Amethystine python (*Liasis amethistinus*) | 28' |
| Indian python (*Python molurus molurus*) | 19'2" |
| Boa constrictor (*Boa constrictor*) | 18'5" |
| King cobra (*Opriophagus hannah*) | 18'4" |
| Black mamba (*Dendraspis polylepis*) | 13'7" |
| Bushmaster (*Lachesis muta*) | 11'4" |
| Taipan (*Oxyuranus scutellatus*) | 11' |
| Australian brown snake (*Pseudonaja texilis*) | 10'-11' |
| Indigo snake (*Drymarchon corais couperi*) | 8'7½" |
| Black rat snake (*Elaphe obsoleta obsoleta*) | 8'5" |
| Bullsnake (*Pituophis melanoleucus sayi*) | 8'4" |

GILA MONSTER.

## VENOMOUS LIZARDS

**Although there are at least as many species of lizards as there are of snakes, only two species of lizards are known to be venomous.** They are the Gila monster (*Heloderma suspectum*) of the southwestern United States and adjacent Mexico and the closely related Mexican beaded lizard (*H. horridum*) from central, western, and southern Mexico.

The two desert-dwelling species belong to the family Helodermatidae and have no close affinity to any other living group of lizards. A 30 million- to 40 million-year-old fossil helodermatid is known from the Oligocene period; this predates the oldest poisonous snake fossils found on this continent by 14 million years.

The first Spanish explorers to encounter the Mexican beaded lizard, around 1577, attributed the venom to its breath, a trait ascribed to the fabulous basilisk. Poisonous breath is still a characteristic occasionally credited to the Gila monster. It is not known whether these beliefs originated with the Spaniards or with other Europeans or whether they were held by the pre-Columbian Indians. Among superstitious people, the notion is also prevalent that the Gila monster has no anus. The poison, they believe, comes from accumulated waste that must thus be voided through the mouth.

The poison glands of these two venomous lizards are in the lower jaw, not in the upper jaw as in snakes. And whereas snakes have two poison fangs in the upper jaw, in these lizards eight to ten upper teeth and six to eleven lower teeth are grooved and the venom must flow along the gums before reaching the teeth. In the manner of snakes, the forked tongue is flicked out and in again, bringing in particles of scent to a pair of pits in the roof of the mouth. These pits are known as Jacobson's organ, after the man who discovered them. Snakes also have this organ and use it in the same way.

The Gila monster and the Mexican beaded

ANOLE.

lizard are very alike. They differ principally in color. Both have a stout body, a large blunt head, powerful lower jaws, small eyes, and an unusually thick tail. Their bodies are covered not with scales but with small tubercles, strongly resembling the pattern of old-fashioned beaded bags.

The habits of the two species are also very similar, although the beaded lizard is less restricted to a desert environment than the Gila monster. Most of the lizard's prey — small birds, eggs, small rodents, and other lizards — is small enough to be taken easily without the use of venom.

Bites from Gila monsters are quite painful, because the lizards have strong jaws and often hold on with great tenacity. The venom itself contains serotonin, a powerful pain-producing substance. There are several reports of fatal Gila monster bites, but only one is accompanied by adequate medical details. The victim in this case was a carnival barker with a bad heart and a history of alcoholism and drug addiction. General symptoms reported after bites include sweating, nausea, thirst, sore throat, ringing in the ears, weakness, rapid breathing, faintness, and collapse. Abnormal electrocardiogram tracings may also be seen.

The first medical report of a bite by a Mexican beaded lizard was in 1970. The victim, an animal dealer, was bitten by a captive specimen. The principal symptoms were extreme pain in the bitten hand and arm, accompanied by nausea, vomiting, and swelling. Most of these subsided after 48 hours.

The Gila monster and the Mexican beaded lizard have developed a curious solution to the problem of survival through times of food shortage. The thick ungainly tail acts as a food reservoir, storing nourishment for the reptiles, to be used during times when forage is scarce. The tail becomes thick and swollen when food is plentiful and thin and attenuated when food is scarce.

## THE MOST POPULAR LIZARD
### Anole

**Commonest of North America's lizards is the anole (*Anolis carolinensis*), erroneously referred to as a chameleon.** This little green fellow, which grows to a length of about 6 inches, may be the most popular pet lizard in the world. Hundreds of thousands of anoles are sold in pet stores every year. These fascinating creatures make ideal pets because they are easy to keep, do not require much space or exotic foods, and will survive for many years with reasonable care.

The anole, which is really a type of small iguana, does not closely resemble the true chameleons of the Old World. True chameleons are much larger lizards from Africa and Asia. The genus *Anolis* is very widely distributed throughout Central and South America and is especially abundant in the West Indies; our own familiar anole ranges across nearly the entire southern half of the United States from Colorado to the Carolinas.

Like the true chameleons, however, anoles have the ability to change their color to suit different occasions. Under ordinary conditions in natural sunlight the anole is a dull brown. But when there is an encounter between two males, amazing changes occur. The pinkish throat fan, or "blanket," becomes distended, the body becomes ash gray, and the two dart at and tangle with each other until one becomes the victor. The vanquished anole scampers off, often minus its tail, and becomes a dull yellow, while the strutting victor becomes a vivid green. Very soon their colors fade back to the normal dull brown.

# IT SQUIRTS BLOOD FROM ITS EYES
*Texas Horned Toad (Lizard)*

**The Texas horned toad (*Phrynosoma cornutum*) represents a family of reptiles made up of fifteen species, all indigenous to western North America.** Despite its name and toadlike appearance, the horned toad is, in fact, a true lizard. It is not able to sever its own tail when grasped by that appendage, as many lizards can, but it can grow a new tail if the original one is accidentally severed.

Looking for all the world like some relic from the Permian period, the horned toad is a strange creature. There is great variation in color among individual specimens, which may be slate gray, brownish, buff, reddish, or yellowish. The horned toad is versatile in reproduction, bearing its young either alive or as eggs to be hatched; there may be thirty or forty to a brood.

As is typical of reptiles, the horned toad is coldblooded and requires heat. It will readily burrow into the earth to escape the cold of a

AMERICAN TOAD.

prairie night. Generally, horned toads frequent sandy locales in arid or semi-arid regions, although some species may be found in mountainous regions to a height of 10,000 feet in some parts of their range.

The Texas horned toad, which reaches a length of 4 to 5 inches, is found in the southwestern United States from Kansas to Arizona and north Mexico. It lives in the ground in the dry plateau country and is seen only during the warm part of the day. As soon as the temperature drops, it digs itself down into the sand by rocking its body from side to side, so that the sand is thrown up over its back.

HORNED TOAD.

An interesting aspect of the creature's behavior is its method of bluffing when threatened. This miniature monster puffs itself up, stands high on its toes with its mouth agape, and charges, hissing as it comes.

But the most striking characteristic of the horned toad is that it is able to squirt blood from its eyes whenever it becomes excited or angry. This is believed to be the result of a rise in blood pressure, which causes the capillaries near the corners of the eye socket to rupture, squirting blood for some distance, sometimes as great as 7 feet.

......................

## IT'S NOT WHAT IT SEEMS
### *Glass Snake*

**This brittle little creature is not a snake at all.** It is a lizard, as proved by its ear openings and movable eyelids, characteristics that snakes don't have.

The eastern glass snake (*Ophisaurus ventralis*), one of three species of glass snakes native to this continent, has a variable coloration. Some specimens are black with bright green spots on each scale; others have yellow spots on their scales that are as highly polished as glass. This animal, in fact, looks very much as if it had been varnished.

Whenever the glass snake is handled by the tail, the reptile disengages it with a single thrust (and then grows a new one). No blood appears, and the tail thrashes about in a livelier manner than when it was attached to the body. In the meantime, the lizard is endeavoring to escape; but it has no external legs and moves by stiff lateral undulations of its body, quite unlike the sinous grace of a snake.

......................

## TOADS AND WARTS

**Some people believe that simply the touch of a toad's skin is sufficient to cause warts to develop, while others think that it is the toad's urine that produces them.** Toads never cause warts, but they do have some annoying habits that may have helped to bring about the idea that they do.

Most toads secrete an irritating and poisonous substance, which in some species may actually burn or irritate the skin of anyone who handles them incautiously. Also, many frogs and toads have a tendency to urinate when they are seized, and if the urine gets into a broken place in the skin, it produces a burning sensation.

Despite their low favor with many people, toads' food habits indicate that they are the most valuable of the amphibians: Most of their food is composed of insects, of which many, such as cutworms, are definitely harmful.

A toad's appetite is truly amazing; one toad's stomach was found to contain sixty-five caterpillars of the gypsy moth (*Porthetria dispar*), an important pest of shade and fruit trees. Under normal circumstances a toad consumes approximately 10,000 insects in three months.

......................

## FIRE ANIMALS
### *Salamanders*

**Salamanders belong to the amphibian order Urodela.** Though similar to lizards in appearance, they have neither claws nor scales, and have no more than four toes as compared to the lizard's five. Salamanders vary tremendously in size, from those that are no bigger than a small earthworm to one, the giant salamander (*Megalobatrachus maximus*) from Japan, that attains a length of over 5 feet. North America is especially rich in salamanders. There are 350 species worldwide, 112 of which are native to North America.

The belief that salamanders had the power to endure fire without harm was current in Biblical times. However, the myth was exploded nearly 2,000 years ago, when Pliny the Elder (A.D. 23–79) told of an experiment in which a salamander was put into fire and, as expected, was burned to a powder. The name

EASTERN
GLASS SNAKE.

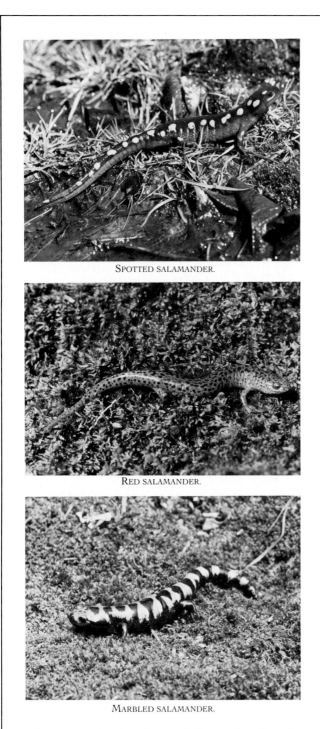

SPOTTED SALAMANDER.

RED SALAMANDER.

MARBLED SALAMANDER.

main immature throughout their lives, as in the case of the mudpuppy (*Necturus maculosus*) and the tiger salamander (*Ambystoma mexicanum*) from Mexico, which do not pass to the adult stage, although they are able to breed.

Such amphibians never lose their external gills. They may develop lungs, but the gills remain with them. Most of these amphibians are born in water and remain there throughout their lives. Neoteny is caused by the thyroid gland, the chief regulator of metamorphosis. Laboratory experiments have shown that when non-neotenic salamander larvae are injected with extracts from the thyroid of neotenic salamanders, there is an immediate transformation — from immature characteristics to mature ones.

Both as a larva and as an adult, the salamander is carnivorous and consumes great quantities of insects of all varieties, in addition to worms. The larger species will even eat frogs and smaller salamanders. In turn, salamanders have many enemies, but they also have a number of ways of defending themselves. Probably the most valuable protection they possess is their skin, which becomes lubricated and makes them slippery and difficult to catch. Some salamanders have the added protection of granular glands, which can exude a foul-smelling secretion. Also, their teeth are often slanted back toward the throat, making it difficult for food and enemies to wriggle free from their grasp.

Like lizards, salamanders have the ability to snap off their tails when they are grasped by this appendage. The animal appears to be in no way incapacitated, and there is little or no blood. It soon grows a new tail, not quite as long as the original one but just as useful. Salamanders are also able to change their color somewhat, usually to a darker shade.

Salamanders are found almost entirely in the northern temperate climates, except in extreme regions like the arctic wastes and high mountain peaks.

In North America, very little distinction is

of these animals, derived from the Greek, meaning "fire animal," is a misnomer indeed, for the salamander shuns heat and requires a great deal of moisture in order to live.

Salamanders lay jelly-covered eggs, usually in water. The larvae maintain external gills throughout their larval life, losing them as they gradually change into adult salamanders. Some salamanders exhibit neoteny; that is, they remade between newts and salamanders; newts are generally considered as just a type of salamander. Superficially, newts and salamanders are very much alike, exhibiting only minor differences. Newts are more confined to an aquatic life and are sometimes called water salamanders. Also, a newt has a slimmer body than a salamander, terminating in a tail that is flattened at the sides. The body of a salamander is rounded. Finally, newts, but not salamanders, shed their skin periodically. The old skin begins to break at the mouth and peels away from the body in one piece.

Some of the more familiar native salamanders include the tiger salamander (*Ambystoma tigrinum*), spotted salamander (*A. maculatum*), Jefferson salamander (*A. jeffersonianum*), long-tailed salamander (*Eurycea longicauda*), red salamander (*Pseudotriton ruber*), and red-spotted newt (*Diemictylus viridescens viridescens*).

The greater siren (*Siren lacertina*) is North America's largest salamander, a neotenic species that ranges from the District of Columbia south to Alabama and Florida and that may attain a record length of 36 inches.

The United States has the added distinction of playing host to both the smallest salamander and the smallest newt in the world. The smallest salamander is the pygmy salamander (*Desmognathus wrighti*), which is restricted in its range to Tennessee, North Carolina, and Virginia. Adult specimens may be no more than 1¾ inches long. The smallest newt is believed to be the striped newt (*Notophthalmus perstriatus*) of the southeastern United States. Adult specimens average slightly over 2 inches in length.

......................

## A CURE FOR GOITER

**The best-known example of neoteny is the axolotl.** The name *axolotl* was first given to a dark, yellow-spotted, gilled salamander found in some lakes around Mexico City. At that time, zoologists were unable to decide on the classification of this creature; based on the belief that the strange animal spent all its life in the water, it was considered a fully aquatic species of salamander.

The problem of the axolotl's classification was solved in 1865. Several specimens had bred successfully at the Jardin des Plantes in Paris, when one day someone noticed that the young of one brood had lost its gills and tails and had quite a different coloration. They had, in fact, turned into mature salamanders.

Study revealed that these transformed axolotls were simply tiger salamanders (*Amystoma mexicanum*), almost identical to a species common in many areas of the United States. The most amazing part of the whole discovery — since neoteny was unheard of at the time — was that under certain environmental conditions, these immature forms actually reproduced although retaining all the other features of the larval forms.

It is now known that the basic cause of neoteny is a lack of thyroxine, the hormone secreted by the thyroid gland, which controls metabolism. If this secretion is upset in humans, several bodily disorders occur, including the formation of a goiter, a swelling in the neck caused by the expansion of the thyroid gland. When thyroid extract from cattle is administered to humans, their goiter is often cured; when it is administered to axolotls, they change into adult tiger salamanders.

Tiger salamanders in Wyoming and the Rocky Mountain region regularly exhibit neoteny, and people there are prone to goiter. These conditions have been traced to a lack of iodine in the water, for iodine is an essential component of thyroxine. In these cases, the administration of iodine, rather than thyroxine, is all that is needed to bring about the metamorphosis of the salamander or the cure of goiter.

However, iodine treatment or thyroid extract is not the only way of turning axolotls into salamanders. Sometimes axolotls sent to a dealer or a laboratory change into adults shortly after being received. Apparently, the jolting during travel is sufficient to effect the change.

One may conclude that certain advantages must be conferred on the axolotls by having the capacity to remain totally aquatic or change into mature salamanders. In hot, dry climates, where body water has to be conserved, freshwater animals have an advantage over land animals. Since the lakes where the axolotls live are unlikely to dry up, they always have all the water they need. And in the event that the lakes dry up, they can change into adult salamanders, and thereby enjoy both worlds.

........................

## AMPHIBIOLOGIST?

**A student of birds is called an ornithologist, of mammals a mammalogist, of insects an entomologist, and of reptiles a herpetologist, but there is no generally recognized name for an individual who works with amphibians — frogs, toads, and salamanders.**

Up to now, herpetology has been used to cover both reptiles and amphibians, but as specialization increases, it becomes more common to find specialists in reptiles who are not too well informed about amphibians, and vice versa. It is almost as if we were to use the same word to refer to a person who works with birds and one who works with mammals. The word *amphibiologist* has been coined, but it is a rather awkward mouthful. Whether or not a new word comes into use to refer to the person who works with amphibians, the herpetologists have invented a word to cover both of their interests.

The word *herptile* is now coming into quite general use. Although not found in most dictionaries, it may well appear there before very long. A herptile may be a snake, a turtle, a lizard, a frog, a toad, a newt or a salamander. An interesting fact is that herptiles never stop growing, and if they lived long enough, they would all become monsters.

COLLARED LIZARD.

FEMALE BULL FROG.

## THEY LIKE FRESH FOOD
*Frogs and Toads*

**Frogs and toads will not eat stationary insects. They appear to view movement as an indication of freshness and good taste.** A frog or toad can flip its tongue out 2 or 3 inches and retrieve a moving insect in less than one fifth of a second—faster than the human eye can see. This ability results from a unique muscle structure that enables the frog to thrust its tongue outward, snare its prey on the sticky end, and withdraw the tongue to its base—in the front of the mouth, rather than the throat, as in most other animals.

. . . . . . . . . . . . . . . . . . . . . . .

## A SENSITIVE CRUSTACEAN
*The American Lobster*

**This ancient creature has survived and multiplied over millions of years and has developed a sensory ability that is millions of times more acute than that of man.** The lobster is a solitary, nearly blind, nocturnal invertebrate with hard, protective armor covered with tiny hairlike appendages. These appendages are sensory filaments that function as tasters or smellers, receptors of chemical information, that enable the lobster to locate prey at a great distance. The lobster, whose brain is the size of a pea, is an effective predator because of this extraordinary sensory capacity. Unfortunately, it is this same ability that leads the lobster so unfailingly to the lobsterman's traps.

Lobsters also use this sense of smell when they mate. The female lobster sends a chemical message to the male, who then admits her to his chamber. She enters and molts, shedding her hard shell. She must be impregnated within a short time of this molting. This the male does while exercising tender concern not to damage her soft flesh. After the coupling, the male and female stay together for seven to ten days, the male guarding the female until her new shell is grown.

The lobster's larger claw is slower-moving but more powerful than its smaller claw. The

COMMON LOBSTER.

smaller claw is used for catching fast-moving prey; the large claw is used to crush the mussels, crabs, and clams that lobsters dine on.

The American lobster (*Homarus americanus*) is the most common and the largest of the three main types of clawed lobsters. Lobsters appear to live in communities of up to several hundred, and they demonstrate a certain degree of friendly social contact with each other, as well as the usual rivalries seen in many species. Its greatest rival is the crab, against which a lobster of equal size is usually the victor.

As a consequence of its special sensory, predatory, and defensive systems, the lobster lives as long as most long-lived land-based mammals — about forty years.

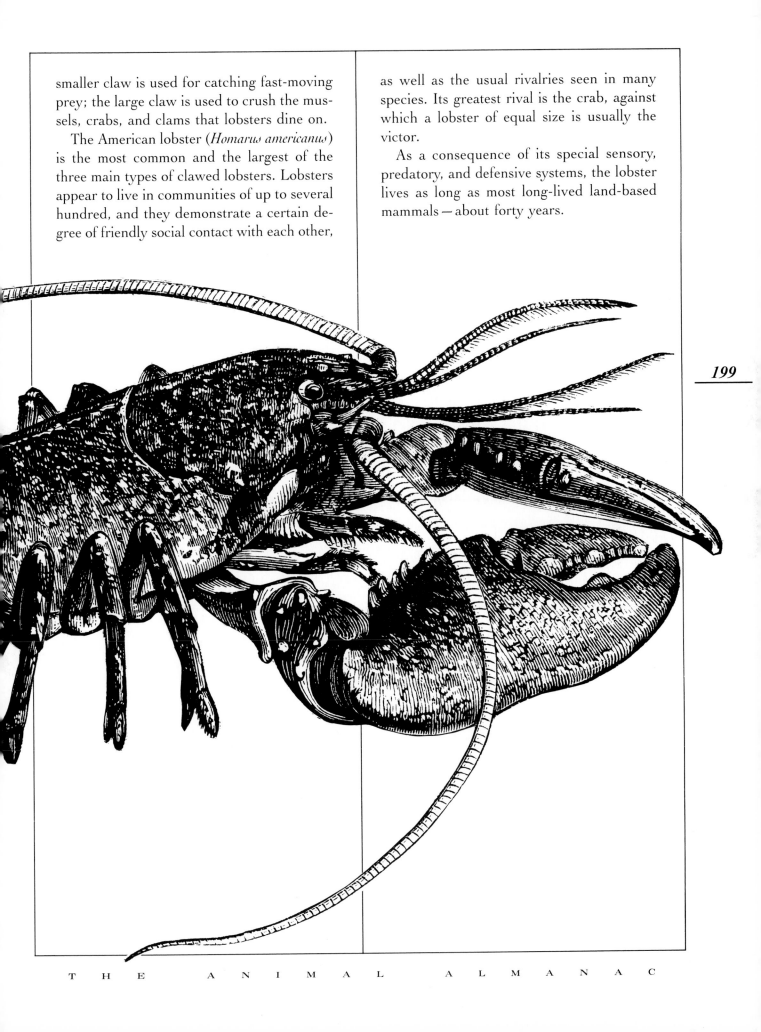

# September

Although beautiful, the first signs of autumn are often sad as well, and we are reminded that even the most successful forms of life can die off. For example, passenger pigeons once abounded in flocks numbering in the billions, but they have completely disappeared. Also extinct are the North American penguin, the great auk, the Steller's sea cow, the eastern elk, and many other species that survived for millions of years and that have died out only since the European settlement of North America.

Fortunately, not all threatened species become extinct. The buffalo population, which had declined from an estimated 60 million to perhaps less than a dozen individual creatures, is happily restored to the tens of thousands. As it happens, the scorpion is one creature whose extinction we need not fear. Unfriendly as it is, the scorpion stands a good chance of outliving most North American animals and humans in the most terrible of disasters: It is extraordinarily resistant to atomic radiation, able to withstand doses up to 200 times greater than humans can withstand.

OPPOSITE: BULL BISON.

# SEPTEMBER

BULL ELK.

## 1

Last passenger pigeon, Martha, died in the Cincinnati Zoo in 1914.

. . . . . . . . . . . .

## 2

*National Observer* reported three people mauled to death by black bears at Anchorage, Alaska, in 1963.

## 3

Very large specimen of ocean sunfish, the world's heaviest bony fish, captured off Santa Catalina Islands, California, in 1919. It measured 10 feet 11 inches in length and 10 feet 9 inches between the dorsal and anal fins.

. . . . . . . . . . . .

## 6

First pronghorn discovered above the mouth of the Niobrara River near the South Dakota border during the Lewis and Clark expedition in 1804.

Alabama adopted the common flicker, erroneously called "yellowhammer," as the state bird in 1927.

. . . . . . . . . . . .

## 7

Only recorded sighting of an anhinga in Canada — at Wellington, Ontario, in 1904.

## 9

Large flocks of the almost extinct Eskimo curlew reported in their wintering grounds in Uruguay in 1880.

. . . . . . . . . . . .

## 11

World Wildlife Fund (International) formed in Zurich, Switzerland, in 1961.

. . . . . . . . . . . .

## 13

Haleakala National Park, Hawaii, established in 1960.

. . . . . . . . . . . .

## 15

Largest northern pike (46 pounds 2 ounces) caught in North America taken in the Sacandaga Reserve, New York, in 1940.

Charles Darwin and the *Beagle* dropped anchor at Chatham Island, in the Galapagos in 1835.

Bryce Canyon National Park, Utah, established in 1928.

## 16

Record number of broad-winged hawks seen in one day was 11,392 over Hawk Mountain, Pennsylvania, in 1948.

Charles Darwin, the first naturalist to see the giant Galapagos tortoises, saw his first specimens on Chatham Island, in the Galapagos, in 1835.

Captain Meriwether Lewis's diary for this day in 1804 reads: "This scenery already rich pleasing and beautiful was still further hightened by immense herds of Buffaloe, deer Elk and Antelopes which we saw in every direction feeding on the hills and plains. I do not think I exaggerate when I estimate the number of Buffaloe which could be comprehended at one view to amount to 3,000."

. . . . . . . . . . . .

## 20

Large bull northern elephant seal (15 feet 7 inches long, estimated 5,000 pounds) towed into San Diego Harbor in 1929, after being killed by swordfish fishermen about 40 miles off Point Loma, California.

ALASKAN BROWN BEAR.

## 22

Largest Kodiak bear (1,670 pounds) ever recorded died in the Cheyenne Mountain Zoological Park, Colorado Springs, Colorado, in 1955.

Largest muskellunge (69 pounds 15 ounces) caught with rod and line taken in the St. Lawrence River, New York, in 1957.

## 23

Lewis and Clark expedition returned to St. Louis, Missouri, in 1806.

Grizzly bear killed by a hunting guide in the San Juan Mountains of Colorado in 1979. The animal had been presumed extinct in that state since 1951.

FLICKER.

Last passenger pigeon allegedly observed in the wild shot at St. Vincent, Quebec, in 1907.

. . . . . . . . . . . .

## 25

Sequoia National Park, California, established in 1890.

Yellow-breasted chat discovered in Caribou Island, Thunder Bay, Ontario, in 1979, its most northerly occurrence.

. . . . . . . . . . . .

## 26

Pipevine swallowtail butterfly, essentially of the southern United States, found at Caribou Island, Thunder Bay, Ontario, in 1979 — by far its most northerly occurrence.

. . . . . . . . . . . .

## 29

Only specimen of a timber rattlesnake to be recorded at Point Pelee, Ontario, occurred in 1918.

203

## BUTTERFLY MIGRANT
### *Monarch*

The monarch butterfly (*Danaus plexippus*) is the only North American insect proven to exhibit true migrational behavior. A number of other insect species occur in the northern part of the continent as summer immigrants from the south, and a few butterfly species have been observed flying south in the fall. But whether they can be termed truly migrational has yet to be determined.

In its strictest sense, migration denotes a continuous movement from one area to another with periodic return to the place of origin. However, in the case of insect migration, it is usually taken to mean a one-way movement with no return flight for the participants. Instead, their offspring make the return flight.

The range of the monarch corresponds to that of the milkweed, the insect's food plant, which can be found over most of North America. Seasonally, though, the butterflies are more numerous in certain areas: They spend the summer months and breed in the northern United States and southern Canada and migrate south in the fall.

Each spring and fall there is a movement of monarchs from one range to the other. The fall migration is, of course, the more spectacular, augmented as it is by a new generation of monarchs moving south. Their numbers build to a peak every five to seven years.

During their flight, the monarchs reach speeds of 30 miles per hour. The longest recorded flight is more than 1,800 miles, from Ontario to the Sierra Madre Mountains, their wintering ground in central Mexico.

Perhaps the most baffling aspect of this migration is the fact that every year a new crop of butterflies undertakes this trip with no aid or direction from the previous generation—their elders have died out by departure time.

North America's famous migrant butterfly has also found its way to Great Britain, Japan, the Canary Islands, Australia, and many other faraway places. The first monarch to appear in Great Britain was at Neath, South Wales, in 1876. Since then, more than 200 specimens have been observed.

........................

## MODEL AND MIMIC
### *Monarch and Viceroy*

Butterflies are among the greatest mimics of the animal world. An excellent example of mimicry involves the monarch (*Danaus plexippus*). The caterpillar of the monarch feeds

EASTERN TIMBER RATTLESNAKE.

on the leaves of the milkweed plant *(Asclepias* sp.), which are very acrid. The ultimate butterfly thus becomes unpalatable and is afforded much protection from most predators, which have come to avoid the butterfly's orange and black warning coloration. The viceroy *(Basilarchia archippus)*, a butterfly species belonging to a distinctly different family, is perfectly edible, but has managed to simulate the orange and black color pattern of the monarch to such a great degree that it too is afforded protection from predators—by *appearing* to be unpalatable.

This phenomenon is known as Batesian mimicry, after Henry Walter Bates, the famous nineteenth-century explorer and lepidopterist. It should be noted, however, that the theory of mimicry is not accepted by all authorities; some opponents of butterfly mimicry regard the color and pattern likeness as simply a remarkable coincidence.

. . . . . . . . . . . . . . . . . . . . . .

## THE WRONG RATTLESNAKE FOR DINNER

One of the most bizarre incidents involving a rattlesnake occurred in September of 1979, when C. Kenneth Dodd, a herpetologist with the U.S. Fish and Wildlife Service, discovered that Pennsylvania timber rattlesnakes were being featured on the menu of Dominique's, a French restaurant in Washington, D.C.

Without much ado, Dodd wrote the proprietor a letter protesting that the snake is protected by the state of Pennsylvania, and that it is illegal to use it for commercial purposes. Dominique D'Erimo, the restaurateur, promptly substituted a nonendangered Texas rattlesnake for the Pennsylvania variety.

Interior Secretary Cecil D. Andrus learned of the incident when he read of the letter in a *Washington Star* gossip column and noted that Dodd had written it on official departmental stationery.

Shortly afterward, Dodd received a notice of "proposed termination" from U.S. Fish and Wildlife director Lynn C. Greenwalt, who accused Dodd of meddling and writing "unauthorized correspondence" and jeopardizing "endangered species legislation."

The matter received enthusiastic coverage by the media, and Interior Secretary Andrus was inundated with letters from environmental groups and professional associations protesting the unwarranted firing.

Pat Schroeder and John H. Dingell, Democratic representatives from Colorado and Michigan, respectively, rallied to Dodd's side, demanding a full and detailed explanation from Andrus, with Dingell predicting that if the business was not settled to everybody's satisfaction, there would be "blood and guts, hair and hide all over the wall."

Andrus thought the idea that anyone could be concerned about rattlesnakes was "humorous," and predicted that the furor would quickly die down, telling reporters, "I hate rattlesnakes." But the pressure from environmentalists and others soon induced Andrus to reverse his position, and Dodd was duly reinstated in his job.

. . . . . . . . . . . . . . . . . . . . . . .

## ABUNDANCE IS NO GUARANTEE OF SURVIVAL
*Passenger Pigeon*

Undoubtedly the most famous of North America's former inhabitants was the passenger pigeon (*Ectopistes migratorius*). Ironically, this species was the most numerous of all birds, and before 1840 was estimated to have numbered between 5 billion and 9 billion individuals. Even the great naturalist John James Audubon, who predicted the decline of many na-

PASSENGER PIGEON.

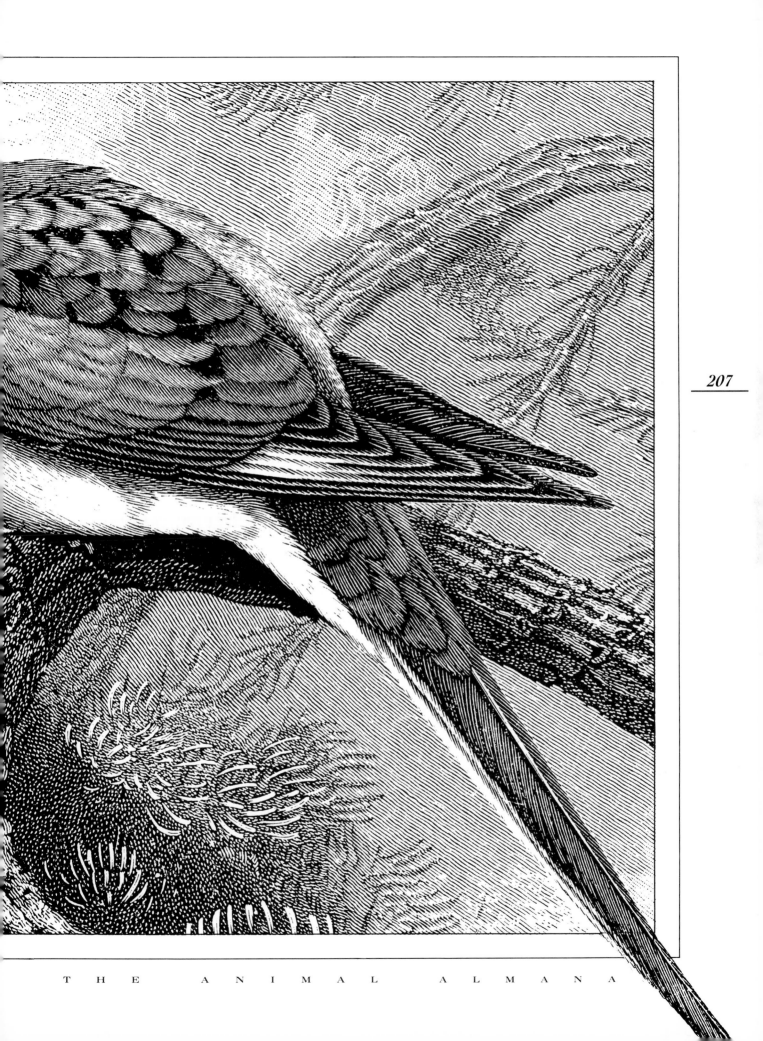

tive birds, could see no danger for the passenger pigeon because it was so abundant.

The passenger pigeon was essentially a North American forest species, long-tailed and graceful, with a slate blue back and head and a reddish breast. The breast muscles were strong; the bird flew about 60 miles an hour. Summering in huge flocks in the hardwood wilderness of Canada and the northern United States and wintering in the southern United States, the passenger pigeon fed largely on beech nuts and was good to eat, tastier than wild duck. The largest-known nesting site was in Wisconsin, where the awesome dimensions were placed at 75 miles by 10 to 15 miles, an area of at least 740 square miles, shared by an estimated 136 million birds.

Audubon described a continuous flight of passenger pigeons that lasted for three days in 1813. And Alexander Wilson, the father of American ornithology, saw a flock near Frankfort, Kentucky, about 1808, and said it contained at least 2,230,272,000 individuals.

One flock of passenger pigeons seen by Major W. R. King in 1866 at Mississauga, Ontario, is the largest flock of birds to ever be recorded. King reported that it took 14 hours for the flock to pass overhead, and for several days after smaller flocks of weaker or younger birds continued to fly past. It has been calculated that this flock of birds contained 3,717,120,000 pigeons.

The sudden and complete disappearance of the passenger pigeon is probably the most remarkable in all zoological history. Their extinction was brought about by the unlimited killing of these birds, which were a valuable source of food. A dozen pigeons could be bought for less than a dollar at local markets; the breast meat was eaten, and the wings and back feathers were used to fill potholes in the road. The birds' habit of nesting in huge colonies made them an easy target for the guns and nets of the thousands of professional hunters who caught them for profit. The destruction of the eastern deciduous forest that contained their feeding, nesting, and roosting areas was also a contributing factor.

Roosting passenger pigeons were attacked by hunters armed with guns, poles, clubs, even pots of sulphur, and hundreds of birds were killed nightly. Similar methods of destruction were employed when the birds were nesting. At this sea-

SHOOTING PASSENGER PIGEONS.

son the squabs were especially desired, and the trees were shaken or felled to obtain them. When the hunters had taken what they wanted, droves of hogs were released beneath the nesting trees to feed on the remaining birds. At one of the last-known large passenger pigeon nesting sites, near Petoskey, Michigan, an estimated 1 million birds were killed during the 1878 nesting season.

Between 1850 and 1880 the passenger pigeon population declined dramatically. The billions were reduced to millions, the millions to thousands. Tentative warnings by naturalists were ignored, the assumption being that the flocks were somewhere else where the nut crop was better.

Since reproduction success decreased with the decline in numbers, and since the pigeons only laid one egg at a time, this species was unable to maintain its reproductive level. The last positively recorded wild passenger pigeon, according to E. H. Forbush, was a female said to have been shot at Bar Harbor, Maine, in the summer of 1904. It was mounted in July of that year by J. Bert Baxter, a taxidermist from Bangor, but its whereabouts are now unknown.

The species became extinct when the last living specimen, Martha, died in the Cincinnati Zoological Gardens on September 1, 1914.

# September Reading

## LOST FOREVER
### *Extinct Animals*

**The direct effects of humans, the ultimate predators, and the mutilation of the surroundings that accompanied their settlement, have been most harmful to wildlife.** In the course of the human advance into the New World, the forests, the rivers, the plains, and the prairies suffered changes more drastic than all those undergone during the centuries following the last glaciation.

The settlers in North America and their descendants have not lived here long, yet they have created a record of extinction of various species and subspecies of native wildlife that is appalling. At least sixty-three animals that once flourished on this continent are gone, most disappearing in the twentieth century.

As the world has evolved, extinction has been the ultimate fate of most life forms. Two thirds of the species of animals and plants known to have existed are now extinct. Natural extinction is a slow process: A species evolves over millennia, and then, as conditions gradually change and new life forms appear, the animal or plant fails to adjust fully to the new environment and it disappears, equally slowly, to be supplanted by creatures better able to survive.

For example, dinosaurs were enormously successful while the world was a much warmer place than it is now, but when the earth's climate became cooler, these huge reptiles were gradually replaced by warmblooded mammals, better able to withstand temperature extremes.

Human-made extinction, however, is quite a different situation; it is final and does not provide new species to replace those that have disappeared.

It is generally believed that of all the life forms known to exist, at least two or three vertebrates, and two or three plant species, are becoming extinct through habitat loss each year. If we consider all species, including invertebrates, this figure rises to at least one in ten species extinct every year. In ten years this could become one species per hour. By the year 2000, over 1 million species could be extinct.

The following list represents the alarmingly large roster of animals that have become extinct in North America (including Hawaii) since 1600:

Eastern elk
Merriam elk
Queen Charlotte Island caribou
Eastern bison
Badland's bighorn sheep
Leaf-nosed bat
Southern California kit fox
Puerto Rican nesophones
Steller's sea cow
Gull Island vole
Atlantic gray whale
Great Plains wolf
Cascade Mountain wolf
Mogollon Mountain wolf
Southern Rocky Mountain wolf
Texas wolf
Newfoundland wolf
Great auk
Labrador duck
Passenger pigeon

OVERLEAF: PASSENGER PIGEONS.

Carolina parakeet
Louisiana parakeet
Culebra Puerto Rican parrot
Mauge's parakeet
Palas cormorant
Oahu
Hawaii akialoa
Lanai akialoa
Oahu akialoa
Lanai alauwahio          Ula-ai-hawane
Greater amakihi          Townsend's bunting
Laysan apapane           Guadalupe petrel
Grosbeak finch           Black-capped petrel
Heath hen                San Pecos leopard frog
Kioea                    Thicktail chub
Greater koafinch         White-lined topminnow
Lesser koafinch          Pahrump Ranch killifish
Black mamo               Leon Springs pupfish
Hawaii mamo              Tecopa pupfish
Laysan millerbird        Utah Lake sculpin
Oahu nukupuu             Big Spring spinedace
Hawaii o'o               Pahranagat spinedace
Molokai o'o              Ash Meadows springfish
Oahu o'o                 Raycraft Ranch springfish
Laysan rail              Harelip sucker
Sandwich rail            Longjaw cisco
Lanai thrush             Snail darter
Oahu thrush              Blue pike

## THE ORIGINAL PENGUINS
### The Great Auk

**Once there were penguins in the Northern Hemisphere.** In fact, the penguins of the south, not at all related, were named for them because of their resemblance to these northern birds. The original penguin, better known as the great auk or garefowl (*Pinguinis impennis*), has been extinct since 1844. It was hunted by humans for centuries, for like the dodo and the Steller's sea cow, it was too easy to kill.

The great auk was the largest member of its family, standing about 3 feet high. It resembled the familiar penguin in its coloring, and was an equally good swimmer. The bird could swim so swiftly that pursuers in rowboats could not overtake it. But the auk was slow and ungainly on land and could be captured easily. And since its meat was considered a delicacy, and its body was covered in a thick layer of fat that was useful as fuel, the great auk was the target of hunters.

The bird's main breeding ground was the north, from Russia and Scandinavia in the east, to Canada in the west. But fossils of great auks have been discovered on the Italian coast and along the Atlantic shoreline from Maine to Florida. The great auk is also depicted in prehistoric cave murals in northern Spain. It is certain that the Vikings hunted the great auk from Iceland to Newfoundland. By A.D. 100 it was no longer very common on the Eu-

GREAT AUK.

ropean side of the Atlantic, but in the west it existed in such multitudes that the raids by the Norsemen had no effect on the bird's numbers.

Late in the fifteenth century, fishermen from Portugal, Spain, and France began to go boldly westward in quest of codfish. In their journeys they discovered the outlying islands on which the great auk nested. Here they clubbed the birds to death by the hundreds and loaded them aboard the boats. They ate some fresh and salted down the rest to be eaten during the voyage.

The large eggs of the great auk were also collected in huge quantities, causing a serious threat to the survival of the species, since each bird laid only one egg during a season. But so many millions of auks lived on the islands that no one could imagine a time when there would be none left.

John Cabot encountered great auks on the Labrador coast in 1497. And an entry in the journal of French explorer Jacques Cartier describes the meeting between man and auk on Funk Island off Newfoundland in 1534. Cartier had sent two boatloads of men ashore to gather provisions. They found the island crowded with great auks, so trusting they let the men approach them.

The slaughter continued all during the sixteenth and seventeenth centuries. Still, by 1730 millions of great auks remained in Greenland, according to explorer and missionary Hans Egede.

Toward the end of their existence, fifty auks remained on Eldey Island, off Iceland. Museum directors encouraged the killing of these remaining rare birds because they wanted stuffed specimens for their collections. Fabulous prices were offered for a complete skin, a skeleton, or an unbroken egg of the great auk. Between 1830 and 1844 one bird after another was hunted down, until only two individuals remained.

On that fateful day — June 3, 1844 — three fishermen hired by an Icelandic bird collector made a trip to Eldey Island. There the last of the great auks were slaughtered, and the one last egg smashed.

Only once has a species been destroyed in the name of science. The greed and cruelty of the hunters reduced the great auk to a handful of survivors, but it was the museum directors, not the fishermen, who brought down the final curtain.

On March 5, 1971, a stuffed specimen of a great auk in summer plumage was purchased at an auction at Sotheby's in London for £9,000 — the highest price ever paid for a stuffed bird specimen. The purchaser, the director of the Iceland Natural History Museum, later stated that his museum had been prepared to go as high as £23,000.

SEA OTTER.

## Endangered and Threatened Species of North America

The current roster of vanishing animals on this continent is an awesome one. The following endangered and threatened species and subspecies appear on the U.S. Department of the Interior, Fish and Wildlife Service's federal register of endangered species in North America. There are 191 endangered species and 38 threatened species.

*Endangered Mammals*
Gray bat
Hawaiian hoary bat
Indiana bat
Ozark big-eared bat
Virginia big-eared bat
Wood bison

Woodland caribou
Eastern cougar
Cedros Island mule deer
Columbian white-tailed deer
Key deer
Utah prairie dog
Black-footed ferret
Northern swift fox
San Joaquin kit fox
Jaguar
Jaguarandi
Florida manatee
Margay
Ocelot

JAGUAR.

Florida panther
Peninsula pronghorn
Sonoran pronghorn
Salt marsh harvest mouse
Morro Bay kangaroo rat
Hawaiian monk seal
Delmarva peninsula fox squirrel
Blue whale°
Bowhead whale°
Finback whale°
Gray whale°
Humpback whale°
Right whale°
Sei whale°
Sperm whale°
Gray wolf (Eastern timber)°
Red wolf

*Threatened Mammals*
Grizzly bear
Southern sea otter

*Endangered Birds*
Hawaii akepa
Maui akepa
Kauai akialoa
Akiapolaau
Short-tailed albatross
Yellow-shouldered blackbird
Masked bobwhite (quail)
California condor
Hawaiian coot
Mississippi sandhill crane
Whooping crane
Hawaiian creeper
Molokai creeper

Oahu creeper
Hawaiian crow
Eskimo curlew
Palau ground dove
Hawaiian duck
Laysan duck
Bald eagle
American peregrine falcon
Arctic peregrine falcon
Laysan finch
Nihoa finch
Palau fantail flycatcher
Hawaiian gallinule
Aleutian Canada goose
Hawaiian goose (nene)
Hawaiian hawk
Crested honeycreeper
Everglade kite
La Perouse's megapode
Nihoa millerbird
Tinian monarch
Nukupuu
Kauai o'o
Palau owl
Palila
Ou
Puerto Rican parrot
Thick-billed parrot
Maui parrotbill
Brown pelican
Hawaiian dark-rumped petrel
Puerto Rican plain pigeon
Poo-uli
Attwater's greater prairie chicken
California clapper rail
Light-footed clapper rail
Yuma clapper rail
San Clemente sage sparrow
San Clemente loggerhead shrike
Cape Sable seaside sparrow
Dusky seaside sparrow
Santa Barbara song sparrow
Ponape mountain starling
Hawaiian stilt
California least tern
Large Kauai thrush
Molokai thrush
Small Kauai thrush
Bachman's warbler
Kirtland's warbler
Puerto Rican whip-poor-will
Great Ponape white-eye
Ivory-billed woodpecker
Red-cockaded woodpecker

*Threatened Birds*
Newell's Manx shearwater

*Endangered Reptiles*
Culebra giant anole
Mona boa
Puerto Rican boa
Virgin Islands tree boa
American crocodile
Monito gecko
Blunt-nose leopard lizard
St. Croix ground lizard
San Francisco garter snake
Green sea turtle
Kemp's Ridley sea turtle
Olive Ridley sea turtle
Leatherback sea turtle

*Threatened Reptiles*
American alligator
Mona ground iguana
Coachella Valley fringe-toed lizard
Island night lizard
New Mexican ridgenosed rattlesnake
Atlantic salt marsh snake
Eastern indigo snake
Desert tortoise
Loggerhead sea turtle

*Endangered Amphibians*
Santa Cruz long-toed salamander
Slender desert salamander
Texas blind salamander
Houston toad
Pine Barrens treefrog

*Threatened Amphibians*
Golden coqui
Red Hills salamander
San Marcos salamander

*Endangered Fish*
Pahranagat bonytail
Bonytail chub
Borax Lake chub
Humpback chub
Mohave chub
Alabama cavefish
Cui-ui
Kendall Warm Springs dace
Ash Meadows speckled dace
Moapa dace
Fountain darter
Maryland darter

Overleaf: Leatherback turtle.

Okaloosa darter
Watercress darter
Big Bend gambusia
Clear Creek gambusia
Goodenough gambusia
Pecos gambusia
San Marcos gambusia
Pahrump killifish
Scioto madtom
Comanche Springs pupfish
Devil's Hole pupfish
Owen's River pupfish
Warm Springs pupfish
Colorado River squawfish
Unarmored three-spine stickleback
Shortnose sturgeon
Gila topminnow
Totoaba
Gila trout
Woundfin

*Threatened fish*
Slender chub
Spotfin chub
Bayou darter
Leopard darter
Slackwater darter
Yellowfin madtom
Arizona trout
Greenback cutthroat trout
Lahontan cutthroat trout
Paiute cutthroat trout
Little Kern golden trout

*Endangered Snails*
Iowa Pleistocene snail
Manus Island tree snail
Virginia fringed mountain snail

*Threatened Snails*
Chittenango ovate amber snail
Flat-spired three-toothed snail
Noonday snail
Painted snake coiled forest snail
Stock Island snail

*Endangered Clams*
Alabama lamp pearly mussel
Appalachian monkeyface pearly mussel
Birdwing pearly mussel
Cumberland bean pearly mussel
Cumberland monkeyface pearly mussel
Curtis' pearly mussel
Dromedary pearly mussel
Fat pocketbook pearly mussel
Fine-rayed pigtoe pearly mussel

SPERM WHALE.

Green-blossom pearly mussel
Higgin's eye pearly mussel
Nicklin's eye pearly mussel
Pale lilliput pearly mussel
Pink musket pearly mussel
Rough pigtoe pearly mussel
Sampson's pearly mussel
Shiny pigtoe pearly mussel
Tampico pearly mussel
Tuberculed-blossom pearly mussel
Turgid-blossom pearly mussel
White cat's eye pearly mussel
White warty-back pearly mussel
Yellow-blossom pearly mussel
Orange-footed pimpleback
Tan riffle shell clam

*Endangered Crustaceans*
Hay's Spring amphipod
Socorro isopod

*Threatened Crustaceans*
Madison Cave isopod

*Endangered Insects*
El Segundo blue butterfly
Lange's metalmark butterfly
Lotis blue butterfly
Mission blue butterfly
Palos Verde blue butterfly
San Bruno elfin butterfly
Smith's blue butterfly

*Threatened Insects*
Delta green ground beetle
Valley elderberry longhorn beetle
Bahama swallowtail butterfly
Oregon silverspot butterfly
Schaus swallowtail butterfly
Kern primrose sphinx moth

*Listed as endangered on the United States World List

# BACK FROM THE EDGE OF EXTINCTION

*American Bison*

**It is ironic that the American bison (*Bison bison*), commonly called buffalo, should have almost reached the edge of extinction, when at its peak it undoubtedly formed the greatest large mammal congregations that ever existed on earth.** Huge herds of bison moved like a black sea across the plains, covering them for miles around.

Before the settlers arrived in North America, the bison's range covered one third of the entire land. It was found in the eastern states from New York south to Florida, west to the Rocky Mountains, and north to central Alaska. The total number of bison was almost beyond comprehension: An estimation has placed the total population at better than 60 million animals. Most experts agree that this estimate is reliable.

When the settlers began their westward drive over the North American plains, the bison was slaughtered at an alarming rate. However, an estimated 40 million bison still survived in the west as late as 1830, and it was not until the construction of the Central Pacific and the Union Pacific railroads in 1869 that the herds noticeably dwindled.

The last days of the bison began in the 1870s, but even then they appeared to march without end. Near Fort Hays, Kansas, in September 1871, a troop of the Sixth Cavalry came upon a herd that numbered in the hundreds of thousands. "For six days," reported the young commander, "we continued our way through this enormous herd, during the last three of which it was in constant motion across our path." He found it impossible to "approximate the millions."

BISON MOTHER AND CALF.      OVERLEAF: BISON BULLS FIGHTING.

Some of the killing by the settlers was for meat and hides, but much of it was for sport. In many instances, even when bison were killed for food, only the tongue was used. It is estimated that ignorance of the methods of curing hides resulted in the saving of only one out of every three or four hides.

In the late 1800s, professional bison hunters, such as William F. Cody, better known as "Buffalo Bill," were hired to supply food for the crews working on the railroads: "I killed buffalo for the railroad company for twelve months, and during that time the number I brought into camp was kept account of and at the end of that period I had killed 4,280 buffalo." Between 1872 and 1874 well over 3 million animals were shot.

The bison might have completely disappeared had not an Indian named Walking Coyote saved four bison calves from slaughter in 1873, during a hunting expedition along the Milk River in northwestern Montana. Also, a Winnipeg, Manitoba, fur dealer saved another five calves in the following year.

By 1914 Walking Coyote's calves had 745 descendants. In that year, these 745 bison and the 87 offspring of the calves saved in Winnipeg were released in Wood Buffalo National Park in the Northwest Territories. By 1954 the offspring of the original nine calves numbered 40,000, making the comeback of the American bison one of North America's greatest conservation victories.

........................

## THE RAREST NORTH AMERICAN MAMMAL?
### *Black-Footed Ferret*

**The title of rarest North American mammal may well belong to the black-footed ferret (*Mustela nigripes*). The total population has probably not exceeded a hundred individuals in decades. Throughout the continent between 1946 and 1953, about seventy specimens were seen in forty-two different locations; one third of them were dead.**

FERRET.

Since 1979, the black-footed ferret has generally been regarded as being extirpated in Canada; its headquarters appears to be in South Dakota, though there have been some recent reports of sightings from Wyoming and elsewhere.

The black-footed ferret is largely nocturnal, which probably accounts for its description by John James Audubon and John Bachman as late as 1851, two years after they had received a specimen collected near the Platte River, close to Fort Laramie, Wyoming. At that time they were hard at work on the paintings and text for their monumental work on mammals *The Viviparous Quadrupeds of North America* and were delighted to receive the skin of this rare weasel. It was at least another 24 years before the next specimen was reported.

........................

## THE MOST POISONOUS SPIDER
### *Black Widow*

**Although all of the 25,000 species of spiders are poisonous, only a few are dangerous to humans.**

The most dangerous of these in North America, and indeed in the entire world, is the black widow spider, whose bite is capable of killing a human being. Fortunately, death from these bites is rare. One biologist who suffered no ill effects from the bites of several kinds of tarantulas had to be hospitalized after he had been bitten by a black widow.

Three species of black widow spiders occur on this continent, the best known being *Latrodectus mactans*. It is widely distributed in North America, even being found in parts of southern Canada, but it is far more common in the south. The female of the species contains the venom; the much smaller male is quite harmless.

The black widow is called this because the female is black and has a most unfortunate habit of eating the male after they have mated. She has a body about as large as the end of one's middle finger and a leg spread of about an inch. The species is readily distinguished by the red or orange spot on the underside of the body, but the hourglass shape of the body and the coal black color make the spider easy to recognize even without seeing the red spot.

Fortunately, black widow spiders are shy and retiring by nature and bite only when frightened or disturbed. According to *The Guinness Book of Animal Facts and Feats* (Guinness Superlatives Ltd., 1982), a 1945 report by Thorp and Woodson informs us that there were 1,291 reported cases of black widow bites in the United States (578 in California) between 1726 and 1943, with 55 of these being fatal. Most fatalities involved children or elderly people in rural areas.

Although it is young children and elderly individuals who are most likely to die from a black widow bite, a bite from this spider to anyone of any age should always be treated with the utmost concern. On September 21, 1947, the famous actor Harry Carey died of heart complications resulting from a black widow bite during the making of the film *Red River* in Arizona.

The venom of the black widow spider is neurotoxic, and the resulting symptoms include excruciating pain, temporary paralysis, and profuse perspiration, followed by nervousness and acute anxiety, to the extent where victims were convinced they were going insane.

A victim of black widow bite should see a physician at once. Doctors now have treatments that relieve the symptoms of the bite within a relatively short time, usually by an injection of calcium gluconate or a similar substance.

A series of experiments conducted some time ago to determine the toxicity of this spider's venom showed it was fifteen times more potent than the venom of the prairie rattlesnake (*Crotalus terrificus*). Interestingly enough, the Gosiute Indians of Utah at one time smeared their arrowheads with a mixture of black widow and rattlesnake venom when hunting for game.

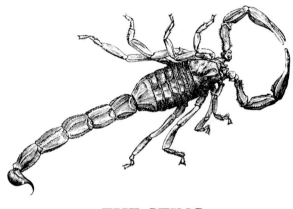

## THE STING
### *Scorpion*

**Scorpions are probably the oldest known arachnids (an order that also includes spiders, ticks and mites); some species of arachnids lived 400 million years ago.** There are 700 known species of scorpions, ranging in size from *Pandinus imperator* of West Africa, which can measure 9 inches from the top of the head to the end of the sting, to *Microbuthus pusillus* of the Red Sea coast, which grows to only half an inch.

The world's most dangerous scorpion is probably the large North African species *Androctonus australis*, which can deliver a massive dose of neurotoxic venom that can kill a human in four hours and a dog in about seven minutes. Another contender for most dangerous scorpion is the Palestine yellow scorpion (*Leiurus quinquestriatus*), whose extensive range covers eastern North Africa through the Middle East to the shores of the Red Sea. Fortunately, the amount of venom it delivers is very small and adults are rarely endangered. However, young children are especially vulnerable, and a number of fatalities of children under five have resulted from the sting of this species.

The scorpions of the genus *Centruroides*, found in the deserts of Mexico, southern Arizona, and New Mexico, pose a threat, and one species, *Centruroides sculpturatus*, is highly venomous. According to Roger Caras, *C. sculpturatus* and *C. gertschi* were responsible for 64 deaths in Arizona between 1929 and 1948 (Stahnke, 1950) – about 2,500 people are stung by scorpions in this state each year – and over a period of thirty-five years approximately 1,600 people died in Mexico from scorpion stings (in most cases the sting entered the sole of the bare foot).

*The Guinness Book of Animal Facts and Feats* (Guinness Superlatives Ltd., 1982) reports that it was formerly believed that a scorpion would sting itself to death if it were surrounded by a ring of fire, but scientific evidence doesn't support such an idea. A scorpion will, not unnaturally, lash out with its tail when threatened, but it has not been known to deliver a self-induced sting. It is known, however, that scorpions in combat have the ability to sting each other to death, indicating that scorpion venoms have different degrees of toxicity.

Experiments have revealed that scorpions can survive massive doses of atomic radiation for weeks on end. Scorpions in the area of France's atomic-bomb tests in the Sahara showed no ill effects from sustained doses of gamma rays of up to 100,000 roentgens; they succumbed only when the radiation level reached 150,000 roentgens. This level of radiation is astonishingly high when compared to the level — *700* roentgens — that is usually fatal to humans and other higher animals.

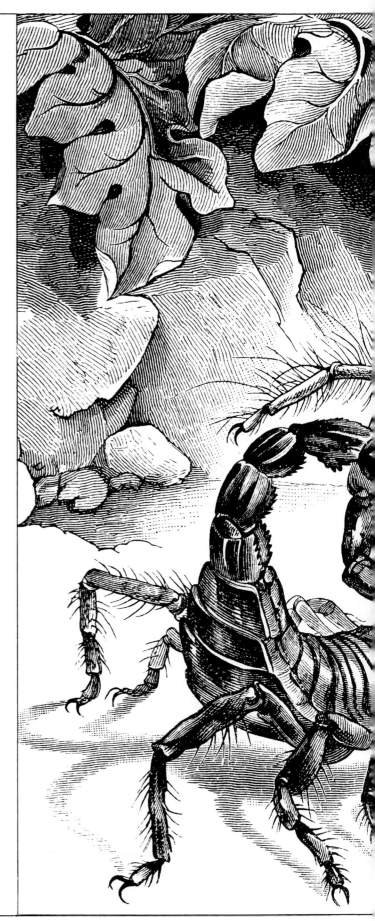

SCORPION ATTACKING SPIDER.

# CHARMING THE BIRDS OUT OF THE TREES
*Foxes*

**Foxes have traditionally been credited with an extraordinary amount of cunning.** This may be attributed to their custom of using a particular strategem called *charming* to attain their end.

A story told often is of a fox observing rabbits feeding. Knowing that the rabbits will scatter and run into their burrows at its approach, the fox rolls about on the ground in order to attract their attention. Next it chases its tail as if it were a kitten, while the rabbits gaze, enraptured, at the performance. All the while, the crafty animal is edging closer to the rabbits, until a sudden straightening of its body enables it to grasp the nearest victim in its jaws.

Eyewitness accounts of the charming of foxes are so numerous that there is no doubt as to their authenticity. However, a rational explanation of the foxes' unusual behavior is possible: Being naturally playful, foxes, like many other mammals, appear to behave with complete abandon as they bound about and somersault and so on. Birds and rabbits seeing these strange antics are fascinated, and are forced to watch out of curiosity. A fox behaving in this fashion and finding prey species attracted to it might capitalize on this tactic by using it deliberately. Such ability to learn is well within the range of the fox's intelligence; but more than likely the act of charming is conducted without any preconceived notion.

. . . . . . . . . . . . . . . . . . . . . .

# LIVING MOUSE TRAP
*The Red Fox*

**The red fox (*Vulpes vulpes*) is a fairly common animal in most parts of the continent, even in highly populated urban areas, but it is secretive in its habits and is therefore seldom seen.** This animal comes in many different color phases—cross, silver, and black foxes being the same species in different outfits. All phases are fairly common except the black, which is usually rare. Some time ago, when fox fur was in great demand, the most prized possession was a fur piece of silver fox. Fortunately, fox fur is no longer especially popular, and hunting and breeding of these foxes for commercial purposes has greatly declined.

The fox has long been credited with great wisdom and cunning, a reputation that is well earned. In hunting, the red fox is the picture of alertness, and is indeed most wary and cunning. It will approach even familiar objects with extreme caution, always pausing to inspect the area for any possible danger. This inborn wariness has enabled the red fox to survive against enormous odds, for this animal has many enemies in addition to humans, such as lynxes, wolves, fishers, and eagles.

When foxes make their home close to agricultural districts, they may acquire a taste for poultry, and thus incur the wrath of the farmer. However, the percentage of poultry taken by foxes is usually relatively small; and before the farmers reach for their guns to eliminate this supposed threat to their livestock, it would be well for them to know that the red fox is the greatest devourer of mice ever created. It also consumes large amounts of noxious insects. The red fox devotes much time and patience to the capturing of mice. And this in itself is a good reason why this handsome and intelligent animal should be allowed to go about its business unhindered by human persecution.

. . . . . . . . . . . . . . . . . . . . . .

# A FOX THAT CLIMBS TREES
*The Gray Fox*

**The gray fox (*Urocyon cineroargenteus*) is a little-known species that inhabits thick woodlands and brush country from southern Canada to southwestern South America, where its shy and retiring habits keep it from being seen.** Unlike other foxes that are mainly terrestrial, the gray fox spends much of its time in trees. No doubt, this compensates for its not being a fast runner. Nor can it cover long distances at the full speed of other foxes, as its legs are somewhat shorter than theirs are.

Although the animal catches most of its prey on the ground, it readily takes to trees whenever it is pursued, and when it is seeking out fruits in season. It can run up a leaning trunk with ease, and can even climb up a perfectly perpendicular trunk, gripping it with its forelimbs, while pushing upwards with its clawed hindfeet. Once treebound, the gray fox can leap from branch to branch as nimbly as a marten or a squirrel.

The climbing superiority of the gray fox over the more familiar red fox can best be illustrated by this tragic incident: A gray fox was discovered dead in a tree with the tip of its tail caught on a forked twig. It was also stuck in a second fork. The fox's desperate efforts to free itself were obvious from the extensive scarring of the bark. The point of the story is that none of the twigs in that tree were more than three quarters of an inch thick, and most were close to two fifths of an inch proving that the gray fox climbs higher limbs than the red fox.

Fox.

# October

The most inspiring sight of the year may be the gathering and migration of geese in October. Along the Atlantic flyway, not far from the bustle of New York City, the vast V's and Y's of hundreds of geese cross the skies,

the wing tip of each goose set slightly behind and to the left or right of the wing tip before it. As geese cross the horizon, emitting their faint and lonely sound, the single or double formations are so long that they nearly cover the full range of vision. Birds flying in formation generate a cloud of life in the sky, as do millions of bats (which constitute a fifth of the mammals on this continent) as they launch forth from their dark, daytime repose. Directed by reflected sound, these bats consume thousands of tons of insects in just a few hours. The squirrel is very energetic in this season, unlike the bat. Autumn is the time when this creature prepares for survival — by gathering hundreds of acorns, beechnuts, and seeds to see it through the cold months to come.

OPPOSITE: BULL MOOSE.

# OCTOBER

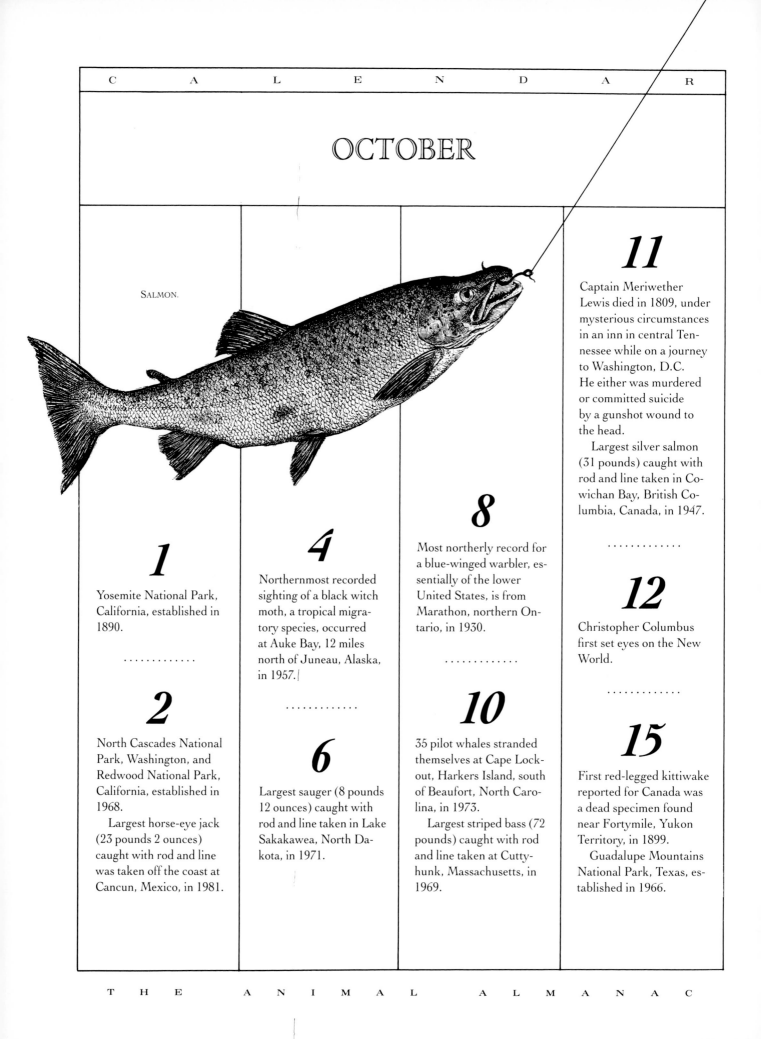

SALMON.

**1**

Yosemite National Park, California, established in 1890.

. . . . . . . . . . . .

**2**

North Cascades National Park, Washington, and Redwood National Park, California, established in 1968.

Largest horse-eye jack (23 pounds 2 ounces) caught with rod and line was taken off the coast at Cancun, Mexico, in 1981.

**4**

Northernmost recorded sighting of a black witch moth, a tropical migratory species, occurred at Auke Bay, 12 miles north of Juneau, Alaska, in 1957.

. . . . . . . . . . . .

**6**

Largest sauger (8 pounds 12 ounces) caught with rod and line taken in Lake Sakakawea, North Dakota, in 1971.

**8**

Most northerly record for a blue-winged warbler, essentially of the lower United States, is from Marathon, northern Ontario, in 1930.

. . . . . . . . . . . .

**10**

35 pilot whales stranded themselves at Cape Lockout, Harkers Island, south of Beaufort, North Carolina, in 1973.

Largest striped bass (72 pounds) caught with rod and line taken at Cuttyhunk, Massachusetts, in 1969.

**11**

Captain Meriwether Lewis died in 1809, under mysterious circumstances in an inn in central Tennessee while on a journey to Washington, D.C. He either was murdered or committed suicide by a gunshot wound to the head.

Largest silver salmon (31 pounds) caught with rod and line taken in Cowichan Bay, British Columbia, Canada, in 1947.

. . . . . . . . . . . .

**12**

Christopher Columbus first set eyes on the New World.

. . . . . . . . . . . .

**15**

First red-legged kittiwake reported for Canada was a dead specimen found near Fortymile, Yukon Territory, in 1899.

Guadalupe Mountains National Park, Texas, established in 1966.

## 16

Captain Meriwether Lewis first described a small bird that "appeared to be passing into the dormant stage," in 1805. This was the first mention of the poor-will, our only hibernating bird.

. . . . . . . . . . . .

## 17

Ocean sunfish, largest of all bony fishes, was landed on the deck of an American liner after crashing through the grand rail in 1926. It was 6 feet long and 6 feet 10 inches between the dorsal and anal fins, and weighed about 800 pounds.

. . . . . . . . . . . .

## 19

Zion National Park, Utah, established in 1919.

Largest silver redhorse (5 pounds 2 ounces) caught with rod and line taken from Shelbyville, Indiana, in 1980.

. . . . . . . . . . . .

## 21

Marine Mammal Protection Act signed into law in 1972.

## 22

Longest-lived animal in the world believed to be a Madagascar radiated tortoise that was allegedly given to the King of Tonga in 1773, by Captain James Cook. The animal was still alive in 1966, making it over 200 years old.

. . . . . . . . . . . .

## 23

Prior to the acceptance of the theory of evolution following Charles Darwin's *"Origin of Species"* in 1859, authorities believed the earth had been created on this day in 4004 B.C. at 9 o'clock in the morning.

South Dakota Federated Women's Clubs adopted the western meadowlark as their state bird in 1931.

. . . . . . . . . . . .

## 26

Largest bluefin tuna caught with rod and line taken in Auld's Cove, Nova Scotia, Canada, in 1979. It weighed an incredible 1,496 pounds.

BOTTLE-NOSE DOLPHIN.

## 27

Largest Dolly Varden (32 pounds) caught with rod and line taken in Lake Pend, Oreille, Idaho, in 1949.

. . . . . . . . . . . .

## 29

First and only sighting of a vermilion flycatcher in Canada was at Toronto, Ontario, in 1949. The specimen was collected by James L. Baillie, Jr. and deposited at the Royal Ontario Museum.

. . . . . . . . . . . .

## 30

Scientists collecting aquarium specimens off the Gulf Coast of the Florida panhandle exploded dynamite under water close to a pod of bottle-nosed dolphins in 1954. One of the dolphins was stunned by the blast. Another specimen swam over and supported it under its flippers to keep it afloat. The entire group of dolphins stayed with the injured one until it recovered.

233

## THE FRIENDLY OWL
### *The Saw-whet Owl*

The Toronto Island Bird Sanctuary, between Hanlan's Point and Center Island, Toronto, Ontario, has long been regarded as one of the best sites for migrating saw-whet owls *(Aegolius acadicus)* in North America; over a hundred specimens are regularly banded here each year.

The migration begins the first week in October and continues to the second week in November, with a peak period around mid-October. As mice constitute the mainstay of the owls' diet, whenever there is a mouse shortage in their area, owls are forced to seek food elsewhere. Under normal circumstances, they tend to spend the winter seeking sustenance in favorable locations in the southern parts of their breeding grounds. Their breeding range extends from southern Alaska south to Mexico.

Saw-whet owls spend the daylight hours sleeping or perched motionless and well concealed in willows. At this time they are unusually tame and easily approached, allowing themselves to be handled without showing any sign of alarm. This trait makes them easy prey to their archenemy, the barred owl *(Strix varia)*. Saw-whet owls become active with the onset of dusk. In flight their chunky bodies and short, rounded wings are somewhat suggestive of the American woodcock *(Philohela minor)*.

Only 7 or 8 inches long, the saw-whet owl is the smallest owl species in eastern North America. It varies from fawn brown to a grayish brown, with white spots on its wings. Its underparts are pale and prominently streaked with chestnut brown. Bright yellow eyes are set in a conspicu-

ous facial disk. The saw-whet owl may be readily distinguished from the screech owl *(Otus asio)* by its lack of ear tufts, and from the boreal owl *(Aegolius funereus)* by its smaller size and lack of white spots on the crown.

The bird's rather unusual name is derived from one of its calls, which sounds like a large-toothed saw being filed.

..........................

## THE ONLY FLYING MAMMALS
### *Bats*

Although bats exist almost everywhere, their secretive ways and nocturnal life style usually keep them out of sight. In fact, a fifth of all mammals are bats, and they are second in number only to the rodents. There are 18 families of bats, comprising about 900 species, of which about 100 are found north of the southern Mexican border. Worldwide, sizes of bats range from the kalong *(Pteropus niger)* of Indonesia, with a wingspan of up to 5 feet 7 inches and a weight of 2 pounds or more, to the West African tiny pipistrelle *(Pipistrellus nanulus)*, the smallest-known bat. Specimens of tiny pipistrelles have a wingspan of about 6 inches and weigh about 0.88 ounce, which means they rival the Etruscan pygmy shrew *(Suncus etruscus)* for the title of "smallest living mammal."

Bats, the only true flying mammals, rival birds in their powers of flight and are among the most unusual of nature's adaptations. The bones of the wing are the same as those in the human arm and hand, but the bat's hand expands to form the highly maneuverable wing.

A bat's natural radar equipment enables it to avoid collision with obstacles by detecting the echo of its squeaks and chirps. The voices of some bats are pitched so high that the sounds are beyond the range of human hearing and can be detected only on the sensitive filament of a sound track.

Bats appear to have few enemies. Cats, raccoons, weasels, snakes, owls, and hawks catch some, but humans are probably their greatest destroyer today. Specimens that get into buildings are killed indiscriminately, and many are collected for scientific and public health studies. Unseasonably bad weather can cause widespread destruction. It is known, for example, that large numbers of bats

OPPOSITE: OWLS.

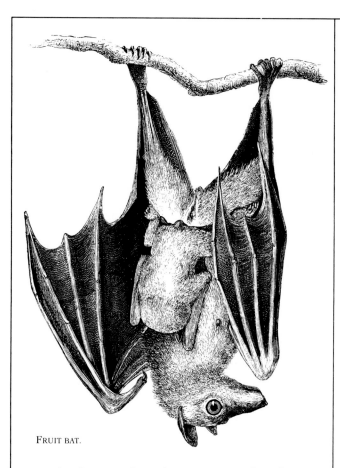

FRUIT BAT.

perish when caught in heavy rains. Others have died when the entrance to the cave they sought to enter was blocked by snow. Sudden floods sometimes fill caves, drowning the bats, although they seem to recognize caves that flood regularly and avoid hibernating in them.

Some bats form extremely large colonies. Mexican free-tailed bats *(Tadarida brasiliensis)* form the largest colonies of any mammal; some Texas caves contain as many as 20 million individuals. Each evening as virtual clouds of Mexican free-tails emerge from many caves in the southwestern United States and Mexico, one can hear the muffled roar of the simultaneous fluttering of tens of thousands of bat wings. The largest colonies require more than 100,000 pounds of insects nightly, and to obtain them, bats may cover more than a hundred miles in a single night.

Although bats play a useful role by helping to keep insects like mosquitoes under control, they are not at all popular. Their summer colonies are usually not appreciated by humans who share dwellings with them, for bat droppings are smelly. And in spite of their small size, bats are ferocious fighters; they will bare their teeth and fight vi-

ciously with little provocation. They will not, however, entangle themselves in your hair.

.......................

## BATS THAT FISH
*Mexican Fishing Bat*

One of the most bizarre bats is the Mexican fishing bat *(Pizonyx vivesi)*, one of two Mexican species that fish for a living. The huge feet and claws look for all the world like pitchfork tines.

The Mexican fishing bat is found on the coast and islands of the Gulf of California, where it regularly roosts in the crevices of cliffs rising from the sea. On some remote islands it inhabits spaces beneath rocks in the ground or even old turtle shells.

With the approach of nightfall, the fishing bat swoops low over the water in search of food. It locates fish through sonar, which echoes from its tiny dorsal fins or from the surface ripples. The bat then drags its huge claws through the water until it seizes its prey. Unlike most bats, the Mexican fishing bat is an adept walker.

## RABID BATS

It was first noticed in 1953 that insect-eating bats can carry the virus of rabies. They are thought to pick up the virus when they migrate south and come into contact with bats that have a diet of blood. Fortunately, the percentage of infected bats in North America is relatively low. Some infected bats give no sign of being diseased, while others appear sick, and some become aggressive.

Because rabies in humans is fatal if it is permitted to develop to the stage where symptoms are observed, bats should be handled only if precautions are taken to prevent them from biting. Children, in particular, should be warned against handling bats.

A person who is bitten should cleanse the wound immediately and report to a physician without delay. If possible, the bat should be caught for examination at a government animal pathology laboratory. Prompt action is vital, as delay could prove fatal.

YOUNG RED-TAILED HAWK.

# HAWK MOUNTAIN

Undoubtedly, the finest spot in North America for observing autumnal hawk migrations is Hawk Mountain in Pennsylvania. Probably more bird watchers from more states in the union have assembled on the rocky prow here than at any other spot on the continent. Each fall, 11,000 to 12,000 bird watchers visit Hawk Mountain, about one for every two and a half hawks that pass over. Quite apart from the view of the hawk migration the lookout affords, there is no place like it for watching bird watchers watching birds.

The Hawk Mountain site was established in 1934 and now covers about 2,000 acres of privately owned forest bordering Berks and Schuylkill counties. It was the first wildlife sanctuary in the world specifically set apart to protect birds of prey. Since its inception nearly 50 years ago, 232 bird species have been identified within the sanctuary.

The sanctuary was established to stop the shooting of the migratory hawks. By 1925 hawk shooting had become an extremely popular "sport" among local hunters, and thousands of these birds were shot from the spectacular vantage point on the crest of the Kittatinny Ridge. On a Sunday when record numbers of birds are observed, 300 or more hunters might be blazing away at the living targets. The object was simply to bring the birds down for attestations of marksmanship and the pleasure of seeing them plummet to earth. The corpses were never retrieved, and the high percentage of wounded were left to rot slowly in the woods.

The first effort to stop the killing of these raptors began in 1932. Richard H. Pough (a leading conservationist and author of the Audubon Bird Guides) visited the mountain and described in detail the mindless slaughter he encountered there. After seeing 60 birds shot and picking up 230 corpses with the aid of two friends, he came back and wrote an article about the massacre, containing a letter sent to the executive secretary of the Pennsylvania Board of Game Commissioners requesting that an investigation be made on "conditions on Blue Mountain [Hawk Mountain] with a view to insuring better enforcement of existing laws and, also, in the future to detail wardens to restrict hunters from shooting protected birds dur-

OVERLEAF: GOLDEN EAGLES AND PREY.

G. Mützel n. Leben.

ADULT RED-TAILED HAWK.

ing the autumnal hawk-flight." Photographs taken by Pough documented the information in the article.

Happily, in 1934 the slaughter ended at Hawk Mountain with the establishment of the sanctuary, but elsewhere in Pennsylvania the slaughter of migratory hawks persisted until 1957.

In 1957 protection of hawks during September and October was gradually extended to a portion of the state, and Bake Oven Knob, owned by the Pennsylvania Game Commission, became a prime observation point for hawk watchers. Then in 1969 Pennsylvania adopted the "model hawk law," under which all birds of prey are protected, except those caught actually attacking domestic livestock. The Migratory Bird Treaty of 1936 between the United States and Mexico was expanded in 1972 to include all hawks, with no exceptions. The killing of hawks is now a federal offense, and yet these birds are still gunned down in certain quarters.

The most abundant hawk seen at Hawk Mountain during fall migrations is the broad-winged hawk (*Buteo platypterus*). These birds make up two thirds of all the birds of prey that pass over the area. As many as 17,000 may be counted in a season, thereby numbering all other hawks combined. The record number of broad-wings reported from Hawk Mountain in the course of one day was 11,392 on September 16, 1948.

The broad-wing invasion occurs in September, with the most spectacular flights between September 15 and September 20. By October the mass of these birds has passed through the central states and is then replaced by the sharp-shinned hawks (*Accipiter striatus*).

The sharp-shins begin coming through in September, and for the first week or two of October they greatly predominate over other hawks in the migration lanes. The hawk migration is now at its peak, with the sharp-shins far outnumbering any other species; more than 8,000 have been counted in a season here.

The golden eagles (*Aquila chrysaetos*), which can occur quite regularly at the sanctuary late in the season, are a special attraction. But perhaps the most sought-after bird at Hawk Mountain is the peregrine falcon (*Falco peregrinus*). This endangered species has never been common here, but it did hit a peak of forty-four in 1941. The red-tailed hawks (*Buteo jamaicensis*) arrive after the sharp-shins have tapered off, and by the time the red-tails trail off in late November or early December, more than 4,000 of these large buteo hawks have passed over Hawk Mountain.

Approach roads to the sanctuary are Pennsylvania Routes 895 to the west and 143 to the east, and a rural road clearly marked with Hawk Mountain Sanctuary signs connecting the two state highways.

For further information, write: Hawk Mountain Sanctuary Association, Route 2, Kempton, Pennsylvania 19529.

# October Reading

## THE RETURN
## OF THE TRUMPETERS
### *Trumpeter Swans*

**In the early part of the century, the trumpeter swan (*Olor buccinator*), largest of all waterfowl, was generally considered to be a candidate for extinction.** "This magnificent bird belongs to a vanishing race," wrote the great ornithologist Arthur Cleveland Bent of this species in 1925.

Just how many trumpeter swans once existed on this continent is not known, but they must have been plentiful. An account from North Carolina in 1709 refers to "great flocks in the winter," and in 1795 Samuel Hearne of the Hudson's Bay Company recorded that the Indians took great numbers of these birds for their feathers as well as for food.

Trumpeter swans remained plentiful until the end of the eighteenth century, when the powerful Hudson's Bay Company began to

TRUMPETER SWAN.                    OVERLEAF: TRUMPETER SWAN BY AUDUBON.

241

take control of all trade and swan skins became regarded as valuable articles of trade. (The famous bird artist John James Audubon selected quills from the trumpeter swan for sketching the feet and claws of small birds, because they were hard yet also elastic.)

Large-scale slaughter ensued, and the number of trumpeter swans dwindled rapidly. An indication of the decimation of the swans can readily be seen in the records of the Hudson's Bay Company, in which a total of 17,671 bird skins, largely of trumpeter swans, were listed as sold between 1853 and 1877. The population steadily decreased from 1,312 in 1854 to 122 in 1877, and during the next two or three years the traffic in swan skins practically ceased.

It was the Migratory Bird Convention Act of 1916 that started the protection that resulted in a comeback for these birds. The treaty put a closed season on swans (and other migratory birds) in Canada and in the United States and later (1936) in Mexico.

In 1933 the United States breeding population consisted of only 69 birds and was restricted to Yellowstone National Park and nearby areas such as Red Rock Lakes in southwestern Montana (established two years later as Red Rock Lakes Migratory Waterfowl Refuge).

The Red Rock Lakes flock grew with the establishment of the 40,000-acre refuge in 1935. Within three years its population had doubled to 98, and by 1944 it had jumped to 207. The figure stood at 417 in 1951, and since then the population has stablized, with about 500 birds producing 100 cygnets a year. In 1955 six trumpeter swans were removed from the Red Rock Lakes flock to the Delta Waterfowl Research Station in Manitoba. Stock from Red Rock Lakes has also been transferred to the National Elk Refuge in Oregon, the Ruby Lake National Wildlife Refuge in Nevada, and the Lacreek National Wildlife Refuge in South Dakota.

The aim of this transplantation program is to supply the nucleus of a new population to many available habitats in the Northwest in hopes of reestablishing the swans in some of their old areas. The trumpeter swans have nested successfully in all these locations.

Efforts are continuing to restore the trumpeter swan to its former breeding range. If the program of transplanting is to succeed, however, the bird's former breeding marshes must be saved. Continued vigilance and the determination of an informed public are needed to prevent unnecessary destruction of the swan's breeding habitat.

So far, reestablishment efforts have brought the trumpeter swan back to a population that numbers between 9,000 to 10,000 free-flying individuals. Compared to the known total of 69 trumpeters half a century ago, this is certainly an encouraging statistic.

Accordingly, in 1969 the species was officially removed from the International Union for Conservation of Nature and Natural Resources' list of rare and endangered species, making the saving of the trumpeter swan one of the brightest pages in the history of wildlife conservation.

........................

# THE GREAT INVADER
## *Cattle Egret*

**Undoubtedly, the most successful case of a bird's extension of its range within recent years is that of the cattle egret (*Bubulcus ibis*).**

This species, long an inhabitant of Africa and southern Asia, apparently crossed the south Atlantic and entered South America around 1930. It first appeared in Florida in 1948, and the very same year it traveled to Australia. In the past few decades, far from behaving in the reticent manner of the usual exotic bird, the cattle egret has established itself in several states and has visited widely on this continent. Though its coming was inadvertent, the cattle egret has since its initial landing in the Guianas (now Guyana),

CATTLE EGRET.

pushed northward in increasing numbers to reach Newfoundland, Saskatchewan, Washington, and British Columbia.

Ornithologists were startled by this explosion of egrets. Although no satisfactory official explanation has been found, all agree that the main reason for the bird's success has been the lack of native competition. Feeding chiefly on insects disturbed by browsing cattle, egrets fill an ecological niche no native species had learned to adjust to so precisely.

Today cattle egrets are found throughout most of the eastern states, all along the Gulf Coast into Texas, west to California and Washington, and up into New Brunswick and Newfoundland. Nesting has occurred as far north as Ontario. Egrets have also spread into many other areas where they were formerly unknown, such as most of South Africa and Europe, southeast Asia, and Australia. The story of the cattle egret is an outstanding example of a bird's extension of its range.

## GIVEAWAY TOOTH MARKS

**No members of the deer family — domestic cattle, sheep, and goats — have front teeth (incisors).** Deer get most of their food by browsing small branches and leaves from trees and shrubs. Because of this lack of teeth, it is easy to tell what kind of animal has nipped off twigs along the trail. If the twigs are broken off, it is the work of deer, but if they are cut smoothly as with a knife, it is the work of a rabbit, beaver, or some other rodent that has sharp cutting teeth both top and bottom.

．．．．．．．．．．．．．．．．．．．．．．

## IT'S DOUBLE-JOINTED
### *Red Squirrel*

**The red squirrel (*Tamiasciurus budsonicus*) is equipped with ball and socket joints that allow it to turn its feet completely around, back to front, something that few mammals**

247

BEAVER.

RED SQUIRREL.

learn to live with them. Although less common than deer, in several ways moose present a greater driving hazard, because they move more slowly and are more likely to be standing in the middle of the road or wandering the highway on a dark night. In this way, many of these huge animals are killed each year. Watchful driving and moderate speeds are necessary to avoid this terrible carnage.

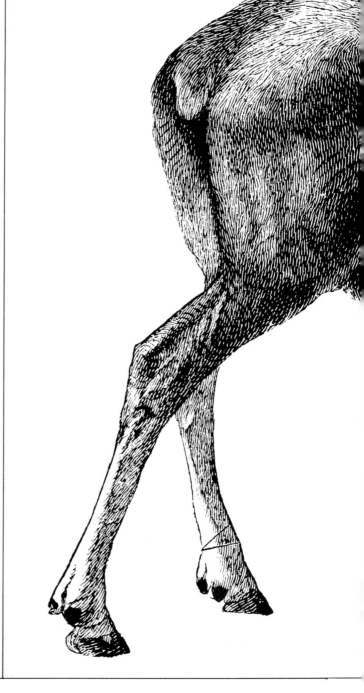

**are able to do.** The next time you are scolded by a squirrel while it hangs head downward on a tree trunk, look carefully at its hind feet. The toes will very likely be pointing toward the top of the tree. This explains why a cat, which doesn't have this capacity though it is otherwise a good climber, is afraid to come down after it goes up, and why, if it does come down, it comes tail end first.

..........................

## THE MONARCH OF THE NORTH WOODS
### *Moose*

**The moose (*Alces alces*), monarch of the north woods, is the largest of all deer; consequently, it has few natural enemies.** Wolves prey on moose to some extent, but wolves have difficulty killing moose, for they are formidable fighters. As a game animal, the moose is eagerly hunted by humans, both for the large quantity of meat and for their tremendous palmated antlers, which may have a span of 6 feet from tip to tip. The antlers are shed annually, and the new ones are at first covered with "velvet," such as seen on the more familariar white-tailed deer (*Odocoileus virginianus*).

There is no more thrilling sight than that of a fully antlered moose. But if we want to go on having the pleasure of seeing them, we must

MOOSE.

# A THREATENED TROPHY
*Bighorn Sheep*

**Early in the nineteenth century, great numbers of bighorn sheep (*Ovis canadensis*) could be found on the slopes and in the foothills of the Rocky Mountains.** But their numbers began to plunge when they were picked off at random by adventurers and hungry prospectors.

This population reduction occurred principally in the second half of the nineteenth century; and the rate of decline accelerated when domestic sheep and cattle were introduced into their grazing areas, competing with the bighorn for food. Thus the bighorn sheep disappeared from much of their previous range, as they were forced to retreat farther and farther into the higher reaches of the mountain passes.

Canadian naturalist/author Ernest Thompson Seton estimated that there were about 1½ to 2 million bighorn sheep on the North American continent at the beginning of the century. Today, fewer than 20,000 of these magnificent animals are thought to survive throughout the entire Rocky Mountain region.

Among the threats facing this animal today comes from epidemic diseases and parasites transmitted from domestic livestock; many bighorns die each year from such ailments as diarrhea and scabies. Also, bighorns need large wilderness areas. They thrive best when their population density is small. When they are crowded in small, concentrated areas, they are more susceptible to epidemic diseases such as pneumonia, and a weakening from lungworms, which cause many deaths among them.

## Record Longevities for Terrestrial Mammals

| | |
|---|---|
| Asiatic elephant (*Elephas maximus*) | 69 years |
| African elephant (*Loxodonta africana*) | 55 |
| Hippopotamus (*Hippopotamus amphibius*) | 54 |
| Chimpanzee (*Pan troglodytes*) | 51 + |
| Short-beaked spiny anteater (*Tachyglossus aculeatus*) | 49 |
| Great Indian rhinoceros (*Rhinoceros unicornis*) | 47 |
| European brown bear (*Ursus arctos*) | 47 |
| Mandrill (*Mandrillus sphinx*) | 46 |
| Lowland gorilla (*Gorilla g. gorilla*) | 40 + |
| Chapman's zebra (*Equus burchelli antiquorum*) | 40 |
| Brown capuchin (*Cebus paraguayanus*) | 37 |
| Orangutan (*Pongo pygmaeus*) | 34 |
| Bison (*Bison bison*) | 33 |
| Hoolock gibbon (*Hylobates hoolock*) | 32 + |
| Sumatran rhinoceros (*Rhinoceros sumatrensis*) | 32 |
| Malayan tapir (*Tapirus indicus*) | 30 |
| African lion (*Panthera leo*) | 29 |
| Giraffe (*Giraffa cameleopardalis*) | 28 |
| Bactrian camel (*Camelus bactriarus*) | 27 |
| Cape buffalo (*Syncerus caffer*) | 26 |
| Black lemur (*Lemur macaco*) | 25 |
| Ratel (*Mellivora capensis*) | 24 |
| Two-toed sloth (*Chloepus didactylus*) | 23 |
| Tiger (*Panthera tigris*) | 22 |
| Llama (*Llama peruana*) | 21 |
| Common porcupine (*Hystrix cristata*) | 20 |
| Common wombat (*Vombatus hirsutus*) | 19 |
| Sumatran porcupine (*Hystrix longicauda*) | 18 |
| Sambar (*Rusa unicolor*) | 17 |
| Red kangaroo (*Macropus rufa*) | 16 |
| Indian otter (*Amblonyx cinerea*) | 15 |
| Red fox (*Vulpes vulpes*) | 14 |
| Gray kangaroo (*Macropus major*) | 13 |
| Common marmoset (*Callithrix jacchus*) | 12 |
| American marten (*Martes americana*) | 11 |
| Golden marmoset (*Leontocebus rosialia*) | 10 |
| Capybara (*Hydrochoerus hydrochoeris*) | 9 |
| Gray squirrel (*Sciurus carolinensis*) | 8 |
| Australian native cat (*Dasyurus quoll*) | 7 |
| Coypu (*Myocaster coypus*) | 6 |
| Algerian hedgehog (*Erinoceus algirus*) | 5 |
| Lesser Egyptian gerbil (*Gerbillus gerbillus*) | 4 |
| Black rat (*Rattus rattus*) | 3 |
| Common hamster (*Cricetus cricetus*) | 2 |
| Pygmy shrew (*Sorex minutus*) | 1 |

## THE BEAR WITH ITS OWN SNOW TIRES
*Polar Bear*

**Most people think of the polar bear (*Ursus maritimus*) as having always lived at the North Pole and nowhere else.** Actually, the North Pole is too far north for even a polar bear to survive. However, individual bears have been seen in the frozen Arctic Ocean as far as 88 degrees north latitude — only 2 degrees from the North Pole. A most unusual record was that of an old female that was shot

POLAR BEAR.

near Peribonca, Lake St. John district, in Quebec on or about October 29, 1938.

Polar bears lived farther south of their current range during the last glacial period. In 1690 a German naturalist named Von Siebold reported that polar bears reached the northern island of Japan and that they were once more common in the Bering Strait and in Iceland than they are now.

Polar bears are almost totally absent from the Canadian arctic islands because the coastal inshore ice does not break up every summer to provide suitable areas of open water for seals, on which the bears prey. Off the coast of Alaska and northeastern Greenland, the conditions are particularly well suited for seals.

The polar bear is unique among bears because it has its own snow tires. The bottoms of its paws are covered with short, stiff hairs, which not only keep the paws warm but also give the bear good traction on the slippery ice and snow. On all other species of bears, the undersides of the paws are quite devoid of hair.

OVERLEAF: *THE PEACEABLE KINGDOM* BY WILLIAM HALLOWELL.

## A Plurality of Mammals

The following are some terms currently in vogue in the English language to describe mammals in groups:

A sloth of bears
A clowder of cats
A gang of elk
A pack of hounds,
    wolves, or mules
A skulk of foxes
A herd of horses, cows
    or sheep
A pride of lions
A labor of moles
A troop of monkeys
A drove of pigs or sheep
A school of porpoises
A pod (or gam) of whales
    or seals
A sounder of swine
A rout of wolves
A stud of mares

A kindle of kittens
A singular of boars
A colony of rabbits
A band of gorillas
A cete of badgers
A down of hares
A leap of leopards
A leash of greyhounds
A litter of pigs
A mute of hounds
A pair of horses
A sounder of boars
A sleuth of bears
A span of mules
A tribe (or trip) or goats
A mob (troop) of
    kangaroos
A yoke of oxen

........................

## ODD COLOR PHASES

**A pure white bird in a flock of house sparrows (*Passer domesticus*), or a completely white American robin (*Turdus migratorius*), is reported from time to time, though a white** specimen (albino) of any species can, of course, occur.

Albinism, from the Latin *albus*, meaning "white," can occur even in plants, but partial albinism is most often noticed. The offspring of true albino parents are always albinos. There are records of two white female robins with normally colored mates rearing normally colored broods, one for three, and the other for four, successive years.

Any abnormality in an offspring is usually caused by an inheritance factor. For instance, if two parents, though normally colored, each carry inheritance factors for white, about a quarter of their brood should be white. But only rarely do such individuals come together as parents, and their progeny are not always as expected.

Odd color phases are most likely to be seen during the autumn, and most of these are albino or partially albino birds. But complete black phases (melanism) and red phases (erythrism) also occur. A black squirrel is a color phase of the gray squirrel (*Sciurus carolinensis*), and there have been black chipmunks (*Tamias* sp.) and black raccoons (*Procyon lotor*). In some areas of North America, the common color of the garter snake (*Thamnophis* sp.) is black, and in other areas it is bright red.

SHORT-TAILED WEASEL.

# CAMELS AND BUTTERFLIES

**Camels roamed the southwestern United States during the middle of the last century.** These animals were descended from a herd of thirty-four specimens that were imported from North Africa by the U.S. government in 1856 to be used as pack animals in expeditions across the arid desert.

Secretary of State Jefferson Davis had become alarmed by the fact that communications in the southwest were delivered haphazardly, if at all. A major problem was that the horses frequently died during the long treks across the parched land. And while most of the eastern United States was comfortably settled, the southwest was still as much a trackless wilderness as it had been during the early days of its discovery.

At any rate, Secretary Davis conceived the idea that camels, being natural desert animals, would be a logical choice for use as pack animals in military expeditions across the arid wasteland. The first shipment of these animals duly arrived from North Africa and was stationed at a military garrison near present-day Kerrville in Texas.

Unfortunately, the camels turned out to be touchy, independent beasts, biting, kicking, and spitting at the mule skinners, who displayed little patience with the new animals in their charge. The camels spooked the cavalry horses and frightened civilians. Many cowboys refused to ride them, since by this time they had developed a close association with the horse. Indians feared them and killed them at sight.

With the eruption of the Civil War, the experiment was abandoned, and the unfortunate camels were either sold or turned out to fend for themselves. It is said that they wandered the desert until around 1901, occasionally producing young, and turning up now and then like phantoms to startle inhabitants and travelers.

Legend has it that a small lavender blue butterfly from the camel's African homeland was accidentally imported in the fodder upon which the camels had been bedded. Their chrysalids, lodged in the straw, were scattered all around the ground at the garrison, until they emerged into butterflies in the hot Texas sun. From thence, they supposedly fluttered hither and yon across the Texas countryside.

Alas, no one has seen them from that day to this! It appears that the butterflies were only able to mate and reproduce in the company of the camels; the hooves of the large animals left deep holes in the sand, trapping the spring water, which was crucial for the butterflies during their brief breeding season. Thus the butterflies disappeared along with the camels.

257

# November

Although many animals have made arrangements to reside elsewhere for the winter, a few may remain near their autumn habitats. To make life somewhat more comfortable for birds during the months ahead, you may want to offer these winter residents refreshments of sunflower seeds, peanuts, raisins, suet, millet, and corn. A single request, however: If you start to feed them now, please be certain not to disappoint them later. They will come to rely on you for sustenance and will certainly starve to death if you discontinue feeding before spring.

Entire species of animals have found year-round lodgings elsewhere or vanished altogether when their environment failed to sustain them. Gone are the days when farmers on this continent lived in dread of the catamount, the cougar, the bobcat, or the lynx.

If it were not for the attention given to preserving the great whales, this mammal would surely have vanished altogether from the ocean depths of this earth. Traveling thousands of miles, these intelligent creatures manage to communicate over long distances in mysterious musical voices, evading their predators in a watery, weightless oceanic world.

Opposite: Mountain lion.

# NOVEMBER

Winter feeding for birds can commence this month.

In November 1970 a 30-foot-long marine animal described by local police as a sea serpent was washed up on a beach near Scituate, Massachusetts. It was later positively identified as a basking shark.

In late November 1977 about 500 dead and dying blackbirds and pigeons landed on the streets of San Luis Obispo, California. No local spraying had occurred and no explanation was offered.

**1**

Probably the last recorded sighting of Dawson caribou (4 specimens) was made about 3½ miles inland from Virago Sound, British Columbia, Canada, in 1908.

**2**

Largest-known invertebrate, the Atlantic giant squid, killed after it ran aground in Thimble Tickle Bay, Newfoundland, Canada, in 1878. It was 55 feet long and weighed an estimated 2,500 pounds.

**11**

A black phoebe, bird of the southwestern United States and adjacent Mexico, first reported from Canada in Vancouver, British Columbia, in 1936.

**12**

Georg Wilhelm Steller, naturalist and explorer who gave his name to Steller's sea cow and Steller's jay, died of pneumonia in the northern Siberian town of Tyumen in 1746.

**13**

Last report of extinct longjaw cisco made near Long Point, Lake Erie, Ontario, when 26 specimens were collected in 1957.

**15**

Highest price ever paid for bird's egg was £330.75 for an egg of the extinct great auk sold in London, England, in 1934. The bird became extirpated in North America in 1785, and became totally extinct in 1844.

**17**

1-cent stamp issued in the United States depicting the bald eagle, the national emblem, in 1851. This stamp and the Canadian stamp with the beaver on it, issued the same year, were the first ones to appear with animals on them.

**18**

California condor discovered during the Lewis and Clark expedition in 1805. An entry in Captain William Clark's diary reads: "Rubin Fields Killed a Buzzard of the Large Kind."

CALIFORNIA CONDOR.

## 22

Eastern cougar, an endangered species, attacked a human in New Brunswick, Canada, 1951. It was reported by Bruce S. Wright in the January-March 1953 issue of the *Canadian Field Naturalist*. Truculent specimens are not unknown, although the great majority of cougars are extremely timid.

. . . . . . . . . . . . .

## 24

Charles Darwin's *Origin of Species* published in 1859.

SWORDFISH.

## 30

A fisherman died after being speared through the back by a swordfish off the coast of Baja California, Mexico, in 1957.

Young male humpback whale found stranded at Corolla, North Carolina, in 1973. It was still alive on December 4 but died early the following day.

BLUE WHALE BEING FLENSED.

# FEEDING BIRDS IN WINTER

*I*n northern latitudes, when the snow lies thick on the ground and covers much of the birds' natural food, the birds must seek other food elsewhere, often far from their natural habitat. At times like these, feeding stations can attract a great many birds, particularly if the operator pays careful attention to the different requirements of birds.

Some birds like seeds, others fruit. Sunflower seeds, suet, and peanuts (unsalted) are all popular foods that can be placed out to attract winter birds. The sunflower seeds are for grosbeaks, cardinals, and chickadees; the suet for woodpeckers and nuthatches; and the peanuts for the blue jays.

Birds that come to feeders will generally accept a wide variety of foods. Most birds will take bread crumbs, raisins, crushed pecans, and oatmeal as supplements to their diet.

It is important to keep your feeders clean at all times. Birds can get diseases from moldy food. Throw out the leftover food from the previous day before putting out fresh food. Egg shells are especially valuable to female birds and should be provided, for the females need the calcium to build up the shells of their own eggs. A receptacle filled with fresh water from which your birds can drink is also necessary.

If you start feeding birds in winter, it is important to keep it up through the entire season. Don't stop winter feeding once you have started; your birds will perish if they have become dependent on you for food.

For a backyard you need only a small feeding table with a roof for shelter; for a window sill all you need is a tray. Bird feeders need not be elaborate to attract birds. It is more important that they be put in a place where the birds using them will be safe from cats and squirrels.

The three cold winter months are among the most interesting of the year in many respects for bird watchers. During this period some of the most colorful perching birds are down from the far north. The more regular visitors include evening grosbeaks *(Hesperiphona vespertina)*, pine grosbeaks *(Pinicola enucleator)*, red crossbills *(Loxia curvirostra)*, white-winged crossbills *(L. leucoptera)*, pine siskins *(Spinus pinus)*, common redpolls *(Acanthis flammea)*, purple finches *(Carpodacus purpureus)*, snow bun-

SWALLOWS ON MIGRATION.

FINCHES.

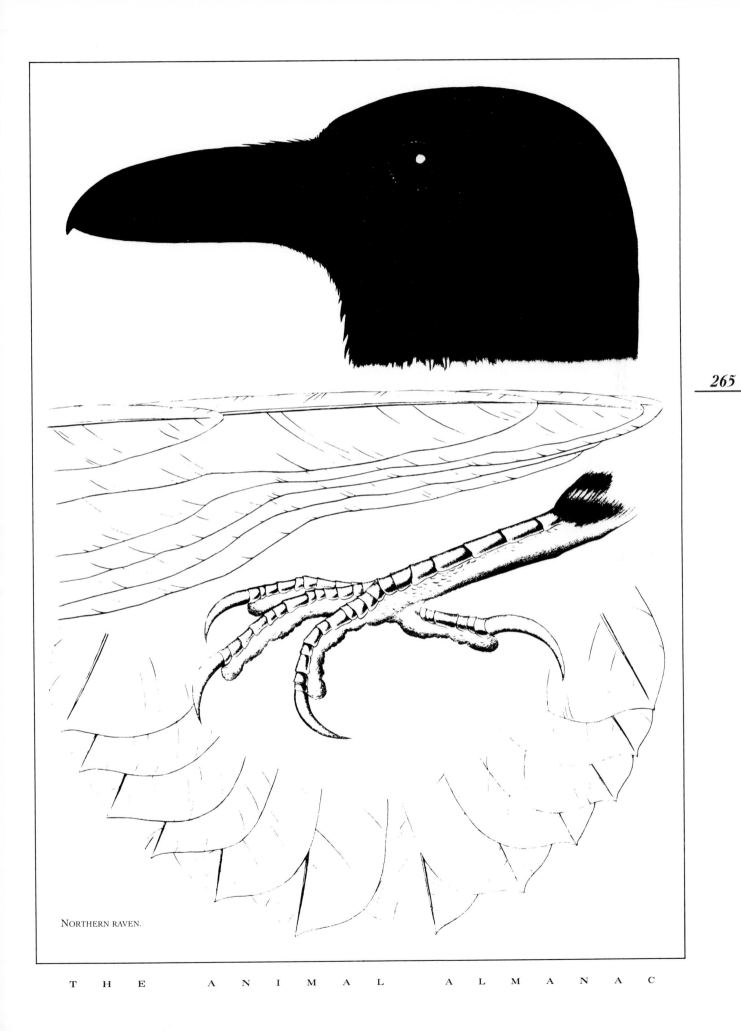

NORTHERN RAVEN.

tings *(Plectrophenax nivalis)*, and Lapland long-spurs *(Calcarius lapponicus)*.

Apart from northern visitors, there are also many resident winter species found within close proximity to your own home, such as black-capped chickadees *(Parus atricapillus)*, white-breasted nuthatches *(Sitta carolinensis)*, downy woodpeckers *(Dentrocopos pubescens)*, hairy woodpeckers *(D. villosus)*, blue jays *(Cyanocitta cristata)*, dark-eyed juncos *(Junco hyemalis)*, tree sparrows *(Spizella arborea)*, and that most beautiful of winter residents, the cardinal *(Cardinalis cardinalis)*.

keep the water from freezing. If a piece of tile is not available, another method that works well is to use a 10-inch or 12-inch clay flowerpot as a base on which to support the pan of water above the light. A large flowerpot saucer or a garbage pail cover makes an excellent water tray. In any case, be sure to use a well-insulated, weatherproof extension cord to connect the light to an outdoor electrical outlet, so that short circuits and blown-out fuses will not result. If the birdbath can be set up on a wide outside window ledge where a short cord can be used, so much the better. And when

## WINTER BIRDBATH

To add to the attractiveness of your winter bird-feeding station, consider providing some means of drinking and bathing facilities for your winged visitors. In rural areas nature usually provides some open water in rapidly flowing streams, but in cities birds may have difficulty locating unfrozen water during severely cold periods.

The simplest way to provide this service is merely to set out a pan of warm water at the same time every day. Of course, on a really frosty day it will freeze over in a few minutes and be of no further use. Some steady source of heat below it would prevent this from happening.

If a length of pipe tile can be obtained, it makes a fine base for supporting a pan of water and provides a protected space where a 100-watt light bulb can be suspended to provide the necessary heat to

the birds have lost their initial fear, you will have an excellent chance for close-up observations of them when they come to drink and bathe.

## OUR ONLY HIBERNATING BIRD
### *Poor-Will*

The phenomenon of migration was unknown to us two centuries ago, and not surprisingly, it was believed that birds, along with other animals, spent the winter in a state of hibernation. The most popular assumption was that they slept under mud at the bottom of ponds.

This notion has, of course, been ridiculed by our more enlightened, sophisticated selves. How-

WHIP-POOR-WILL.

ever, it has been discovered that at least one species of native bird does, in fact, hibernate throughout the winter.

The poor-will (*Phalaenoptilus nuttallii*), a member of the goatsuckers, has been found in the foothills of the Sierra Nevada huddled in rock crevices or in the hollow of saguaros (giant cacti), with no detectable heartbeat and a body temperature many degrees below its normal temperature.

The Hopi Indians have long referred to the poor-will as "Holchko," meaning "the sleeper." Mormon settlers and Arizona prospectors also made references to the unique behavior of this bird, but their tales were totally discounted until December 29, 1946. On that day biologist Edmund Jaeger found a hibernating specimen in a cold canyon bottom.

In late November of 1947, Edmund Jaeger found the poor-will again "dead to the world" in the same spot. Testing the bird's internal temperature, he discovered it was 64.4 degrees Fahrenheit instead of the 106 degrees Fahrenheit that is normal for a bird. When Jaeger returned to the site in February 1948, the poor-will had lost very little weight; it woke up while being banded and flew away. But since it carried an identification band, it could be positively established that the same bird occupied the rock niche for a third season in 1948 and a fourth in 1949.

Since then, other hibernating poor-wills have been discovered, including one that was brought in to the Desert Trailside Museum north of Tucson, Arizona, in 1953. During its five-day stay there in an unheated building, the bird's temperature dropped every night to 55.7 degrees Fahrenheit, only to rise again during the day.

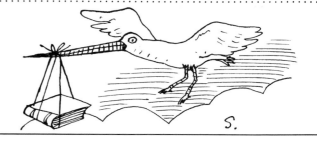

S.

## GOATSUCKERS

**In ancient Europe people believed that birds belonging to the family Caprimulgidae, which include the whip-poor-will** (*Caprimulgus vociferus*) **and the common nighthawk** (*Chordeiles minor*)**, were capable of milking goats.** Superstitious farmhands, observing these birds hovering over their goats with mouths agape, assumed that they sucked milk from the teats of goats. Thus they became known as goatsuckers.

In reality, the birds were searching for insects that the goats stirred up while they were grazing. Goatsuckers are entirely insect-eaters. They have small beaks but enormously large mouths, which enable them to catch flying insects on the wing.

A characteristic that goatsuckers share with owls is their noiseless flight, made possible by the softness of their feathers. Owls, of course, prey largely on mammals, and silent flight is obviously of advantage to them, but one does not think of insects as being very sensitive to sound.

Whip-poor-wills and nighthawks are ground nesters and do not bother to build a nest. Perhaps because the birds themselves are so well camouflaged, a real nest would attract notice to the eggs and the young. Instead, these birds pick a spot on the ground where their mottled plumage blends so completely that you can pass within a yard or two of a brooding bird without ever seeing it.

The whip-poor-will, so called for its monotonous repetitions of its call, is usually first heard around the second week in April. A naturalist once counted over 1,000 repetitive calls from a whip-poor-will without a single break.

OPPOSITE:
TIMBER WOLF.

RED DEER.

# THE BALANCE OF NATURE
*Essential Predators*

**The creatures chiefly singled out to bear the brunt of human destructiveness are undoubtedly the predators, or meat-eaters**. They hunt game regarded by humans as theirs alone. The war on predators has been waged with little scientific knowledge of their roles in the scheme of things and little moral regard for our responsibility to conserve our environment.

In pioneer days, extermination seemed more rational. Frontier people worked hard against great odds to carve their little clearings out of the forest; they could not afford to have their hard-won fields and herds destroyed. In many cases, it was literally "them or us."

That was an era of abundance. But unfortunately the attitude survived for generations after the danger was past. As recently as 1958, it was part of the game warden's job in Ontario's Algonquin Provincial Park to eliminate wolves. Predators were bountied in protected areas because sportsmen and naturalists alike assumed that flesh-eating animals were the cause of the decline in the numbers of game animals. They mistakenly thought that the key to successful game management was the elimination of any species that preyed on game. Their ignorance has proven costly to other animals and, ultimately, to themselves.

Consider the story of the Kaibab Plateau in Arizona, established in 1906 as a natural game reserve. This vast area had been inhabited for centuries by a herd of 4,000 deer, together with a thrifty population of cougars. This reserve could have maintained 30,000 deer. When the reserve was established, however,

deer shooting was terminated and government hunters were told to clean out the predators.

Within 25 years, the kill was reported as 781 cougars, 30 timber wolves, 4,889 coyotes, and uncounted numbers of eagles. As expected, the deer population increased. By 1924 the total deer herd had reached 100,000 individuals.

Then came the inevitable — and unexpected! Deer died of starvation by the thousands, and the survivors ate every available leaf and twig, destroying almost 90 percent of the range. Though shooting was resumed and a thousand deer were taken annually, the numbers still declined. By 1930 there were 20,000 deer left; by 1940, only 10,000. It was a tragic, costly mistake repeated many times over in other parks.

The lesson is simple: A given range will support only a certain number of animals, whether game or domestic. Predators take only small numbers, usually the weakest, from the animals they prey on and are essential to the maintenance of a healthy population. Predators are, therefore, a vital part of our environment, and an essential element in a balanced and healthy wildlife population.

........................

## BIG CAT REDISCOVERED
*Cougar*

**The cougar (*Felis concolor*) once had the greatest range of any New World mammal**. It was found from northern British Columbia east to Nova Scotia and all the way south to Patagonia at the tip of South America. Throughout this vast area, it was known by a wide variety of names, including cougar, puma (in South America), mountain lion, panther, painter, Indian devil, catamount, screamer, and king cat.

Civilized humans and cougars couldn't live on the same ground, and the cougars retreated, gradually vanishing as the wilderness did. Cougars on this continent are, for the most part, now confined to regions of the west.

PUMA.

The eastern cougar (*F. c. cougar*), a subspecies found in the eastern regions of North America, once ranged from Ontario, Quebec, and the maritime provinces of Canada south to Florida. It was assumed to have become extinct during the nineteenth century; the last complete specimen preserved was killed near Barnard, Vermont, on November 24, 1881.

But, in 1948, Bruce S. Wright, director of the Northeastern Wildlife Station in Fredericton, New Brunswick, reported that he had personally seen a wild specimen, and that he had in his possession a complete mounted specimen that had been trapped east of Little St. John Lake in Somerset County, Maine.

Then in 1954 plaster casts of cougar tracks were made in Nova Scotia for the first time in history, and cougar sightings have since come from the Gaspé Peninsula in Quebec, Ontario, and the Maritime provinces. In March 1959 a family group of one large and two smaller cougars wandered into the outskirts of Montreal, Quebec; and the following year, the trail of a freak specimen with five toes on its forepaw was discovered in Maine.

It is believed that the eastern cougar was never especially common even in the earlier days, but many were killed with little record. The animal persisted in some numbers until about the middle of the nineteenth century, after which time it was supposedly hunted to extinction. Wright maintained in 1972 that the total number of eastern cougars on the continent, principally in New Brunswick and Maine, probably didn't exceed a hundred individuals and was likely to be smaller. Happily, however, it is not extinct, as was once believed.

. . . . . . . . . . . . . . . . . . . . . . .

## RARE TROPICAL CATS

**North Americans are, for the most part, conversant with the cougar (Felis concolor), the bobcat (Lynx rufus), and the Canada lynx (L. canadensis), for these are the wild cats**

OPPOSITE: JAGUAR.

JAGUAR.

**most frequently encountered on this continent.** However, there are four tropical species that may be found, although rarely, at the extreme southern part of the United States.

The most easily identifiable of these is the jaguar (*Panthera onca*). Largest of the New World cats, and resembling a very heavy set leopard with a shorter tail, this magnificent predator formerly prowled the North American continent north to central California and east to Louisiana. It was also an established species north to the Red River in Arkansas, and a number of debatable early records have even placed the jaguar as occurring as far east as the Appalachian range.

An account of the coastal Carolinas in 1711 notes that "Tygers . . . are more to the Westward. . . . I once saw one that was larger than

273

a Panther [cougar], and seemed to be a very bold Creature.... It seems to differ from the Tyger of Asia and Africa."

Peter Matthiessen in *Wildlife in America* (Penguin, 1978) states that: The animal was last recorded in California from Palm Springs in 1860, and in New Mexico in 1903. The jaguar must now be considered as extirpated from the United States as a breeding species, although occasional specimens wander infrequently into extreme southern Texas and southeastern Arizona. Recent records are from Texas in 1948 and Arizona in 1949 and 1971.

The jaguar inhabits low coastal forests in Mexico, from the mouth of the Rio Grande southward into Argentina, where it preys largely on deer, capybaras, tapirs, peccaries, and various small mammals. An excellent swimmer, it sometimes pursues and preys on caimans in tropical streams. Almost everywhere, the jaguar is known as "El Tigre."

Unfortunately, the jaguar has been relentlessly hunted for being a livestock killer and for its valuable coat. Dr. Carl Koford estimated in a recent survey that there were fewer than 1,000 individuals left in Mexico and fewer than 100 in Argentina.

The ocelot (*Felis pardalis*) is another southern spotted cat that has been heavily hunted for its fur. Fortunately, the Endangered Species Act has made importation of the furs of this species into the United States illegal, and some Latin American countries also officially protect these rare cats.

Considerably smaller than the jaguar, with an even more beautifully marked coat, the ocelot blends perfectly with the dappled sun-and-shadow world that it inhabits. This animal usually rests by day, hidden by the foliage in its forest and brushland home, and comes forth at night to hunt small and medium-size prey, such as rabbits, monkeys, pacas, agoutis, iguanas, fish, frogs, and various species of birds.

The Mexicans, who hunted ocelots when they were more abundant, not only took the pelts but also consumed the meat and blood. Traditionally, this was to increase the health and strength of the hunter. Currently, the ocelot is an extremely rare animal in the United States, and although it frequents three counties in southern Texas, it will probably follow close behind the jaguar.

Looking for all the world like a diminutive copy of the ocelot is the margay (*F. wiedii*), a little-known animal in the United States. In fact, its status as an American mammal is based largely on a single specimen found at Eagle Pass on the Rio Grande of Texas, over a century ago. The animal is presumed to be nocturnal, and the ultrasecretiveness of its habits may account for the extreme paucity of records. The margay is referred to as "tiger cat" by the Mayans of the Yucatan.

The jaguarundi (*F. yagouaroundi*) is probably the least-known cat on the continent. This is an elongated, dark-hued, low-slung cat that bears a superficial resemblance to a weasel and consequently is called "otter cat." The jaguarundi prefers to hunt at dusk and during the twilight hours.

It has always been a rare mammal in the United States and is becoming even rarer as its habitat, the wild thickets and dense lowland forest, is cleared for ranching and farm use. Rodents, other smaller mammals, and fish form the mainstay of the jaguarundi's diet.

This rare animal comes in two distinct colors, one a dark smoky gray, the other russet. Both color phases regularly interbreed. Within its restricted range in North America, the jaguarundi inhabits the chaparral country of Arizona and southern Texas.

The jaguar, ocelot, margay, and jaguarundi are all officially recognized as endangered species in North America.

........................

## PLAYING POSSUM

Undoubtedly, one of the strangest of our native mammals is the Virginia opossum (*Didelphis virginiana*), the only species of mar-

OPOSSUM AND YOUNG.

supial represented in North America. It probably evolved in Mexico late in the Pleistocene Period and today ranges from Canada to Costa Rica. Except for a few species inhabiting tropical America, all other marsupials, or pouched animals, are restricted to the regions of Australia and New Guinea.

The Virginia opossum is similar to the species first discovered by Vicente Yanez Pinzon in 1500 in Brazil. It was a female carrying young. Yanez Pinzon, who had shared in another major discovery eight years earlier as captain of the *Nina*, under Christopher Columbus, took this incredible animal back to Spain, where he showed it to King Ferdinand and Queen Isabella: They were among the first Europeans to set eyes on this unusual, pouched creature.

This is the animal that gave rise to the expression "playing possum." When danger threatens, the opossum may sink into a nervous paralysis — a catatonic state lasting a few minutes to several hours, depending on how long it takes for the attacker to be fooled by

"PLAYING POSSUM."

OVERLEAF:
BABY OPOSSUMS.

SIX-WEEK OLD OPOSSUM.

the feint. Its weathered-looking ears and bare tail add to the deathly effect, and as a final touch the animal draws back its lips to expose its teeth in a horrible grimace. When the danger has passed, the "corpse" comes to life again.

The name opossum is derived from the Algonquin Indian name *apasum*, meaning "white animal." It was introduced to western civilization in 1608 in Captain John Smith's description of the animal from Virginia: "An Opassum hath an head like a Swine, and a taile like a Rat, and is of the bigness of a Cat. Under her belly she hath a bagge, wherin shee lodgeth . . . and sucketh her young."

The Virginia opossum was rare or absent north of present-day Virginia and Ohio when Europeans began colonizing this continent. Today the species is in all the New England states and southern Canada, where it is probably at the northern limit of its range.

## WHALE SLAUGHTER

**The vital need for a ban on commercial whaling has been evident in the light of previous whale-hunting activities.**

All eight species of great whales have become rare and endangered due to the relentless hunting of whalers. Every year tens of thousands of whales are slaughtered by a handful of nations that refuse to abandon the dead-end whaling industry and that ignore the ten-year moratorium unanimously recommended by the United Nations Conference on the Environment.

Unfortunately, the whaling industry is big business. Huge convoys of ships roam the seas surrounding Antarctica searching for whales. These fleets, equipped with sonar helicopters, long-range explosive harpoons, and factory

HUMPBACK WHALES.

ships, can reduce an 80-foot whale to nothing in less than an hour.

Whaling is one of the cruelest and most barbaric of all hunting activities. The whale is killed with a 200-pound, 6-foot-long iron harpoon that is shot from a cannon. The harpoon head contains a time-fuse grenade that literally blows the whale's entrails apart seconds after impact. The animal may spend hours in agony, and more than one harpoon may be necessary to kill it.

The senselessness of this whale slaughter is best illustrated by the fact that there are readily available substitutes for all products that are obtained from whales. These include animal feed, industrial oils, fertilizer, perfume, soap, shampoo, gelatin, and margarine. Every single whale-by-product can be replaced by inexpensive substitutes in goodly supply.

The rate of the killing of these giant mammals during the past ten years has been positively alarming. On the average, 1 whale has been killed every 13 minutes — over 100 every day. In 1976 alone, almost 40,000 whales were killed throughout the world.

## A PHASE-OUT ON WHALING

**Perhaps the greatest victory for wildlife conservation occurred in the summer of 1982 when a complete ban on commercial whaling was declared at the International Whaling Commission meeting at Brighton, England.**

A three-year phase-out of commercial whaling will be completed by the 1985–1986 season. Said a jubilant Sir Peter Scott, "This is a great breakthrough. After 25 years of coming to these meetings this is the highest spot of all. I don't think any species will have gone in three years' time; the danger of extinction has disappeared."

But the battle is not yet over. Whaling nations such as Japan and Norway are threatening to continue whaling and are waging a major press campaign against the three-year phase-out. Japan, the largest whaling nation, has threatened to leave the commission and says it may lodge an objection to the ban.

However, should Japan defy the International Whaling Commission's decision after 1986, the Pelly Amendment to the U.S. Fisher-

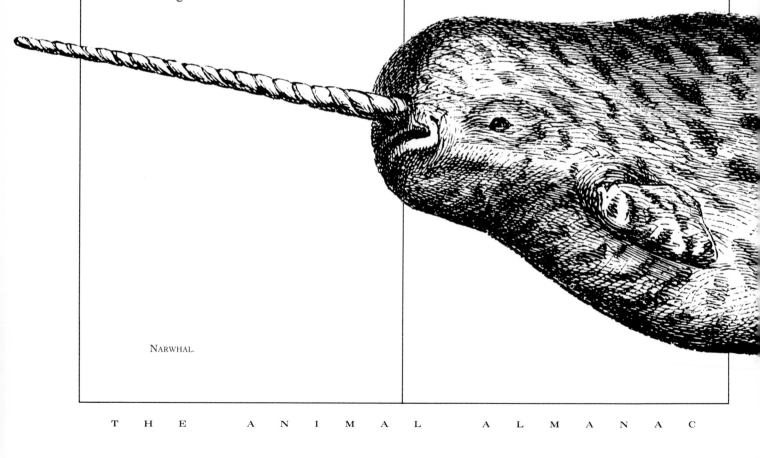

NARWHAL.

man's Protection Act of 1967 and the Packwood-Magnuson amendment to the U.S. Fishery Conservation and Management Act of 1976 would be called into effect. Under these laws, the United States is required to prohibit the importation of fish products from a nation that disregards an International Whaling Commission ruling.

........................

## THE UNICORN FISH
*Narwhal*

**According to mythology, the unicorn was a horselike creature with a single horn growing from its forehead.** No such creature has ever been known to exist, but the term *unicorn*, or *unicorn fish*, is sometimes applied to the narwhal (*Monodon monoceros*), a type of toothed whale that grows to a length of 15 to 16 feet and is found primarily in arctic waters.

The peculiar development of one of its teeth is responsible for the name of unicorn. Both male and female narwhals are born with a number of teeth, but these shortly degenerate, except for two in the upper jaw. These two teeth

HUNTING NARWHALS.

seldom become functional in the female, but in the male narwhal the left tooth continues to grow. It grows forward straight through the upper jaw and lip, spiraling upon itself in a clockwise direction.

The right tooth normally does not develop even in the male, but occasional specimens have been collected in which both teeth had grown into tusks, and for some unknown reason, both the tusks spiraled in the same direction. Exact measurements are few, but it is probable that they sometimes grow to a

281

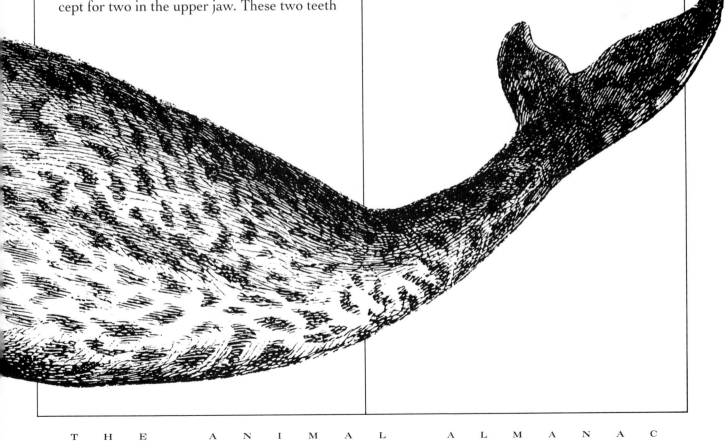

length of 9 to 10 feet. The function of this enormous tooth is not definitely known.

## Record Measurements for Whales

| | Length | Weight |
|---|---|---|
| Blue whale | | |
| (Balaenoptera musculus) | 110'2½" | 190° ton |
| Fin whale | | |
| (Balaenoptera physalus) | 90' | 97° |
| Sei whale | | |
| (Balaenoptera borealis) | 72' | 45° |
| Sperm whale | | |
| (Physeter catodon) | 67'10" | 72° |
| Greenland whale | | |
| (Balaena mysticetus) | 67' | 83° |
| Humpback whale | | |
| (Megaptera novaeangliae) | 65' | 64° |
| Right whale | | |
| (Balaena glacialis) | 60' | 71 |
| Bryde's whale | | |
| (Balaenoptera edeni) | 59' | 31.5 |
| Pacific gray whale | | |
| (Eschrichtius gibbonsus) | 51' | 39 |
| Berardius whale | | |
| (Berardius bairdi) | 41' | 16.5 |
| Piked whale | | |
| (Balaenoptera acutorostrata) | 34' | 9 |

° Estimated weight

........................

# THE SEA WOLF
## Killer Whale

**Fearful of neither human nor beast, the killer whale (Orcinus orca) is renowned for its strength and ferocity.** Although rarely exceeding 25 feet in length, these largest of porpoises habitually attack whales several times their own size, often tearing the larger mammals to pieces.

One of the chief victims of "Orca" is the Californian gray whale (Eschrichtius robustus) which, although it may be 50 feet long, becomes paralyzed with fear when confronted by a school of killer whales. At such times the gray whale will turn on its back, with flippers outstretched, and lie helpless at the surface.

Approaching its victim at high speed, a killer whale will put its nose against its victim's lips, force the mouth open, and gouge out great chunks of the soft, spongelike tongue. At the same time, other killer whales are tearing at the giant body and literally eating the victim whale alive.

In captivity, the killer whale often displays strong affection for humans and great intelligence.

........................

# THE LARGEST ANIMAL
## Blue Whale

**The blue whale (Balaenoptera musculus) is the largest animal that has ever lived, exceeding even the biggest dinosaurs.** The largest accurately measured specimen on record was a female landed at an Argentine Whaling Station, South Georgia, in 1912 that was 110 feet 2½ inches long.

Another female, measuring 96 feet 9 inches, brought into the shore station at Prince Olaf, South Georgia, around 1931, was calculated to weigh 163.7 tons, exclusive of blood, judging by the number of cookers that were filled by the animal's blubber, meat, and bones. The total weight of this whale was believed to be 174 tons.

In November 1947 a weight of 190 tons was reported for a 90-foot 9-inch blue whale weighed piecemeal by the Russians during the first cruise of the Slava whaling fleet in the Antarctic, but this figure was a misprint and should have read 140 tons.

On the principle that the weight should vary as the cube of linear dimensions, a 100-foot blue whale in good condition should weigh about 160 tons, but in the case of pregnant females, the weight could be as much as 190 to 200 tons, equivalent to the weight of thirty-five African elephants.

The blue whale is one of the eight species of great whales that have become rare and endangered due to relentless hunting over the years by humans. It is listed on the United States World List as an endangered species.

KILLER WHALE.

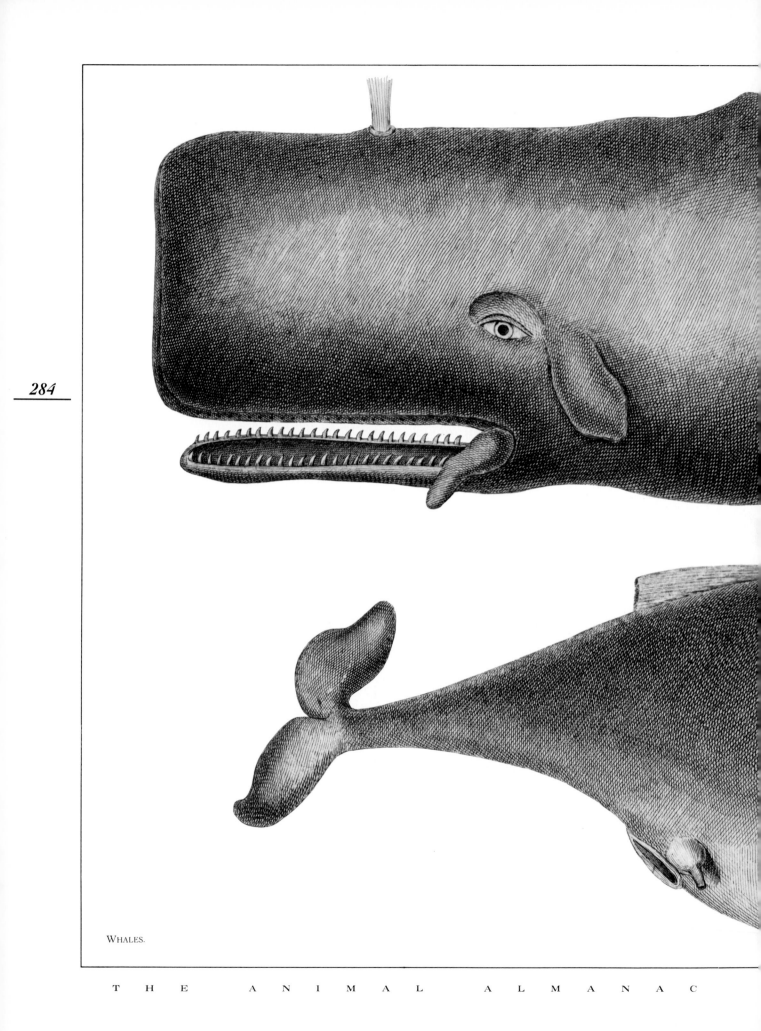

WHALES.

## ECHO-LOCATION
### *Dolphins*

**In the underwater world of the dolphin, dependence on vision, except at close range, would be inefficient and ineffective; consequently, the dolphin has come to depend on echo-location.** They are able to locate objects by bouncing sound waves off them, in much the same way that people use electronic equipment in antisubmarine warfare, under the name of *sonar*.

While swimming, a dolphin emits a steady clicking sound, whose frequency increases when it is approaching an object. The returning clicks indicate to the dolphin the direction in which the object is traveling, and its distance away. In 1961, marine biologist Kenneth Norris blindfolded a dolphin and had it swim through a maze of thin threads and wires. Miraculously, the dolphin was able to detect and avoid the threads, some of which were only 0.2 mm in diameter.

Although these high-frequency sounds cannot be detected by human ears, they can, apparently, be felt under certain circumstances. Don C. Reed, chief diver at Marine World/ Africa U.S.A. in San Francisco, said that when swimming among dolphins with the hood of his wet suit down and his neck uncovered, he felt "featherlike touches" on the back of his neck. Other divers in the company of dolphins have experienced similar sensations.

Other animals are known to use sonar. Bats are perhaps the best-known users of this system, but echo-location is also used by whales, certain seals, hippopotamuses, several birds (most notably, the oil-bird) and possibly by rats, shrews, and penguins.

BOTTLE-NOSE DOLPHIN.

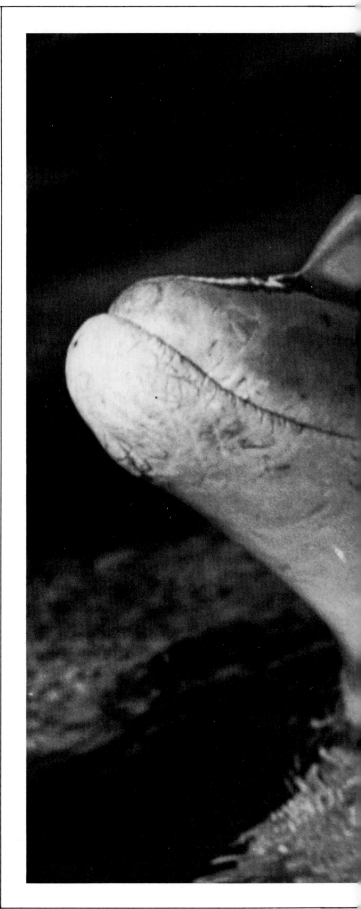

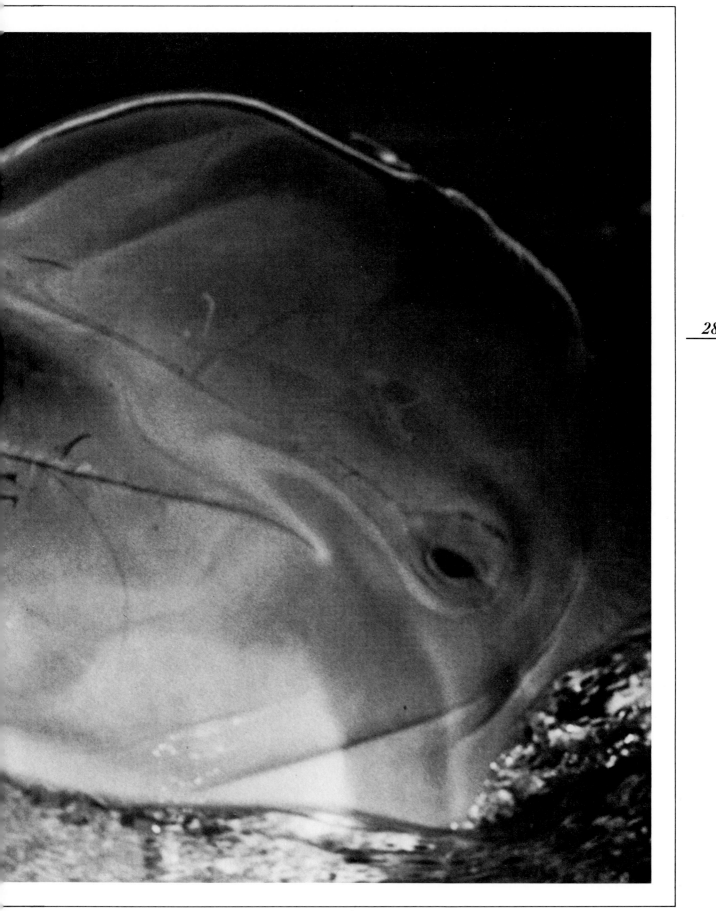

# December

As the earth turns its northern pole furthest from the sun, the bitter weather that comes with December darkness imposes its greatest demands on North American wildlife. Like people, most of the animals in the temperate and arctic regions—from bears, to rodents, to reptiles, and even to insects—direct their thoughts to shelter and are now inclined toward long winter naps. With the harvest of a fruitful summer stored away—in the fat of their bodies and in the hoards of nuts, seeds, or honey—most animals can retreat from the cold without fear of hunger or starvation.

Other creatures, especially those with hooves, are now obliged to face active but trying times. Deer, elk, moose, caribou, bison, sheep, antelope, goats, and others travel along seemingly endless tracks within millions of acres of forests, plains, and mountains.

During the ten days between Christmas and New Year's Day, lovers of the outdoors can celebrate by joining the Christmas bird count. Annually, thousands of bird watchers conduct an extensive count of thousands of species of birds in order to study the fluctuations in bird population from year to year.

BEAVER
CUTTING DOWN TREE.

# DECEMBER

**1**

Virgin Islands National Park established in 1956.

. . . . . . . . . . . .

**2**

Largest alligator gar (279 pounds) caught with rod and line taken in the Rio Grande River, Texas, in 1951.

WOLF.

**6**

Margaret Morse Nice, noted ornithologist, born in Amherst, Massachusetts, in 1883.

. . . . . . . . . . . .

**7**

Last authenticated sighting of a black-footed ferret in Canada in 1937.

**8**

14 men determined to save the American bison met in the Lion House of the New York Zoological Society's Bronx Zoo and organized the American Bison Society in 1905.

. . . . . . . . . . . .

**9**

Xerces Society founded in 1971, to preserve endan-

gered insects and their habitats.

Petrified Forest National Park, Arizona, established in 1962.

. . . . . . . . . . . .

**10**

A fin whale (4,900 pounds, 22 feet long) beached itself at Cape Henlopen, Delaware, in 1973. It died the same day.

. . . . . . . . . . . .

**12**

Last reported Labrador duck shot over Long Island, New York, in 1872.

. . . . . . . . . . . .

**24**

European jacksnipe first reported in North America at Makkovik Bay, Labrador, in 1927.

BISON.

## 25

Christmas Bird Count begun by Frank M. Chapman, renowned ornithologist and editor of *Bird Lore*, in 1900.

. . . . . . . . . . . .

## 27

Charles Darwin set sail on the *Beagle* for South America and the Galapagos Islands in 1831.

## 28

President Richard M. Nixon signed the Endangered Species Act into law in 1973.

LONGNOSED GAR.

## 29

Possibly the only authenticated report of a wolf attack on a human in North America occurred near Poulin, Ontario, Canada, in 1942. The animal was believed to be rabid.

Biologist Edmund Jaeger discovered the first hibernating poor-will in 1946.

. . . . . . . . . . . .

## 31

According to local tradition the last herd of eastern bison was wiped out in 1799 near the present town of Weikeot in Union County, Pennsylvania.

## THE ANIMAL THAT LAUNCHED A FUR INDUSTRY
### *Beaver*

It is difficult to believe that an animal as abundant as the beaver (*Castor canadensis*) could once have been close to extinction.

Many North American mammals have suffered from the effects of the early fur trade, though no species, with the exception of the bison, was as greatly affected as the beaver by hunting and trapping. Peter Matthiessen in *Wildlife in America* (Penguin, 1978) states that: Exploited from the outset for its rich dense fur, the beaver started to decline in North America as early as 1638, when the compulsory use of its fur in the manufacture of hats was decreed by King Charles I.

Fashionable Europeans demanded felt hats, and the soft beaver fur resulted in the most luxurious felt of all. Because the process of felt making involved large amounts of mercury, many hatters were literally mad, their brains addled by mercury poisoning.

Hats varied considerably in size and shape: Some hats were tall, some squat, and others drooping. For several decades the demand for beaver fur remained strong as fur trappers spread across the continent, seeking fresh supplies as old ones diminished. This preference for beaver fur lasted for 200 years, which makes the beaver the best example of a fur-bearing animal whose numbers were drastically affected by human exploitation.

The history of the fur trade in North America is essentially a history of the beaver.

Up to 17,000 beaver pelts a year were taken to be sold in London and Edinburgh, most being used to make felt for hats. Generally speaking, the cooler the climate, the richer the fur. Prime beaver pelts are found where the average yearly temperature is below 35 degrees Fahrenheit.

Trapping became more and more effective with the use of steel traps. By 1812 beavers were scarce everywhere east of the Rocky Mountains, although they were still plentiful west of that region. However, there too trapping would later reduce their numbers. About 153,000 pelts were collected annually between 1860 and 1870. Shortly after the turn of the century, beavers also became very scarce in the west because of trapping and settlement.

Over much of the continent the big rodent had become extirpated. Many large regions were completely without beavers during most of the first half of this century. Had the French and Italian stylists not shifted their interest to the silk hat, the beaver might well have followed the great auk and the Steller's sea cow to a human-made oblivion.

......................

## CHRISTMAS BIRD COUNT

Most bird watchers get their first chance to make a contribution to science by taking part in a bird census. For bird watchers, the chief census is the annual Audubon Christmas Bird Count.

The Christmas Count was started in 1900 by the famous ornithologist Frank M. Chapman as a substitute for the Christmas Hunt, then a popular holiday pastime. The popularity of this Christmas census has greatly exceeded expectations and is now operating in virtually every state and province in North America and Mexico, including all Central American countries, the West Indies, and the northern rim (Caribbean side) of South America.

Since 1900, when the first census attracted 27 bird watchers in 25 small areas, the Christmas Bird Count has expanded to more than 1,275 counts throughout North America, with more than 30,000 participants. Such massive participation has re-

BEAVER CUTTING DOWN TREE.

sulted in tallies of more than 120 million birds in a single counting season.

The immediate purpose of the census is to count every bird found within a given area on one day within a ten-day period that includes Christmas and New Year's Day. During one 24-hour period, participants count as completely as possible all birds within a 30-mile radius of a specific point. There is no limit to the number of participants in a count; in some areas 100 persons now participate. The entire area is divided into sections and a team of counters is assigned to comb each section thoroughly.

The 83rd Christmas Bird Count (for the winter of 1982-1983) represents the efforts of 36,426 observers who recorded a total of 93,963,639 birds in 1,453 counts. One of the highlights of this count was the number of alcids reported on the north Atlantic coast. Thick-billed murres figured in 13 counts, while dovekies were noted in 21. St. Anthony, Newfoundland, recorded the greatest number, with 13,713 thick-billed murres, 9,720 dovekies, and 585 black guillemots in day-long gale-force winds.

Here is the result of the 83rd Audubon Christmas Bird Count for the Brooklyn-Long Island region of New York. The 111 species and 97,283 individuals are given in order of numbers observed:

| | |
|---|---:|
| Herring gull | 59,501 |
| Great black-backed gull | 9,269 |
| Ring-billed gull | 4,639 |
| Brant | 3,750 |
| Starling | 3,080 |
| Black duck | 2,525 |
| Canvasback | 1,787 |
| Greater scaup | 1,705 |
| Rock dove | 1,291 |
| Bonaparte's gull | 1,221 |
| Canada goose | 1,120 |
| Yellow-rumped warbler | 841 |
| Bufflehead | 818 |
| American wigeon | 558 |
| Ruddy duck | 473 |
| Mallard | 419 |
| House sparrow | 361 |
| Mourning dove | 314 |
| Dunlin | 270 |
| Sanderling | 257 |
| Snow bunting | 230 |

| | |
|---|---:|
| Red-breasted merganser | 223 |
| White-throated sparrow | 208 |
| House finch | 185 |
| Red-winged blackbird | 156 |
| Brown-headed cowbird | 154 |
| Snow-goose (white race) | 152 |
| Song sparrow | 140 |
| Dark-eyed junco | 125 |
| Common crow | 122 |
| Shoveler | 105 |
| Blue jay | 74 |
| Cardinal | 70 |
| Tufted titmouse | 65 |
| Gadwall | 62 |

SHOVELLER DUCK.

MERGANSER DUCK.

| | | | |
|---|---:|---|---:|
| Cormorant | 30 | Greater white-footed goose | 1 |
| White-breasted nuthatch | 28 | Red-shouldered hawk | 1 |
| Purple finch | 25 | Peregrine falcon | 1 |
| Downy woodpecker | 24 | Clapper rail | 1 |
| Red-breasted nuthatch | 22 | Common snipe | 1 |
| American goldfinch | 22 | Red knot | 1 |
| Marsh hawk | 21 | Iceland gull | 1 |
| American coot | 20 | Common merganser | 1 |
| Black-hooded parakeet | 17 | Saw-whet owl | 1 |
| Purple sandpiper | 17 | Hairy woodpecker | 1 |
| Savannah sparrow | 14 | Ruby-crowned kinglet | 1 |
| American kestrel | 13 | Orange-crowned warbler | 1 |
| Short-eared owl | 13 | Palm warbler | 1 |
| Common grackle | 12 | Sharp-tailed sparrow | 1 |
| Common goldeneye | 11 | | |
| Bald eagle | 11 | | |
| Great blue heron | 11 | | |
| Black-crowned night heron | 11 | | |
| Bobwhite | 10 | | |
| White-winged scoter | 10 | | |
| White-crowned sparrow | 7 | | |
| Pied-billed grebe | 7 | | |
| Red-tailed hawk | 7 | | |
| Fish crow | 7 | | |
| Sharp-shinned hawk | 6 | | |
| Killdeer | 5 | | |
| Rough-legged hawk | 4 | | |
| Field sparrow | 4 | | |
| Greater yellowlegs | 4 | | |
| Laughing gull | 4 | | |
| Belted kingfisher | 4 | | |
| Brown creeper | 4 | | |
| Common loon | 3 | | |
| Gannet | 3 | | |
| Snowy egret | 3 | | |
| Goshawk | 3 | | |
| Barn owl | 3 | | |
| Eastern meadowlark | 3 | | |
| Red-necked grebe | 2 | | |
| Pintail | 2 | | |
| Redhead | 2 | | |
| Cooper's hawk | 2 | | |
| Black-bellied plover | 2 | | |
| Monk parakeet | 2 | | |
| Cedar waxwing | 2 | | |
| Rusty blackbird | 2 | | |
| Rufous-sided towhee | 2 | | |
| Savannah sparrow (Ipswich race) | 2 | | |
| Red-throated loon | 1 | | |
| Green heron | 1 | | |

Participants: Berry Baker, Walter Berger, Jean and Ronald Bourke, Barbara Bromfield, Irving and Jean Cantor, Lee Cohen, Marie and Paul Cohen, Eileen Conyers, Bob Cook, Jerry Digen, Jean Dorman, Harry Gavers, George and Henry Karsch, Judy Katz, Roy Leaf, Jose Machado, Bob Marvin, Jay Pituccheli, John Plummer, Fritz Polatsek, Oscar and Ruth Posner, Peter Post, A. and G. Roberts, Richard Rosenblum, Jonathan Rosenthal, Maurice Russak, Starr Saphir, Sy Schiff, Marge Searles, Jane Shumsky, David Simon, Martin Sohoner, Bill Starika, Tim Styles, Esther Swayer, Robert Wade, Gill Wald, Will Wilkens, George Wood, and John Yrizarry (compiler).

Anyone wishing to participate in a Christmas Bird Count should write to: AMERICAN BIRDS, 950 Third Avenue, New York, N.Y. 10022.

. . . . . . . . . . . . . . . . . . . . . . .

# THE WINTER SLEEP OF ANIMALS

**W**inter in the temperate and extremely cold areas of our continent is a hard time for wild animals. People provide food and shelter for themselves and their domestic animals, but the creatures of the wild must fend for themselves.

Although some birds remain with us during the cooler weather, most species migrate to warmer climes. But land-bound animals are not able to get away and must meet the problems of winter as best they can. Many temperate-climate mammals are active all winter, but others go into a sort of sleep and are often not seen again until the spring.

HIBERNATING CHIPMUNK.

Such animals are said to hibernate (from the Latin verb *hibernare*, meaning "to pass the winter").

If a hibernating animal is taken from its wintering place, it is found to be cold and stiff and at first glance appears to be dead. Closer examination reveals that it is breathing but at a very slow rate. Most hibernating animals do not remain asleep throughout the winter but are for some of the time in a partial stupor in which they are warm to the touch. They may even wake up completely and emerge from their dens to take food and drink before retiring again for another period of hibernation.

The groundhog (*Marmota monax*) spends the winter in a deep underground burrow. It enters hibernation rather slowly in a series of progressively drowsy stages extending over several days. When it is in complete hibernation, its heartbeat is 95 percent slower than normal, its breathing is 96 percent slower than normal, and its temperature drops to 37 or 38 degrees Fahrenheit. Waking is a far more rapid process and may occur if the animal is disturbed to any extent. The breathing, heartbeat, and temperature all rise rather dramatically, and within a few hours the animal is totally awake.

Groundhogs are occasionally seen in January during some milder days of winter, but generally they do not emerge from their burrows until March. Hoary marmots (*Marmota caligata*), the western mountain species that live near the foot of the mountain, retire earlier than those that live in the higher, colder areas. The time of going into hibernation is probably determined less by temperature than by the physical state of the animal. Marmots do not hibernate until they have accumulated a store of fat.

The meadow jumping mouse (*Zapus hudsonius*)

GROUNDHOG.

hibernates in a leaf-lined nest 2 or 3 feet underground. This species enters hibernation during the fall and doesn't reappear until the warm days of spring—which probably makes this small mammal our most complete hibernator.

The chipmunk (*Tamias* sp.) retires into its burrow for the winter, but some doubt exists about the completeness of its sleep. Unlike most hibernating creatures, the chipmunk stores up food in its burrow for the harsh winter ahead. It is probable, therefore, that this animal is awake and active some of the time and partially or completely asleep at other times.

The striped skunk (*Mephitis mephitis*) dens up for the winter in a deep underground burrow, while the raccoon (*Procyon lotor*) prefers a hollow tree. Both appear to be light sleepers and awaken readily, usually emerging quite a few times during the winter.

The black bear (*Ursus americanus*) has long been considered the ideal example of a hibernating animal, but this may be somewhat of a misconception. It is very doubtful that a bear ever hibernates as completely as the groundhog or the chipmunk. A bear may use a cave or a hollow log, or claw itself a space under an upturned root for its winter quarters; or it may simply lie down under a tree and, there, pass into a hibernating stupor. If disturbed, a bear may leave its winter quarters and seek a new den. In common with most hibernating animals, bears are likely to awaken several times before finally emerging in the spring.

Like the chipmunk, many nonhibernating animals, such as the beaver (*Castor canadensis*) and the red squirrel (*Tamiasciurus hudsonicus*), also store up winter food supplies. The beaver stores pieces of trees under water where it can get to them whenever ice covers the pond, and the red squirrel stores nuts and seeds in hollow trees or logs. Squirrels frequently have many such storehouses. Both species are active throughout the winter, although they may remain in their nests for long periods when the weather is unusually cold.

Reptiles and amphibians also pass the winter in an inactive state. Snakes go underground. Turtles and frogs take shelter in mud at the bottom of ponds or beneath moss and leaves. These animals differ from mammals in that they are coldblooded, which means that their temperature is the same as the air or water around them. In summer, when the atmosphere is warm, their bodies are also warm, but when the cooler weather approaches, their bodies become so cold that they are unable to move. Before this happens, reptiles and amphibians must retire to places where they are not exposed to the elements. There they pass the winter in an inactive state until the warm weather returns.

Mammals and birds, being warmblooded, are able to regulate their own temperatures, which enables them to be active throughout the year. Mammals that hibernate, therefore, are behaving somewhat like reptiles, in that the temperature of their bodies falls far below their normal temperatures.

Insects hibernate in all stages of development. Some hibernate as eggs, some as young larvae, full-grown larvae, pupae, and adults. Insects will seek out any sheltered and safe retreat to spend the winter months. The soil is an ideal place for hibernation, since insects can descend below the frost line, or at least below the line of critical temperature, and are safe from most predators. When moisture exists in the soil, the temperature of the surrounding area rises and gives added protection against frost. Low temperatures are without doubt the all-important element in inducing hibernation in insects. The boll weevil (*Anthonomus grandis*) begins to hibernate when the mean temperature reaches 55 degrees Fahrenheit. The weevil hibernates in the larval, pupal, or adult stage, as is the case with all related groups of this insect.

Perhaps the best-known and most striking form of insect hibernation is that of the giant silk moths (family Saturniidae). The larvae of these large moths spin thick cocoons around themselves, usually wrapping the cocoons in a leaf or two and attaching themselves to their respective food trees. The thickness of the silken cocoon gives adequate protection against frost but, alas, not always from the beaks of hungry birds.

The cocoons of the luna moth (*Tropaea luna*), polyphemus (*Telea polyphemus*), and cecropia (*Hyalophora cecropia*) are perhaps those most commonly seen in most parts of the continent. Often, the polyphemus cocoon falls to the ground from its attachment. The cecropia cocoon is especially noticeable because it is attached lengthwise to a twig and is the largest cocoon of all the insects.

# December Reading

## ABUNDANT DEER

**The aptness of the name "white-tail" for the Virginia deer (*Odocoileus virginianus*) is obvious to anyone who has startled a deer in the forest**. Off it goes into the woods with leaps of 15 to 20 feet, its tail upright, flashing white danger signals at every jump. Nature has given it marvelous hearing and scent to protect it from enemies, but its eyesight is not the best. It seems to regard all motionless objects downwind as features of the landscape.

The adults have two strongly contrasted coats each year, brownish gray in the winter and reddish brown in the summer. The red pelage is conspicuous, but the deer depends on the heavy foliage to protect it from sight. During the winter when the trees are bare, the countershaded dark body blends perfectly with the bushes and branches. The spotted coat of the fawn and its deathlike stillness are wonderful safeguards. The baby is left in the forest cover for a month or more by the mother and hardly moves during that time.

The deer that inhabit the north face grave danger during the winter, for the heavy snows make food scarce and travel difficult. Their small, sharp hooves and slim legs sink deep into the snow with each step. Instinct, however, provides deer with a way to obtain food

BLACK-TAILED DEER.

WHITE-TAILED BUCKS.

under these adverse conditions. They gather together in parties in dense growth where food is plentiful, remaining throughout the season and forming a "yard" by keeping a network of hard-beaten paths over the snow in order to reach the leaves on which they feed.

The white-tailed deer is as abundant today as it was at the time of the colonization of this continent. This is eloquent testimony to the safeguards nature has given them.

## SUCCESSFUL INVADERS
### *Coyotes*

**The coyote or brush wolf (*Canis latrans*) has embarked on one of the most remarkable range extensions on this continent; it has traveled toward the Atlantic Coast through Illinois, Indiana, Ohio, Pennsylvania, and even New Jersey.** Coyotes from Minnesota have also headed east through Michigan toward Maine, southern Ontario, and New York at an average rate of about 16 miles a year.

Partly because the adaptable coyote coexists so successfully with humans, there seems to be little limit to its expansion. Coyotes are natural wanderers anyway and are known to travel up to 40 or 50 miles in one night. Overpopulation in the existing range and the availability of new habitats, such as those created by farming practices that draw mice and other rodents, are among the reasons cited for the animal's eastward movement. Some biologists even suggest that the coyote has moved in to fill the niche left by vanishing wolves.

Eastern coyotes are larger than their western counterparts and may weigh more than 50 pounds. Most likely, they picked up wolf genes in Ontario and mated with domestic or wild dogs elsewhere.

In the considered opinion of many investigators, the normal food habits of most coyotes are more beneficial than harmful, but villainous habits are occasionally developed by individuals. Unhappily, the death of an infant girl in California can be directly attributed to a coyote attack outside the child's home.

The coyote problem is, however, usually a local one, and although it can be serious, it should probably not be taken as an excuse to persecute the entire coyote clan. Coyotes not only make a considerable contribution to the control of harmful rodents, they are also important scavengers. The scavenger role is especially noteworthy in protected overcrowded refuges, where starvation takes its toll of deer and other game animals.

*301*

## THE BIG BAD WOLF?

**Traditionally, wolves have been held in ill repute, and attitudes toward them have been mostly negative.** Early settlers feared for their lives because they were often in close proximity to these animals as they worked their small farms hacked out of the wilderness. The lonely, mournful howl of the wolf instilled fear in even the most stout-hearted pioneer.

Recently, attitudes have begun to change, as people realize that wolves are not a threat to their personal safety and are only rarely a threat to their livestock. There is no authenticated case of a timber wolf (*Canis lupus*) seriously harming a human in North America. The incidence of rabies among wolves is extremely low. Only one attack on a human by a rabid wolf has been reported — and the man was not bitten or seriously hurt. Workers who trap and tag wolves find it unnecessary to drug the animals during tagging operations and never carry firearms, which demonstrates that wolves are not savage.

Today people realize that wolves have positive value and should remain an integral part of our fauna in large parks and wilderness areas. In Michigan's Isle Royale National Park and in Ontario's Algonquin Provincial Park, wolves are a major tourist attraction; many people travel hundreds of miles in the hopes of hearing or seeing a wolf. Tape-recorded wolf howls, or human imitations of wolf howls, are used to elicit responses from wild wolves. This participation of wolf howlers is most popular, and interest continues to grow as more people take the opportunity to listen to wild wolves.

# *APPENDIX*
# I

## CLASSIFICATION OF INVERTEBRATE ANIMALS

This list comprises the Arthropods frequently seen on land or in fresh water.

*Phylum Arthropoda — Arthropods*

*Subphylum Invertebrata — Invertebrates*

*Class Crustacea — Crustaceans*

Order Branchiopoda — Fairy shrimps and water fleas

Order Copepoda — Copepods

Order Ostracoda — Ostracods

Order Amphipoda — Beach fleas and sand fleas

Order Isopoda — Sowbugs and pillbugs

Order Decapoda — Lobsters, crayfish, crabs, and shrimps

*Class Diplopoda — Millipedes*

*Class Chilopoda — Centipedes*

*Class Symphyla — Symphilids* (rarely seen)

*Class Tardigrada — Waterbears and tardigrades* (rarely seen)

*Class Arachnida — Spiders*

Order Scorpionia — Scorpions

Order Chelonethida —
Pseudoscorpions

Order Phalangida — Harvestmen and daddy-longlegs

Order Acarina — Mites, ticks, and chiggers

Order Araneida — Spiders (Tarantulas)

*Class Insecta — Insects*

Order Thysanura — Bristletails, silverfish, and firebrats

Order Collembola — Springtails and snow-fleas

Order Ephemeroptera — Mayflies

Order Odonata — Dragonflies and damselflies

Order Orthoptera — Grasshoppers, locusts, katydids, crickets, mantids, walking sticks, and cockroaches

Order Isoptera — Termites

Order Plecoptera — Stoneflies

Order Dermaptera — Earwigs

Order Psocoptera — Psocids, booklice, and barklice

Order Mallophaga — Chewing lice and biting lice

Order Anoplura — Sucking lice

Order Thysanoptera — Thrips

Order Hemiptera — Cicadas, froghoppers, treehoppers, leafhoppers, aphids, plant lice, white-flies, and scale insects

Order Neuroptera — Lacewings, ant lions, dobsonflies, and alderflies

Order Coleoptera — Beetles and weevils

Order Strepsiptera — Twisted-winged insects (rarely seen)

Order Mecoptera — Scorpionflies

Order Trichoptera — Caddisflies

Order Lepidoptera — Butterflies and moths

Order Diptera — True flies, midges, mosquitoes, gnats, and sheepticks

Order Siphonaptera — Fleas

Order Hymenoptera — Bees, ants, wasps, hornets, sawflies, horntails, ichneumons, chalcids, and braconids.

## CLASSIFICATION OF VERTEBRATE ANIMALS

This classification system is widely used and is one of many available.

*Subphylum Vertebrata — Vertebrates*

*Class Agnatha — Jawless Vertebrates*

*Class Placodermi — Placoderms* (extinct)

*Class Chondrichthyes — Cartilaginous fish* (Sharks, rays)

*Class Osteichthyes — Bony fish*

*Class Amphibia —*
*Amphibians*

*Class Reptilia — Reptiles*

*Class Aves — Birds*

*Class Mammalia — Mammals*

*Subclass Prothotheria — Marsupials*

*Subclass Eutheria — Placental mammals*

Order Insectivora — Moles, shrews, and others

Order Dermoptera — Flying lemurs
Order Chiroptera — Bats
Order Primates — Monkeys, apes, and humans
Order Pholidota — Pangolins
Order Lagomorpha — Rabbits and hares
Order Rodentia — Rodents
Order Cetacea — Whales, dolphins, and porpoises
Order Carnivora — Carnivores
Order Tubulidentata — Aardvark
Order Proboscidea — Elephants
Order Hyracoidea — Coneys or rock rabbits
Order Sirenia — Sea cows (Manatees and dugongs)
Order Perissodactyla — Odd-toed ungulates (Horses, rhinoceroses)
Order Artiodactyla — Even-toed ungulates (Cows, deer, pigs)

# MAMMALS OF NORTH AMERICA

It is believed that mammals first made their appearance on the earth 180 million to 190 million years ago, at a time when our planet was dominated by reptiles.

The first mammalian features, however, were exhibited in lizardlike reptiles known as pelycosaurs, which date back 280 million years or more, long before the evolution of true mammals. Although not necessarily the direct ancestors of modern-day mammals, pelycosaurs were among the first creatures to display early mammalian features. Instead of having uniform teeth as in other reptiles, many pelycosaurs had front teeth approaching mammalian incisors; behind these were large canines comparable to the molars and premolars of mammals.

The age of the true mammals didn't occur until some 60 million years ago, after the descendants of mammal-like reptiles began to assert their preeminence. This dates them to the Pleistocene period, which is regarded as the first epoch in the Age of Mammals, from 63 million to 58 million years ago.

It is impossible to know with any certainty what the first mammals were, or what they looked like, but they are believed to have been small, shrewlike creatures, probably nocturnal, arboreal insect-eaters.

One possible candidate for earliest mammal is melanodon, which lived in North America about 160 million years ago, and whose remains are among the oldest-known mammalian fossils. Paleontologists suspect that melanodon might well have been the ancestor of all modern mammals, but nothing is known about its history.

About 4,230 mammal species exist today, and 461 mammalian species and subspecies are known to occur in North America.

Virginia opossum
Masked shrew
Pribilof shrew
Mount Lyell shrew
Carmen Mountain shrew
Southeastern shrew
Vagrant shrew
Ornate shrew
Inyo shrew
Ashland shrew
Dwarf shrew
Tule shrew
Suisun shrew
Large-toothed shrew
Water shrew
Glacier Bay water shrew
Pacific water shrew
Smoky shrew
Arctic shrew
Gaspé shrew
Long-tailed shrew
Trowbridge's shrew
Merriam's shrew
Saussure's shrew
Mexican long-tailed shrew
Pygmy shrew
Short-tailed shrew
Southern short-tailed shrew
Swamp short-tailed shrew
Least shrew
Mexican small-eared shrew
Goldman's small-eared shrew
Desert shrew
Shrew-mole
Townsend's mole
Coast mole
Broad-footed mole
Hairy-tailed mole
Eastern mole
Star-nosed mole
Leaf-chinned bat
California leaf-nosed bat
Hog-nosed bat
Mexican long-nosed bat
Sanborn's long-nosed bat
Hairy fruit-eating bat

Highland fruit-eating bat
Common vampire bat
Hairy-legged vampire bat
Greater funnel-eared bat
Little brown myotis
Yuma myotis
Southeastern myotis
Gray myotis
Cave myotis
Keen's myotis
Long-eared myotis
Miller's myotis
Southwestern myotis
Fringed myotis
Indiana myotis
Long-legged myotis
California myotis
Small-footed myotis
Flat-headed myotis
Mexican fishing bat
Silver-haired bat
Western pipistrelle
Eastern pipistrelle
Big brown bat
Red bat
Seminole bat
Hoary bat
Northern yellow bat
Southern yellow bat
Evening bat
Allen's yellow bat
Spotted bat
Mexican big-eared bat
Townsend's big-eared bat
Rafinesque's big-eared bat
Allen's big-eared bat
Pallid bat
Mexican free-tailed bat
Pocketed free-tailed bat
Big free-tailed bat
Western mastiff bat
Underwood's mastiff bat
Wagner's mastiff bat
Nine-banded armadillo
Pika
Volcano rabbit
Pygmy rabbit

BEAVER.

Brush rabbit
Marsh rabbit
Eastern cottontail
New England cottontail
Nuttall's cottontail
Desert cottontail
Swamp rabbit
Snowshoe hare
Alaskan hare
Arctic hare
White-tailed jackrabbit
Black-tailed jackrabbit
White-sided jackrabbit
Antelope jackrabbit
Mountain beaver
Eastern chipmunk
Alpine chipmunk
Least chipmunk

Yellow-pine chipmunk
Townsend's chipmunk
Yellow-cheeked chipmunk
Allen's chipmunk
Siskiyou chipmunk
Sonoma chipmunk
Merriam's chipmunk
Cliff chipmunk
Colorado chipmunk
Red-tailed chipmunk
Gray-collared chipmunk
Long-eared chipmunk
Lodgepole chipmunk
Panamint chipmunk
Uinta chipmunk
Palmer's chipmunk
Buller's chipmunk
Woodchuck or groundhog

Yellow-bellied marmot
Hoary marmot
Olympic marmot
Vancouver Island marmot
Harris' antelope squirrel
White-tailed antelope
　squirrel
Texas antelope squirrel
Nelson's antelope squirrel
Townsend's ground
　squirrel
Washington ground
　squirrel
Idaho ground squirrel
Richardson's ground
　squirrel
Uinta ground squirrel
Belding's ground squirrel

Columbian ground squirrel
Arctic ground squirrel
Thirteen-lined ground
　squirrel
Mexican ground squirrel
Spotted ground squirrel
Perote ground squirrel
Franklin's ground squirrel
Rock squirrel
California ground squirrel
Baja California rock
　squirrel
Mohave ground squirrel
Round-tailed ground
　squirrel
Golden-mantled ground
　squirrel
Cascade golden-mantled

ground squirrel
Sierra Madre mantled
  ground squirrel
Black-tailed prairie dog
Mexican prairie dog
White-tailed prairie dog
Utah prairie dog
Gunnison's prairie dog
Gray squirrel
Mexican gray squirrel
Collie's squirrel
Western gray squirrel
Abert's squirrel
Fox squirrel
Peters' squirrel
Allen's squirrel
Nayarit squirrel
Arizona gray squirrel
Red squirrel
Douglas' squirrel
Southern flying squirrel
Northern flying squirrel
Southern pocket gopher
Northern pocket gopher
Western pocket gopher
Mountain pocket gopher
Camas pocket gopher
Michoacan pocket gopher
Plains pocket gopher
Desert pocket gopher
Texas pocket gopher
Southeastern pocket
  gopher
Colonial pocket gopher
Sherman's pocket gopher
Cumberland pocket
  gopher
Buller's pocket gopher
Alcorn's pocket gopher
Yellow-faced pocket
  gopher
Merriam's pocket gopher
Queretaro pocket gopher
Smoky pocket gopher
Taylor's pocket gopher
Zinser's pocket gopher
Llano pocket gopher
Olive-backed pocket
  mouse
Plains pocket mouse
Great Basin pocket mouse
White-eared pocket mouse
Yellow-eared pocket
  mouse

Silky pocket mouse
Little pocket mouse
Arizona pocket mouse
San Joaquin pocket mouse
Long-tailed pocket mouse
Bailey's pocket mouse
Hispid pocket mouse
Desert pocket mouse
Little desert pocket mouse
Sinaloan pocket mouse
Rock pocket mouse
Nelson's pocket mouse
Goldman's pocket mouse
Narrow-skulled pocket
  mouse
Lined pocket mouse
San Diego pocket mouse
Anthony's pocket mouse
California pocket mouse
Spiny pocket mouse
Dark kangaroo mouse
Pale kangaroo mouse
Ord's kangaroo rat
Chisel-toothed kangaroo rat
Big-eared kangaroo rat
Narrow-faced kangaroo rat
Agile kangaroo rat
Heermann's kangaroo rat
Giant kangaroo rat
Panamint kangaroo rat
Stephens' kangaroo rat
San Quintin kangaroo rat
Banner-tailed kangaroo rat
Nelson's kangaroo rat
Texas kangaroo rat
Desert kangaroo rat
Phillips' kangaroo rat
Merriam's kangaroo rat
Fresno kangaroo rat
Painted spiny pocket
  mouse
Mexican spiny pocket
  mouse
Marsh rice rat
Silver rice rat
Plains harvest mouse
Sonoran harvest mouse
Eastern harvest mouse
Western harvest mouse
Salt marsh harvest mouse
Volcano harvest mouse
Sumichrast's harvest
  mouse
Fulvous harvest mouse

Hairy harvest mouse
Mexican harvest mouse
Cactus mouse
Desert mouse
Turner Island Canyon
  mouse
Angel Island mouse
Hooper's mouse
Merriam's mouse
California mouse
Deer mouse
Sitka mouse
Oldfield mouse
Black-eared mouse
White-footed mouse
Cotton mouse
Canyon mouse
Brush mouse
Texas mouse
White-ankled mouse
Chihuahuan mouse
San Esteban Island mouse
Southern wood mouse
Pinon mouse
Rock mouse
Plateau mouse
El Carrizo deer mouse
Blackish deer mouse
Jico deer mouse
Florida mouse
Golden mouse
Pygmy mouse
Northern grasshopper
  mouse
Southern grasshopper
  mouse
Hispid cotton rat
Jaliscan cotton rat
Arizona cotton rat
Tawny-bellied cotton rat
Allen's cotton rat
White-eared cotton rat
Yellow-nosed cotton rat
Volcano mouse
Eastern woodrat
Southern plains woodrat
White-throated woodrat
Nelson's woodrat
Bolanos woodrat
Turner Island woodrat
Desert woodrat
Bryant's woodrat
Anthony's woodrat
San Martin Island woodrat

Stephens' woodrat
Goldman's woodrat
Mexican woodrat
Tamaulipan woodrat
Dusky-footed woodrat
Bushy-tailed woodrat
Diminutive woodrat
Northern red-backed vole
Southern red-backed vole
California red-backed vole
Heather vole
White-footed vole
Red tree vole
Meadow vole
Beach vole
Gull Island vole (extinct)
Montane vole
Gray-tailed vole
California vole
Townsend's vole
Tundra vole
Long-tailed vole
Coronation Island vole
Mexican vole
Rock vole
Yellow-cheeked vole
Creeping vole
Insular vole
Prairie vole
Woodland vole
Jalapan pine vole
Singing vole
Water vole
Sagebrush vole
Round-tailed muskrat
Muskrat
Brown lemming
Southern bog lemming
Northern bog lemming
Collared lemming
St. Lawrence Island col-
  lared lemming
Labrador collared lemming
Meadow jumping mouse
Western jumping mouse
Pacific jumping mouse
Woodland jumping mouse
American porcupine
Baird's beaked whale
North Atlantic beaked
  whale
Tropical beaked whale
Gervais' beaked whale
True's beaked whale

DOLPHIN.

North Pacific beaked whale
Moore's beaked whale
Japanese beaked whale
Goose-beaked whale
Northern bottlenose whale
Sperm whale
Pygmy sperm whale
Dwarf sperm whale
Beluga
Narwhal
Spotted porpoise
Spinner dolphin
Striped porpoise
Rough-toothed porpoise
Common dolphin
Bottlenose dolphin
Gill's bottlenose dolphin
Northern right-whale dolphin
White-beaked dolphin
Atlantic white-sided dolphin
Pacific white-sided dolphin
Killer whale
Risso's dolphin
False killer whale
Long-finned pilot whale
Short-finned pilot whale
Pygmy killer whale
Harbor porpoise
Dall's porpoise
Gray whale
Fin whale
Sei whale
Minke whale
Bryde's whale
Blue whale
Humpback whale
Right whale
Bowhead
Coyote
Red wolf
Gray or timber wolf
Arctic fox
Red fox
Kit fox
Swift fox
Gray fox
Insular gray fox
Black bear
Grizzly or Alaskan brown bear
Polar bear

Ringtail
Raccoon
Coatimundi
Marten
Fisher
Ermine
Least weasel
Long-tailed weasel
Black-footed ferret
Mink
Sea mink (extinct)
Wolverine
American badger
Spotted skunk
Striped skunk
Hooded skunk
Hog-nosed skunk
Eastern hog-nosed skunk
River otter
Sea otter
Jaguar
Cougar
Ocelot
Margay
Jaguarundi
Canada lynx
Bobcat
Northern fur seal
Guadalupe fur seal
Northern sea lion
California sea lion
Walrus
Harbor seal
Ribbon seal
Ringed seal
Harp seal
Bearded seal
Gray seal
West Indian monk seal
Hooded seal
Northern elephant seal
Manatee
Collared peccary
Wapiti
Mule deer
White-tailed deer
Moose
Caribou
Pronghorn
Bison
Rocky Mountain goat
Muskox
Bighorn sheep
Dall's sheep

# BIRDS OF NORTH AMERICA

Fossil remains of the earliest-known bird were first discovered in Bavaria, West Germany, in 1861. Known as archaeopteryx, it is estimated to have lived 140 million years ago.

It looked so much like a reptile, with its well-developed teeth and long, lizardlike tail, that it would easily have passed for one, except for this important difference: The fossil clearly revealed that the wings bore feathers, a feature peculiar to birds.

Archaeopteryx wasn't like a modern bird, nor was it like a true reptile; in fact, it was a link between the two kinds of animals. Slightly larger than a crow, and almost totally reptilian except for the feathers, it could probably only glide from tree to tree.

It is known as an "ancestral" bird, which means that from this bird all others have descended. In due course, true birds evolved, such as hesperornis, an ancient form of loon, 4 or 5 feet long; and ichyornis, a small ternlike bird. Modern birds evolved, however, early in the Age of Mammals, 63 million to 36 million years ago, when primitive forms of ostriches, pelicans, herons, and ducks made their appearance.

Of all the higher animals living today, birds are undoubtedly the most beautiful and, except for fish, the most numerous. Yet the bird species that exist today are only a small fraction of the total number of bird species that have ever lived. It has been estimated that since archaeopteryx first took to the air, 1,634,000 different bird species may have existed.

Currently, between 8,700 and 8,900 bird species are known to exist worldwide, divided into 27 separate orders, with about 5,300 of these species being songbirds (Passeriiformes).

The American Ornithologists Union's checklist of North American birds (as of July 3, 1982) currently lists 927 species:

Red-throated loon
Arctic loon
Common loon
Yellow-billed loon
Least grebe
Pied-billed grebe
Horned grebe
Red-necked grebe
Eared grebe
Western grebe
Wandering albatross

Short-tailed albatross
Black-footed albatross
Laysan albatross
Shy albatross
Yellow-nosed albatross
Northern fulmar
Cape petrel
Black-capped petrel
Dark-rumped petrel
White-necked petrel
Mottled petrel

FLAMINGO.

Murphy's petrel
Kermadec petrel
Herald petrel
Cook's petrel
Bonin petrel
Black-winged petrel
Bulwer's petrel
Jouanin's petrel
Streaked shearwater
Cory's shearwater
Pink-footed shearwater
Flesh-footed shearwater
Greater shearwater
Wedge-tailed shearwater
Buller's shearwater
Sooty shearwater
Short-tailed shearwater
Christmas shearwater
Manx shearwater

Black-vented shearwater
Townsend's shearwater
Little shearwater
Audubon's shearwater
Wilson's storm-petrel
White-faced storm-petrel
British storm-petrel
Fork-tailed storm-petrel
Leach's storm-petrel
Ashy storm-petrel
Band-rumped storm-petrel
Wedge-rumped storm-
   petrel
Black storm-petrel
Guadalupe storm-petrel
Sooty storm-petrel
Least storm-petrel
White-tailed tropicbird
Red-billed tropicbird

Red-tailed tropicbird
Masked booby
Blue-footed booby
Red-footed booby
Northern gannet
American white pelican
Brown pelican
Great cormorant
Double-crested cormorant
Olivaceous cormorant
Brandt's cormorant
Pelagic cormorant
Red-faced cormorant
Anhinga
Magnificent frigatebird
Great frigatebird
Lesser frigatebird
American bittern
Least bittern
Great blue heron (incl.
   white phase)
Great egret
Chinese egret
Little egret
Snowy egret
Little blue heron
Tricolored heron
Reddish egret
Cattle egret
Green-backed heron
Black-crowned night heron
Yellow-crowned night
   heron
White ibis
Scarlet ibis
Glossy ibis
White-faced ibis
Roseate spoonbill
Jabiru
Wood stork
Greater flamingo
Fulvous whistling-duck
Black-bellied whistling-
   duck
Tundra swan
Whooper swan
Trumpeter swan
Mute swan
Bean goose
Pink-footed goose
Lesser white-fronted
   goose
Greater white-fronted
   goose

Snow goose
Ross's goose
Emperor goose
Brant
Barnacle goose
Canada goose
Hawaiian goose
Wood duck
Green-winged teal
Baikal teal
Falcated teal
American black duck
Mottled duck
Mallard
Hawaiian duck
Laysan duck
Spot-billed duck
White-cheeked pintail
Northern pintail
Garganey
Blue-winged teal
Cinnamon teal
Northern shoveler
Gadwall
Eurasian widgeon
American widgeon
Common pochard
Canvasback
Redhead
Ring-necked duck
Tufted duck
Greater scaup
Lesser scaup
Common eider
King eider
Spectacled eider
Steller's eider
Labrador duck (extinct)
Harlequin duck
Oldsquaw
Black scoter
Surf scoter
White-winged scoter
Common goldeneye
Barrow's goldeneye
Bufflehead
Smew
Hooded merganser
Common merganser
Red-breasted merganser
Ruddy duck
Masked duck
Black vulture
Turkey vulture

California condor
Hook-billed kite
Swallow-tailed kite
Black-shouldered kite
Everglades kite
Mississippi kite
Bald eagle
White-tailed eagle
Steller's sea eagle
Northern harrier
Sharp-shinned hawk
Cooper's hawk
Northern goshawk
Common black hawk
Harris' hawk
Gray hawk
Roadside hawk
Red-shouldered hawk
Broad-winged hawk
Short-tailed hawk
Swainson's hawk
White-tailed hawk
Zone-tailed hawk
Hawaiian hawk
Red-tailed hawk
Ferruginous hawk
Rough-legged hawk
Golden eagle
Crested caracara
Eurasian kestrel
American kestrel
Merlin
Aplomado falcon
Peregrine falcon
Gyrfalcon
Prairie falcon
Gray partridge
Black francolin
Erckel's francolin
Gray francolin
Chukar
Japanese quail
Kalij pheasant
Red junglefowl
Ring-necked pheasant
Spruce grouse
Blue grouse
Willow ptarmigan
Rock ptarmigan
White-tailed ptarmigan
Ruffed grouse
Sage grouse
Greater prairie chicken
Lesser prairie chicken

Sharp-tailed grouse
Wild turkey
Montezuma quail
Northern bobwhite
Scaled quail
Elegant quail
Gambel's quail
California quail
Mountain quail
Helmeted guineafowl
Yellow rail
Black rail
Corncrake
Clapper rail
King rail
Virginia rail
Sora
Hawaiian rail
Laysan rail
Paint-billed crake
Spotted rail
Purple gallinule
Common moorhen
Eurasian coot
American coot
Limpkin
Sandhill crane
Common crane
Whooping crane
Double-striped thick-knee
Lapwing
Black-bellied plover
Greater golden plover
Lesser golden plover
Mongolian plover
Snowy plover
Wilson's plover
Ringed plover
Semipalmated plover
Piping plover
Little ringed plover
Killdeer
Mountain plover
Dotterel
American oystercatcher
American black oyster-
    catcher
Black-necked stilt
American avocet
Northern jacana
Greenshank
Greater yellowlegs
Lesser yellowlegs
Marsh sandpiper

Spotted redshank
Wood sandpiper
Solitary sandpiper
Willet
Wandering tattler
Gray-tailed tattler
Common sandpiper
Spotted sandpiper
Terek sandpiper
Upland sandpiper
Eskimo curlew
Whimbrel
Bristle-thighed curlew
Slender-billed curlew
Far East curlew
Eurasian curlew
Long-billed curlew
Black-tailed godwit
Hudsonian godwit
Bar-tailed godwit
Marbled godwit
Ruddy turnstone
Black turnstone
Surfbird
Great knot
Red knot
Sanderling
Semipalmated sandpiper
Western sandpiper
Rufous-necked stint
Little stint
Temminck's stint
Long-toed stint
Least sandpiper
White-rumped sandpiper
Baird's sandpiper
Pectoral sandpiper
Sharp-tailed sandpiper
Purple sandpiper
Rock sandpiper
Dunlin
Curlew sandpiper
Stilt sandpiper
Spoonbill sandpiper
Broad-billed sandpiper
Buff-breasted sandpiper
Ruff
Short-billed dowitcher
Long-billed dowitcher
Jack snipe
Common snipe
Pintailed snipe
Eurasian woodcock
American woodcock

Wilson's phalarope
Red-necked phalarope
Red phalarope
Pomarine jaeger
Parasitic jaeger
Long-tailed jaeger
Great skua
South polar skua
Laughing gull
Franklin's gull
Little gull
Black-headed gull
Bonaparte's gull
Heermann's gull
Band-tailed gull
Mew gull
Ring-billed gull
Herring gull
California gull
Thayer's gull
Iceland gull
Lesser black-backed gull
Slaty-backed gull
Yellow-footed gull
Western gull
Glaucous-winged gull
Glaucous gull
Great black-backed gull
Black-legged kittiwake
Red-legged kittiwake
Ross's gull
Sabine's gull
Ivory gull
Gull-billed tern
Caspian tern
Royal tern
Elegant tern
Sandwich tern
Roseate tern
Common tern
Arctic tern
Aleutian tern
Forster's tern
Least tern
Gray-backed tern
Bridled tern
Sooty tern
White-winged tern
Black tern
Brown noddy
Black noddy
Blue-gray noddy
White tern
Black skimmer

QUAIL DRAWINGS BY L.A. FUERTES.

Dovekie
Thick-billed murre
Razorbill
Great auk (extinct)
Black guillemot
Pigeon guillemot
Common murre
Marbled murrelet
Kittlitz's murrelet
Xantus' murrelet
Craveri's murrelet
Ancient murrelet
Cassin's auklet
Parakeet auklet
Least auklet
Whiskered auklet
Crested auklet
Rhinoceros auklet
Tufted puffin
Atlantic puffin
Horned puffin
Chestnut-bellied sand-
    grouse
Rock dove
Scaly-naped pigeon
White-crowned pigeon
Red-billed pigeon
Bank-tailed pigeon
Ringed turtle dove
Spotted dove
Zebra dove
White-winged dove
Zenaida dove
Mourning dove
Passenger pigeon (extinct)
Inca dove
Common ground-dove
Ruddy ground-dove
White-tipped dove
Key West quail-dove
Ruddy quail-dove
Budgerigar
Rose-ringed parakeet
Monk parakeet
Carolina parakeet (extinct)
Thick-billed parrot
Canary-winged parakeet
Red-crowned parrot
Eurasian cuckoo
Oriental cuckoo
Black-billed cuckoo
Yellow-billed cuckoo
Mangove cuckoo
Roadrunner

Smooth-billed ani
Groove-billed ani
Barn owl
Oriental scops owl
Flammulated owl
Eastern screech owl
Western screech owl
Whiskered screech owl
Great horned owl
Snowy owl
Hawk owl
Northern pygmy owl
Ferruginous pygmy owl
Elf owl
Burrowing owl
Spotted owl
Barred owl
Great gray owl
Long-eared owl
Boreal owl
Saw-whet owl
Lesser nighthawk
Common nighthawk
Antillean nighthawk
Common pauraque
Poor-will
Chuck-will's-widow
Buff-collared nightjar
Whip-poor-will
Jungle nightjar
Black swift
White-collared swift
Chimney swift
Vaux's swift
White-throated needletail
Common swift
Fork-tailed swift
White-throated swift
Antillean palm swift
Green violet-ear
Broad-billed hummingbird
White-eared hummingbird
Berylline hummingbird
Rufous-tailed hummingbird
Buff-bellied hummingbird
Violet-crowned hummingbird
Blue-throated hummingbird
Magnificent hummingbird
Plain-capped starthroat
Bahama woodstar
Lucifer hummingbird
Ruby-throated hummingbird
Black-chinned hummingbird
Anna's hummingbird

Costa's hummingbird
Calliope hummingbird
Bumblebee hummingbird
Broad-tailed hummingbird
Rufous hummingbird
Allen's hummingbird
Elegant trogon
Eared trogon
Hoopoe
Ringed kingfisher
Belted kingfisher
Green kingfisher
Wryneck
Lewis' woodpecker
Red-headed woodpecker
Acorn woodpecker
Gila woodpecker
Golden-fronted wood-
  pecker
Red-bellied woodpecker
Yellow-bellied sapsucker
Red-breasted sapsucker
Williamson's sapsucker
Ladder-backed wood-
  pecker
Nuttall's woodpecker
Downy woodpecker
Hairy woodpecker
Stricktland's woodpecker
Red-cockaded woodpecker
White-headed woodpecker
Three-toed woodpecker
Black-backed woodpecker
Northern flicker
Pileated woodpecker
Ivory-billed woodpecker
Northern beardless tryan-
  nulet
Olive-sided flycatcher
Greater pewee
Western wood pewee
Eastern wood pewee
Yellow-bellied flycatcher
Acadian flycatcher
Willow flycatcher
Least flycatcher
Hammond's flycatcher
Dusky flycatcher
Gray flycatcher
Western flycatcher
Buff-breasted flycatcher
Black phoebe
Eastern phoebe
Say's phoebe

Vermilion flycatcher
Dusky-capped flycatcher
Ash-throated flycatcher
Nutting's flycatcher
Great crested flycatcher
Brown-crested flycatcher
La Sagra's flycatcher
Great kiskadee
Sulphur-bellied flycatcher
Variegated flycatcher
Tropical kingbird
Couch's kingbird
Cassin's kingbird
Thick-billed kingbird
Western kingbird
Eastern kingbird
Gray kingbird
Loggerhead kingbird
Scissor-tailed flycatcher
Fork-tailed flycatcher
Rose-throated becard
Skylark
Horned lark
Purple martin
Cuban martin
Gray-breasted martin
Southern martin
Tree swallow
Violet-green swallow
Bahama swallow
Northern rough-winged
  swallow
Bank swallow
Cliff swallow
Cave swallow
Barn swallow
House martin
Gray jay
Steller's jay
Blue jay
Black-throated magpie-jay
Green jay
Brown jay
Scrub jay
Gray-breasted jay
Pinyon jay
Clark's nutcracker
Black-billed magpie
Yellow-billed magpie
American crow
Northwestern crow
Mexican crow
Fish crow
Hawaiian crow

Chihuahuan raven
Common raven
Black-capped chickadee
Carolina chickadee
Mexican chickadee
Mountain chickadee
Siberian tit
Boreal chickadee
Chestnut-backed chickadee
Bridled titmouse
Varied tit
Plain titmouse
Tufted titmouse
Verdin
Bushtit
Red-breasted nuthatch
White-breasted nuthatch
Pygmy nuthatch
Brown-headed nuthatch
Brown creeper
Red-vented bulbul
Red-whiskered bulbul
Cactus wren
Rock wren
Canyon wren
Carolina wren
Bewick's wren
House wren
Winter wren
Sedge wren
Marsh wren
American dipper
Japanese bush-warbler
Middendorff's grasshop-
  per-warbler
Millerbird
Wood warbler
Dusky warbler
Arctic warbler
Golden-crowned kinglet
Ruby-crowned kinglet
Blue-gray gnatcatcher
Black-tailed gnatcatcher
Black-capped gnatcatcher
Red-breasted flycatcher
Siberian flycatcher
Gray-spotted flycatcher
Eleaio
Siberian rubythroat
Bluethroat
White-rumped shama
Wheatear
Eastern bluebird
Western bluebird

Mountain bluebird
Townsend's solitaire
Hawaiian thrush
Small Kauai thrush
Veery
Gray-cheeked thrush
Swainson's thrush
Hermit thrush
Wood thrush
Eurasian blackbird
Eyebrowed thrush
Dusky thrush
Fieldfare
Redwing
Clay-colored robin
Rufous-backed robin
American robin
Varied thrush
Aztec thrush
Greater necklaced laugh-
  ing-thrush
Melodious laughing-thrush
Red-billed leiothrix
Wrentit
Gray catbird
Northern mockingbird
Bahama mockingbird
Sage thrasher
Brown thrasher
Long-billed thrasher
Bendire's thrasher
Curve-billed thrasher
California thrasher
Crissal thrasher
Le Conte's thrasher
Siberian accentor
Yellow wagtail
Gray wagtail
White wagtail
Black-backed wagtail
Brown tree-pipit
Olive tree-pipit
Pechora pipit
Red-throated pipit
Water pipit
Sprague's pitpt
Bohemian waxwing
Cedar waxwing
Phainopepla
Brown shrike
Northern shrike
Loggerhead shrike
European starling
Common myna

Crested myna
Kauai oo
Oahu oo
Bishop's oo
Hawaii oo
Kioea
Japanese white-eye
White-eyed vireo
Bell's vireo
Black-capped vireo
Gray vireo
Solitary vireo
Yellow-throated vireo
Hutton's vireo
Warbling vireo
Philadelphia vireo
Red-eyed vireo
Black-whiskered vireo
Bachman's warbler
Blue-winged warbler
Golden-winged warbler
Tennessee warbler
Orange-crowned warbler
Nashville warbler
Virginia's warbler
Colima warbler
Lucy's warbler
Northern parula
Tropical parula
Yellow warbler
Chestnut-sided warbler
Magnolia warbler
Cape May warbler
Black-throated blue warbler
Yellow-rumped warbler
Black-throated gray warbler
Townsend's warbler
Hermit warbler
Black-throated green warbler
Golden-cheeked warbler
Blackburnian warbler
Yellow-throated warbler
Grace's warbler
Pine warbler
Kirtland's warbler
Prairie warbler
Palm warbler
Bay-breasted warbler
Blackpoll warbler
Cerulean warbler
Black-and-white warbler

American redstart
Prothonotary warbler
Worm-eating warbler
Swainson's warbler
Ovenbird
Northern waterthrush
Louisiana waterthrush
Kentucky warbler
Connecticut warbler
Mourning warbler
MacGillivray's warbler
Common yellowthroat
Gray-crowned yellowthroat
Hooded warbler
Wilson's warbler
Canada warbler
Red-faced warbler
Painted redstart
Slate-throated redstart
Fan-tailed warbler
Golden-crowned warbler
Rufous-capped warbler
Yellow-breasted chat
Olive warbler
Bananaquit
Stripe-headed tanager
Hapatic tanager
Summer tanager
Scarlet tanager
Western tanager
Crimson-collared grosbeak
Cardinal
Pyrrhuloxia
Yellow grosbeak
Rose-breasted grosbeak
Black-headed grosbeak
Blue bunting
Blue grosbeak
Lazuli bunting
Indigo bunting
Evening grosbeak
Varied bunting
Painted bunting
Dickcissel
Red-crested cardinal
Yellow-billed cardinal
Olive sparrow
Green-tailed towhee
Rufous-sided towhee
Brown towhee
Abert's towhee
White-collared seedeater
Yellow-faced grassquit

Black-faced grassquit
Saffron finch
Bachman's sparrow
Botteri's sparrow
Cassin's sparrow
Rufous-winged sparrow
Rufous-crowned sparrow
American tree sparrow
Chipping sparrow
Clay-colored sparrow
Brewer's sparrow
Field sparrow
Worthen's sparrow
Black-chinned sparrow
Vesper sparrow
Lark sparrow
Black-throated sparrow
Sage sparrow
Five-striped sparrow
Lark bunting
Savannah sparrow
Baird's sparrow
Grasshopper sparrow
Henslow's sparrow
Le Conte's sparrow
Sharp-tailed sparrow
Seaside sparrow
Fox sparrow
Song sparrow
Lincoln's sparrow
Swamp sparrow
White-throated sparrow
Golden-crowned sparrow
White-crowned sparrow
Harris' sparrow
Dark-eyed junco
Yellow-eyed junco
McCown's longspur
Smith's longspur
Chestnut-collared longspur
Little bunting
Rustic bunting
Gray bunting
Pallas' reed-bunting
Common reed-bunting
Snow bunting
McKay's bunting
Bobolink
Red-winged blackbird
Tricolored blackbird
Tawny-shouldered blackbird
Eastern meadowlark
Western meadowlark

Yellow-headed blackbird
Rusty blackbird
Brewer's blackbird
Great-tailed grackle
Boat-tailed grackle
Common grackle
Bronzed cowbird
Brown-headed cowbird
Black-vented oriole
Orchard oriole
Hooded oriole
Streak-backed oriole
Spot-breasted oriole
Altamira oriole
Audubon's oriole
Northern oriole
Scott's oriole
Chaffinch
Brambling
Rosy finch
Pine grosbeak
Common rosefinch
Purple finch
Cassin's finch
House finch
Red crossbill
White-winged crossbill
Common redpoll
Hoary redpoll
Pine siskin
Lesser goldfinch
Lawrence's goldfinch
American goldfinch
European goldfinch
Oriental greenfinch
Yellow-fronted canary
Common canary
Bullfinch
Hawfinch
Laysan finch
Nihoa finch
Ou
Palila
Lesser koa-finch
Greater koa-finch
Grosbeak finch
Maui parrotbill
Common amakihi
Anianiau
Greater amakihi
Hawaiian akialoa
Kauai akialoa
Nukupuu
Akiapolaau

| | |
|---|---|
| Hawaii creeper | Poo-uli |
| Kauai creeper | House sparrow |
| Maui creeper | Eurasian tree sparrow |
| Molokai creeper | Red-cheeked cordonbleu |
| Oahu creeper | Lavender fire-finch |
| Akepa | Orange-cheeked waxbill |
| Ula-ai-hawane | Black-rumped waxbill |
| Iiwi | Red avadavat |
| Hawii mamo | Warbling silverbill |
| Black mamo | Nutmeg mannikin |
| Crested honeycreeper | Chestnut mannikin |
| Apapane | Java sparrow |

# REPTILES OF NORTH AMERICA

Until about 65 million years ago, reptiles were the dominant animals on the earth. They flourished for about 160 million years, adapting to every kind of environment: swamps, deserts, forests, grasslands, rivers, lakes, even the sea and the air.

Then, at the end of the Cretaceous period, the Age of Reptiles came to an abrupt (in terms of geologic time) and mysterious end. We know from fossil remains that all the dinosaurs and four fifths of the other reptiles, including the flying species, completely disappeared.

Of the 16 orders of reptiles known to have roamed the earth, only 4 have survived to the present time. The turtles (Chelonians), the crocodiles (Crocodilians), and the tuatara (Rhynochocephalia) are in decline; there are just 250 species of turtles, 23 species of crocodilians, and a single species of tuatara currently surviving. Only the fourth order, the lizards and snakes (Squamata), has continued to proliferate and adapt to a changing world.

Despite their extremely diversified forms, the members of the four orders of reptiles have in common a dry skin covered with horny plates or scales. In contrast to the amphibians from which they are descended, reptiles are relatively independent of water, and even those that live in an aquatic environment, such as the sea turtles, come ashore to lay their eggs. All reptiles once had four legs like lizards, but snakes lost theirs, and the sea turtles modified their crawling limbs into flippers.

The reptile and amphibian family trees date way back to the crossopterygian fishes, which existed toward the end of the Devonian period 300 million years ago. Reptiles are believed to have originated from the so-called stem reptiles, which roamed the earth early in the Permian period 215 million years ago. From these evolved the Chelonia, ancestor of modern turtles; the Thecondontia, the forebears of the dinosaurs, and in turn, the ancestors of the crocodiles; and the Eosuchia, which evolved into today's lizards and snakes. Another branch of the Eosuchia produced the tuatara, a solitary relic of an ancient world.

Apart from the tuatara, the turtles are the most primitive of modern-day reptiles. Fossil remains date back to the Triassic period in the dawn of the Age of Reptiles about 200 million years ago. The earliest turtle fossils are found in Triassic deposits in Germany, and appeared almost as we know them today; they have remained relatively unchanged down through the ages.

CHAMELEONS.

The unique feature of turtles is the shell, which is divided into two parts: the upper part is known as the carapace; the lower, the plastron. The sections of these are called scutes, or plates.

Crocodiles have also come down through the ages relatively unchanged, though early crocodilians appeared to have been larger than modern-day species. Phobosuchus, or "horror crocodile," which lived in the lakes and swamps of what are now the states of Montana and Texas about 75 million years ago, measured up to 50 feet in length and had a 6-foot-long skull. The gavial (*Rhamphosuchus* sp.), which lived in what is now northern India about 7 million years ago, also reached a length of 50 feet.

Snakes (Serpentes) are the newest suborder of reptiles, having descended directly from lizards dur-ing the Lower Cretaceous period, when the Age of Reptiles was coming to an end. Lizards and snakes together consist of about 5,700 species, and are by far the largest, as well as the most modern, branch of the reptiles. Pythons and boas (Boids) are the most primitive of living snakes; vestiges of hind legs are present as "spurs" and are usually visible on either side of the vent.

Of the 250 species of turtles found today, 46 are native to North America; and 3 crocodilians occur here (including one introduced species) out of 23 species worldwide. There are approximately 3,000 lizard species on earth, of which 105 (including established exotics) may be encountered here; and of the world's 2,700 snake species, North America's contribution is also 114 species.

CHAMELEONS.

COLLARED LIZARD.

| | |
|---|---|
| American alligator | Ringed sawback |
| American crocodile | False map turtle |
| Snapping turtle | Alabama map turtle |
| Alligator snapping turtle | Texas map turtle |
| Striped mud turtle | Diamondback terrapin |
| Yellow mud turtle | Eastern box turtle |
| Mexican mud turtle | Western box turtle |
| Sonora mud turtle | Desert tortoise |
| Mud turtle | Berlandier's tortoise |
| Razor-backed musk turtle | Gopher tortoise |
| Flattened musk turtle | Loggerhead |
| Loggerhead musk turtle | Green turtle |
| Stinkpot | Hawksbill |
| Alabama red-bellied turtle | Atlantic ridley |
| River cooter | Olive ridley |
| Cooter | Leatherback |
| Florida red-bellied turtle | Florida softshell |
| Painted turtle | Smooth softshell |
| Red-bellied turtle | Spiny softshell |
| Pond slider | Texas banded gecko |
| Spotted turtle | Big Bend gecko |
| Wood turtle | Banded gecko |
| Western pond turtle | Yellow-headed gecko |
| Bog turtle | Leaftoed gecko |
| Chicken turtle | Reef gecko |
| Blanding's turtle | Green anole |
| Barbour's map turtle | Zebra-tailed lizard |
| Cagle's map turtle | Greater earless lizard |
| Yellow-blotched sawback | Collared lizard |

Desert collared lizard
Reticulate collared lizard
Desert iguana
Blunt-nosed leopard lizard
Leopard lizard
Spot-tailed earless lizard
Lesser earless lizard
Keeled earless lizard
Banded rock lizard
Texas horned lizard
Coast horned lizard
Short-horned lizard
Flat-tailed horned lizard
Round-tailed horned lizard
Desert horned lizard
Regal horned lizard
Chuckwalla
Clark's spiny lizard
Blue spiny lizard
Sagebrush lizard
Mesquite lizard
Yarrow's spiny lizard
Desert spiny lizard
Canyon lizard
Western fence lizard
Texas spiny lizard
Granite spiny lizard
Crevice spiny lizard
Bunch grass lizard
Eastern fence lizard
Rose-bellied lizard
Striped plateau lizard
Florida scrub lizard
Coachella Valley fringed-
  toed lizard
Fringed-toed lizard
Mojave fringed-toed lizard
Long-tailed brush lizard
Small-scaled tree lizard
Common tree lizard
Side-blotched lizard
Northern alligator lizard
Panamint alligator lizard
Slender glass lizard
Island glass lizard
Eastern glass lizard
Gila monster
California legless lizard
Granite night lizard
Island night lizard
Desert night lizard
Jungle runner
Giant spotted whiptail
Gray checkered whiptail

Chihuahuan spotted whip-
  tail
Gila whiptail
Texas spotted whiptail
Orange-throated whiptail
Little striped whiptail
Laredo striped whiptail
New Mexican whiptail
Plateau spotted whiptail
Racerunner
Sonoran spotted whiptail
Checkered whiptail
Western whiptail
Desert-grassland whiptail
Plateau striped whiptail
Green lizard
Ruin lizard
Coal skink
Mole skink
Five-lined skink
Gilbert's skink
Southeastern five-lined
  skink
Broad-headed skink
Many-lined skink
Great Plains skink
Prairie skink
Western skink
Four-lined skink
Sand skink
Ground skink
Worm lizard
Texas blind snake
Western blind snake
Rubber boa
Rosy boa
Glossy snake
Worm snake
Scarlet snake
Banded sand snake
Western shovel-nosed
  snake
Sonoran shovel-nosed
  snake
Kirtland's snake
Racer
Black-striped snake
Sharp-tailed snake
Ringneck snake
Indigo snake
Speckled racer
Corn snake
Rat snake
Trans-Pecos rat snake

Green rat snake
Fox snake
Mud snake
Rainbow snake
Mexican hook-nosed snake
Western hook-nosed snake
Desert hook-nosed snake
Western hognose snake
Eastern hognose snake
Southern hognose snake
Night snake
Prairie kingsnake
Common kingsnake
Gray-banded kingsnake
Sonora mountain king-
  snake
Milk snake
California mountain king-
  snake
Cat-eyed snake
Sonora whipsnake
Coachwhip
Striped racer
Striped whipsnake
Green water snake
Plain-bellied water snake
Southern water snake
Harter's water snake
Diamondback water snake
Northern water snake
Brown water snake
Rough green snake
Smooth green snake
Mexican vine snake
Saddle leaf-nosed snake
Spotted leaf-nosed snake
Pine-gopher snake
Graham's crayfish snake
Glossy crayfish water
  snake
Queen snake
Pine woods snake
Long-nosed snake
Big Bend patch-nosed
  snake
Mountain patch-nosed
  snake
Swamp snake
Ground snake
Short-tailed snake
Brown snake
Red-bellied snake
Mexican black-headed
  snake

Southeastern crowned snake
Flat-headed snake
Plains black-headed snake
Rim Rock crowned snake
Western black-headed
  snake
Florida crowned snake
Big Bend black-headed
  snake
Chihuahuan black-headed
  snake
Yaqui black-headed snake
Short-headed garter snake
Butler's garter snake
Western aquatic garter
  snake
Black-necked garter snake
Western terrestrial garter
  snake
Mexican garter snake
Checkered garter snake
Northwestern garter snake
Western ribbon snake
Plains garter snake
Narrow-headed garter
  snake
Eastern ribbon snake
Common garter snake
Lyre snake
Lined snake
Rough earth snake
Smooth earth snake
Arizona coral snake
Texas coral snake
Eastern coral snake
Copperhead
Cottonmouth
Eastern diamondback rat-
  tlesnake
Western diamondback rat-
  tlesnake
Sidewinder
Timber rattlesnake
Rock rattlesnake
Speckled rattlesnake
Black-tailed rattlesnake
Twin-spotted rattlesnake
Red diamond rattlesnake
Mojave rattlesnake
Tiger rattlesnake
Western rattlesnake
Ridge-nosed rattlesnake
Massasauga rattlesnake
Pygmy rattlesnake

The following exotic species have been inadvertently introduced and are living in a wild, natural state in Florida.

COMMON IGUANA

Spectacled caiman
Indo-Pacific gecko
Mediterranean gecko
Ocellated gecko
Ashy gecko
Crested anole
Large-headed anole
Bark anole
Knight anole
Brown anole
Spiny-tailed iguana
Common iguana
Curly-tailed lizard

# AMPHIBIANS OF NORTH AMERICA

It is relatively certain that amphibian ancestors gave rise to the reptiles, which in turn came from fish ancestors like the crossopterygiis.

Although living amphibians are easily distinguished from reptiles, many fossil forms of these groups of animals are very similar. However, amphibians retain an ancient dependence on water: Some live in it most of the time, most need it to breed in, and all require it to keep from becoming dehydrated. During their larval stages, amphibians are fishlike, breathing through gills. As adults, they can be characterized by their skin, which, unlike that of reptiles, is moist and scaleless.

Three orders of living amphibians are recognized: the caecilians (Apoda), limbless creatures resembling earthworms and the most primitive; the newts, salamanders, and sirens (Urodella); and the frogs and toads (Anura), which comprise, worldwide, the largest group.

Approximately 3,150 species of amphibians occur throughout the world; these consist of about 100 species of caecilians, 350 species of salamanders, and nearly 2,700 species of frogs and toads.

Caecilians occur chiefly in the Tropics and are not represented in North America. Frogs and toads number a modest 83 species on this continent, while salamanders are better represented in North America than anywhere else on earth, with 109 species, including endemic sirens, mole salamanders, and amphiumas.

Hellbender
Dwarf siren
Lesser siren
Greater siren
Black-spotted newt
Striped newt
Eastern newt
Rough-skinned newt
Red-bellied newt
California newt
Alabama waterdog
Gulf Coast waterdog
Neuse River waterdog
Mudpuppy
Dwarf waterdog
Two-toed amphiuma
One-toed amphiuma
Three-toed amphiuma
Ringed salamander
California tiger salamander
Flatwoods salamander
Northwestern salamander
Jefferson salamander
Blue-spotted salamander
Mabee's salamander
Long-toed salamander
Spotted salamander
Marbled salamander
Silvery salamander
Mole salamander
Small-mouthed salamander
Tiger salamander
Tremblay's salamander
Cope's giant salamander
Pacific giant salamander
Olympic salamander
Green salamander
Clouded salamander
Black salamander
Sacramento mountain salamander
Arboreal salamander
Desert slender salamander
California slender salamander
Garden slender salamander
Channel Islands slender salamander
Relictual slender salamander
Kern Canyon slender salamander
Tehachapi slender salamander

Oregon slender salamander
Seepage salamander
Southern dusky salamander
Ouachita dusky salamander
Dusky salamander
Imitator salamander
Seal salamander
Mountain dusky salamander
Black-bellied salamander
Black mountain dusky salamander
Pygmy salamander
Ensatina
Two-lined salamander
Junaluska salamander
Cascade cavern salamander
Long-tailed salamander
Cave salamander
Many-ribbed salamander
San Marcos salamander
Texas salamander
Dwarf salamander
Comal blind salamander
Valdina Farms salamander
Oklahoma salamander
Tennessee cave salamander
Spring salamander
Limestone salamander
Mount Lyell salamander
Shasta salamander
Shovel-nosed salamander
Red Hills salamander
Caddo Mountain salamander
Red-backed salamander
Zigzag salamander
Dunn's salamander
Del Norte salamander
Fourche Mountain salamander
Slimy salamander
Valley and Ridge salamander
Appalachian woodland salamander
Larch Mountain salamander
Crevice salamander
Jemez Mountains salamander

Netting's salamander
Rich Mountain salamander
White-spotted salamander
Ravine salamander
Southern red-backed sal-
amander
Shenandoah salamander
Siskiyou Mountain sala-
mander
Van Dyke's salamander
Western red-backed sala-
mander
Wehrle's salamander
Weller's salamander
Yonahlossee salamander
Mud salamander
Red salamander
Many-lined salamander
Texas blind salamander
Grotto salamander
Tailed frog
Mexican burrowing toad
Plains spadefoot
Couch's spadefoot
Western spadefoot
Eastern spadefoot
Great Basin spadefoot
Crawfish frog
Red-legged frog
Rio Grande leopard frog
Plains leopard frog
Foothill yellow-legged frog
Cascades frog
Bullfrog
Green frog
Las Vegas leopard frog
Pig frog
River frog
Mountain yellow-legged
frog
Relict leopard frog
Pickerel frog
Northern leopard frog
Spotted frog
Mink frog
Southern leopard frog
Wood frog
Tarahumara frog
Carpenter frog
Eastern narrow-mouthed
frog
Great Plains narrow-
mouthed frog
Sheep frog

Colorado River toad
American toad
Western toad
Yosemite toad
Great Plains toad
Green toad
Black toad
Canadian toad
Houston toad
Giant toad
Southwestern toad
Red-spotted toad
Oak toad
Sonoran green toad
Texas toad
Southern toad
Gulf Coast toad
Woodhouse's toad
Northern cricket frog
Southern cricket frog
Pine Barrens treefrog
Canyon treefrog
Bird-voiced treefrog
California treefrog
Cope's gray treefrog
Common gray treefrog
Green treefrog
Spring peeper
Mountain treefrog
Pine Woods treefrog
Barking treefrog
Pacific treefrog
Squirrel treefrog
Little grass frog
African clawed frog (intro-
duced into California)
Cuban treefrog
Mountain chorus frog
Brimley's chorus frog
Spotted chorus frog
Southern chorus frog
Ornate chorus frog
Strecker's chorus frog
Chorus frog
Burrowing treefrog
Mexican treefrog
Puerto Rican doqui
Greenhouse frog
Barking frog
White-lipped frog
Rio Grande chirping frog
Spotted chirping frog
Cliff chirping frog

# FRESHWATER FISH OF NORTH AMERICA

Fish evolved in the Devonian period between 405 million and 345 million years ago. The earliest fish, known as ostracoderms, were jawless and bottom-dwelling forms, such as thelodus and pteraspis, that were to become the ancestors of all vertebrate animals. Heavily armored and with primitive sucking mouths, they failed to survive the competition of more advanced fish with hinged jaws.

Before the ostracoderms died out at the end of the Devonian period, fish with true jaws had already arrived on the scene. This new feature freed certain fish from a bottom-dwelling existence. With jaws, which developed from the front gill arches, fish could eat larger, tougher food; they now began to move more freely through the water in search of more varied prey. The first fish with jaws were known as placoderms, so called because of the hard, armorlike covering of their bodies.

Except for some tropical species, such as the lung fish (*Polypterus* sp.) and the climbing perch (*Anabus testudinosus*), fish have never adapted themselves to any form of land living. Like snakes, they have neither eyelids nor ears; they receive sound as vibrations transmitted along a lateral nerve that is plainly discernible on a speckled trout (*Salvelinus fontinalis*). Fish have a fairly well developed sense of taste and can communicate with their own kind by grunts, squeals, and other sounds that have been picked up and classified by sonar. A lake trout (*S. namaycush*) that has been boated will utter a recognizable sound of fright.

The ages of scaled fish can be determined by the number of rings, like trees. Biologists can determine the ages of scaleless fish, such as sturgeon and catfish, by examining the skull structures at the point where the ears would be if there were any.

Modern-day fish are so numerous and diversified that they are no longer grouped together in one class but are broken down into three: these are the Agnatha, or jawless fish, represented by the lampreys and hagfishes; the Chondrichthyes, comprising the cartilaginous fish such as sharks, rays, and chimaeras; and the Osteichthyes or bony fish, which alone include about half the world's vertebrate species.

The total freshwater fish fauna of North America consists of 712 species and subspecies (not including introduced exotics):

Sea lamprey
Pacific lamprey
River lamprey
Arctic lamprey
Chestnut lamprey
Silver lamprey
Ohio lamprey
Darktail lamprey
American brook lamprey
Western brook lamprey
Northern brook lamprey
Southern brook lamprey
Allegheny brook lamprey
*Lampetra folletti* (no common name)
Kern brook lamprey
Pit-Klamath brook lamprey
Gulf brook lamprey
Miller Lake lamprey
Pacific brook lamprey
Klamath River lamprey
Atlantic sturgeon
Atlantic stingray
Bull shark
Green sturgeon
Lake sturgeon
Shortnose sturgeon
White sturgeon
Pallid sturgeon
Shovelnose sturgeon
Paddlefish
Spotted gar
Longnose gar
Alligator gar
Shortnose gar
Florida gar
Bowfin
Machete
Ladyfish
Tarpon
Alabama shad
Dolly Varden
Blueback herring
Slipjack herring
American shad
Alewife
Gizzard shad
Hickory shad
Threadfin shad
Scaled sardine
Atlantic thread herring
Bay anchovy
Goldeye

Bear Lake whitefish
Bonneville cisco
Bonneville whitefish
Pink salmon
Chum salmon
Coho salmon
Kokanee (Sockeye salmon)
Chinook salmon
Cutthroat trout
Rainbow trout
Atlantic salmon
Arctic char
Brook trout
Lake trout
Golden trout
Arizona trout
Gila trout
Silver trout
Angayukaksurak char
Delta smelt
Alaska blackfish
Longjaw cisco
Cisco (Lake herring)
Arctic cisco
Blater
Deepwater cisco
Kiyi
Bering cisco
Blackfin cisco
Shortnose cisco
Least cisco
Shortjaw cisco
Lake whitefish
Broad whitefish
Atlantic whitefish
Pygmy whitefish
Round whitefish
Mountain whitefish
Inconnu
Arctic grayling
Pond smelt
Rainbow smelt
Longfin smelt
Eulachon
Mooneye
Central mudminnow
Olympic mudminnow
Eastern mudminnow
Redfin pickerel
Grass pickerel
Chain pickerel
Northern pike
Muskellunge

Chiselmouth
Mexican tetra
Northern redbelly dace
Longfin dace
Redside dace
Finescale dace
Rosyside dace
Desert dace
Largescale stoneroller
Mexican stoneroller
Cutlips minnow
Brassy minnow
Silvery minnow
Devil's River minnow
Roundnose minnow
Silverjaw minnow
Tonguetied minnow
Lake chub
Silver chub
Gravel chub
Peamouth
Hornyhead chub
Alvord chub
Utah chub
Tui chub
Blue chub
Leatherside chub
Thicktail chub
Humpback chub
Sonora chub
Bonytail chub
Chihuahua chub
Arroya chub
Rio Grande chub
Yaqui chub
Roundtail chub
Flame chub
Cypress minnow
Plains minnow
River chub
Speckled chub
Bigeye chub
Slender chub
Oregon chub
Streamline chub
Sturgeon chub
Highback chub
Blotched chub
Thicklip chub
Lined chub
Sicklefin chub
Spotfin chub
Rosyface chub
Clear chub

Santee chub
Least chub
*Lavinia exilicauda* (no common name)
California roach
White River spinedace
Pahranagat spinedace
Virgin spinedace
Little Colorado spinedace
Spikedace
Moapa dace
Hardhead
Redspot chub
Redtail chub
Bluehead chub
Bigmouth chub
Bull chub
Golden shiner
Pugnose shiner
Emerald shiner
Bridle shiner
River shiner
Common shiner
Bigmouth shiner
Pugnose minnow
Blackchin shiner
Spottail shiner
Rosyface shiner
Spotfin shiner
Sand shiner
Redfin shiner
Mimic shiner
Bluntnose minnow
Fathead minnow
Northern squawfish
Blacknose dace
Longnose dace
Leopard dace
Speckled dace
Redside shiner
Creek chub
White shiner
Whitemouth shiner
Highfin shiner
Texas shiner
Pallid shiner
Comely shiner
Satinfin shiner
Rosefin shiner
Popeye shiner
Burrhead shiner
Blacktip shiner
Blackspot shiner
Rough shiner

Red River shiner
Pretty shiner
Bigeye shiner
Tamaulipas shiner
Smalleye shiner
Ghost shiner
Blue shiner
Ocmulgee shiner
Alabama shiner
Bluestripe shiner
Bluntface shiner
Crescent shiner
Ironcolor shiner
Chihuahua shiner
Redlip shiner
Greenfin shiner
Greenhead shiner
Rainbow shiner
Warpaint shiner
Dusky shiner
Bigmouth shiner
Fluvial shiner
Broadstripe shiner
Beautiful shiner
Ribbon shiner
Whitetail shiner
Tallapoosa shiner
Arkansas River shiner
Wedgespot shiner
Redeye chub
Bluehead shiner
Sailfin shiner
Highscale shiner
Rio Grande shiner
Bannerfin shiner
Tennessee shiner
Mountain shiner
Longnose shiner
Yellowfin shiner
Red shiner
Taillight shiner
Cape Fear shiner
Whitefin shiner
Ozard minnow
Kiamichi shiner
Sharpnose shiner
Ozark shiner
Peppered shiner
Coastal shiner
Duskystripe shiner
Chub shiner
Swallowtail shiner
Proserpine shiner
Fieryblack shiner

Cherryfin shiner
Saffron shiner
Sabine shiner
New River shiner
Sandbar shiner
Roughhead shiner
Silverband shiner
Flagfin shiner
Bluntnose shiner
Mirror shiner
Silverstripe shiner
Telescope shiner
Weed shiner
Topeka shiner
Tricolor shiner
Skygazer shiner
Blacktail shiner
Bluenose shiner
Steelcolor shiner
Coosa shiner
Altamaha shiner
Bleeding shiner
Bandfin shiner
Sacramento blackfish
Riffle minnow
Fatlips minnow
Suckermouth minnow
Kanawha minnow
Stargazing minnow
Blackside dace
Southern redbelly dace
Mountain redbelly dace
Slim minnow
Bullhead minnow
Woundfin
Clear Lake splittail
Splittail
Sacramento squawfish
Colorado squawfish
Umpqua dace
Lahontan redside shiner
Sandhills chub
Loach minnow
Fallfish
Pearl dace
Quillback
River carpsucker
Highfin carpsucker
Longnose sucker
Bridgelip sucker
White sucker
Largescale sucker
Mountain sucker
Lake chubsucker

Northern hog sucker
Bigmouth buffalo
Spotted sucker
Smallmouth buffalo
Utah sucker
Yaqui sucker
Desert sucker
Bluehead sucker
Webug sucker
Owen's sucker
Sonora sucker
Flannelmouth sucker
Lost River sucker
Modoc sucker
Sacramento sucker
Rio Grande sucker
Klamath smallscale sucker
Santa Ana sucker
Klamath largescale sucker
Tahoe sucker
Warner sucker
Shortnose sucker
Cui-ui
June sucker
Blue sucker
Creek chubsucker
Sharpfin chubsucker
Alabama hog sucker
Roanoke hog sucker
Black buffalo
Harelip sucker
Bigeye jumprock
Blackfin sucker
West Mexican redhorse
Rustyside sucker
Greater jumprock
Torrent sucker
Humpback sucker
Silver redhorse
River redhorse
Golden redhorse
Black redhorse
Copper redhorse
Shorthead redhorse
Greater redhorse
Black bullhead
Yellow bullhead
Brown bullhead
V-lip redhorse
Blacktail redhorse
Smallfin redhorse
Gray redhorse
Striped jumprock
Snail bullhead

Flat bullhead
Channel catfish
White catfish
Blue catfish
Headwater catfish
Yaqui catfish
Spotted bullhead
Stonecat
Flathead catfish
Hardhead catfish
Tadpole madtom
Brindled madtom
Ozark madtom
Smoky madtom
Elegant madtom
Mountain madtom
Slender madtom
Checkered madtom
Yellowfin madtom
Black madtom
Carolina madtom
Orangefin madtom
Least madtom
Margined madtom
Ouachita madtom
Speckled madtom
Brown madtom
Neosho madtom
Northern madtom
Caddo madtom
Scioto madtom
Widemouth blind cat
Toothless blind cat
American eel
Ozark cavefish
Northern cavefish
Spring cavefish
Pirate perch
Sand roller
Atlantic needlefish
White River springfish
Railroad Valley springfish
Leon Springs pupfish
Devil's Hole pupfish
Comanche Springs pupfish
Conchos pupfish
Desert pupfish
Amargosa pupfish
Pecos River pupfish
Owens pupfish
Red River pupfish
Salt Creek pupfish
White Sands pupfish
Sheephead minnow

Banded killifish
Pahrump killifish
Ash Meadows killifish
Marsh killifish
Gulf killifish
Spotfin killifish
California killifish
Bayou killifish
Speckled killifish
Seminole killifish
Waccamaw killifish
Plains killifish
Pygmy killifish
Bluefin killifish
Rainwater killifish
Whiteline topminnow
Northern studfish
Golden topminnow
Banded topminnow
Northern starhead
  topminnow
Eastern starhead
  topminnow
Saltmarsh topminnow
Lined topminnow
Blackstripe topminnow
Plains topminnow
Starhead topminnow
Blackspotted topminnow
Southern studfish
Flagfish
Rivulus
Mosquitofish
Least killifish
Gila topminnow
Mummichog
Burbot
Atlantic tomcod
Goldeneye gambusia
Big Bend gambusia
Largespring gambusia
San Marcos gambusia
Clear Creek gambusia
Pecos gambusia
Mangrove gambusia
Blotched gambusia
Brook silverside
Tidewater silverside
Waccamaw silverside
Atlantic silverside
Opossum pipefish
Gulf pipefish
Swordspine snook
Fat snook

Tarpon snook
Snook
Fourspine stickleback
Brook stickleback
Threespine stickleback
Blackspotted stickleback
Ninespine stickleback
Trout-perch
White perch
White bass
Yellow bass
Striped bass
Rock bass
Yellow perch
Smallmouth bass
Largemouth bass
Shadow bass
Roanoke bass
Sacramento perch
Flier
Mud sunfish
Redbreast sunfish
Green sunfish
Pumpkinseed
Bluegill
Longear sunfish
White crappie
Black crappie
Sauger
Walleye
Everglades pygmy sunfish
Okefenokee pygmy sunfish
Banded pygmy sunfish
Blackbanded sunfish
Bluespotted sunfish
Banded sunfish
Warmouth
Orangespotted sunfish
Dollar sunfish
Redear sunfish
Spotted sunfish
Bantam sunfish
Redeyed bass
Suwannee bass
Spotted bass
Guadalupe bass
Eastern sand darter
Greenside darter
Rainbow darter
Iowa darter
Fantail darter
Least darter
Johnny darter
Crystal darter

Naked sand darter
Florida sand darter
Western sand darter
Southern sand darter
Scaly sand darter
Sharphead darter
Coppercheek darter
Mud darter
Cumberland snubnose
  darter
Teardrop darter
Orangefin darter
Blenny darter
Slackwater darter
Bluebreast darter
Greenfin darter
Bluntnose darter
Ashy darter
Creole darter
Carolina darter
Coosa darter
Arkansas darter
Logperch
Channel darter
Blackside darter
River darter
Choctawhatchee darter
Coldwater darter
Blackside snubnose darter
Brown darter
Cherry darter
Arkansas saddled darter
Fountain darter
Savannah darter
Swamp darter
Slough darter
Rio Grande darter
Harlequin darter
Christmas darter
Turquoise darter
Blueside darter
Greenbreast darter
Yoke darter
Kanawha darter
Stripetail darter
Greenthroat darter
Longfin darter
Redband darter
Spotted darter
Pinewoods darter
*Etheostoma meadiae* (no
  common name)
Smallscale darter
Yellowcheek darter

Lollypop darter
Niangua darter
Watercress darter
Barcreek darter
Okaloosa darter
Dirty darter
Finscale saddled darter
Paleback darter
Goldstripe darter
Waccamaw darter
Riverweed darter
Cypress darter
Stippled darter
Orangebelly darter
Bayou darter
Redline darter
Rock darter
Arrow darter
Saluda darter
Maryland darter
Sawcheek darter
Tennessee snubnose darter
Slabrock darter
Orangethroat darter
Spottail darter
Speckled darter
Striated darter
Gulf darter
Swannanoa darter
Missouri saddled darter
Seagreen darter
Tippecanoe darter
Trispot darter
Tuscumbia darter
Variegated darter
Striped darter
Glassy darter
Redfin darter
Banded darter
Backwater darter
Amber darter
Tangerine darter
Goldline darter
Blotchside logperch
Piedmont darter
Bluestripe darter
Gilt darter
Freckled darter
Longhead darter
Bigscale logperch
Longnose darter
Blackbanded darter
Stripeback darter
Yellow darter

Sharpnose darter
Bronze darter
Leopard darter
Shield darter
Slenderhead darter
Roanoke logperch
Roanoke darter
Dusky darter
Olive darter
Snail darter
Stargazing darter
Grevalle jack
Gray snapper
Striped mojarra
Spotfin mojarra
Bigfish
Silver perch
Spotted seatrout
Spot
Atlantic croaker
Red drum
Freshwater drum
Atlantic spadefish
Rio Grande perch
Tule perch
Mountain mullet
White mullet
Fat sleeper
Spotted sleeper
Spinycheek sleeper
Bigmouth sleeper
Yellowfin goby

River goby
Tidewater goby
Longjaw mudsucker
Violet goby
Blackfin goby
Darter goby
Slashcheek goby
Freshwater goby
Naked goby
Code goby
Clown goby
Green goby
Coastrange sculpin
Prickly sculpin
Mottled sculpin
Slimy sculpin
Shorthead sculpin
Torrent sculpin
Spoonhead sculpin
Deepwater sculpin
Rough sculpin
Black sculpin
Piute sculpin
Banded sculpin
Utah Lake sculpin
Bear Lake sculpin
Potomac sculpin
Shoshone sculpin
Riffle sculpin
Marbled sculpin
Wood River sculpin
Margined sculpin

Reticulate sculpin
Pit sculpin
Klamath Lake sculpin
Pygmy sculpin

Slender sculpin
Bay whiff
Southern flounder
Hogchocker

## EXOTIC FISH

The following fish species have been inadvertently introduced into North American fresh waters, where they are living in a wild, free state, most of them in Florida.

Brown trout
Carp
Goldfish
Tench
Grass carp
Ide
Bitterling
Rudd
Oriental weatherfish
Walking catfish
Armored catfish
Medaka
Pike killifish
Guppy
Shortfin molly
Amazon molly

Porthole livebear
Green swordtail
Southern platyfish
Variable platyfish
Oscar
Black acara
Firemouth
Convict cichlid
Jack Dempsey
Banded cichlid
Jewelfish
Blue tilapia
Blackchin tilapia
Mozambique tilapia
Redbelly tilapia
Croaking gourami

# APPENDIX
# II

## NATIONAL PARKS OF THE UNITED STATES

The national park system commenced in 1872 when Yellowstone National Park was established. Since that time forty-eight national parks have been formed in order to preserve America's wildlife heritage. The national parks are under the jurisdiction of the National Park Service of the U.S. Department of the Interior.

Denali National Park and Preserve
P.O. Box 9
McKinley Park, Alaska 99755

Gates of the Arctic National Park and Preserve
P.O. Box 74680
Fairbanks, Alaska 99707

Glacier Bay National Park and Preserve
P.O. Box 1089
Juneau, Alaska 99802

Katmai National Park and Preserve
P.O. Box 7
King Salmon, Alaska 99613

Kenai Fjords National Park
General Delivery
Seward, Alaska 99664

Kobuk Valley National Park
General Delivery
Kotzebue, Alaska 99752

Lake Clarke National Park and Preserve
1011 East Tudor Road
Anchorage, Alaska 99503

Wrangell–St. Elias National Park and Preserve
P.O. Box 29
Glenn Allen, Alaska 99588

Grand Canyon National Park
P.O. Box 129
Grand Canyon, Arizona 86023

Hot Springs National Park
P.O. Box 1860
Hot Springs, Arizona 71901

Petrified Forest National Park
Arizona 86028

Channel Island National Park
1699 Anchors Way Drive
Ventura, California 93003

Kings Canyon National Park
Three Rivers, California 93271

Lassen Volcanic National Park
Mineral, California 96063

Redwood National Park
1111 Second City
Crescent City, California 95531

Sequoia National Park
Three Rivers, California 93271

Yosemite National Park
P.O. Box 577
Yosemite, California 95389

Mesa Verde National Park
Colorado 81330

Rocky Mountain National Park
Estes Park, Colorado 80517

Biscayne National Park
P.O. Box 1369
Homestead, Florida 33030

Everglades National Park
P.O. Box 279
Homestead, Florida 33030

Haleakala National Park
P.O. Box 537
Makawao, Hawaii 96768

Hawaii Volcanoes National Park
Hawaii National Park, Hawaii 96718

Mammoth Cave National Park
Mammoth Cave, Kentucky 42259

Acadia National Park
Route 1, Box 1
Bar Harbor, Maine 04609

Isle Royale National Park
87 North Ripley Street
Houghton, Michigan 49931

Voyageurs National Park
P.O. Box 50
International Falls, Minnesota 56649

Glacier National Park
West Glacier, Montana 59936

Carlsbad Caverns National Park
3225 National Parks Highway
Carlsbad, New Mexico 88220

Guadalupe Mountains National
Park
3225 National Parks Highway
Carlsbad, New Mexico 88220

Theodore Roosevelt National Park
Medora, North Dakota 58645

Crater Lake National Park
P.O. Box 7
Crater Lake, Oregon 97604

Badlands National Park
P.O. Box 6
Interior, South Dakota 57750

Wind Cave National Park
Hot Springs, South Dakota 57747

Great Smoky Mountains National
Park
Gatlinburg, Tennessee 37738

Big Bend National Park
Texas 79834

Arches National Park
446 S. Main Street
Moab, Utah 84532

Bryce Canyon National Park
Bryce Canyon, Utah 84717

Canyonlands National Park
446 S. Main Street
Moab, Utah 84532

Capitol Reef National Park
Torrey, Utah 84775

Zion National Park
Springdale, Utah 84767

Shenandoah National Park
Route 4, Box 292
Luray, Virginia 22835

Virgin Islands National Park
P.O. Box 806
Charlotte Amalie
St. Thomas, Virgin Islands 00801

Mount Rainier National Park
Tahoma Woods
Star Route
Ashford, Washington 98304

North Cascades National Park
800 State Street
Sedro Woolley, Washington 98284

Olympic National Park
600 East Park Avenue
Port Angeles, Washington 98362

Grand Teton National Park
P.O. Drawer 170
Moose, Wyoming 83101

Yellowstone National Park
P.O. Box 168
Wyoming 82190

# NATIONAL PARKS
# OF CANADA

The national parks system of Canada was started in 1885 when Banff National Park in Alberta was established. There are currently twenty-eight wildlife reserves under the jurisdiction of Parks Canada.

Banff National Park
Banff
Alberta T0L 0C0

Elk Island National Park
Site 4, R.R. 1
Fort Saskatchewan
Alberta T8L 2N7

Jasper National Park
Jasper
Alberta T0E 1E0

Waterton Lakes National Park
Waterton Park
Alberta T0K 2M0

Glacier National Park
Box 350
Revelstoke
British Columbia V0E 2S0

Kootenay National Park
Box 220
Radium Hot Springs
British Columbia V0A 1G0

Mount Revelstoke National Park
Box 350
Revelstoke
British Columbia V0E 2S0

Pacific Rim National Park
Box 280
Ucluelet
British Columbia V0R 3A0

Yoho National Park
Box 99
Field
British Columbia V0A 1G

Riding Mountain National Park
Wasagaming
Manitoba R0J 2H0

Fundy National Park
Alma
New Brunswick E0A 1B0

Kouchibouguac National Park
Kent County
New Brunswick E0A 2A0

Gros Morne National Park
Box 130
Rocky Harbour
Bonne Bay
Newfoundland A0K 4N0

Terra Nova National Park
Glovertown
Newfoundland A0G 2L0

Auyuitiuq National Park
Auyuitiuq, Pangnirtung
Northwest Territories X0A 0R0

Nahanni National Park
Postal Bag 300
Fort Simpson
Northwest Territories X0E 0N0

Wood Buffalo National Park
Fort Smith
Northwest Territories X0E 0P0

Cape Breton Highlands National Park
Ingonish Beach
Cape Breton
Nova Scotia B0C 1L0

Kejimkujik National Park
Box 36
Maitland Bridge
Nova Scotia B0T 1N0

Georgian Bay Islands National Park
Honey Harbour
Ontario P0E 1E0

Point Pelee National Park
R.R. 1
Leamington
Ontario N8H 3H4

Pukaskwa National Park
Box 550
Marathon
Ontario P0T 2E0

St. Lawrence Islands National
Park
Box 469, R.R. 3
Mallorytown
Ontario K0E 1R0

Prince Edward Island National
Park
Box 487
Charlottetown
Prince Edward Island C1A 7L1

Forillon National Park
Box 1220
Gaspé
Quebec G0C 1R0

La Mauricie National Park
Box 758
Shawinigan
Quebec G9N 6V9

Prince Albert National Park
Box 100
Waskesiu Lake
Saskatchewan S0J 2Y0

Kluane National Park
Mile 1019 Alaska Highway
Haines Junction
Yukon Territory Y0B 1L0

For further information regarding
national parks in Canada write to:

Information
Director General, Parks Canada
Department of Indian and
Northern Affairs
400 Laurier Avenue West
Ottawa, Ontario
Canada K1A 0H4

# NATIONAL WILDLIFE
# REFUGES

On March 14, 1903, President Theodore Roosevelt issued an Executive Order to set aside Pelican Island, on the east coast of Florida, as a bird sanctuary. Thus Pelican Island became the first of 390 national wildlife refuges created to save America's dwindling wildlife. The National Wildlife Refuge System is under the jurisdiction of the U.S. Department of the Interior, Fish and Wildlife Service.

Choctaw National Wildlife Refuge
2704 Westside College Avenue
Jackson, Alabama 36545

Eufaula National Wildlife Refuge
Route 2, Box 97-B
Eufaula, Alabama 36027

Wheeler National Wildlife Refuge
P.O. Box 1643
Decatur, Alabama 35602

Arctic National Wildlife Refuge
Room 266 Federal Building
101-12th Avenue
Box 20
Fairbanks, Alaska 99701

Izembek National Wildlife Range
Pouch 2
Cold Bay, Alaska 99571

Kenai National Moose Range
Box 500
Kenai, Alaska 99611

Kodiak National Wildlife Refuge
Box 825
Kodiak, Alaska 99615

Clarence Rhode National Wildlife
Refuge
P.O. Box 346
Bethel, Alaska 99559

Cabeza Prieta National Wildlife
Refuge
P.O. Box 1032
Yuma, Arizona 85364

Imperial National Wildlife Refuge
P.O. Box 2217
Martinez Lake, Arizona 85364

Kofa National Wildlife Refuge
P.O. Box 1032
Yuma, Arizona 85364

Felsenthal National Wildlife Refuge
P.O. Box 279
Crossett, Arkansas 71635

Holla Bend National Wildlife
Refuge
P.O. Box 1043
Russellville, Arkansas 72801

Wapanocca National Wildlife
Refuge
P.O. Box 279
Turrell, Arkansas 72384

White River National Wildlife
Refuge
P.O. Box 308
De Witt, Arkansas 72042

Havasu National Wildlife Refuge
1406 Bailey Avenue
P.O. Box A
Needles, California 92363

Humboldt Bay National Wildlife
Refuge
P.O. Box 1386
Eureka, California 95501

Kern-Pixley National Wildlife
Refuges
P.O. Box 219
Delano, California 93215

Klamath Basin National Wildlife
Refuges
Route 1, Box 74
Tule Lake, California 96134

Modoc Refuge
P.O. Box 1610
Alturas, California 96101

Sacramento National Wildlife
Refuge
Route 1, Box 311
Willows, California 95988

Salton Sea National Wildlife
Refuge
P.O. Box 247
Calipatria, California 92233

San Francisco Bay National
Wildlife Refuge
3849 Peralta Boulevard
Fremont, California 94536

San Luis–Merced National
Wildlife Refuge
P.O. Box 2176
Los Banos, California 93635

Arapaho National Wildlife Refuge
P.O. Box 457
Walden, Colorado 80480

Browns Park National Wildlife
Refuge
Greystone Route
Maybell, Colorado 81640

Monte Vista National Wildlife
Refuge
P.O. Box 511
Monte Vista, Colorado 81144

Bombay Hook National Wildlife
Refuge
R.D. 1, Box 147
Smyrna, Delaware 19977

Prime Hook National Wildlife
Refuge
R.D. 1, Box 195
Milton, Delaware 19968

Chassahowitzka National Wildlife
Refuge
Route 2, Box 44
Homosassa, Florida 32646

J.N. "Ding" Darling National
Wildlife Refuge
P.O. Drawer B
Sanibel, Florida 33957

Florida Keys National Wildlife
Refuge
P.O. Box 510
Big Pine Key, Florida 33043

Lake Woodruff National Wildlife
Refuge
P.O. Box 488
De Leon Springs, Florida 32028

Loxahatchee National Wildlife
Refuge
Route 1, Box 278
Boynton Beach, Florida 33437

Merritt Island National Wildlife
Refuge
P.O. Box 6504
Titusville, Florida 32780

St. Marks National Wildlife Refuge
P.O. Box 68
St. Marks, Florida 32355

St. Vincent National Wildlife
Refuge
Apalachicola, Florida 32320

Okefenokee National Wildlife
Refuge
P.O. Box 117
Waycross, Georgia 31501

Piedmont National Wildlife Refuge
Round Oak, Georgia 31080

Savannah National Wildlife Refuge
Complex
P.O. Box 8487
Savannah, Georgia 31402

Hawaiian & Pacific Islands
National Wildlife Refuge Complex
300 Ala Moana Boulevard
Room 5302
P.O. Box 50167
Honolulu, Hawaii 96850

Hanalei & Huleia National Wildlife
Refuges
P.O. Box 87
Kilauea
Kauai, Hawaii 96754

Camas National Wildlife Refuge
Hamer, Idaho 83425

Deer Flat National Wildlife Refuge
P.O. Box 448
Nampa, Idaho 83651

Grays Lake National Wildlife
Refuge
Box 837
Soda Springs, Idaho 83276

Kootenai National Wildlife Refuge
Star Route 1, Box 160
Bonners Ferry, Idaho 83805

Minidoka National Wildlife Refuge
Route 4
Rupert, Idaho 83350

Crab Orchard National Wildlife
Refuge
P.O. Box J
Carterville, Illinois 62918

Mark Twain National Wildlife
Refuge (Calhoun, Batchtown, and
Gilbert Lake Divisions)
Box 142
Brussels, Illinois 62013

Mark Twain National Wildlife
Refuge (Quincy, Headquarters,
and Gardner Divisions)
P.O. Box 225
Quincy, Illinois 62301

Mark Twain National Wildlife
Refuge (Chautauqua, Meredosia,
and Cameron Divisions)
R.R. 2
Illinois 62644

Muscatatuck National Wildlife
Refuge
P.O. Box 631
Seymour, Indiana 47274

Mark Twain National Wildlife
Refuge (Louisa, Keithsburg, and
Big Timber Divisions)
R.R. 1
Wapello, Iowa 52653

De Soto National Wildlife Refuge
Route 1, Box 114
Missouri Valley, Iowa 51555

Flint Hills National Wildlife Refuge
P.O. Box 128
Hartford, Kansas 66854

Catahoula National Wildlife Refuge
P.O. Drawer LL
Jena, Louisiana 71342

D'Arbonne National Wildlife
Refuge
P.O. Box 3065
Monroe, Louisiana 71201

Delta-Breton National Wildlife
Refuges
Venice, Louisiana 70091

Lacassine National Wildlife Refuge
Route 1, Box 186
Lake Arthur, Louisiana 70549

Sabine National Wildlife Refuge
M.R.H. Box 107
Hackberry, Louisiana 70645

Moosehorn National Wildlife
Refuge
Box X
Calais, Maine 04619

Blackwater National Wildlife
Refuge
Route 1, Box 121
Cambridge, Maryland 21613

Eastern Neck National Wildlife
Refuge
Route 2, Box 225
Rock Hall, Maryland 21661

Great Meadows National Wildlife
Refuge
191 Sudbury Road
Concord, Massachusetts 01742

Monomoy National Wildlife Refuge
c/o Massachusetts Audubon Society
Wellfleet Bay Wildlife Sanctuary
Box 236
South Wellfleet, Massachusetts
02663

Parker River National Wildlife
Refuge
Plum Island
Newburyport, Massachusetts 01950

Seney National Wildlife Refuge
Star Route
Seney, Michigan 49883

Shiawassee National Wildlife
Refuge
6975 Mower Road
Saginaw, Michigan 48601

Agassiz National Wildlife Refuge
Middle River, Minnesota 56737

Big Stone National Wildlife Refuge
25 N.W. Second Street
Ortonville, Minnesota 56278

Rice Lake National Wildlife Refuge
R.R. 2
McGregor, Minnesota 55760

Sherburne National Wildlife Refuge
Route 2
Zimmerman, Minnesota 55398

Tamarac National Wildlife Refuge
Rural Route Box 66
Rochert, Minnesota 56578

Hillside National Wildlife Refuge
P.O. Box 107
Yazoo City, Mississippi 39194

Mississippi Sandhill Crane National
Wildlife Refuge
Gautier, Mississippi 39553

Noxubee National Wildlife Refuge
Route 1, Box 84
Brooksville, Mississippi 39739

Yazoo National Wildlife Refuge
Route 1, Box 286
Hollandale, Mississippi 38748

Mark Twain National Wildlife
Refuge (Clarence Cannon and
Delair Division)
P.O. Box 88
Annada, Missouri 63330

Benton Lake National Wildlife
Refuge
P.O. Box 450
Black Eagle, Montana 59414

Bowdoin National Wildlife Refuge
P.O. Box J
Malta, Montana 59538

Medicine Lake National Wildlife
Refuge
Medicine Lake, Montana 59247

Metcalf National Wildlife Refuge
P.O. Box 257
Stevensville, Montana 59870

National Bison Range
Moiese, Montana 59824

Red Rock Lakes National Wildlife
Refuge
Monida Star Route, Box 15
Lima, Montana 59739

Charles M. Russell Refuge
P.O. Box 110
Lewistown, Montana 59457

Crescent Lake National Wildlife
Refuge
Star Route
Ellsworth, Nebraska 69340

Fort Niobrara National Wildlife
Refuge
Hidden Timber Star Route
Valentine, Nebraska 69201

Desert National Wildlife Refuge
1500 North Decatur Boulevard
Las Vegas, Nevada 89108

Ruby Lake National Wildlife
Refuge
P.O. Box 649
Elko, Nevada 89801

Sheldon Hart Mountain
Denio, Nevada 89404

Stillwater National Wildlife Refuge
P.O. Box 592
Fallon, Nevada 89406

Brigantine National Wildlife Refuge
P.O. Box 72
Oceanville, New Jersey 08231

Great Swamp National Wildlife
Refuge
R.D. 1, Box 148
Basking Ridge, New Jersey 07420

Bitter Lake National Wildlife Refuge
P.O. Box 7
Roswell, New Mexico 88201

Bosque del Apache National
Wildlife Refuge
Box 1246
Socorro, New Mexico 87801

Las Vegas National Wildlife Refuge
P.O. Box 1070
Las Vegas, New Mexico 87701

Maxwell National Wildlife Refuge
P.O. Box 276
Maxwell, New Mexico 87728

Iroquois National Wildlife Refuge
R.D. 1
Casey Road
Bason, New York 14013

Montezuma National Wildlife
Refuge
R. D. 1, Box 1411
Seneca Falls, New York 13148

Target Rock National Wildlife
Refuge
Lloyd Neck
Huntington, New York 11743

Mattamuskeet National Wildlife
Refuge
Route 1, Box N-2
Swanquarter, North Carolina 27885

Pea Island National Wildlife Refuge
P.O. Box 1026
Manteo, North Carolina 27954

Pee Dee National Wildlife Refuge
P.O. Box 780
Wadesboro, North Carolina 28170

Pungo National Wildlife Refuge
P.O. Box 267
Plymouth, North Carolina 27962

Arrowwood National Wildlife
Refuge
Pingree, North Dakota 58476

Audubon National Wildlife Refuge
Coleharbor, North Dakota 58531

Des Lacs National Wildlife Refuge
Box 578
Kenmare, North Dakota 58746

Ottawa National Wildlife Refuge
1400 West State Route 2
Oak Harbor, Ohio 43449

Optima National Wildlife Refuge
P.O. Box 628
Guymon, Oklahoma 73942

Salt Plains National Wildlife Refuge
Route 1, Box 76
Jet, Oklahoma 73749

Sequoyah National Wildlife Refuge
P.O. Box 398
Sallisaw, Oklahoma 74995

Tishomingo National Wildlife
Refuge
P.O. Box 248
Tishomingo, Oklahoma 73460

Washita National Wildlife Refuge
Route 1, Box 68
Butler, Oklahoma 73625

Wichita Mountains Wildlife Refuge
Box 448
Cache, Oklahoma 73527

Hart Mountain National Antelope
Refuge
P.O. Box 111
Lakeview, Oregon 97630

Malheur National Wildlife Refuge
P.O. Box 113
Burns, Oregon 97720

Umatilla National Wildlife Refuge
P.O. Box 239
Umatilla, Oregon 97882

Erie National Wildlife Refuge
R.D. 2, Box 191
Guys Mills, Pennsylvania 16327

Tinicum National Environmental
Center, Suite 104
Scott Plaza 2
Philadelphia, Pennsylvania 19113

Ninigret National Wildlife Refuge
Box 307
Charlestown, Rhode Island 02813

Cape Romain National Wildlife
Refuge
Route 1, Box 191
Awendaw, South Carolina 29429

Carolina Sandhills National
Wildlife Refuge
Route 2, Box 130
McBee, South Carolina 29101

Santee National Wildlife Refuge
P.O. Box 158
Summerton, South Carolina 29148

Reelfoot National Wildlife Refuge
Box 98
Samburg, Tennessee 38254

Cross Creeks National Wildlife
Refuge
Route 1, Box 229
Dover, Tennessee 37058

Hatchie National Wildlife Refuge
Brownsville, Tennessee 38012

Tennessee National Wildlife Refuge
P.O. Box 849
Paris, Tennessee 38242

Aransas National Wildlife Refuge
P.O. Box 100
Austwell, Texas 77950

Attwater Prairie Chicken National
Wildlife Refuge
P.O. Box 518
Eagle Lake, Texas 77434

Buffalo Lake National Wildlife Refuge
P.O. Box 228
Umbarger, Texas 79091

Hagerman National Wildlife Refuge
Route 3, Box 123
Sherman, Texas 75090

Laguna Atascosa National Wildlife
Refuge
P.O. Box 2683
Harlingen, Texas 78550

Muleshoe National Wildlife Refuge
P.O. Box 549
Muleshoe, Texas 79347

San Bernard–Brazoria National
Wildlife Refuge
P.O. Drawer 1088
Angleton, Texas 77515

Santa Ana National Wildlife Refuge
Route 1, Box 202A
Alamo, Texas 78516

Bear River Migratory Bird Refuge
P.O. Box 459
Brigham City, Utah 84302

Fish Springs National Wildlife
Refuge
Dingway, Utah 84022

Ouray National Wildlife Refuge
447 East Main Street
Vernal, Utah 84078

Missisquoi National Wildlife Refuge
R.F.D. 2
Swanton, Vermont 05488

Back Bay National Wildlife Refuge
Pembroke Office Park
Pembroke Building
No. 2, Suite 218
Virginia Beach, Virginia 23462

Chincoteague National Wildlife
Refuge
P.O. Box 62
Chincoteague, Virginia 23336

Mason Neck National Wildlife
Refuge
9502 Richmond Highway
Lorton, Virginia 22079

Great Dismal Swamp National
Wildlife Refuge
P.O. Box 349
Suffolk, Virginia 23434

Presquile National Wildlife Refuge
P.O. Box 620
Hopewell, Virginia 23860

Columbian White-Tailed Deer
National Wildlife Refuge
Route 1, Box 376-C
Cathlamet, Washington 98612

Columbia National Wildlife Refuge
P.O. Drawer F
Othello, Washington 99344

Willapa National Wildlife Refuge
Ilwaco, Washington 98624

McNary National Wildlife Refuge
P.O. Box 308
Burbank, Washington 99323

Nisqually National Wildlife Refuge
2625 Parkmont Lane
Building A-2
Olympia, Washington 98502

Ridgefield National Wildlife
Refuge
P.O. Box 457
Ridgefield, Washington 98642

Turnbull National Wildlife Refuge
Route 3, Box 385
Cheney, Washington 99004

Aleutian Islands National Wildlife
Refuge
Box 5251
FPO Seattle, Washington 98791

Horicon National Wildlife Refuge
Route 2
Mayville, Wisconsin 53050

Necedah National Wildlife Refuge
Star Route West
Necedah, Wisconsin 54646

Trempealeau National Wildlife
Refuge
Route 1
Trempealeau, Wisconsin 54661

National Elk Refuge
Box C
Jackson, Wyoming 83001

Seedskadee National Wildlife Refuge
P.O. Box 67
Green River, Wyoming 82935

. . . . . . . . . . . . . . . . . .

For further information on national
wildlife refuges, write to the office
in the appropriate region:

U.S. Fish and Wildlife Service
1011 East Tudor Road
Anchorage, Alaska 99503

U.S. Fish and Wildlife Service
P.O. Box 25486
Denver Federal Center
Denver, Colorado 80225

U.S. Fish and Wildlife Service
P.O. Box 95067
Atlanta, Georgia 30347
(includes Puerto Rico and Virgin
Islands)

U.S. Fish and Wildlife Service
One Gateway Center
Suite 700
Newton Corner, Massachusetts
02158

U.S. Fish and Wildlife Service
Federal Building
Fort Snelling
Twin Cities, Minnesota 55111

U.S. Fish and Wildlife Service
P.O. Box 1306
Albuquerque, New Mexico 87103

U.S. Fish and Wildlife Service
Lloyd 500 Building
Suite 1692
500 Northeast Multnomah Street
Portland, Oregon 97232
(includes Hawaii and Pacific Islands)

# ZOOLOGICAL GARDENS OF THE UNITED STATES

Birmingham Zoo
2630 Cahaba Road
Birmingham, Alabama 35223

Montgomery Zoo
Box 3313
329 Vandiver Boulevard
Montgomery, Alabama 36109

Alaska Zoo
Box 1730S
Star Route H
Anchorage, Alaska 99507

The Research Ranch
Box 44
Elgin, Arizona 85611

Ollson's Rare Bird Farm
Route 1, Box 152
Glendale, Arizona 85301

Cheetahs Unlimited
5105 East Exeter
Phoenix, Arizona 85018

Phoenix Zoo
Box 5155
Phoenix, Arizona 85010

Tropical Gardens Zoo
6232 North 7th Street
Phoenix, Arizona 85014

Arizona–Sonora Desert Museum
Route 9, Box 900
Tucson, Arizona 85704

Randolph Park Zoo
900 S. Randolph Way
Tucson, Arizona 85716

Wild Wilderness
Route 3, Box 309
Gentry, Arkansas 72734

Little Rock Zoological Gardens
1 Jonesboro Drive
Little Rock, Arkansas 72205

Charles Paddock Zoo
9305 Marchant Avenue
Atascadero, California 93422

California Alligator Farm
Box 236
Buena Park, California 90621

San Diego Wild Animal Park
Route 1, Box 725E
Escondido, California 92025

Sequoia Park Zoo
Box 1018
Eureka, California 95501

Roeding Park Zoo
894 W. Belmont Avenue
Fresno, California 93728

T. Wayland Vaughan Aquarium-
Museum, Scripps Institution of
Oceanography
La Jolla, California 92093

Lion Country Safari, Inc.
8800 Moulton Parkway
Laguna Hills, California 92653

Micke Grove Zoological Gardens
11793 N. Micke Grove Road
Lodi, California 95240

Los Angeles Zoo
5333 Zoo Drive
Los Angeles, California 90027

Applegate Zoo
Box 2068
Merced, California 95340

Oakland Zoo
9777 Golf Links Road
Oakland, California 94605

Living Desert Reserve
Box 1775
Palm Desert, California 92260

Hanna-Barbera Marineland
Box 937
Rancho Palos Verdes, California
90274

Marine World–Africa USA
Marine World Parkway
Redwood City, California 94065

Sacramento Zoo
3930 W. Land Park Drive
Sacramento, California 95822

San Diego Zoo
Box 551
San Diego, California 92112

San Francisco Zoological Gardens
Zoo Road and Skyline Boulevard
San Francisco, California 94132

Steinhart Aquarium
Golden Gate Park
San Francisco, California 94118

San Jose Baby Zoo
1300 Senter Road
San Jose, California 95112

Prentice Park Zoo
20 Civic Center Plaza
Santa Ana, California 92701

Santa Barbara Zoological Gardens
Box 4758
Santa Barbara, California 93103

Institute for Herpetological
Research
Box 2227
Stanford, California 94305

Busch Bird Sanctuary
1600 Roscoe Boulevard
Van Nuys, California 91406

Cheyenne Mountain Zoological
Park
Box 158
Colorado Springs, Colorado 80901

Denver Zoological Gardens
City Park
Denver, Colorado 80205

Beardsley Zoological Gardens
Noble Avenue
Bridgeport, Connecticut 06610

Moran Nature Center and Zoo
Municipal Building
New London, Connecticut 06320

Children's Museum of Hartford
950 Trout Brook Drive
West Hartford, Connecticut 06119

National Aquarium
Room B-037
Department of Commerce
Washington, D.C. 20008

Sante Fe Community College
Biological Park and Teaching Zoo
3000 N.W. 83rd Street
Gainesville, Florida 32601

Jacksonville Zoological Park
8605 Zoo Road
Jacksonville, Florida 32218

Crandon Park Zoological Gardens
4000 Crandon Boulevard
Key Biscayne, Florida 33149

Miami Seaquarium
30 Rickenbacker Causeway
Miami, Florida 33149

Monkey Jungle
Box 246
Goulds, Florida 33170

Sea World of Florida
7007 Sea World Drive
Orlando, Florida 32809

Skye Hye Zoological Park
Box 510
Ponte Vedra Beach, Florida 32083

Marineland, Inc.
(Marineland of Florida)
Route 1, Box 122
St. Augustine, Florida 32084

Central Florida Zoological Park
P.O. Drawer 2078
Sanford, Florida 32771

Life Fellowship
New Age Ranch
Route 1, Box 64N
Seffner, Florida 33584

Busch Gardens (The Dark Continent)
Box 9158
Tampa, Florida 33674

Dreher Park Zoological Gardens
1301 Summit Boulevard
West Palm Beach, Florida 33405

Chehaw Wild Animal Park
Route 18, Box 97
Albany, Georgia 31701

Atlanta Zoological Park
800 Cherokee Avenue, S.E.
Atlanta, Georgia 30315

Honolulu Zoo
Queen Kapiolani Park
Honolulu, Hawaii 96815

Maui Zoological and Botanical
Garden
County of Maui
Wailuku, Hawaii 96793

Sea Life Park
Makapuu Point
Waimanalo, Hawaii 96795

Boise City Zoo
1104 Royal Boulevard
Boise, Idaho 83706

Arrington's Animal Park
Box 881
Idaho Falls, Idaho 83401

Small Animal Lab and Farm, Inc.
401 W. Golf Road
Arlington Heights, Illinois 60005

Miller Park Zoo
Box 3157
Bloomington, Illinois 61701

Chicago Zoological Park
(Brookfield Zoo)
Golf Road
Brookfield, Illinois 60513

Lincoln Park Zoological Gardens
2200 N. Cannon Drive
Chicago, Illinois 60614

John G. Shedd Aquarium
1200 South Lake Shore Drive
Chicago, Illinois 60605

Wildlife Prairie Park
R.R. 1
Taylor Road
Hanna City, Illinois 61536

Glen Oak Zoo
2218 N. Prospect
Peoria, Illinois 61603

Henson C. Robinson Children's
Zoo
Box 5052
Springfield, Illinois 62705

Wolf Park
North American Wildlife Park
Foundation
Battle Ground, Indiana 47920

Mesker Park Zoo
Bement Avenue
Evansville, Indiana 47712

Fort Wayne Children's Zoo
3411 Sherman Street
Fort Wayne, Indiana 46808

Irving Game Farm
R.R. 5
Greenfield, Indiana 46140

Indianapolis Zoological Park
3120 East 30th Street
Indianapolis, Indiana 46218

Washington Park Zoological
Gardens
Washington Park
Michigan City, Indiana 46360

Potawatomi Park Zoo
10006 35th Street
South Bend, Indiana 46615

Weed Park Zoo
City Hall
Muscatine, Iowa 52761

Lee Richardson Zoo
Box 499
Garden City, Kansas 67846

Brit Spaugh Zoo
Box 215
Great Bend, Kansas 67530

Ralph Mitchell Zoo
Route 4
Independence, Kansas 67301

Sunset Zoological Park
1725 Poyntz
Manhattan, Kansas 66502

Topeka Zoological Park
635 Gage Boulevard
Topeka, Kansas 66606

Sedgwick County Zoo
5555 Zoo Boulevard
Wichita, Kansas 67212

Louisville Zoological Garden
1100 Trevilian Way
Louisville, Kentucky 40213

James P. Heady Kiddieland Zoo
Box 295
Forest Park Station
Springfield, Massachusetts 01108

Alexandria Zoological Park
Box 71
Alexandria, Louisiana 71301

Greater Baton Rouge Zoo
Box 60
Baker, Louisiana 70714

Louisiana Purchase Gardens and
Zoo
Box 123
Monroe, Louisiana 71201

Audubon Park and Zoological
Gardens
Box 4327
New Orleans, Louisiana 70118

Hamel's Zoo
50 Dixie Garden Loop
Shreveport, Louisiana 71105

Aqualand
Route 3
Bar Harbor, Maine 04609

Baltimore Aquarium
Inner Harbor CCCB
Lombard and Market Streets
Baltimore, Maryland 21202

Baltimore Zoo
Druid Hill Park
Baltimore, Maryland 21217

Salisbury Zoo
750 South Park Drive
Salisbury, Maryland 21801

Catoctin Mountain Zoological Park
Route 3, Box 126
Thurmont, Maryland 21788

Capron Park Zoo
County Street
Attleboro, Massachusetts 02703

Boston Zoological Society
c/o Franklin Park Zoo
Boston, Massachusetts 02121

New England Aquarium
Central Wharf
Boston, Massachusetts 02110

Sealand of Cape Cod, Inc.
Route 6A
Brewster, Massachusetts 02631

Binder Park Zoo
7500 Division Street
Battle Creek, Michigan 49017

John Ball Zoological Gardens
301 Markeb S.W.
Grand Rapids, Michigan 49503

Potter Park Zoo
1301 South Pennsylvania Avenue
Lansing, Michigan 48910

Detroit Zoological Park
Box 39
Royal Oak, Michigan 48008

Saginaw Children's Zoo
1694 South Washington
Saginaw, Michigan 48601

Minnesota Zoological Gardens
555 Wabasha Street
St. Paul, Minnesota 55102

Duluth Zoological Gardens
7210 Fremont Street
Duluth, Minnesota 55807

Saint Paul's Como Zoo
Midway Parkway and Kaufman Drive
St. Paul, Minnesota 55103

Kamper Zoological Park
107 17th Avenue
Hattiesburg, Mississippi 39401

Jackson Zoological Park
2918 West Capitol Street
Jackson, Mississippi 39209

Max Allen's Zoological Gardens
Highway 54 South
Route 3
Eldon, Missouri 65026

Kansas City Zoo
Swope Park
Kansas City, Missouri 64132

Saint Louis Zoological Park
Forest Park
St. Louis, Missouri 63110

Dickerson Park Zoo
3043 North Fort
Springfield, Missouri 65803

McRoberts Game Farm
Box 55
Gurley, Nebraska 69141

Lincoln Children's Zoo
2800 A Street
Lincoln, Nebraska 68502

Henry Doorly Zoo
10th and Deer Park Boulevard
Omaha, Nebraska 68107

Riverside Park Zoo
1818 Avenue A
Scottsbluff, Nebraska 69361

Las Vegas Valley Zoo
Box 4036
Las Vegas, Nevada 89106

Cohanzick Zoo
City Park
Mayor Aitken Drive
Bridgeton, New Jersey 08302

Safari Park
Great Adventure
Box 120
Jackson, New Jersey 08527

Van Saun Park Zoo
Forrest Avenue
Paramus, New Jersey 07652

Terry Lou Zoo
1451 Raritan Road
Scotch Plains, New Jersey 07076

Space Farms Zoo and Museum
R.D. 3
Sussex, New Jersey 07461

Turtle Back Zoo
560 Northfield Avenue
West Orange, New Jersey 07052

Bergen County Wildlife Center
Crescent Avenue
Wyckoff, New Jersey 07481

Alameda Park Zoo
Box 205
Alamogordo, New Mexico 88310

Rio Grande Zoological Park
903 Tenth Street S.W.
Albuquerque, New Mexico 87102

Ross Park Zoo
60 Morgan Road
Binghamton, New York 13903

Buffalo Zoological Gardens
Delaware Park
Buffalo, New York 14214

Catskill Game Farm, Inc.
R.D. 1, Box 92
Catskill, New York 12414

Snyder's Darien Lake Zoo
9993 Allegheny Road
Corfu, New York 14036

Central Park Zoo
830 Fifth Avenue
New York, New York 10021

New York Aquarium
Boardwalk and West 8th Street
Brooklyn, New York 11224

New York Zoological Park
Bronx Park
Bronx, New York 10460

The Prospect Park Zoo
Empire Boulevard & Flatbush Avenue
Brooklyn, New York 11215

The Queens Zoo
Flushing Meadows-Corona Park
Flushing, New York 11368

Staten Island Zoo
614 Broadway
Staten Island, New York 10310

Seneca Park Zoo
2222 St. Paul Street
Rochester, New York 14621

Burnet Park Zoo
412 Spencer Street
Syracuse, New York 13204

Utica Zoo
Steele Hill Road
Utica, New York 13501

North Carolina Zoological Park
Route 4, Box 73
Asheboro, North Carolina 27203

Dakota Zoo
Box 711
Bismarck, North Dakota 58501

Roosevelt Zoo
Box 538
Minot, North Dakota 58701

Akron Children's Zoo
500 Edgewood Avenue
Akron, Ohio 44307

Sea World of Ohio, Inc.
1100 Sea World Drive
Aurora, Ohio 44202

Cincinnati Zoo
3400 Vine Street
Cincinnati, Ohio 45220

The Cleveland Aquarium
601 East 72nd Street
Cleveland, Ohio 44103

Parkman Zoological Gardens
(Jean Mar, Inc.)
1763 Coventry Road
Cleveland Heights, Ohio 44118

Dayton Museum of Natural History
"Animal Fair"
2629 Ridge Avenue
Dayton, Ohio 45414

Darby Dan Farm
R.R. 1
Galloway, Ohio 43119

Sealand Aquarium
310 Buckeye
Huron, Ohio 44839

Kings Island
Box 400
Kings Mills, Ohio 45034

Columbus Zoological
Gardens
9990 Riverside Drive
Powell, Ohio
43065

Toledo Zoological Gardens
2700 Broadway
Toledo, Ohio 43609

Oklahoma City Zoo
Route 1, Box 1
Oklahoma City, Oklahoma 73111

Tulsa Zoological Park
5701 E. 36th Street N.
Tulsa, Oklahoma 74115

Washington Park Zoo
4001 S.W. Canyon Road
Portland, Oregon 97221

Wildlife Safari
Box 600
Winston, Oregon 97496

Clyde Peeling's Reptiland, Ltd.
Box 66
Allenwood, Pennsylvania 17810

Erie Zoo
Box 3268
653 Shunpike Road
Erie, Pennsylvania 16508

Gettysburg Game Park
R.D. 1
Fairfield, Pennsylvania 17320

Lake Tobias and Animal Haven
R.D. 4
Halifax, Pennsylvania
17302

Philadelphia Zoological Garden
34th and Girard Avenue
Philadelphia, Pennsylvania 19104

The Pittsburgh Zoo
Box 5250
Pittsburgh, Pennsylvania 15206

Nay Aug Park Zoo
Nay Aug Park
Scranton, Pennsylvania 18510

Pocona Wild Animal Farm
R.D. 1
Stroudsburg, Pennsylvania 18360

Safari Park, Inc.
777 Bayamon
Puerto Rico 00619

Roger Williams Park Zoo
Elmwood Avenue
Providence, Rhode Island 02905

Riverbanks Zoological Park
500 Wildlife Parkway
Columbia, South Carolina 29210

Greenville Zoological Park
Cleveland Park
Greenville, South Carolina 29601

Brookgreen Gardens
A Society for South-
eastern Flora and Fauna
Murrells Inlet, South Carolina
29576

Bear Country U.S.A.
Route 2, Box 628
Rapid City, South Dakota 57701

Black Hills Reptile Garden
Box 620
Rapid City, South Dakota 57709

Bramble Park Zoo
Bramble Park
Watertown, South Dakota 57201

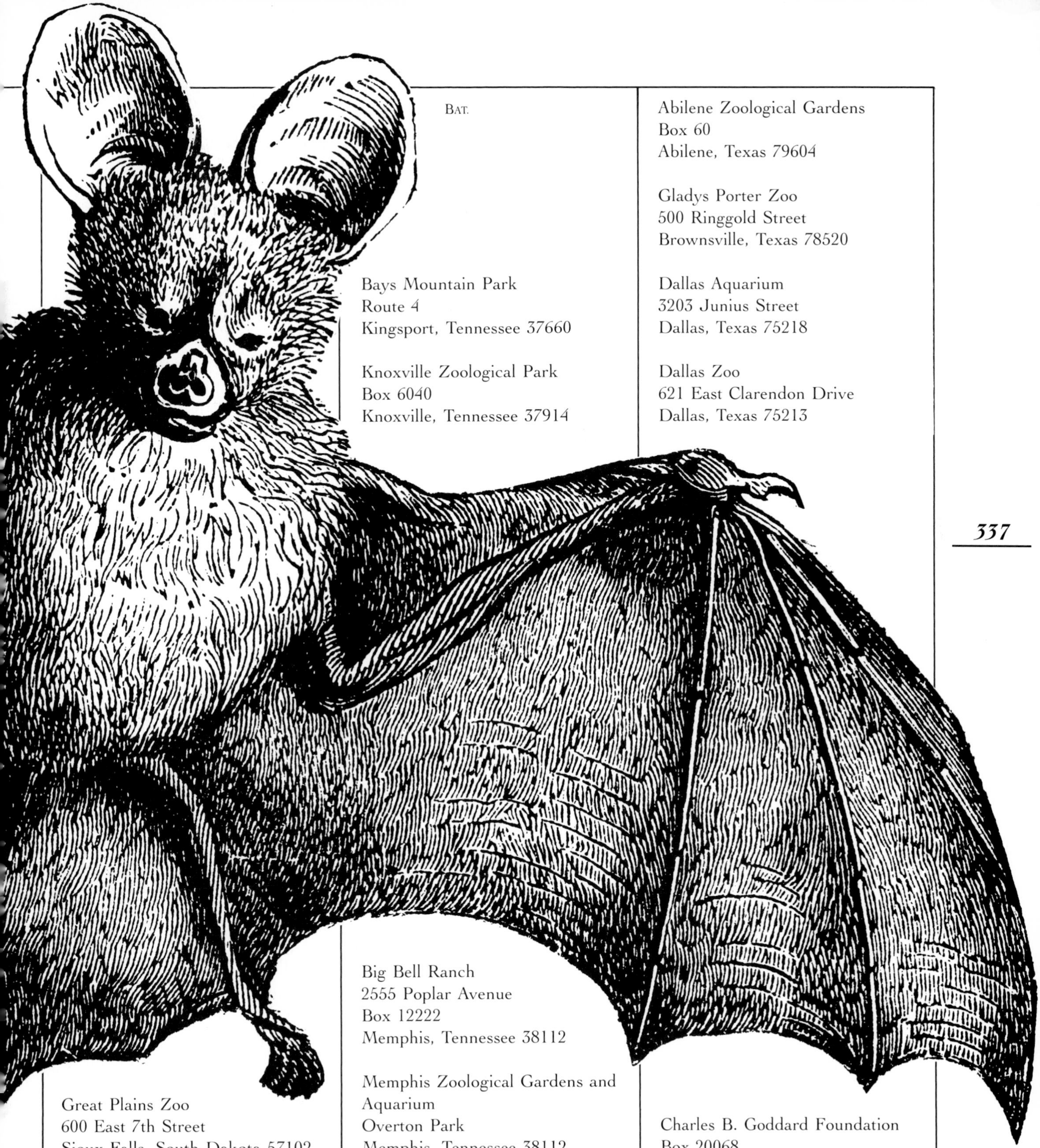

BAT.

Bays Mountain Park
Route 4
Kingsport, Tennessee 37660

Knoxville Zoological Park
Box 6040
Knoxville, Tennessee 37914

Abilene Zoological Gardens
Box 60
Abilene, Texas 79604

Gladys Porter Zoo
500 Ringgold Street
Brownsville, Texas 78520

Dallas Aquarium
3203 Junius Street
Dallas, Texas 75218

Dallas Zoo
621 East Clarendon Drive
Dallas, Texas 75213

Big Bell Ranch
2555 Poplar Avenue
Box 12222
Memphis, Tennessee 38112

Memphis Zoological Gardens and
Aquarium
Overton Park
Memphis, Tennessee 38112

Opryland, U.S.A.
Box 2138
Nashville, Tennessee 37214

Great Plains Zoo
600 East 7th Street
Sioux Falls, South Dakota 57102

Tennessee Game Farm
Route 2, Box 192
Joelton, Tennessee 37080

Charles B. Goddard Foundation
Box 20068
Dallas, Texas 75220

El Paso Zoological Park
Evergreen and Paisano
El Paso, Texas 79905

Fort Worth Zoological Park
2727 Zoological Park Drive
Fort Worth, Texas 76110

The Waterfall Ranch
2500 Fort Worth National Bank
Building
Fort Worth, Texas 76102

Camp Cooley Ranch
Route 3
Franklin, Texas 77856

Amigita Grande Ranch
11003 Wickwood
Houston, Texas 77024

The Houston Zoological Gardens
Box 1562
Houston, Texas 77001

Ellen Trout Zoo
P.O. Drawer 190
Lufkin, Texas 75901

Y. O. Ranch
Mountain Home, Texas 78058

San Antonio Zoological Gardens
and Aquarium
3903 North St. Mary's Street
San Antonio, Texas 78212

Caldwell Children's Zoo
Box 428
Tyler, Texas 75710

Central Texas Zoo
Route 10, Box 173E
Waco, Texas 76708

Hogle Zoological Garden
Box 8475
Salt Lake City, Utah 84108

Tracy Aviary
589 East 13th South
Salt Lake City, Utah 84105

Kings Dominion
Box 166
Doswell, Virginia 23047

Natural Bridge Zoological Park
Route 1, Box 560
Natural Bridge, Virginia 24578

Lafayette Zoological Park
3500 Granby Street
Norfolk, Virginia 23504

The Seattle Aquarium
Pier 59
Waterfront Park
Seattle, Washington 98101

Northwest Trek
Box 580
Eatonville, Washington 98328

Woodland Park Zoological
Gardens
5500 Phinney Avenue North
Seattle, Washington 98103

Olympic Game Farm
Route 3, Box 903
Sequim, Washington 98382

Walk in the Wild
Box 14258
Spokane, Washington 99214

Oglebay's Good Zoo
Oglebay Park
Wheeling, West Virginia 26003

Aqualand "K" Street
Boulder Junction, Wisconsin
54512

Henry Vilas Park Zoo
702 South Randall Avenue
Madison, Wisconsin 53715

Milwaukee County Zoological Park
10001 West Bluemound Road
Milwaukee, Wisconsin 53226

# NATURAL HISTORY MUSEUMS OF NORTH AMERICA
# UNITED STATES

Anniston Museum of Natural
History
The John B. Lagarde Environmental
Interpretive Center
Anniston, Alabama 36201

Jean P. Haydon Museum
Pago Pago, Alabama 96799

University of Alabama Museum of
Natural History
University, Alabama 35486

The Aquary Museum
Tucson, Arizona 85705

Arizona-Sonora Desert Museum
Tucson, Arizona 85704

Museum of Northern Arizona
Flagstaff, Arizona 86001

Pratt Museum
Homer, Arkansas 99603

Alexander Lindsay Junior Museum
Walnut Creek, California 94596

Desert Museum
Randsburg, California 93554

Codding Museum of Natural History
Santa Rosa, California 95405

Coyote Point Museum for
Environmental Education
San Mateo, California 94401

Death Valley Museum
Death Valley, California 92328

The Discovery Center
Fresno, California 93703

Eastern California Museum
Independence, California 93526

El Dorado Nature Center
Long Beach, California 90815

Hi-Desert Nature Museum
Yucca Valley, California 92284

Los Gatos Museum
Los Gatos, California 95031

Morro Bay State Park Museum of
Natural History
Morro Bay, California 93442

Mousley Museum of Natural
History
Yucaipa, California 92399

Museum of Vertebrate Zoology
Berkeley, California 94720

Natural History Museum
San Diego, California 92112

Natural History Museum of Los
Angeles County
Los Angeles, California 90007

The Oakland Museum
Oakland, California 94607

Pacific Grove Museum of Natural
History
Pacific Grove, California 93950

Palm Springs Desert Museum, Inc.
Palm Springs, California 92263

Santa Barbara Museum of Natural
History
Santa Barbara, California 93105

Museum of Vertebrate Zoology
Berkeley, California 94720

Denver Museum of Natural History
Denver, Colorado 80205

May Natural History Museum
Colorado Springs, Colorado 80906

University of Colorado Museum
Boulder, Colorado 80309

The Bruce Museum
Greenwich, Connecticut 06830

Children's Museum of Hartford
West Hartford, Connecticut 06119

Peabody Museum of Natural
History
New Haven, Connecticut 06520

Stamford Museum & Nature Center
Stamford, Connecticut 06903

Delaware Museum of Natural
History
Greenville, Delaware 19807

Brevard Museum, Inc.
Cocoa, Florida 32922

Florida State Museum
Gainesville, Florida 32611

Columbus Museum of Arts &
Sciences, Inc.
Columbus, Georgia 31906

Emory University Museum
Atlanta, Georgia 30322

Fernbank Science Center
Atlanta, Georgia 30307

Savannah Science Museum, Inc.
Savannah, Georgia 31405

University of Georgia Museum of
Natural History
Athens, Georgia 30602

Bernice Pauahi Bishop Museum
Honolulu, Hawaii 96819

Idaho Museum of Natural History
Pocatello, Idaho 83209

Burpee Museum of Natural History
Rockford, Illinois 61103

Chicago Academy of Sciences
Museum of Ecology
Chicago, Illinois 60614

Field Museum of Natural History
Chicago, Illinois 60605

Illinois State Museum
Springfield, Illinois 62706

Lincoln Memorial Garden and
Nature Center
Springfield, Illinois 62707

Museum of Natural History
University of Illinois
Urbana, Illinois 61801

The Children's Museum
Indianapolis, Indiana 46208

Indiana State Museum
Indianapolis, Indiana 46204

Joseph Moore Museum
Richmond, Indiana 47374

Ellsworth College Museum
Iowa Falls, Iowa 50126

Grout Museum of History and
Science
Waterloo, Iowa 50701

Museum of Natural History
Iowa City, Iowa 52240

Fort Hays State University
Museums
Hays, Kansas 67601

Pittsburg State University Natural
History Museum
Pittsburg, Kansas 66762

Richard H. Schmidt Museum of
Natural History
Emporia, Kansas 66801

Berea College Museums
Berea, Kentucky 40404

John James Audubon Museum
Henderson, Kentucky 42420

Lafayette Natural History Museum
& Planetarium
Lafayette, Louisiana 70503

Louisiana Nature Center, Inc.
New Orleans, Louisiana 70127

Louisiana Wildlife Museum
New Orleans, Louisiana 70130

Museum of Zoology
Baton Rouge, Louisiana 70893

The Zigler Museum
Jennings, Louisiana 70546

Museum of Zoology
Baton Rouge, Louisiana 70893

L. C. Bates Museum
Hinckley, Maine 04944

Maine State Museum
Augusta, Maine 04333

Nylander Museum
Caribou, Maine 04736

Calvert Marine Museum
Solomons, Maryland 20688

Cylburn Museum
Baltimore, Maryland 21209

The Berkshire Museum
Pittsfield, Massachusetts 01201

Blue Hills Trailside Museum
Milton, Massachusetts 02186

Cape Cod Museum of Natural
History
Brewster, Massachusetts 02631

Museum of Comparative Zoology
Cambridge, Massachusetts 02138

Museum of Zoology
Amherst, Massachusetts 01003

Holyoke Museum — Wistariahurst
Holyoke, Massachusetts 01040

The Pratt Museum of Natural History
Amherst, Massachusetts 01002

Call of the Wild Museum
Gaylord, Michigan 49735

Center for Cultural and Natural
History
Mount Pleasant, Michigan 48858

Fort De Buade Museum, Inc.
St. Ignace, Michigan 49781

Grand Rapids Public Museum
Grand Rapids, Michigan 49503

Kingman Museum of Natural
History
Battle Creek, Michigan 49017

The Wayne State University
Museum of Natural History
Detroit, Michigan 48202

University of Michigan
Museum of Zoology
Ann Arbor, Michigan 48109

James Ford Bell Museum of
Natural History
Minneapolis, Minnesota 55455

John Martin Frazier Museum of
Natural Science
Hattiesburg, Mississippi 59401

Jurica Natural History Museum
Marine Education Center
Biloxi, Mississippi 39530

Mississippi Museum of Natural
Sciences
Jackson, Mississippi 39202

Babler Nature Interpretive Center
Chesterfield, Missouri 63017

Kansas City Museum of History
& Science
Kansas City, Missouri 64123

Missouri State Museum
Jefferson City, Missouri 65101

Museum of Science & Natural
History
St. Louis, Missouri 63105

St. Joseph Museum
St. Joseph, Missouri 64501

Stephens Museum of Natural
History
Fayette, Missouri 65248

Earth Science Museum
Loma, Montana 59460

Scriver Museum of Montana
Wildlife
Browning, Montana 59417

Northern Montana College
Collections
Havre, Montana 59501

Hastings Museum
Hastings, Nebraska 68901

Fontenelle Forest Nature Center
Bellevue, Nebraska 68005

Lehman Caves National Monument
Baker, Nevada 89311

Museum of Natural History
University of Nevada
Las Vegas, Nevada 89154

Annie E. Woodman Institute
Dover, New Hampshire 03820

Libby Museum
Wolfeboro, New Hampshire 03894

Mount Washington Museum
Gorham, New Hampshire 03581

Bergen Community Museum
Paramus, New Jersey 07652

New Jersey State Museum
Trenton, New Jersey 08625

Paterson Museum
Paterson, New Jersey 07501

Princeton University Museum of
Natural History
Princeton, New Jersey 08544

Trailside Nature & Science Center
Mountainside, New Jersey 07092

Carlsbad Municipal Fine Arts &
Museum
Carlsbad, New Mexico 88220

Museum of New Mexico
Santa Fe, New Mexico 87501

Natural History Museum
Portales, New Mexico 88130

University of New Mexico Biology
Department
Albuquerque, New Mexico 87131

Alley Pond Environmental Center
Douglaston, New York 11363

American Museum of Natural
History
New York, New York 10024

Bear Mountain Trailside Museums
Bear Mountain, New York 10911

Buffalo Museum of Science
Buffalo, New York 14211

Children's Museum of History
Natural History and Science at
Utica
Utica, New York 13501

Museum of Natural History
Pawling, New York 12564

New York State Museum
Albany, New York 12230

Trailside Nature Museum
Cross River, New York 10518

Buffalo Museum of Science
Buffalo, New York 14211

The Nature Museum
Charlotte, North Carolina 28209

North Carolina State Museum
Raleigh, North Carolina 27611

Schiele Museum of Natural History
and Planetarium, Inc.
Gastonia, North Carolina 28052

Weymouth Woods–Sandhills
Nature Preserve Museum
Southern Pines, North Carolina
28387

Charlotte Nature Museum, Inc.
Charlotte, North Carolina 28202

Buffalo Trails Museum
Epping, North Dakota 58843

University of North Dakota
Zoology Museum
Grand Forks, North Dakota 58202

Cincinnati Museum of Natural
History
Cincinnati, Ohio 45202

Cleveland Museum of Natural
History
Cleveland, Ohio 44106

Dayton Museum of Natural History
Dayton, Ohio 45414

Ehrhart Museum
Antwerp, Ohio 45813

Lake Erie Nature and Science
Center
Bay Village, Ohio 44140

Trailside Nature Center & Museum
Cincinnati, Ohio 45220

The A. D. Buck Museum of
Natural History & Science
Tonkawa, Oklahoma 74653

Oklahoma State University
Museum of Natural & Cultural
History
Stillwater, Oklahoma 74078

Klamath County Museum
Klamath Falls, Oregon 97601

Oregon High Desert Museum
Bend, Oregon 97701

Southern Oregon State College
Museum of Vertebrate Natural
History
Ashland, Oregon 97520

Oregon State University
Museum of Natural History
Corvallis, Oregon 97331

Academy of Natural Sciences of
Philadelphia
Philadelphia, Pennsylvania 19103

Carnegie Museum of Natural History
Carnegie Institute
Pittsburgh, Pennsylvania 15213

Roger Williams Park Museum
Providence, Rhode Island 02905

Big Thicket Museum
Saratoga, Texas 77585

Brazos Valley Museum of Natural
Science
Bryan, Texas 77801

Brazosport Museum of Natural
Science
Brazosport, Texas 77566

Dallas Museum of Natural History
Dallas, Texas 75226

El Campo Museum of Art, History
& Natural Science
El Campo, Texas 77437

El Paso Centennial Museum
University of Texas at El Paso
El Paso, Texas 79968

Heard Natural Science Museum &
Wildlife Sanctuary
McKinney, Texas 75069

Houston Museum of Natural Sciences
Houston, Texas 77030

McAllen International Museum
McAllen, Texas 78501

The Museum
Texas Tech University
Lubbock, Texas 79409

Outdoor Nature Programs
City of Austin Parks & Recreation
Department
Austin, Texas 78703

Strecker Museum
Waco, Texas 76703

Welder Wildlife Foundation
Sinton, Texas 78387

Capitol Reef National Park Visitor
Center
Torrey, Utah 84775

Dinosaur Natural History State
Museum
Vernal, Utah 84078

John Hutchings Museum of
Natural History
Lehi, Utah 84043

Monte L. Bean Life Science
Museum
Provo, Utah 84602

Utah Museum of Natural History
Salt Lake City, Utah 84112

Discovery Museum
Essex Junction, Vermont 05452

D. Ralph Hostetter Museum of
Natural History
Harrisonburg, Virginia 22801

Oyster Museum of Chinco
Chincoteague, Virginia 23336

Puget Sound Museum of Natural
History
Tacoma, Washington 98416

The Whale Museum
Friday Harbor, Washington 98250

Charles R. Conner Museum
Pullman, Washington 99164

Explorers Hall
Washington, D.C. 20036

National Museum of Natural
History
Washington, D.C. 20560

Kenosha Public Museum
Kenosha, Wisconsin 53140

Milwaukee Public Museum
Milwaukee, Wisconsin 53233

The Museum of Natural History
Stevens Point, Wisconsin 54481

Dale Warren's Wildlife Exhibit, Inc.
Dubois, Wyoming 75226

## CANADA

B. J. Hales Museum of Natural
History
Brandon, Manitoba
Canada

British Columbia Provincial
Museum
Victoria, British Columbia
Canada

Lynn Canyon Ecology Center
North Vancouver, British Columbia
Canada

Manitoba Museum of Man & Nature
Winnipeg, Manitoba
Canada

Museum of Natural History
Regina, Saskatchewan
Canada

The New Brunswick Museum
St. John, New Brunswick
Canada

Nova Scotia Museum
Halifax, Nova Scotia
Canada

Queen Charlotte Islands Museum
Skidegate, British Columbia
Canada

Quetico Provincial Park Museum
Atikokan, Ontario
Canada

Vancouver Museum
Vancouver, British Columbia
Canada

The Cowan Vertebrate Museum
Vancouver, British Columbia
Canada

## WILDLIFE AND ENVIRONMENTAL ORGANIZATIONS IN THE UNITED STATES

American Association for
Conservation Information
Game and Fish Commission
2 Capitol Mall
Little Rock, Arkansas 72201

American Cetacean Society
P.O. Box 2698
San Pedro, California 90731

Committee for the Preservation
of the Tule Elk
5502 Markland Drive
Los Angeles, California 90022

Conservation Associates
3844 Leak lane,
Loomis, California 95650

Desert Fishes Council
407 West Line Street
Bishop, California 93514

Desert Tortoise Council
350 Golden Shore Drive
Long Beach, California 90802

Eaton Canyon Nature Center
1750 North Altadena Drive
Pasadena, California 91107

Federation of Western Outdoor Clubs
93 Via Ventura
Monterey, California 93940

North American Native Fishes
Association
P.O. Box 88073
Emeryville, California 94462

North American Peregrine Foundation
354 Country Road 229
Durango, California 81301

Pacific Coast Entomological Society
Dr. Paul Arnaud
c/o California Academy of Sciences
Golden Gate Park
San Francisco, California 94118

Point Reyes Bird Observatory
P.O. Box 321
Bolinas, California 94924

San Diego Natural History Society
Natural History Museum
P.O. Box 1390
San Diego, California 92112

Society for the Preservation of Birds
of Prey
Box 891
Pacific Palisades, California 90272

Western Bird Banding Association
California State University,
Long Beach
Department of Biology
Long Beach, California 90840

The American Humane Association
P.O. Box 1266
Denver, Colorado 80201

The Wilson Ornithological Society
Department of Fishery and Wildlife
Biology
Colorado State University
Fort Collins, Colorado 80523

The Conservation and Research
Foundation
Box 1445
Connecticut College
New London, Connecticut 06320

The Joint Conservation Committee
Society of Amphibians and Reptiles
Department of Interpretation
Florida State Museum
University of Florida
Gainesville, Florida 32611

Society for the Study of Amphibians
and Reptiles
Gainesville Field Station
National Fish and Wildlife Laboratory
2820 E. University Avenue
Gainesville, Florida 32601

Boone and Crockett Club
50 South LaSalle Street
Chicago, Illinois 60690

Ducks Unlimited, Inc.
P.O. Box 66300
Chicago, Illinois 60666

Field Museum of Natural History
Roosevelt Road & Lake Shore Drive
Chicago, Illinois 60605

J.N. "Ding" Darling Foundation, Inc.
3663 Grand Street
Des Moines, Iowa 50312

Kansas Entomological Society
Waters Hall
Kansas State University
Manhattan, Kansas 66502

Lepidopterists Society
c/o Dr. Charles V. Covell, Jr.
University of Louisville
Louisville, Kentucky 40208

Center for Natural Areas
Northeast Office  Box 98
South Gardner, Maine 04359

American Fisheries Society
5410 Grosvenor Lane
Bethesda, Maryland 20014

Audubon Naturalists Society
of the Central Atlantic States, Inc.
6412 Garnett Drive
Chevy Chase, Maryland 20015

Entomological Society of America
4603 Calvert Road
College Park, Maryland 20740

American Orchid Society
Botanical Museum of Harvard
University
Cambridge, Massachusetts 02138

Xerces Society
Mrs. Jo Brewer, Associate Director
300 Islington Road
Auburndale, Massachusetts 02166

American Society of Ichthyologists
& Herpetologists
c/o The Museum of Zoology
University of Michigan
Ann Arbor, Michigan 48109

Southeastern Fishes Council
Drawer Z
Mississippi State, Mississippi 39762

Wild Canid Survival Center
Wolf Sanctuary
P.O. Box 16204
St. Louis, Missouri 63105

Inland Bird Banding Association
Route 2, Box 26
Wisner, Nebraska 68791

The Ecological Society of America
Department of Biology
4505 Maryland Parkway
University of Nevada
Las Vegas, Nevada 89109

Porpoises News
Chipmunk Falls
Weare, New Hampshire 03281

American Littoral Society
Sandy Hook Highlands, New Jersey
07732

Sierra Club
National Wildlife Committee
Box 2471
Trenton, New Jersey 08607

Association of Interpretive Naturalists
12312 Marshall Court, N.E.
Albuquerque, New Mexico 87112

Whooping Crane Conservation
Association, Inc.
New Mexico Department of Game
and Fish
Villagra Building
Santa Fe, New Mexico 87503

American Nature Study Publications
R.D. 1
Homer, New York 13077

American Society of Mammalogists
Department of Forest Zoology
State University of New York
College of Science and Forestry
Syracuse, New York 13210

Clem and Jethro Memorial Fund
89–25 Rutledge Avenue
Glendale, New York 11227

Garden Club of America
598 Madison Avenue
New York, New York 10022

National Audubon Society
950 Third Avenue
New York, New York 10022

Xerces Society
Mr. Robert Dirig, Acting Director
TIEG Office
334 Plant Science Building
Cornell University
Ithaca, New York 14850

Conservation Committee —
Association of Southeastern
Biologists
St. Andrew's Presbyterian College
Laurinburg, North Carolina 28352

American Malacological Union
Museum of Zoology
Ohio State University
1813 N. High Street
Columbus, Ohio 43210

International Fund for Animal Welfare
28001 West Oakland Road
Bay Village
Cleveland, Ohio 44140

North American Wolf Society
P.O. Box 12071
Columbus, Ohio 43212

Game Conservationists International
P.O. Box 1378
Fort Worth, Texas 76101

Game Bird Breeders, Aviculturists,
Zoologists, and Conservationists
1155 East 4780 South
Salt Lake City, Utah 84117

Raptor Research Foundation
Department of Zoology
167 WIDB
Brigham Young University
Provo, Utah 84602

American Institute of Biological
Sciences, Inc.
4101 Wilson Boulevard
Arlington, Virginia 22209

Arctic Institute of North America
3426 N. Washington Boulevard
Arlington, Virginia 22201

The Izaak Walton League of America
1800 North Kent Street
Suite 806
Arlington, Virginia 22209

National Association of Biology
Teachers
11250 Roger Bacon Drive
Reston, Virginia 22090

The Nature Conservancy
Suite 800
1800 North Kent Street
Arlington, Virginia 22209

Outdoor Writers Association
of America
Heron Hill
Locustville, Virginia 23404

American Committee for
International Wildlife Protection, I
c/o Wildlife Society
Suite 611
7107 Wisconsin Avenue, N.W.
Washington, D.C. 20014

American Ornithologists Union
National Museum of Natural History
Smithsonian Institution
Washington, D.C. 20560

American Rivers Conservation Council
317 Pennsylvania Avenue, S.E.
Washington, D.C. 20003

Animal Protection Institute
613 Pennsylvania Avenue, S.E.
Washington, D.C. 20003

Animal Welfare Institute
P.O. Box 3650
Washington, D.C. 20007

Botanical Society of America
Office of Endangered Species
Fish and Wildlife Service
Department of the Interior
Washington, D.C. 20240

Center for Natural Areas
1525 New Hampshire Avenue, N.W.
Washington, D.C. 20036

Chamber of Commerce of the
United States
Natural Resources and Environ-
mental Quality
1615 H Street, N.W.
Washington, D.C. 20062

Committee for Humane Legislation
210 Massachusetts Avenue, N.E.
Washington, D.C. 20002

Conservation Education Association
Department of Agriculture
Room 6202
South Building
Washington, D.C. 20250

The Conservation Foundation
Suite 300
1717 Massachusetts Avenue, N.W.
Washington, D.C. 20036

Defenders of Wildlife
1244 19th Street, N.W.
Washington, D.C. 20036

Environmental Defense Fund, Inc.
1525 18th Street, N.W.
Washington, D.C. 20036

Environmental Policy Center
317 Pennsylvania Avenue, S.E.
Washington, D.C. 20003

Friends of Animals, Inc.
1707 H Street, N.W.
Suite 1005
Washington, D.C. 20006

Friends of the Earth
620 C Street, S.E.
Washington, D.C. 20003

Fund for Animals, Inc.
1765 P Street, N.W.
Washington, D.C. 20036

Herpetologists League
National Fish & Wildlife Laboratory
National Museum of Natural History
Washington, D.C. 20560

Humane Society of the United States
c/o Mrs. Sue Pressman
Director, Wildlife Protection
2100 L Street, N.W.
Washington, D.C. 20037

Institute of Laboratory Animal
Resources
National Research Council
2101 Constitution Avenue
Washington, D.C. 20418

International Association for Fish &
Wildlife Agencies
1412 16th Street, N.W.
Washington, D.C. 20036

National Parks and Conservation
Association
1701 18th Street, N.W.
Washington, D.C. 20009

National Wildlife Federation
1412 16th Street, N.W.
Washington, D.C. 20036

Office of Endangered Species
Fish & Wildlife Service
U.S. Department of the Interior
Washington, D.C. 20240

Endangered Species Program
Smithsonian Institution
Washington, D.C. 20560

The Wildnerness Society
1901 Pennsylvania Avenue, N.W.
Washington, D.C. 20006

The Wildlife Society
7101 Wisconsin Avenue, N.W.
Suite 611
Washington, D.C. 20014

World Wildlife Fund
1319 18th Street, N.W.
Washington, D.C. 20036

American Association of Zoological
Parks and Aquariums
Oglebay Parks
Wheeling, West Virginia 26003

The Brooks Bird Club
Department of Natural Resources
Box 67
Elkins, West Virginia 26241

General Federation of Women's
Clubs
204 East Washington Street
Poynette, Wisconsin 53995

Island Resources Foundation
P.O. Box 4187
St. Thomas, U.S. Virgin Islands
00801

# WILDLIFE AND ENVIRONMENTAL ORGANIZATIONS IN CANADA

Arctic Institute of North America
2920 24 Avenue N.W.
Calgary, Alberta T2N 1N4

Alpine Club of Canada
P.O. Box 1026
Banff, Alberta T0L 0C0

Boreal Circle
Boreal Institute for Northern
Studies
CW 401
Biological Sciences Building
University of Alberta
Edmonton, Alberta T6G 2E9

Canadian Wolf Defenders
Box 3480
Station D
Edmonton, Alberta T5L 4J3

Arctic International Wildlife Range
Society
c/o Dr. Andrew Thompson
Faculty of Law
University of British Columbia
Vancouver, British Columbia
V6T 1W5

Greenpeace Foundation
2623 W. Fourth Avenue
Vancouver, British Columbia
V6K 1P8

International Wildlife Protection
Association
P.O. Box 728
Kamloops, British Columbia
V2C 5M4

Association for the Protection of
Fur-Bearing Animals
1316 East 12th Avenue
Vancouver, British Columbia
V5N 1Z9

Outdoors Unlimited
200–1326 Johnston Road
White Rock, British Columbia
V4B 3Z2

Ducks Unlimited (Canada)
1495 Pembina Avenue
Winnipeg, Manitoba R3T 2E2

International Atlantic Salmon
Foundation
P.O. Box 429
St. Andrews, New Brunswick
E0G 2X0

International Fund for Animal
Welfare, Inc.
P.O. Box 1011
Fredericton, New Brunswick
E3B 5B4

Canada–U.S. Environmental
Council
Canadian Nature Federation
Suite 203
75 Albert Street
Ottawa, Ontario K1P 6G1

The Elsa Wild Animal Appeal of
Canada
P.O. Box 864, Postal Station K
Toronto, Ontario M4P 2H2

International Council for Bird
Preservation
Dr. A. J. Erskine, Secretary
1215 Agincourt Road
Ottawa, Ontario K2C 2H8

World Wildlife Fund (Canada)
Mr. Monte Hummel, Director
60 St. Clair Avenue East, Suite 201
Toronto, Ontario M4V 1M9

Canadian Amphibian and
Reptile Conservation Society
Barbara Froom, Editor
8 Preston Place
Toronto, Ontario M4N 2S9

Canadian Arctic Resources
Committee
46 Elgin Street
Room 11
Ottawa, Ontario K1P 5K6

Canadian Association for Humane
Trapping
c/o Marietta J.B. Lash
Executive Secretary
Box 934
Station F
Toronto, Ontario M4Y 2N9

Canadian Canoe Association
c/o Mrs. J.M. Matheson
Executive Director
333 River Road
Vanier, Ontario K1L 8B9

Canadian Committee for the
International Union for Conservation
of Nature and Natural Resources
422 Finch Avenue
Pickering, Ontario L1V 1H8

Canadian Environmental Law
Association
1 Spadina Crescent
Suite 303
Toronto, Ontario M5S 2J5

Canadian Exploration Group
P.O. Box 1635
Peterborough, Ontario K2B 6B3

Canadian Federation of Humane
Societies
900 Pinecrest Road
Ottawa, Ontario K2B 6B3

Canadian Forestry Association
185 Somserset Street West
Suite 203
Ottawa, Ontario K2P 0J2

Canadian National Sportsmen's
Shows
Box 168
Toronto–Dominion Center
Toronto, Ontario M5K 1H8

Canadian Nature Federation
75 Albert Street
Suite 203
Ottawa, Ontario K1P 6G1

Canadian Parks
333 River Road
Vanier, Ontario K1L 8B9

Canadian Wildlife Federation
1673 Carling Avenue
Ottawa, Ontario K2A 1C4

Fisheries Council of Canada
77 Metcalfe Street
Suite 603
Ottawa, Ontario K1P 5L6

National and Provincial Parks
Association of Canada
47 Colborne Street
Suite 308
Toronto, Ontario M5E 1E3

National Survival Institute
2175 Victoria Park Avenue
Scarborough, Ontario M1R 1V6

Heritage Canada
P.O. Box 1358
Station B
Ottawa, Ontario K1P 5R4

Atlantic Salmon Association
1405 Peel Street
Montreal, Quebec H3A 1S5

threatened, 218
Cuckoo, 90, 105
Curlew, Eskimo, 63, 85, 132, 177, 202
Cutworms, 53

**D**

Darwin, Charles, 33, 42, 136, 202–3, 233, 260, 291
Deer, 58, *58*, 67, *153*, 247–48, 268–70, 274, 289, 300–01, *300–1*
Dinosaurs, 24–29, *26–29*, 209, 282
Dipper, American, 70
Dog, 41, 93
Dolly Varden, 233
Dolphin, 233, 286, *286–87*, 308–09
Dovekies, 294
Drum, 85
Duck, 96; black, 72; harlequin, 70; Labrador, 290; pintail, *72*; ring-necked, *73*; shoveller, *295*; wood, *73*
Dugong, 23

**E**

Eagle, 41, 49, 57–58, 91, 106, 112, 226; bald, *20*, 21, 70, 73, 131, 133–35, *135*, 146–47, *147*, 154, 260, 270; golden, 45, 131, 146–47, 238–39
Egret: cattle, 72, 244–47, *245*; great, 72, 155–59, *156–57*
Elephant, 50
Elk, 131, *131*, *179*, 201–3, *202*, 289
Endangered Species legislation, 274, 282
England, 20, 38–39, 87–88
Ermine, 67
Eskimos, 81, 163
Evolution, Theory of, 20, 63. *See* Darwin, Charles

**F**

Falcon, 56–57; Aplomado, 133; lanner, 56; peregrine, 132, 150–52, *150*; prairie, 70
Ferret, black-footed, 21, 49, 106–7, 151, 222, *222*, 290
Finch , 22, 38, *264*; gold-, 35, 63; purple, 35, 262, 264
Fish, 22, 72, 236; endangered, 215, 218; exotic, 324; freshwater, 17, 93; of North America, 320–24; record weights of, 101–3; threatened, 218
Fisher, 50, 52, 226
Flamingo, 154
Flicker, 39, 92
Flies, 83. *See* Insects
Florida, 22–23, 31, 42, 62, 73–74, 152–59, 165–66, 218, 244
Flycatcher, 105, 112, 233
Fossils, 33, 310; living, 33
Fox, 58, 106, 226–27; gray, 226–27, *228–29*; red, 92, 226–27
Franklin, Benjamin, 134, 146
Frog, 22, 96, 184, 194–98, 299; Blanchard's cricket, 124
Fuertes, Louis Agassiz, 90, 312
Fulmar, 136

**G**

Gannet, *136*, 136–37
Gar, alligator, 290; longnosed, *291*; spotted, 33, *33*
Gecko, 176
Gnatcatcher, blue-gray, 122
Goatsucker, 57, 267–68
Godwit, Hudsonian, 132, 150–51
Goldeneye, Barrow's, 70
Goose, Canada, *125*, 231
Gopher, pocket, 129
Grackle, 39

Grasshopper, 53, 56, 170–71, *170–71*
Grayling, 177
Grosbeak, 22, 38, 262; blue, 35; evening, 35, 262; pine, 262; rose-breasted, 35
Groundhog, 41, *41*, 44–45, *44*, 61, 298, *298*; — Day, 42, 44.
Grouse, ruffed, 125
Grub, 53; hop, 53; white, 53
Guillemot, black, 137, 294
Gull: great black-breasted, 137; herring, *151*, 132, 137

**H**

Halibut, 151
Hallowell, William, 253
Harriers, 57
Hawk, 39, 41, 49, 58, 91, 105, *105*, 112, *122*, 129, 203, 234, 237, 240, 268; broad-tailed, 203; buteo, 57, 240; Cooper's, 61; ferruginous, 70; marsh, 56; red-shouldered, 57, 73, *73*, *112*; red-tailed, *57*, 58, 237, 240, *240*; rough-legged, 58, sharp-shinned, 122, *122*, 240; short-tailed, 154; Swainson's, 39
Heath hen, 62
Hedgehog, 163
Heron: black-crowned night, 72; great blue, 72; white, 158
Herptiles, 196
Herring, 33
Hibernation, 44, 233, 266, 297–99
Hinckley, Ohio, 61, 63, 70–71; "Buzzard Day" at, 70
Hummingbird, 91, *91*, 105, 177; bee, 106; buff-bellied, 177; ruby-throated, 91

**I**

Ibis: glossy, 73; white, 72, *76–77*
Iceland, 62, 132, 212–13
Indians, 20, 72, 189, 223, 241, 267
Insects, 91–92, 179–81, 299; endangered, 290

**J**

Jacobson's organ, 189
Jaguar, 214, *214*, *272*, 273–74, *274*
Jaguarundi, 274
Jay, 19; blue, 266; gray, 22; Steller's, 150, 260

**K**

Kangaroo rat, 172, *172*
Katydid, 124, 171
Kelsey, Henry, 133, 138, 177
Killdeer, 146
Kingbird, 106, 112, *112*; Cassin's, 132; tropical, 106
Kite, 56–57; swallow-tailed, 73
Kittiwake, black-legged, 137

**L**

Lark: horned, 41; meadow, 42, *42*, 63, 145–46
Lemming, Labrador collared, 45
Lewis, Capt. Meriwether, 107–9, 132–33, 177, 203, 232–33
Lewis and Clark Expedition, 20, 63, 106–9, 132–33, 177, 202–3
Limpkin, 73
Linnet, Brewster's, 119
Lizard, 143, 175, *188*, 189–96, *197*, 316–17; anole, 190; Gila monster, *188–89*, 189–90; glass snake, 192; horned toad, 175, 191–92, *191*; Mexican beaded, 189–90; venomous, 189
Loon, common, *18*, 34–

# PHOTO CREDITS

AMERICAN MUSEUM OF NATURAL HISTORY, COURTESY OF THE LIBRARY SERVICES DEPARTMENT. Pp. 4–5 (far left), 16 (center), 18, 19, 21 (top), 40, 47, 48 (right), 61, 62 (bottom), 64 (top left), 93, 104, 110, 111, 114 (top right), 117, 123, 148, 162, 179, 188–189, 201, 210–211, 212, 216–217, 218, 222, 252–253, 262–263, 264, 265, 266, 270–271, 278 (left), 284–285, 300 (bottom), 301 (right), 308–309, 313 (both).

THE BETTMANN ARCHIVE. Pp. 1, 43 (top left), 172, 190, 208, 302–303, 316–317.

Peter Bisset, A.R.P.S.: p. 112 (top).

BUREAU OF BIOLOGICAL SURVEY. P. 46.

BUREAU OF SPORT FISHERIES AND WILDLIFE. Winston E. Banko: p. 241; Luther Goldman: 183; E.P. Haddon: 15 (center), 106; H.W. Henshaw: 291 (top); Karl W. Kenyon: 63; D.W. Pfitzer: 20 (top right); Fred Sibley: 62 (top).

LEONARD LEE RUE ENTERPRISES. P. 258; Len Rue, Jr.: cover photo; pp. 68–69, 91, 213, 230, 250–251, 294–295 (bottom); Leonard Lee Rue III: 2–3, 14 (far right), 17 (far right), 35 (top), 39 (top), 42 (bottom left), 43 (bottom), 48 (left), 49, 52 (top), 53 (both), 54–55, 60, 66 (left), 73, 76–77, 80 (right), 82, 83 (all), 84, 105, 107, 108–109, 112 (bottom), 113, 120–121, 128–129, 130, 133 (top), 135, 136, 137, 140, 141, 164 (top), 173, 175, 176, 178, 182, 191 (top), 194 (all), 196–197, 198 (top), 200, 202, 203 (bottom), 204–205 (bottom), 219, 220–221, 231, 233 (all), 237, 246, 247, 248 (top left), 269, 272, 275 (all), 286–287, 288, 289 (both), 293, 301 (top left), 302 (top left), 306; Charles C. Sumners: 57 (right); Fred Tilly: 240; Irene Vandermolen: 16 (far left), 17 (center), 20 (left), 45, 92, 138, 154–155 (all), 156–157, 168–169, 174, 245, 256, 276–277, 297, 298.

THE NATIONAL AUDUBON SOCIETY/JOHN JAMES AUDUBON. Pp. 6-7, 79, 89, 242–243.

NATIONAL OCEANIC AND ATMOSPHERIC ADMINISTRATION. P. 283; R.M. Gilmore: p. 261 (bottom).

NEW YORK PUBLIC LIBRARY PICTURE COLLECTION. Pp. 12, 17 (far left), 58, 70, 74–75, 118, 122, 228–229.

NEW YORK STATE HISTORICAL ASSOCIATION, COOPERSTOWN. *The Peaceable Kingdom* by William Hallowell, pp. 254–255.

PHOTRI. Irene Vandermolen: p. 204 (top).

Pitseolak: p. 14 (center).

PROVINCE OF ONTARIO, MINISTRY OF NATURAL RESOURCES. P. 234; G. Brown: p. 144; Ted Jenkins: 125.

Bill Russell: p. 80 (top).

THE WINNIPEG ART GALLERY/GEORGE SWINTON COLLECTION. *Fishes* (1970) pencil drawing by Marjorie Esa, Baker Lake, N.W.T. Canada, reproduced by permission of the artist, p. 324.

The text was set in Cochin by U.S. Lithograph, Inc., New York, New York.

The book was printed and bound in the U.S. by Arcata Graphics Group.